DATE DUE

HEARTS BEATING
FOR LIBERTY

STACEY M. ROBERTSON

HEARTS BEATING
FOR LIBERTY

Women Abolitionists in the Old Northwest

The University of North Carolina Press · Chapel Hill

This book was published with the assistance of the Thornton H. Brooks
Fund of the University of North Carolina Press.

All rights reserved. Manufactured in the United States of America. Designed by Courtney
Leigh Baker and set in Adobe Caslon Pro by Achorn International, Inc. The paper in this
book meets the guidelines for permanence and durability of the Committee on Production
Guidelines for Book Longevity of the Council on Library Resources. The University of
North Carolina Press has been a member of the Green Press Initiative since 2003. Portions
of chapter 1 have been reprinted with permission in revised form from "'The Strength That
Union Gives': Western Women and Pragmatic Antislavery Politics," *American Nineteenth
Century History* 10 (September 2009): 299–315, <http://www.informaworld.com>.

Library of Congress Cataloging-in-Publication Data
Robertson, Stacey M.
Hearts beating for liberty : women abolitionists
in the old Northwest / Stacey M. Robertson.
p. cm.
Includes bibliographical references and index.
ISBN 978-0-8078-3408-4 (cloth : alk. paper)
1. Women abolitionists—Northwest, Old—History—19th century.
2. Abolitionists—Northwest, Old—History—19th century.
3. Antislavery movements—Northwest, Old—History—19th century.
4. Women—Political activity—Northwest, Old—History—19th century.
5. Northwest, Old—History—19th century. 1. Title.
E449.R644 2010
326'.80820977—dc22
2010010138

14 13 12 11 10   5 4 3 2 1

For Evan and Isaac

Contents

Illustrations

Acknowledgments

This book was a joy to research and write in part because of all the wonderful friends, colleagues, librarians, archivists, and students who have provided assistance, support, encouragement, and advice. I apologize if I neglect anyone among the dozens of people who contributed in one way or another to this project over the past decade.

I thank the helpful staff at the Boston Public Library Rare Books Department, the Chicago Historical Society, the Cincinnati Historical Society Library, the Cincinnati Public Library, the Earlham College Library, the Historical Society of Pennsylvania, the Illinois State Historical Library, the Illinois State University Special Collections Department, the Indiana Historical Library, the Indiana State Library, the Kent State University Library, the Knox College Library, the Library Company of Philadelphia, the Massachusetts Historical Society, the Ohio Historical Society, Swarthmore College's Friends Historical Library, the Western Reserve Historical Society, and the Wheaton College Library. I am especially grateful to the institutions that granted me fellowships to conduct research. I spent a week at Oberlin College thanks to Roland Bauman and the Frederick B. Artz Summer Research Grant. Bill Wallach and the Bentley Historical Society offered me the Bordin/Gillette Research Fellowship that enabled me to devote a month to research in Ann Arbor. I spent another delightful and productive month on fellowship at the American Antiquarian Society under the expert guidance of Gigi Barnhill, Joanne Chaison, Paul Erickson, and Caroline Sloat. I also spent a month on fellowship at the Gilder Lehrman Center for the Study of Slavery, Resistance, and Abolition. Dana Schaffer, Melissa McGrath, and David Blight were invaluable in introducing me to the extraordinary resources at Yale University. I also thank my home institution, Bradley University, for two summer research fellowships. Dean Claire Etaugh provided funds that permitted me to attend conferences and conduct research, and I cannot fully express my appreciation for this support. Her friendship and mentorship are even more priceless.

The University of North Carolina Press has been an excellent and professional institution, and I am proud to have my book published by this press. My kindest regards go to Chuck Grench, Katy O'Brien, Paula Wald, and all the other superb staff who have helped transform this manuscript into a book. I am especially indebted to copyeditor Ellen D. Goldlust-Gingrich for her excellent eye and stylistic skill.

I am indebted to all those colleagues and friends who shared ideas with me, read parts of the manuscript, and enriched our shared scholarly community. My Illinois colleagues include Bill Furry, Pat Goitein, Richard John, Channy Lyons, Bob McColley, Bill and Jane Ann Moore, Owen Muelder, and Junius Rodriguez. I am especially pleased to thank my Women's Historians at Middle Illinois Group: Tina Brakebill, Kyle Ciani, Stacy Cordery, Sandra Harmon, Mary Johnson, Karen Leroux, Deborah McGregor, and April Schultz. We've been reading each other's work, encouraging one another, and breaking bread together for nearly a decade. My fellow scholars of the antislavery movement have been a true inspiration over the years: Carol Faulkner, Julie Roy Jeffrey, Michael Pierson, Beth Salerno, Deborah Bingham Van Broekhoven, and Dana Weiner. What would I do without my longtime conference buddies? Thank you dear friends: Ann Boylan, Jim Broussard, Elizabeth Clapp, Chris Clark, Hugh Davis, Dan Dupre, Doug Egerton, Dan Feller, Craig Friend, Craig Hammond, Graham Hodges, Gary Kornblith, Albrecht Koschnik, Scott Martin, Matt Mason, Monique Patenaude, John Quist, Don Ratcliffe, Kyle Roberts, Jonathan Sassi, Mitchell Snay, and Tamara Thornton. I am equally thankful for the aid of independent scholars Kathy Ernst and Judith Harper.

A few people have generously read all (or nearly all) of the manuscript and offered inestimable advice. I am deeply indebted to the anonymous reviewer as well as to Richard Blackett, Stacy Cordery, Stan Harrold, Carol Lasser, and Jim Stewart. Several friends deserve more thanks than I can offer here. Jim Stewart is the best role model, friend, and mentor anyone could ask for. His bighearted spirit and brilliance are truly unmatched. In particular, I will never forget our shared drink in Philadelphia and the advice he gave me about priorities and balance. Stan Harrold pulled no punches in his critique of my work even as he gave me unqualified encouragement and memorable moments at conferences over the years. His friendship is deeply important to me. Pat Cohen has been a source of scholarly and personal inspiration for more than twenty years. She spent countless hours helping me track obscure characters and is the embodiment of munificence. Carol Lasser is my scholarly sister and dear friend. No one has offered more words of uplift and intellectual inspiration.

My community of scholars and friends at Bradley University and in Peoria is boundlessly supportive. I extend earnest gratitude to Patricia Benassi, Rob Faber, Heather Fowler-Salamini, Bob Fuller, Rusty Gates, Emily Gill, Sarah Glover, Greg Guzman, Jackie Hogan, Phil Jones, Barb and Seth Katz, Randy Kidd, Maggie Koehler, Gina Meeks, Amy Scott, Susan Smith, Ryan Stevenson, and Aurea Toxqui. I am happy to offer my appreciation to Bradley president Joanne Glasser for her inspired leadership and the generous friendship she has offered me. I'm not sure what I would have done without the amazing Pat Campbell, who has been a dear friend since I arrived in Peoria. Thanks also go to my friends who have moved on to other institutions: Kerry Ferris, Issam Nassar and Adriana Ponce, and Marjorie Worthington. I give a special shout out to the Blue Scarf Society, Dawn Roberts and Chris Blouch, who have stood with me through good times and bad. I'm not sure that I could have remained sane without my 5:30 A.M. Jazzercise class. Thanks to my fellow predawn exercisers for making it worth the effort, especially on those cold Illinois winter mornings.

My students have provided inspiration, brilliance, and practical aid. I have benefited from their wisdom. I especially thank my dear Courtney Wiersema. I am so proud of her for her smarts, determination, compassion, and good sense. She is now in graduate school. I have not forgotten Arnie Shober, who was my assistant when I began this project years ago. My SHEAR-Mellon students brought joy and intellectual excitement to the summer of 2009. I miss you all. I am particularly grateful to Brian Powers and Wes Skidmore for producing the fabulous maps for this book. Both of you are amazing. And big hugs go to Christy Thomas, my special sweet student from the summer of 2008, and Amy Baxter-Bellamy, who offered her friendship as well as endless pragmatic aid. My coleader, Rich Newman, was the epitome of professionalism, leadership, and cooperative teaching. Our month in Philadelphia was full of laughter, wisdom, inspiration, sushi, and martinis. The memory of our strolls from the B & B to the McNeil Center will always make me smile.

My friends and family have sustained me over the past decade. I could not have completed this project without them. My parents, Scotty and Shirley Robertson, have always encouraged me to think independently and work harder than I thought possible. Scott and Michelle Robertson could not be more generous and supportive. Sharon Robertson remains my first and most important role model. She is still smarter than me and now can beat me at tennis. Marty Craig and John Williams have become a critical part of my extended family in Peoria. They bring laughter, fun, and lively conversation into my life every week. Missy Ruscheinski is a newer member of this family, but I value her friendship more than I can say. My larger community of dear friends across the country makes me feel connected. Rich Newman and Lisa Hermsen are fun, endearing, and compassionate. Our Broadway play tradition is spectacularly enjoyable. Doug Egerton is among the wittiest and most caring people I know. John Quist has offered unqualified friendship and scholarly advice for more than a decade. Carol Lasser and Gary Kornblith have housed, fed, and entertained me time and again, and I adore their hospitality. Debby Applegate and Bruce Tolgan recently entered my life, and they make me feel welcome in their lovely New Haven home with fascinating conversation, champagne, and unadulterated good cheer. I appreciate all my wonderful New Haven friends: Hugh and Jean Davis, Melissa McGrath and Dan Lanpher, and Dana and Sam Schaffer. To my longtime dearest friends, Stephanie Holt and Demetrice Worley, you know how important you are and you know why. I love you both.

To my sons, Evan and Isaac, you are the joy in my heart. You are smart, sweet, talented boys and I am endlessly proud of you. I wrote this book thinking of you—knowing all along it would be dedicated to you.

To Thomas J. Thurston—you taught me to listen to my own song, to hear my heart beat, to love life. You introduced me to the cabaret, Mike Doughty, the art of cooking, sleepy Sundays, and soulful gazing. You are the most generous, loving, beautiful, dazzling partner anyone could hope for. You make my life complete.

HEARTS BEATING FOR LIBERTY

Introduction

The cheese was enormous. It created quite a stir at the lucrative antislavery fair in Boston, an event renowned more for its elegant and tasteful European imports than its dairy products. Fairgoers listened to the eloquence of antislavery luminaries Wendell Phillips and William Lloyd Garrison; perused the slogans on delicately embroidered Scottish-made handbags; admired silver jewelry boxes from London; took in the scent of evergreen, which graced tables throughout Boston's famed Faneuil Hall; and eagerly tasted the western cheese.[1] Betsey Mix Cowles and her sister abolitionists of the Ashtabula County Female Anti-Slavery Society in the Ohio Western Reserve had donated the "stupendous cheese" to the Boston Female Anti-Slavery Society fair.[2] Maria Giddings, the daughter of Ohio abolitionist politician Joshua Giddings, accompanied the cheese to Boston and reported back to Cowles, "I have given its history a dozen times, and all had to taste it."[3] Lizzie Hitchcock, the energetic young editor of the Ohio-based *Anti-Slavery Bugle*, confirmed that the western contribution was "duly appreciated," cheerfully concluding, "The more we can unite the East & West, the better."[4] Symbolic of their commitment to nourishing abolitionism and their respect for local traditions, the Ohio women, many of whom lived on dairy farms, were excited to learn that their distinctive gift attracted a "great deal of attention" and sold quickly.[5] Abby Kelley, a Boston fair leader who had just spent a year lecturing in Ohio, thanked the western women and assured them that compared to the Old Bay State, abolitionists in the West were "active and zealous."[6] Determined to live up to Kelley's praise, the Ohio women sent an even more astounding 197-pound cheese to Boston the following year.[7]

This book explores the contributions of western women to the antislavery movement. It examines individuals, including Betsey Mix Cowles and Lizzie Hitchcock, and groups such as the vibrant Ashtabula County Female Anti-Slavery Society. It shifts the focus from the East to the West, where a large percentage of abolitionists lived and worked in such places as Salem, Ohio, and Raisin, Michigan, and newly developed cities, among them Cincinnati and Chicago. By taking up the perspective of western women, this study forces a reconsideration of antislavery history. How important was the internecine conflict that permeated abolition in the 1840s, for example, when considered from a western grassroots perspective? How did abolitionists negotiate the lines demarcating different brands of antislavery? In answering these questions, this book argues that the environment of the Old Northwest, a region with a complicated history of slavery and racism, abolitionists created a distinct approach characterized by cooperation and flexibility. By highlighting women's activism, this study illuminates the role of grassroots workers and reveals how they built their movement.

By the mid-1840s, when the Ohio cheese made its way from the Western Reserve to Boston, abolitionism in the Northeast had become increasingly discordant. During the 1830s, most supporters agreed that moral suasion should guide the movement. Following the lead of such early African American activists as James Forten and Samuel Cornish, abolitionists denounced the colonization movement, which sought to compensate slaveholders and ship slaves to Africa, and attempted to persuade southerners that slavery was a sin that should be immediately renounced.[8] These immediate emancipationists, led by William Lloyd Garrison, called for racial justice and equality as a central element of their abolitionism.[9] This approach and the movement overall proved unpopular at best. Most Americans in both the North and the South considered slavery a taboo topic. With nearly 2.5 million slaves in the United States by 1840 and the southern economy increasingly driven by King Cotton, southerners considered the institution central to their regional identity.[10] As a result, abolitionists encountered heated and often violent opposition.[11] Toward the end of the 1830s, many abolitionists began to question the efficacy of moral suasion and advocated the development of a third political party, the Liberty Party, which seemed to offer a more pragmatic approach to ending slavery. This seeming rejection of moral suasion concerned other abolitionists, who worried that politics would corrupt and compromise a movement that had been built on virtue and purity of motive. Garrison and his supporters disavowed the third-party movement for these reasons, but they alienated a large contingent of abolitionists by unflinchingly advocating women's equal place in the movement. By 1840, particularly in the East, three overlapping contingents of abolitionists had emerged: the "Old Organization" Garrisonians who remained committed to moral suasion and favored women's equality; the "New Organization" reformers who also favored moral suasion, preferably through the church, but dismissed woman's equality as misguided; and the Liberty Party political abolitionists.[12]

The contentious issue of women's place in the movement was especially important because, as Julie Roy Jeffrey has shown, women made up the "silent majority" of abolitionists.[13] During the 1830s, women organized into separate female antislavery societies, with hundreds—among them Betsey Mix Cowles's cheese-making group—sprouting up across the Northeast and West. These groups continued the tradition of female benevolence begun at the turn of the century by a small minority of women who organized to nurture orphans, aid widows, and save prostitutes. Sustained by the increasingly popular notion that women were naturally moral and virtuous, these charitable organizations brought women out of the home and into public spaces.[14] Abolitionist women followed the lead of their benevolent sisters, citing their moral superiority as the reason for their activism. Men had failed to eliminate the sinful institution of slavery, so women needed to join the fight for emancipation. Abolitionist women differed from their benevolent predecessors, however, because antislavery was an unpopular movement that engendered intense opposition and social ostracism. Moreover, a few abolitionist women in the late 1830s began offering public lectures before audiences that included members of both sexes. These "promiscuous" lectures led to reproach within the movement. Antislavery clergymen in Massachusetts published a circular accusing the public-speaking women of violating the God-ordained role of womanhood and distracting from the movement. These critics, including both men and women, favored a less visible role for women in the movement. Troubled by this strife, some women left the movement to support other reform organizations. Many, however, continued their support for antislavery.

Cowles and hundreds of other western women abolitionists were among those who remained active in the movement. Western abolitionists did not experience the same bitter divide in 1840 as did the Northeast. Moreover, western women's place in abolitionist organizations was not a contentious issue because these activists did not engage in public lectures to "promiscuous" audiences or assume leadership positions in mixed-sex groups and because western antislavery proved adaptable and cooperative. Most western abolitionists worked with both the Liberty Party and the moral suasionists, self-consciously distancing themselves from the eastern conflict. As Cincinnati-based *Philanthropist* editor Gamaliel Bailey preached in 1845, "The policy of the friends of freedom in Ohio has ever been to avoid strife among themselves . . . , never permitting themselves to be drawn in any way to take any part in Eastern controversies."[15]

This cooperative approach meant that women continued their activism unabated. Working as individuals as well as through female and mixed-sex antislavery societies, the women of Ohio, Indiana, Illinois, Michigan, and Wisconsin forged an important space for themselves in the antislavery movement. Like their eastern sisters, they sewed, sponsored fairs, sang in antislavery choirs, hosted prayer groups, and wrote passionate appeals for their cause. But western women also blazed their own paths. They jumped headfirst into the cauldron of Liberty Party politics, vociferously supported the Quaker-led boycott of slave goods (the free produce movement), and tirelessly aided fugitives. These women remained devoted to local grassroots concerns even as they kept on eye on national issues.

Despite these accomplishments, historians have barely noticed western women abolitionists. Even as early as 1864, an article in Garrison's *Liberator*, "Annals of Women's Anti-Slavery Societies," highlighted the leadership, inventiveness, and success of Boston and Philadelphia groups but gave scant attention to western organizations.[16] There are several reasons for this neglect. General abolitionist studies tend to emphasize the East. Boston has always been considered the heart of abolition because it was the home to Garrisonianism. Philadelphia and New York have also received their fair share of attention. Although historians interested in political and cultural antislavery have recently challenged the preeminence of Garrison and his Boston-based wing of abolitionism, the eastern bias in the scholarship remains intact.[17]

Moreover, the relatively few studies of western abolition have largely focused on leading men—Giddings, Bailey, Theodore Weld, James Birney, and, more recently, Owen Lovejoy.[18] Each of these studies tends to highlight a distinct aspect of western abolition, such as third-party politics, religious antislavery, or radical antislavery. No definitive, all-encompassing study of the diversity and complexity of western abolition has been published.

Women's historians have written extensively on female abolitionists over the past several decades, but as with general studies of the movement, the focus is on the East, particularly New York, Boston, and Philadelphia. While important recent scholarship incorporates some western women, these works do not emphasize regional distinctiveness or interconnections.[19] Deborah Bingham Van Broekhoven's insightful work on Rhode Island women abolitionists, for example, emphasizes small-town grassroots activism and reveals how local politics and community controversies affected the movement, but it remains an eastern study.[20] Beth A. Salerno's excellent book on female antislavery societies moves beyond Boston and Philadelphia to introduce us to fascinating smaller groups, including many in the West, and explores "the power and limits of association," but she only briefly addresses the importance of the West as a region.[21] Michael D. Pierson's brilliant study of gender in antislavery politics incorporates the West but does not distinguish it from the East.[22]

This book builds on these studies but complicates their conclusions. By moving the focus from East to West, from urban to rural, we see the movement from a different perspective. The quarrelsome Boston Female Anti-Slavery Society is decentered by the flexible Ohio State Female Anti-Slavery Society. Boasting a membership of dairy farmers from Ashtabula as well as the elite of Cincinnati, this large, inclusive group focused its energy on local issues of central importance to the region—from repealing racist laws to the election of virtuous Liberty men to office. The society's practical approach to the movement, which required women to work cooperatively with men at all levels, highlights the mixed-sex character of western abolition. This pragmatism did not mean that western women abolitionists lacked firmness or failed to challenge entrenched racism. On the contrary, their flexibility allowed them to use whatever tools were available to achieve these goals.

This book also challenges the presumption that western abolition was an eastern import. By 1850, most of the residents of Ohio, Indiana, and Illinois had been born in the West.[23] Westerners were emphatic that their movement was distinct from the eastern movement, although they sought to work in coordination with their colleagues in Boston, New York, and Philadelphia. Even easterners concurred that the West had a certain energy that was lacking in the East. "The West is a mighty theatre for enterprise," wrote Garrison during a visit to Ohio. "Our East is fossilized in contrast. We have gone to seed."[24]

Western abolition experienced a different trajectory than did the movement in the East. While individuals from the Western Reserve to the frontier of Illinois sympathized with the plight of slaves in the early 1830s, formal antislavery organizations did not emerge until the middle of the decade. By 1840, the Old Northwest boasted hundreds of groups, both single sex and mixed sex. This explosion of antislavery organizations resulted from several regional events. The famed 1834 abolitionist debates at Cincinnati's Lane Theological Seminary, which led a large group of students to leave the institution for northern Ohio's more antislavery-friendly Oberlin College, helped to catalyze support for the movement.[25] Weld, one of the Lane rebels and a passionate abolitionist speaker, toured Ohio in 1835–37, sparking further interest in abolition. The 1837 killing of abolitionist editor Elijah Lovejoy in southern Illinois also awakened antislavery sentiment across the Old Northwest. Lovejoy was shot while defending his printing office from a proslavery mob, leading abolitionists across the West to decry the martyrdom of one of their own.[26] Nearly ten years later, the Illinois Female Anti-Slavery Society raised the specter of Lovejoy in their public denunciation of the state's languid abolitionist movement: "How has it been with us in the State of Illinois? Let the blood of Lovejoy answer the question. And where is our redress? What have we done? *We have buried our dead out of our sight.*"[27] Also in 1846, the abolitionist women of Jackson County, Michigan, used the image of a "murdered Lovejoy" to justify their "small" effort in aiding the "poor crushed slave."[28] When the eastern abolitionist movement splintered, the western movement remained relatively stable. By the mid-1840s most abolitionists in the region favored partisan politics as the most efficient method for fighting slavery; those who preferred to work through the church tolerated their political colleagues. Even the region's Garrisonians, who became more vocal and influential when they initiated an Ohio-based antislavery newspaper in 1846, recognized the critical importance of working with the majority non-Garrisonians in their region.

Most easterners thought about the West as a frontier that represented the hope of the future. By the 1850s, it had become an important battleground between slavery and freedom as the North and the South attempted to spread their regional identity into the expanding nation. But this was old news. Slavery and race had always been contested areas in the Old Northwest. Despite article VI of the Northwest Ordinance of 1787, which prohibited slavery from the territory, both slavery and indentured servitude persisted in the region well into the antebellum period. In Indiana and Illinois, slaveholders repeatedly tried to find ways to legalize or subtly institutionalize slavery. Although these attempts eventually failed, antiblack sentiment drove both sides of the slavery debate. During the Indiana and Illinois constitutional debates in 1816 and 1818, slavery opponents employed racist arguments to support their positions. The region's infamous Black Laws emerged during the 1810s and were reinforced and expanded over the next forty years. The measures prohibited blacks from testifying against whites, participating in the militia, voting, and attending public schools. Indiana and Illinois quickly added laws that required bonds for good behavior or banned black immigration to the state. In 1853, Illinois passed the most severe Black Law, which allowed blacks to be sold for a limited period if they did not leave the state within ten days of arriving. Although Michigan and Wisconsin did not become states until 1837 and 1848, respectively, both followed the lead of their southern neighbors and passed a variety of Black Laws. Wisconsin proved slightly less racist than the other states, refusing to approve immigration restrictions, but it also twice failed to pass universal suffrage bills.[29]

The contested history of race relations in the West strongly affected the development of antislavery action among the region's women. Racism and the Black Laws created an environment that demanded a pragmatic abolitionism. Female antislavery societies certainly devoted their energy toward battling slavery in the South, but it was impossible to ignore the situation at home: legislation that allowed for the enslavement of free blacks, the requirement of a five-hundred-dollar good-behavior bond, or the legal exclusion of blacks from the state. Historians have shown that black abolitionists tended to focus on issues that affected daily life for their community, such as education, job opportunities, and racial discrimination.[30] These issues influenced western abolitionism as well. Both male and female abolitionists focused on eliminating the Black Laws, aiding fugitive slaves, and building and sustaining schools for blacks. This approach required that abolitionists of all stripes work together, and women proved especially adept at such collaboration.

Other aspects of the western environment, including the diversity of the population, further demanded cooperation. Though the African American population in the Old Northwest remained small, blacks and whites coordinated their antislavery efforts. Native-born westerners mixed with German, English, and Irish immigrants; New Englanders; Pennsylvanians; southerners; and New Yorkers.[31] The western abolitionist movement mirrored this regional diversity. Virginians such as Mary Brown Davis, who emigrated to Peoria, Illinois, worked with Bostonians, westerners, and even a few European immigrants. Their different backgrounds affected their approach to the movement—some preferred to work through sewing societies, while others chose to mount the podium. Some supported woman's rights, and some shrunk from such a controversial issue. They built bridges and learned to work through their differences.

This book is organized by topic and is loosely chronological. It begins in the 1830s with an exploration of female antislavery societies in Ohio, revealing how the western environment led to a unique trend toward large countywide and statewide groups, phenomena that did not exist in the East. Directed by energetic and experienced leaders, these inclusive groups organized married and unmarried women from small towns and cities and from a variety of different religious backgrounds. Women's organizations also worked closely with local men who supported and nurtured their sister abolitionists. Ohio, which was populated before the rest of the Old Northwest, initiated trends among female antislavery societies that subsequently affected Indiana, Illinois, Michigan, and Wisconsin.

Chapter 2 highlights women's participation in the Liberty Party in the 1840s. Mary Brown Davis forged the way for women to enter partisan politics and use their special "female influence" to affect local and national elections. The Liberty Party proved especially inviting to women because of its focus on the moral issue of slavery and its tendency to organize at the local level, which worked well with women's groups. In particular, the western Liberty Party, with its emphasis on cooperation among different brands of abolitionists, encouraged women to find a place for themselves. Hundreds of women, particularly in Illinois, Indiana, and Michigan, became earnest Liberty Party advocates, helping to elect local candidates and petition for legislative changes through their party.

Chapter 3 explores the free produce movement, a tactic of abolition that sought to undermine slavery through a boycott of slave-made goods. Advocates refused to purchase slave-produced cotton, sugar, rice, and coffee, hoping that a global shunning of these goods would force slave owners to abandon the iniquitous institution. This method of antislavery proved relatively unpopular because it demanded a sacrifice on the part of its supporters—substitutes for these mainstay products were difficult to find. Most historians have associated this movement with its leadership among Philadelphia Quakers, but western women, particularly Quakers in eastern Indiana and central Ohio, were among the most effective and long-term supporters of free produce. Their advocacy was geared toward both the practical goal of ending slavery and the emotional satisfaction of making personal sacrifices in support of freedom. The West, with its down-to-earth frontier women used to eschewing the fineries supplied by large urban centers, proved more effective at nurturing free produce. The region's mixed-sex approach to abolition also helped build free produce, with both sexes working together through Quaker organizations to create viable free-produce stores and publications.

Chapter 4 analyzes antislavery fairs and shows how western women employed this fund-raising method to negotiate among the different brands of abolitionists in their region. Sarah Otis Ernst, a lonely Garrisonian in Cincinnati, built a profitable fair that funded a spectacularly successful annual spring antislavery convention designed to build bridges between the outnumbered Garrisonians and their colleagues across the region. Attracting the nation's leading abolitionists, Ernst's convention allowed her to dictate the terms of abolitionism in the Queen City. Ernst's sister abolitionists in Salem, Ohio, also designed an antislavery fair that nurtured Garrisonians in the West, helping them to sustain their community even as they, too, learned to negotiate with their third-party and religious-antislavery colleagues.

Women lecturers are the subject of chapter 5, which highlights the explosive influence of Abby Kelley's visit to Ohio in the mid-1840s and the plethora of western women who followed in her footsteps. Though inspired by Kelley, most of these women public speakers developed personal styles that catered to their western audiences. Sensitive to the influence of third-party and religious abolitionists, these women focused on topics that appealed to a broad cross-section of their listeners, including the Black Laws, black education, and racial inequity in their region.

Chapter 6 further explores the battle against racism by focusing on the movement's support for escaped slaves as they made their way through the Old Northwest to safer locations. This type of abolitionist activity in the West again forced Garrisonians to work closely with third-party and religious abolitionists. Although historians have traditionally focused on male leaders of the Underground Railroad, western women such as Laura Haviland not only led the way in dozens of escapes and rescues but also defended their unladylike activity as morally driven and thereby wholly appropriate for any good Christian. Moreover, most of the tedious, invisible labor of the Underground Railroad, including feeding, clothing, and housing escaped slaves, was performed by women.

The final chapter chronicles the connections between woman's rights and abolition in the West. As in the East, many western women abolitionists did not turn to woman's rights, but among those who did, the connection seemed obvious and important. The 1850 Salem Woman's Rights Convention was the first and only meeting that excluded men from participating,

but by and large the western movement proved especially inclusive. Abolitionists of all stripes—men and women, black and white—participated in
woman's rights conventions throughout the 1850s. The common theme of
human rights drew abolitionists into woman's rights and helped them to
see their movement as encompassing not just racial equality but full human
equality.

CHAPTER I

Grassroots Activism and
Female Antislavery Societies

The two knew each other by reputation only. Lucy Wright, sister of famed abolitionist Elizur Wright, had just returned home to Tallmadge, Ohio, after spending nearly two years working as a teacher in African American schools in Cincinnati.[1] Betsey Mix Cowles, who lived only eighty miles from Wright, had recently founded the Ashtabula County Female Anti-Slavery Society, which eventually became the largest and most influential women's group in the Old Northwest.[2] In March 1836, Wright wrote to congratulate Cowles for her zealous advocacy of antislavery and to offer encouragement. A year before the Grimké sisters would lecture to "promiscuous" audiences in New York and Boston and four years before Abby Kelley would scandalize many with her election to a leadership position in the American Anti-Slavery Society, Wright understood the burgeoning opposition to women's organized participation in the movement: "Many curl the lip and cast the look of scorn when woman associate their efforts in this cause," she warned. "They fear the strength that union gives so they cry, *out of your sphere ladies*, you have forgotten the modesty and retirement belonging to your sex." Ever optimistic, Wright advised that the "taunts of opponents" could be helpful if they "incline us to temper our ardor with prudence and study wisdom in our measures more than we otherwise should, and if [they] beget in us patience, and meekness under insult it will be worth more than scores of

The Old Northwest. Map created by Brian Powers and William "Wes" Skidmore.

unmeaning compliments." As an experienced abolitionist and a founder of the fast-growing Portage County Female Anti-Slavery Society, Wright had learned that opponents were more likely to be won over with "prudence" and "patience" than with intransigent resistance. Wright concluded her letter by wishing for a mutually beneficial friendship: "We should like well to have company in this matter."[3]

The Ashtabula and Portage County women's abolitionist societies would become closely linked, as Wright desired, with both experiencing explosive growth during their first year. The Ashtabula society enrolled nearly 80 women at its inaugural meeting, and within twelve months it was bursting at the seams with more than 450 members.[4] The Portage group increased tenfold, from 37 to 390 by August 1836.[5] No other female antislavery society in the Northwest or Northeast rivaled them in numbers; the Philadelphia Female Anti-Slavery Society included fewer than 100 members in 1836, while the famed Boston group boasted only 250 members that year.[6]

The New York–based American Anti-Slavery Society highlighted the two Ohio groups in its monthly publication, the *Anti-Slavery Record*. After disparaging those who would "hate" women for their abolitionism, the *Record* "rejoiced" at the "rapid multiplication" of female antislavery societies in Ohio, exclaiming, "Our hearts are cheered" at the success of the two Western Reserve groups.[7]

The efficient and successful Ashtabula and Portage organizations well represent the cooperative, pragmatic abolitionism that came to characterize western female antislavery. As Wright suggested in her letter to Cowles, western women abolitionists favored prudence and patience over zealousness and rigidity. They understood that as women taking an unpopular position on a controversial political issue, they stood on shaky ground. Western women worked toward pragmatic abolitionism by carefully choosing moderate antislavery methods, including a savvy partnership with men, an unprecedented campaign in support of black education, and a nationally influential petition drive. Moreover, in a distinctly western tradition, Ohio women banded together at the county and state levels to create a unified, powerful antislavery voice. Though their membership was almost entirely white, Ohio women's groups also proved deeply committed to racial equality.[8] These Ohio female antislavery societies influenced the development of women's abolition groups in the remainder of the Old Northwest. In the 1840s, more than one hundred such organizations emerged in Indiana, Michigan, Illinois, and Wisconsin. Even as eastern female groups became embroiled in divisive ideological battles, western women embraced cooperation and practical change as their maxim.

Getting Organized

While the colonization movement held sway among those who opposed slavery during the 1820s, William Lloyd Garrison's call for immediate emancipation quickly took hold in the Buckeye State. By 1836, Ohio claimed more antislavery groups than any other state, accounting for 25 percent of the total.[9] Several individuals and events catalyzed this explosion, much of which was centered in southern Ohio.[10] Though abolitionism would take root primarily in western and northern Ohio, the border town of Cincinnati initially experienced the most antislavery activity. The city's large African American community worked diligently to aid fugitive slaves and to undermine the institution through social and economic success.[11] James G. Birney's courageous attempt to publish an antislavery newspaper in Cincinnati and the

1. ASHTABULA COUNTY
Andover (1836)
Ashtabula (1835)
Cherry Valley (1836)
Geneva (1835)
Harpersfield and
Austinburg (1836)
Morgan (1836)
New Lyme (1836)
Rome (1836)
Windsor (1836)

2. FAYETTE COUNTY
County-Wide (1837)
Bloomingburg (1837)

3. HAMILTON COUNTY
Cincinnati (1835)

4. HARRISON COUNTY
Cadiz (1837)

5. KNOX COUNTY
Mount Vernon (1835)

6. LAKE COUNTY
Madison (1838)

7. LICKING COUNTY
Madison (1835)
St. Albans (1836)

8. LORAIN COUNTY
Elyria (1836)
Oberlin (1835)

9. MEDINA COUNTY
Abbeyville (1836)

10. MUSKINGUM COUNTY
County-Wide (1836)

11. PORTAGE COUNTY
County-Wide (1836)

12. ROSS COUNTY
Concord (1838)

13. STARK COUNTY
Canton (1836)

14. TRUMBULL COUNTY
Vernon (1835)

15. WASHINGTON COUNTY
Unionville (1838)

Ohio Female Antislavery Societies, 1835–38. Map created by Brian Powers
and William "Wes" Skidmore.

violent mob opposition that ensued turned many Ohioans into abolition-ists.[12] Finally, when Theodore Weld and a group of ministerial students chose to leave Cincinnati's Lane Seminary in 1834 because it suppressed their abolitionism, the entire state experienced the aftereffects. Oberlin College received a number of the former Lane students, opened its doors to African American students, and quickly became well known as an abolitionist stronghold. Many "Lane rebels" became public advocates for abolitionism, blanketing Ohio with their message of freedom and equality.[13] Early on, they focused attention particularly on women's role in the movement.[14]

A small group of "sisters" who taught in African American schools in Cincinnati brought some of this attention to women. These teachers made quite an impression on the Lane rebels. The Cincinnati educational experiment began when two young men, Augustus Wattles and Marius Robinson, "felt so deeply" the desperate situation of local African Americans that they abandoned Lane Seminary in 1834 to devote themselves full time to the educational needs of the city's black community.[15] Several equally devoted women abolitionists soon joined Wattles and Robinson. Responding to a plea in the *New York Evangelist* to help educate Cincinnati's young black women, Emeline Bishop, Susan Lowe, Phebe Mathews, and Lucy Wright moved to the Queen City in 1834. Several others, including Ohio-born Emily Rakestraw, would join them within a few months. These women lived, worked, and socialized among local African Americans. Their male colleagues expressed awe at the women's devotion. "The Sisters are doing nobly," exclaimed Lane rebel Samuel Wells. "They are everywhere received with open arms. They visit, eat, and sleep with their people and are exerting a powerful influence in correcting their domestic habits."[16] Most of the sisters received little or no compensation for their work and thus went into debt during their time in Cincinnati.[17] They often worked very long days with little respite. "Since you have been in Cincinnati you have taxed your constitution beyond its power of endurance," Marius Robinson warned his wife, Emily.[18] In response to Weld's concern that the women "do not take recreation enough," Bishop bluntly replied, "We have no time to play or laugh or ramble on the hills that surround us. . . . There is now, particularly *now*, so much that demands attention."[19]

Witnessing considerable self-sacrifice and boundless energy on the part of the Cincinnati sisters, the Lane rebels became strong advocates of women's participation in abolition. When Weld, Wattles, Robinson, and a few others began lecturing across Ohio, they shared with their audiences this respect and enthusiasm for women's important role in the movement. However, although the Lane men helped to plant female abolitionism in Ohio, women had already tilled the ground.[20] By 1838, Ohio alone had at least thirty women's abolitionist groups, with more than one hundred others elsewhere in the North.[21]

Cowles, a savvy organizer, helped construct many of these groups. Raised in the small town of Austinburg, in Ashtabula County in the Western Reserve, Cowles understood the difficulty of building a reform community in rural Ohio. The population of Ashtabula County in the 1830s remained below fifteen thousand, though it would nearly double over the next two decades. Most residents were farmers, but the economy was beginning to diversify, with professionals, bankers, and skilled artisans slowly moving into the area.[22] As one scholar argues, "Ohio was a world defined by the proliferation of villages as commercial crossroads sporting banks, stores, churches, and schools, all of them vying to acquire the keys to growth and prosperity."[23] In the 1830s, however, most citizens were focused on making a living on their farms or on finding consumers for their products, with little time left for activism. Residents often lived miles away from one another, making meetings difficult to organize. Recognizing these obstacles, Cowles and her

Betsey Mix Cowles, 1840. Courtesy of Oberlin College Archives.

fellow antislavery converts in Austinburg decided to create a county organization that would meet on a quarterly basis in different locations. This organization would rely heavily on correspondence among the various auxiliaries to maintain its vitality and focus. Local groups would meet more often at convenient sites. With Cowles as its guiding force, the Ashtabula County Female Anti-Slavery Society became Ohio's most energetic, successful abolition group in the mid-1830s.[24]

Founded in the fall of 1835, several months before the Oberlin Female Anti-Slavery Society, the sensible Ashtabula group focused on growth through networking.[25] Reaching out to nearby friends, relatives, and those with reform inclinations, Cowles immediately began a writing campaign to spur the development of more groups across Ashtabula County. She instructed women in the basics of antislavery organizing and tallied the movement's growth in her region. She asked for specific information about the number and names of participants, their activities, and their successes. She gave advice about holding concerts, prayers groups, and petitioning. Without leaving her small town, she became a one-woman antislavery organizer. Even as Weld and his band of Lane rebels traipsed across the state beating the antislavery drum, Cowles inspired hundreds of women across western Ohio to endure social scorn and embrace abolitionism. With sisterly affection and practical guidance, she brought women out of their homes and into civil society.

The women of the Western Reserve took pleasure and motivation from their interaction with Cowles. "I wish much to hear how the cause prospers with you," wrote Wright to Cowles.[26] "We wish to avail ourselves of your experience and correspondence." One of Cowles's most important lessons was the effectiveness of organizing at the county level, a message Wright took to heart. By the fall of 1835, she was working with Ravenna resident Sarah Carpenter to construct a female group in their county. Carpenter, who had been converted to abolition after hearing a lecture by Weld, begged him to return to Ravenna to attend the group's organizational meeting, telling him, "I am confident not a stroke will be struck, not a finger will be lifted if *you* do not come."[27] But Carpenter belied that conclusion in the same letter, explaining that she had already met with the area's most "influential Ladies" and found a "united expression" in favor of forming a county organization. A few months later, several hundred women met in Ravenna to form the Portage County Ladies Anti-Slavery Society, with Lane rebel James Thome regaling the women with a lively address at their inaugural gathering.[28] Despite violent mob attacks at nearby antislavery meetings—in Middlebury, abolitionists were pelted with rotten eggs and broken glass—the women insisted on their right to organize.[29] "It is peculiarly proper that woman should sympathize with the afflicted and oppressed," they proclaimed.[30] Wright served as the group's first secretary. The Portage organization came to rival the Ashtabula group in both size and success, taking lessons from Cowles in how to organize effectively as well as in the importance of both regional and national networking. One of the society's first resolutions was to maintain a close communication with all of its auxiliaries.[31] Learning about the successes and tribulations of other groups offered practical advice and inspiration to the rural women of the Western Reserve.

While Ohio women abolitionists became expert networkers, the Lane rebels also facilitated the development of female groups throughout the state. After Thome left the Portage County meeting, he shared the story of the women there with women in other communities.[32] He visited Canton in March and won over two influential anti-abolitionist sisters, Eleanor Griswold and Lavenia Gordon, who had grown up in a slaveholding Baltimore family and harbored deep-seated racial prejudices.[33] "Both these Ladies were *thoroughly converted*," boasted Thome in a letter to Weld. Just as Carpenter had laid the groundwork by proselytizing to the elite of Ravenna, Griswold and Gordon began "to visit amongst their acquaintances and to labor with the first Ladies of [Canton] to *convert them*."[34] Although an "overflowing congregation" met to pass antiabolition resolutions and the men of Canton proved too "timorous" to create an abolition group, seventeen of the town's women joined a female antislavery society and defended their action as wholly appropriate.[35] "We believe that the females of our country may exert an important influence in accomplishing this desirable object," they declared in the preamble to their constitution. "We consider that we are *not moving out of our proper sphere* as females, when we assume a *public* stand in favor of our *oppressed sisters*."[36]

By the spring of 1836, female abolitionism was flourishing in western Ohio. In only a few months, dozens of town organizations and county societies in Ashtabula, Portage, Wayne, and Muskingum had emerged. In response, Thome and several other Lane rebels joined Wright and other local abolitionists in encouraging women to attend the annual meeting of the Ohio Anti-Slavery Society to be held in Granville in April. "Ladies from all parts of the state are appointing their delegates & marshalling their bands to make a terrible onset on the kingdom of darkness at Granville," Wattles wrote to Cowles.[37] Assuming that Cowles had reservations about public activity, Wattles assured her, "There is no station in life but what may be filled as ably and as beneficially by woman as by man."[38] Although Cowles did not go to Granville, other Ohio women abolitionists attended the meeting in 1836, including several from Ashtabula. Wright, Carpenter, and the Portage County women provided financial support so that the Cincinnati sisters could make the trek.[39] Bishop, Lowe, and Phebe Mathews accompanied Wattles, Birney, and several others to the meeting, where they were joined by dozens of other women.[40]

When the nearly two hundred abolitionists gathered on the morning of April 27, they met in a large barn, nicknamed the Hall of Freedom, because every meetinghouse in town was closed to them.[41] A remonstrance against the antislavery meeting had been publicly circulated by some of the town's most "prominent citizens." This action came as no surprise to the abolitionists. Opposition to their meetings occurred on a regular basis. A mob had disrupted Weld's lecture in Granville a year earlier, and violent disruptions had already occurred at antislavery gatherings in a dozen Ohio towns.[42]

Despite the threat of disorder, Thome spoke "on the responsibilities of *American females* touching slavery."[43] With as many as eighty women listening, Thome rejected the idea of a "proper sphere" that limited women to domestic duties. Women, like men, he avowed, were bound by Christian duty to "be active in furthering every moral enterprize which promotes the common welfare."[44] Although Thome's speech met with no opposition or disruption (he claimed "it took hold of the women mightily"), that spring day in central Ohio ended with violence.[45] Departing along the streets of Granville, the attendees met an angry crowd. Pushing and shoving occurred. Opponents pelted the abolitionists with eggs and tripped and physically accosted some women.[46] Later that evening, when Birney left the home of a local abolitionist "on his *shave-tailed horse*" (thanks to the mob) he was abused "most vilely" and met with a "shower of eggs and curses."[47] This act of disrespect so disturbed Thome that he confessed to Weld, "I could stand no more. I wept."[48]

Even as their male leader was reduced to tears, however, the women ignored the threats and decided to create a state society for female abolitionists, an unprecedented move. Although a few mixed-sex state antislavery societies had previously been created, no other state female societies existed. On April 29, the day after the Ohio Anti-Slavery Society meeting concluded, the women met to organize.[49] Despite fatigue and lingering fear of a renewed mob attack, the women concluded that Ohio's antislavery movement deserved "more energy and efficiency among the females."[50] The women of Muskingum County, which had sent the largest number of representatives to the Ohio Anti-Slavery Society meeting, agreed to act as a "central committee" for the group, ensuring that "interesting intelligence from our past become common property of all."[51] In other words, group members wanted to share knowledge and gain power from their unification. Their more immediate goals included publishing and distributing Thome's *Address to the Females of Ohio* and petitioning their "Fathers and Rulers" in Congress to abolish slavery in the District of Columbia.[52]

For the next ten years, the Ohio State Female Anti-Slavery Society continued to meet annually, share experiences, petition (it gathered more than three thousand signatures), and finance education for African Americans. It prospered because it was pragmatic, flexible, and cooperative. Wright and other leaders highlighted the organization's religious and moral motivations, knowing that this approach would appeal to female neighbors and friends. They firmly established women's right to speak out about slavery but did so tenderly, thus engendering as little opposition as possible. The group cleverly ensured maximum geographical diversity by shifting its leadership to a different location each year. In the late 1830s, the group's central office moved from Muskingum County in central Ohio to Portage County in the northeast part of the state and finally, to Cincinnati in the southwestern corner.[53]

State antislavery societies in Ohio and other northwestern states offered abolitionists an opportunity to bond through shared identity. The women who participated in the anniversaries of the Ohio state organization did so with a sense of themselves as *Ohioans*, distinct from the South and the Northeast. They traveled through bad weather over dreadful roads to reach a meeting that brought them together to battle the most sinful institution in the nation. They came as representatives of their towns and counties, with deep connections and respect for their communities, but they also came to be a part of something larger. Unlike the Boston, Philadelphia, and New York City abolitionists, the small-town, rural folks who dominated the Ohio meetings felt compelled to unite their forces and express themselves as a part of their state's commitment to ending slavery and inequality. Identifying with the ever-expanding and exciting West, Ohio abolitionists prided themselves on leading the way. Not satisfied simply to follow the New England abolitionists, Ohio's antislavery advocates established themselves as important in their own right. The women in particular paved new roads by creating a state group willing to occupy civil society—to give voice to their ideals and their passions. Even as they organized into a separate female society, however, women continued to work closely with their male counterparts, a desirable and politically expedient partnership.

Partnership with Men

Wattles played a key role at the 1838 meeting of the Ohio Female Anti-Slavery Society, speaking extensively in support of various resolutions.[54] The decision to invite Wattles to speak illustrates women's willingness and inclination to work closely with male abolitionists. Ohio female antislavery societies were characterized by their strong partnership with men. The alliance that developed was not one of perfect equality, but one represented more by what Nancy Isenberg has called "co-equality."[55] Male and female abolitionists cooperated in thoughtful ways that quietly expanded on familiar gendered roles and expectations. They agreed that the moral obligation to battle slavery applied equally to both sexes and required men and women to engage in civic action. The nature of that engagement often differed, with men presuming more of the leadership and policymaking roles. Nonetheless, western women's roles proved fluid, and female groups offered space for women to collaborate with men while remaining independent.

This comfortable cooperation manifested itself in both single-sex and mixed-sex antislavery groups throughout Ohio. The Ohio Anti-Slavery Society, which coordinated its annual meetings with the Ohio Female Anti-Slavery Society, welcomed women. The report of the group's anniversary at Mount Pleasant in the spring of 1837 illustrates the group's commitment to female participation.[56] Fifty-eight of the 250 people who enrolled as delegates were women.[57] Several towns, including Muskingum and Oberlin, incorporated men's and women's names into one list even though the women were involved with separate female societies.[58] Maria Sturges, the eloquent and powerful leader of the Muskingum women's group, was listed under the general county organization, along with five other female abolitionists and only three men, suggesting that distinctions between male and female groups were secondary and that abolitionists of both sexes cooperated in communitywide efforts. Even the order of the names reflected relaxed teamwork, as females and males were integrated throughout the list. Often, but not always, the men and women shared surnames, demonstrating the importance of family ties. Husbands and wives, sisters and brothers, fathers and daughters, mothers and sons—all worked side by side in antislavery societies and attended statewide meetings together. Although men dominated the organization's offices and delivered almost all of the public speeches, women's presence meant that they listened to the same lectures, informally discussed and debated the key issues, and engaged in the same grassroots activism.[59]

Female antislavery societies in Ohio expanded on this cooperative spirit by thoughtfully employing men in carefully chosen positions while maintaining control over male participation. The Ashtabula County Female Anti-Slavery Society hired a male agent to visit various towns, galvanize the ladies, and aid them in creating female auxiliaries.[60] Custom and habit meant that few women would be willing or able to take on the role of agent, so hiring Leonard E. Beardsley was a practical decision. The Ashtabula women maintained a semblance of control over the expansion process by writing introductory letters to abolitionist women in the communities Beardsley visited. These combined efforts proved successful, resulting in the organization of eight auxiliary societies in just a few months.[61] Cowles and her abolitionist sisters recognized the importance and expediency of working closely with men.

The Ashtabula group as well as other Ohio female societies found men useful not only as agents but also as advisers and speakers. Few women, especially in the 1830s, were willing to risk social opprobrium by speaking in public. Men, including Lane rebels John Alvord and Amos Dresser, spoke at each of the Ashtabula meetings. The Madison Female Anti-Slavery Society, a vibrant and large northeastern Ohio group, engaged both male and female speakers to regale members.[62] The ladies of the Cadiz Female Anti-Slavery Society eagerly listened to Marius Robinson as well as African American college student Titus Bosfield.[63] Men often attended the meetings of female antislavery societies when well-known speakers appeared.[64] The relationship between male orators and female antislavery societies in Ohio was mutually beneficial. While the itinerant male lecturers enlivened and educated women's groups, the male-run Ohio Anti-Slavery Society saw its coffers filled through the ladies' societies. As official auxiliaries to the state organization, the female groups pledged money to their parent organization. While few groups could match the one hundred dollars promised to the Ohio Anti-Slavery Society by the Portage County women in 1836 and the Putnam women in 1838, even the inexperienced members of the Oberlin Young Ladies Anti-Slavery Society pledged fifty dollars in 1836.[65]

The men and women of the Ohio antislavery movement became a close-knit group in the 1830s. Traveling lecturers stayed in the homes of local abolitionists and often visited repeatedly. Deep and long-lasting friendships developed. Several Lane rebels married Cincinnati sisters. After suffering together through trying times working in African American schools in Cincinnati, Augustus Wattles and Susan Lowe wed in 1837, establishing a robust reform-focused relationship that lasted over many decades. They taught blacks in Ohio through the late 1830s, farmed and hosted abolitionist lecturers in rural Ohio during the 1840s, and moved to Kansas in the mid-1850s to help sustain the abolitionist voice in that violence-torn territory.[66]

No couple better symbolizes the symmetry and success of men's and women's connections in the western abolitionist movement than Marius Robinson and Emily Rakestraw. Robinson and Wattles were the first to leave Lane Seminary to devote their time to teaching local blacks. Rakestraw soon joined them in Cincinnati's schools. The daughter of abolitionist-minded Quakers from New Garden, Ohio, she read about the need for teachers in the Queen City and moved to southern Ohio. Wattles, Rakestraw, and all of the young, single abolitionist teachers in Cincinnati quickly established the type of intense friendships that endured for years, even though most of them eventually went their separate ways. The stressful and exhausting work of connecting with and teaching African Americans who were cautious about working too closely with unknown whites brought together the teachers, as did the antiabolitionist spirit that permeated Cincinnati. The city proved very unwelcoming to white abolitionists who upset the status quo by educating blacks, preaching equality, and condemning slavery. After a year of teaching in Cincinnati, Mathews wrote rather casually to Weld, "An hour or two since we received information well authenticated, that a mob of more than a hundred are devising a plan to tear down our house [but] our confidence in God is unshaken."[67]

The sense of community that developed among the white Cincinnati teachers, both men and women, supplied them with much-needed human sustenance amid widespread condemnation. Even as many of the female teachers boarded within the African American community, they looked to each other for empathy and humor. Rakestraw discovered this source of emotional nourishment as she found herself swept up in the family of Cincinnati abolitionists.[68] Perhaps because of the intensity of this environment, Robinson and Rakestraw had a short courtship. When they wed in November 1836, they found that although they could continue to rely on their friends in Cincinnati, they were completely cut off by the extended Rakestraw family in New Garden. The evidence suggests that the brevity of the young couple's courtship caused the rift. Robinson had not yet met Rakestraw's family at the time of their marriage, and her relatives may also have been alienated by the fact that Robinson was not a Quaker. In any case, the rift caused Emily Robinson agonizing heartache. "My parents have cast me off in the fullness of bitterness, grief, reproach, and scorn," she wrote to her new husband two months after their wedding. "My sisters and other friends whom I have loved too dearly, and still to[o] fondly remember, love me less and care less for me than they did, in by gone days."[69] She missed her New Garden family. After learning from a cousin of the engagement of one of the Rakestraw girls, Emily confessed to Marius, "I feel very anxious about my sister." Emily worried that her sister's fiancé was a dislikable "little chap" who was "too ignorant" to be an abolitionist. She concluded, "Is it not strange they do not write to me?"[70] Between the challenging nature of her work, the hostility of the city, and the alienation of her family, Emily's residency in Cincinnati proved trying. Her fortunes changed when Marius lectured in New Garden and met with her family. Convinced that her family would be "gruff" and distant with her new spouse, Emily advised him to make his stay brief.[71] However, he won over the Rakestraws with his gentle manner and brilliant antislavery lectures.[72]

Although the reunion with her family relieved Emily, both she and Marius found challenging their full-time commitment to the antislavery movement. Marius left on a lecture tour almost immediately after their wedding, while Emily remained in southern Ohio, teaching and struggling to make ends meet. Other abolitionist couples suffered similarly. Edward Weed, a Lane rebel and Mathews's husband, wrote to Emily Robinson, "I left my dear wife Monday at Putnam. [I] do not expect to see her again under two months. What a sad thing it is to be an abolition lecturer's wife? I sympathize with you my dear sister from knowing how my own dear one feels."[73]

Feelings of isolation proved a challenge not only for the Cincinnati teachers and the spouses of antislavery lecturers but also and especially for rural abolitionists in the West. It meant that collaboration among male and female reformers was critical. Estranged from neighbors, colleagues, and churches, abolitionists in places such as Putnam, Cherry Valley, and Granville could not afford to turn away from any potential ally, male or female. Any new addition to the family of abolitionists was immediately embraced, sometimes to the extreme. "Emily Smith is coming will be here in 3 weeks from this time," explained Emily Robinson to Marius. "Br[other] B. likes her very well, but has made no advances toward matrimony yet."[74] Even as they gossiped, these abolitionists clung to one another for a sense of purpose.

Cooperation between men and women in Ohio antislavery was especially important in the face of widespread opposition. Hostility and violence toward abolitionists helped to unveil women's capabilities and made women more aware of the cultural prescriptions that bound their lives. Both sexes freely took social and physical risks in their advocacy of the movement. While lecturing in Ohio during the mid-1830s, Marius Robinson often found that women were remarkably effective and intrepid in defending him against violent mobs. When a hostile group of men threatened an abolitionist gathering in Hartford in 1837, a fearless sister took charge of the situation: "One woman climbed into the meetinghouse at the window, when I was hemmed in by the mob in the pulpit, determined to see what was going on & if possible to aid in my rescue."[75] A year later, when a group of men tried to abduct Robinson from the home of an abolitionist friend in Berlin, Ohio, his hostess stepped in to defend him: "Mrs. Garretson interfered saying, 'if you take him you must take me too,' and . . . she made an effort to close the door & shut out the remainder of the gang." Continued Robinson, "Brute force was the order of the day & it was exercised without respect of person upon all who opposed." The attackers ordered Garretson to step aside; when she refused, one hooligan assured her that he would "'remember her for this,' & pushed her with some violence." She "received two blows one on her arm which sprained her wrist & another on her breast which since occasioned considerable pain and soreness."[76] Robinson suffered even more severely: he was dragged from Garretson's home. The mob then sliced open his leg with a scythe, tarred and feathered him, beat him almost into unconsciousness, and drove him to a nearby town and dumped him. The injuries impaired his health for years and forced him to retire from full-time lecturing. Twelve years later, the repentant city of Berlin invited Robinson to return. Thousands turned out to hear him recount his previous experience in the community and, concluded one attendee, "scarce an eye was without a tear."[77]

Side by side, scuffling with violent opponents, men and women abolitionists in Ohio developed mutual respect. Despite the existence of distinct female antislavery societies, women were never truly separated from men, and the two sexes interacted in all aspects of the movement, developing tight social, political, and activist networks that helped to sustain them in a hostile and isolated environment. Their roles were fluid and often overlapping. Men certainly offered more public addresses and were elected to leadership positions. But women directed large abolitionist groups and even sometimes physically protected and defended their brothers in the face of violent opposition. While male and female Ohio abolitionists pragmatically coordinated their activities, women still initiated and sustained many very successful methods for promoting antislavery. These activities were consistently characterized by a sensible understanding of their hostile environment and the limitations imposed by womanhood.

Publications

At its 1836 organizing meeting, the Ohio Female Anti-Slavery Society promoted one of the most practical, popular, and effective activities for women abolitionists: the financing, distribution, and communal reading of antislavery publications. Irene Ball Allan of Illinois's Peoria Female Anti-Slavery Society proclaimed in 1842 that the dissemination of antislavery newspapers resulted in the conversion of several "bitter" opponents to the movement.[78] Cowles understood the importance of abolition publications and encouraged female groups in the Western Reserve to subscribe to antislavery papers, read aloud from them at meetings, and even write letters for publication.[79] In 1836, the Ohio Female Anti-Slavery Society resolved to raise money to support antislavery publications.[80]

The type of publications the women chose to distribute indicated much about the message they wanted to promote. Distributing Thome's *Address to the Females of Ohio*, for example, allowed women to defend their abolitionist activism without directly engaging in the debate. The *Address* was a response to the objections to women's increased role in the movement voiced by opponents: "It is boldly declared—by those in high places, and echoed by the press—that woman has no duties of a public nature," explained Thome. "We must ever rebuke that selfish exclusiveness, which—arrogating to man the peculiar endowments of intellect and heart—designates every exercise of the same on the part of woman, as impertinent and assuming." He further argued that women as much as men had a religious duty and moral responsibility to confront slavery wherever it existed, whether that place was public or private.[81]

Ohio women quickly transitioned from promoting men's publications to issuing their own. Women's groups initiated a trend of publishing "addresses" instructing other women, men, churches, and slaveholders in the antislavery message and influencing the politics of the movement. In fact, this interstate and interregional form of communication became a popular method of spreading the antislavery message employed by female antislavery societies across the North. Sturges and her Muskingum, Ohio, antislavery sisters led the way by publishing an address "to Christian Females in the Slaveholding States" in the March 1836 *Philanthropist*. Six months before Angelina Grimké published her famous *Appeal to the Christian Women of the South*, Sturges highlighted the commonalities between southern and northern women, arguing that all had a Christian duty to use their influence to help end slavery. Even as she emphasized religion, however, Sturges urged her southern sisters to read the supposedly "treasonable and incendiary" antislavery newspapers, thus encouraging them to become politically aware and educated.[82]

With Ohio paving the way, western women came to specialize in the publication of their own addresses. This method allowed women's groups thoughtfully to voice their abolitionist sentiment without engaging in public oratory. It also allowed them to speak as a group, instead of as individuals, thus providing them with the courage to declare their abolitionism more boldly than might otherwise have been the case. The Chicago Female Anti-Slavery Society distributed countless copies of "an address to females" throughout the region in 1844. The Henry County women circulated an address to the men of Indiana and a separate one to the women of the state. Illinois's Putnam Female Anti-Slavery Society published its "Address to Females" in the Chicago-based *Western Citizen*; the women's group in Wayne County, Indiana, republished the piece a few months later. A year earlier, the Wayne women had published an address to the "professors of Christianity in the United States."[83]

Ohio women also influenced the antislavery movement in the Old Northwest by subscribing to and promoting African American publications. This was a sensible tactic in a region with a highly contentious history of racial conflict. One of the central tenets of the immediate emancipation movement in the 1830s was the elimination of racial discrimination, stereotypes, and oppression in the North, and western women consistently adhered to this principle. When the Ohio Female Anti-Slavery Society held its third annual meeting, in 1838, members resolved "to eradicate the unholy and cruel prejudice against our colored brethren and sisters."[84] The Fayette County Female Anti-Slavery Society declared in 1838, "We hail the 'Colored American,' edited by a colored minister, (as it carries with it demonstrative evidence that talent and piety are not restricted by color or feature,) as an important auxiliary in the anti-slavery enterprise; and that the Treasurer be directed to subscribe for that paper on behalf of the society."[85] In publicly supporting the *Colored American*, the group's forty women hoped to model a commitment to racial equality. They could support the paper's message without declaring it themselves. More than a decade later, Sarah Ernst and the Cincinnati Anti-Slavery Sewing Circle would use funds from their annual fair to subscribe to *Frederick Douglass' Paper* and Henry Bibb's *Voice of the Fugitive*.[86]

Supporting the dissemination of antislavery publications gave western women a practical means of educating themselves and their neighbors. Writing and publishing addresses gave voice to their vision of antislavery and paved the way for other northern women's groups to follow in their footsteps. Reading aloud from *Frederick Douglass' Paper* or the *Colored American* at meetings allowed attendees to learn about the concerns and opinions of free blacks as well as to model cooperation across racial boundaries.

Education

The success of this pragmatic approach to challenging racism in Ohio encouraged women to find other expedient methods for achieving this same goal. Convinced that "ignorance, vice, and suffering" among blacks in the

North was "one of the strongest bulwarks of slavery," many female organizations focused their finances and attention on black education as a way tangibly to address widespread racism.[87] Black Laws excluded African Americans from the public school system in Ohio.[88] Instead of instigating a political fight to eradicate the Black Laws, an effort that would have caused a virulent backlash against the female antislavery movement, the abolitionist women of Ohio chose to support African American educational institutions.[89] Emily Rakestraw Robinson, Lucy Wright, and the other Cincinnati sisters paved the way, demonstrating a commitment to black education that influenced and inspired other women. Female antislavery societies poured extensive time, money, and hard work into the effort to educate their fellow Ohioans.[90] As the Cadiz Female Anti-Slavery Society asserted, "We consider the exclusion of the people of color from the benefit of education, to be a wickedness of the highest magnitude."[91] Though some eastern female antislavery societies battled educational discrimination, none rivaled the expansive efforts of Ohio's female abolitionists. The Philadelphia Female Anti-Slavery Society, for example, helped organize a school for local blacks and financed it for ten years but did not initiate or support other schools.[92] In Boston during the 1830s, women abolitionists did not focus on black education, and such efforts came later and were scattered in Rhode Island.[93] Though the constitution of the Ladies' New-York City Anti-Slavery Society included the "intellectual improvement of the colored people" as a goal, it never became a priority.[94] In Canterbury, Connecticut, Prudence Crandall opened a school for African American girls but was quickly harassed into closing the institution. Connecticut responded by passing a law prohibiting schools from teaching blacks from other states.[95]

Many northern African American women, both free and fugitive, saw education as the key to the future of their community.[96] Antislavery orator Maria Stewart proclaimed in 1832 that "intellectual improvement" could eliminate prejudice.[97] Black women contributed by creating literary societies, becoming teachers, raising money to support schools, and proselytizing about the importance of education. Although evidence regarding the educational efforts of black women in Ohio in the 1830s is lacking, the writings of white abolitionists demonstrate that this effort was very strong among both men and women. In the late 1830s, black Ohioans created the School Fund Institute, which was devoted to building and supporting schools for African American children. Although this organization could not address all of the state's needs, it reveals blacks' consistent efforts to support education.[98] In 1837, according to Augustus Wattles, only four of Ohio's twenty black schools were operated and funded exclusively by African Americans.[99] By 1840, however, blacks had begun to organize to fund new and existing schools: A convention of "colored inhabitants" in Butler County, in southwestern Ohio, met with the sole object of devising "means whereby our children might enjoy the opportunity of receiving the advantages of education."[100] This emphasis on education never wavered among African American Ohioans, especially women. At an 1852 gathering of the "Colored Citizens of Ohio" in Cleveland, a group of "young ladies" from Oberlin presented a banner with the motto, "Education is our greatest Hope!"[101]

Joining African Americans in raising money to support teachers and build schools was the first priority of white Ohio women abolitionists. Encouraged by a *Philanthropist* columnist who wrote under the pen name Amicus in January 1837, the Ohio Female Anti-Slavery Society devoted much of its efforts toward this goal. After delineating the struggles of free black communities in Ohio and bemoaning the paucity of female teachers in these communities, Amicus encouraged female antislavery societies across Ohio to unite and raise money "for the relief of these settlements" and in support of teachers.[102] Several months later, the Ohio Female Anti-Slavery Society recommended "to female societies throughout the state, that they make special efforts to raise funds for the support of colored schools."[103] Groups responded: the Women's Anti-Slavery Society of Cincinnati was created in February 1838 to "ameliorate the condition and promote the education of the colored people."[104] In 1838, the state society went further in its support for black educational opportunities. "While we view with pleasure the efforts made by colored people for the support of their own schools," it asserted, "the magnitude and importance of the work require that our exertions in their behalf should be increased rather than diminished."[105] To that end, the women pledged to raise additional funds to build schoolhouses and support teachers. Over the previous year, they had raised more than three hundred dollars, most of which went toward this goal.[106] As late as 1845, the Ohio state group was crying out for financial support: "If the women of New England could raise fifty thousand dollars to complete the Bunker Hill Monument, a memento of battles and blood, cannot the women of Ohio raise five thousand dollars for the benefit of those immortal minds, that the wheel of slavery has crushed to the earth?"[107]

One way to appeal to female abolitionists for financial support for schools was to highlight the sacrifices of women teachers. White women taught at fourteen of Ohio's twenty black schools in 1837, but several of the institutions still lacked instructors.[108] After several female antislavery societies failed to fulfill their subscriptions to the educational fund in 1837, educational agent Amzi D. Barber wrote a letter to the *Philanthropist* illustrating the desperate needs of female teachers. "Those who come to teach are poor," he explained. "All the teachers ask is enough to comfortably (not extravagantly) feed and clothe them. Ought they not to receive this?"[109] Barber asked why antislavery lecturers were relatively well supported but teachers were ignored. "Let any one who supposes that slavery can be abolished while the colored people remain as they are, come to this city and circulate petitions for the abolition of slavery in DC or for the repeal of obnoxious laws, and he will find his error. The elevation of the colored people is evidently the hinge upon which every thing turns. Why should not the teacher be sustained as well as the lecturer?"[110] The answer may well in part have lain in the fact that men were the lecturers and young single women were the teachers.

As white female abolitionists became increasingly involved with African American education, they developed closer ties to black families. This intimate connection strengthened white women's pragmatic approach to the movement. Those working closely with African Americans recognized the importance of having white women become acquainted with black community and culture before jumping in to "solve" perceived problems. As Amicus explained, blacks had reason to be cautious about white people with "good" intentions.[111] "When some *fair* lady, who has lived for many years within half a mile of their humble dwellings, visits them perhaps, for the first time, to propose some plan for elevating their condition, they regard her with utter incredulity, and though they may yield a languid assent to her proposition, yet a secret suspicion of her motive still lurks within, and they have no heart to co-operate with her designs." He concluded, "The first thing to be done therefore, is to inspire their confidence: until this is effected, all personal efforts in their behalf will be fruitless." Abolitionists such as Augustus and Susan Wattles learned through extensive experience the accuracy of this advice. They traveled and lived in many of Ohio's black communities, gaining the trust of local leaders. In 1837, working in coordination with the Ohio Female Anti-Slavery Society, the Wattleses visited nearly every African American school in the state and published a report on their efforts.[112]

The Ohio Female Anti-Slavery Society emphasized the need for white abolitionists in every community to seek out local blacks and work as partners in the effort toward equal education. "We recommend to societies through the state that they appoint a committee to visit the colored people in their vicinity, give them suitable advice and instruction, enquire into their condition, and report to the committee of Correspondence."[113] Although the emphasis on dispensing "advice and instruction" reflected a patronizing and superior attitude, the connection with locals was important. In 1838, the group suggested that "female societies of each county" should "pledge themselves to procure and support a teacher the coming year" for a black school.[114] The society's leaders further instructed their auxiliaries to "send in a report respecting the condition of the colored people in their respective neighborhoods," thus requiring white women to step outside their comfort zone and into the African American world.[115]

White abolitionists encouraged their sisters to consider becoming teachers in black communities. Many women did so, devoting several years to this difficult and underpaid position.[116] They learned that in many communities, white women who taught blacks were guilty of a serious violation of the racial status quo. Mary Cheney experienced the wrath of the white community in Big Bottom, Ohio, because she refused to be intimidated into leaving town. "It is now four weeks since my school house was torn down," explained Cheney in a desperate letter to Augustus Wattles. "At that time I was addressed in a most profane and uncivil manner, and told to leave the place."[117] Cheney ignored the threats and moved the school to another house. "Since that time there has been a vast amount of oaths, curses, and threatenings heaped upon me. Repeatedly has word been sent to me, that if I was not sent away, they would come and take me out of the house, give me a dress of tar and feathers, and treat me in a manner too inhuman to mention." Despite such threats, Cheney assured Augustus Wattles that she had not been "at all alarmed." However, she explained, the number of her opponents had recently increased to twenty, and they "engaged to mob me, (signed a pledge), being backed up in it by rich men." Moreover, "they are all miserable whiskey drinkers, armed with guns, pistols, dirks, and each a bottle of whiskey." Although Cheney had not yet been driven from her position, she asked Wattles for counsel: "I have nearly concluded to go on again with my school, but don't know what to do." The publication of Cheney's letter in the *Philanthropist* may have raised the hackles of angry abolitionist women and inspired them to increase their financial generosity but did little to encourage other women to enter the field.

Nevertheless, Ohio women abolitionists remained committed to teaching African Americans. By 1840, the Ohio Female Anti-Slavery Society had renamed itself the Ohio Ladies Education Society for the Free People of Color. The new name was more respectable (as a consequence of the term "Ladies") and signaled a more focused approach exclusively geared toward educational opportunities for the state's free blacks.[118] This group would remain active for seven more years.[119] Many women, including Sturges, continued to participate.[120] Assuming that all abolitionist women supported their cause ("All ladies who are members of anti-slavery societies in this State, shall be considered members of this Society"), the group asserted that "every candid mind may see that the degradation of the colored man at the north is one of the strongest bulwarks of slavery at the south."[121] The organization brought together women from starkly different antislavery positions. Evangelical abolitionists Mary Blanchard and Margaret Bailey, both married to leading anti-Garrisonian Cincinnati abolitionists, worked with such radicals as Lydia Irish, an outspoken Quaker.[122] Although eastern Garrisonians would come to view the issue of black education as secondary to and distracting from the "real" issue of emancipation, it offered Ohio women a tangible opportunity to act on their practical, cooperative abolitionist sentiment. The only other well-orchestrated abolitionist method among women in Ohio in the 1830s to rival education was the petition effort.

Petitioning

Among the most influential actions initiated by Ohio women abolitionists in the late 1830s was their petition campaign. This operation symbolized many of the most successful methods of cooperative organizing. It created a statewide network, both involved women at the local level and drew them into the national debate, and allowed women to see the results of their efforts. Petitioning also began to pull women into civil society and even partisan politics. It brought them into direct confrontation with the larger community and forced them to defend their actions as appropriate for women.[123] Although other reform-minded women signed and circulated petitions in the 1830s, abolitionist women sent an astounding number of petitions to Congress. Frustrated politicians responded to this vast influx by passing an 1837 "gag rule" that automatically tabled all such petitions unread.[124]

The abolitionist women of Ohio did not initially address their petition campaign to Congress, however. Instead, they focused on the church. Cowles again led the way in this effort. "I have obtained nearly all the names of the females belonging to this Church," explained Laura M. Wright of Morgan, Ohio, to Cowles in April 1835.[125] This petition apparently protested the church's failure to speak out against slavery. Since most female antislavery societies grounded their abolitionism in religion, it is not surprising that the church's weak position on slavery would cause concern.[126] Many abolitionists would eventually "come out" of their churches and join breakaway antislavery religious institutions.[127] The Ladies' New-York City Anti-Slavery Society asked its members to petition their churches in support of antislavery in 1835.[128] Lucy Wright became involved with a petition "to the General Assembly of the Presbyterian church" in 1836. As she explained, "We think it highly important that our ecclesiastical bodies consider this subject for if ministers of the gospel of Christ forge their brethren in bonds, how can we expect any thing favorable in the halls of legislation?"[129] Sarah Coleman of Andover convinced all of the female church members "on this street" to sign the petition before passing it on to another town.[130] Maria Kellogg of Cherry Valley garnered thirty signatures.[131] Sturges also encouraged the women of Ohio to continue pressuring their churches through petitioning: "Our societies are made up of members from almost every different denomination, and we think that Anti-Slavery memorials to all our ecclesiastical bodies should be gotten up and circulated without delay."[132] Not all female antislavery societies of the Western Reserve, however, so openly criticized the church. Sophia Arnold of the small, rather conservative New Lyme auxiliary confessed to Cowles, "We think it will not be proper to circulate the petition you sent not but I should be perfectly willing to sign the petition myself but most of this Society belong to the Baptist Churches for this reason we think it not best."[133]

While Cowles paved the way for the church petition, Sturges instigated what became known as the "Fathers and Rulers" petition. This particular form, which asked congressmen to abolish slavery in the District of Columbia, would become the most common petition among women abolitionists, with hundreds of copies sent to Washington, D.C., in the 1830s. Female antislavery societies from Rhode Island to Illinois circulated this petition with an enthusiasm that shocked the nation, and the campaign helped to catalyze the organization of the first national meeting of women abolitionists in 1837.[134] Modest and self-effacing, the "Fathers and Rulers" petition offered a "humble memorial" to Congress, an "honorable body" that represented the "guardians of a Christian people."[135] Although among the more tame of the abolitionist petitions, it nonetheless firmly proclaimed that Christian feeling and justice required the nation's legislators to end slavery in the nation's capital. Coating its demand in religion and morality, the petition on one level embraced the woman's sphere. In making demands on politicians and presuming political knowledge, it also clearly brought women into the public sphere.

Western women initiated and guided this important national petition campaign. Although it is not entirely clear who wrote the first version of

this petition, it emerged out of Ohio. Weld is generally credited with authorship because his initials were inscribed at the bottom of one petition with the
date "1834." Historian Susan Zaeske has noted, however, that his authorship
is contradicted by a January 1836 notice in the *Emancipator* that "a woman
from North Carolina who was residing in Putnam, Ohio," had penned the
petition.[136] The idea of circulating a petition to Congress emerged out of the
1836 meeting of the Ohio State Female Anti-Slavery Society. "We consider
it our right, privilege and duty," attendees resolved, "to petition Congress to
abolish slavery in the District of Columbia, and . . . we recommend the circulation of a single petition for the State, in preference to having one in each
county or town."[137] In deciding to work together through a statewide organization, the Ohio women immediately initiated a campaign that they hoped
would benefit the most from a large-scale approach. As Wright explained to
Cowles, "We thought that our united voice might perhaps obtain a more favorable hearing than of a few scattering petitions were sent in."[138] When the
petition was published in the *Philanthropist*, Sturges wrote an accompanying
"Address to the Females in the State of Ohio" that instructed women on the
importance of signing the petition and on how to circulate it.[139] She focused
on regional dignity, woman's rights, and religion. She appealed to western
pride, asserting that as a vital American "outpost," Ohio needed to establish
itself as a model of antislavery virtue. Knowing firsthand that many female
abolitionists took satisfaction in their Ohio roots, Sturges made them feel
the issue at a local level even though the petition was addressed to Congress.
Sturges also responded to the growing critique of female petitioning as outside the woman's domain, warning that "the sphere of female action has been
so narrowed down, as to cause us sometimes to inquire, if the shadows of the
dark ages are returning to dim our hemisphere, and shut out the faint glim-
merings of millennial glory." The women of Ohio, she averred, will not be
"bantered from the field because we are *women*." Finally, Sturges reminded
her readers, "God holds us accountable for all the talents which he has committed to our keeping."[140]

Portage County's female antislavery society led the way in circulating
the petition, largely because the group's secretary, Wright, had participated
in the initial Ohio Female Anti-Slavery Society meeting and was assigned
to work with Sturges on the petition campaign.[141] "We heartily approve of
the circulation of a single petition to Congress through the state," declared
the Portage County Ladies Anti-Slavery Society in May 1836, "and we approve of the appointment of a committee of general correspondence for the
promotion of this end." The Portage women backed their sentiment with

financial support: "We appropriate ten dollars to aid this Com[mittee] in the prosecution of the enterprise."[142] The Portage women "obtained five hundred signers to the memorial" even though "there exists a considerable prejudice against [the] ladies county soc[iety]."[143]

Despite the Portage group's enthusiasm and political savvy, the Central Committee of the Ohio Female Anti-Slavery Society had some difficulty in starting up the campaign. The male leaders of the Ohio State Anti-Slavery Society failed to comply with the women's instructions to provide copies of the petition.[144] As a result, only a small number of petitions were initially sent out. After learning of the problem, Sturges immediately began distributing copies, urging women to circulate them and send them to her "without delay." She pragmatically reminded each petitioner to "provide herself with a small pocket inkstand, and a ready made pen" to get "proper signatures."[145] She even instructed women in how to obtain lower postage rates. Petitions were sent to ten counties, six of which returned them, with a total of 3,127 signatures. Sturges's Muskingum County was the only one to "fill" its petition (with 533 names) and quickly complete its mission.[146]

Sturges's leadership was critical to the success of the Ohio petition campaign, and it sparked further petitioning on the East Coast.[147] "Arrangements are making to circulate among the ladies in the state a petition to Congress to abolish slavery in the District of Columbia that so our united prayers may go up to the rulers of our nation," the Portage women informed the Boston Female Anti-Slavery Society in August 1836.[148] Impressed with the potential impact of this campaign, Anne Warren Weston and the Boston group decided to follow the lead of their Ohio sisters: "We very gratefully acknowledge the suggestion that we have received from the ladies of Ohio, in reference to the District of Columbia. In imitation of their example, we have determined to send petitions to every town in Mass[achusetts] and trust that the result of these efforts will reward us tenfold."[149]

Petitioning encouraged women to step out of their homes and communicate with their neighbors about an issue of grave concern to their communities and their country. It gave them a specific goal and it made them feel connected to the larger antislavery movement. Together, women daringly entered a world that required knowledge, confidence, and commitment, and they preferred to take this step as a group. As Augustus Wattles admitted to Cowles, it is "worse than useless to advise females to take an active part in any public movement unless they feel within them a *self sustaining power*, a *confidence*, that no obstacle can weaken, no opposition subdue."[150] Ohio women experienced opposition in response to petitioning, which pushed at cultural and gender boundaries by clearly giving women political voices. Ohio's astute women therefore constructed a petition that emphasized respectable sincerity and a certain political reticence, thus bringing "feminine" modesty into the political realm.

Conclusion

Ohio's female antislavery societies flourished in the 1830s because of their resiliency and adaptability. Leaders such as Cowles, Wright, and Sturges developed a shrewd, tactical approach that drew their sister Ohioans into the movement and nourished their sense of accomplishment and importance. Ohio's women abolitionists strategically organized at the local, county, and state levels—unlike female antislavery societies in the East—to ensure their strength in numbers and also allow isolated rural women to feel connected to the larger movement. Ohio's women coordinated and negotiated with their brothers in the movement to the benefit of abolitionism overall. They initiated pragmatic campaigns that spoke to regional issues but had national influence.

These trends would significantly affect female antislavery societies in the burgeoning Old Northwest during the ensuing decades. Cooperation and fluidity allowed women in Peoria, Illinois, and Henry County, Indiana, to advocate abolitionism in otherwise hostile states. As the antislavery movement splintered after 1840, with "new" and "old" abolitionists constantly bickering and political abolitionists forging new ground, western women adapted without being drawn into the internecine fight. Many abolitionists in the Old Northwest, both male and female, found the distressing ideological battle lines of the East to be less relevant in their region. Some, like Peoria resident Mary Brown Davis, found that the new Liberty Party offered a wonderful opportunity for abolitionist progress. Inspired by the political actions of the female petitioners of Ohio and beyond, these women eagerly dove into partisan politics.

CHAPTER 2

Abolitionist Women and the Liberty Party

Mary Davis must have been scandalized when a "gentleman" sat in her lap. She had gone to Chicago's City Hall to hear famed abolitionist Frederick Douglass discuss the state's Black Laws, the importance of political antislavery, and the Fugitive Slave Act.[1] A longtime admirer of Douglass, Davis was eager to listen to his lecture. When she arrived, however, the "house was crowded to its utmost capacity—high and low, rich and poor, black and white." At fifty-three years old, she doubted she could stand for the entire talk. Her extensive antislavery experience had taught her that these meetings often ran longer than three hours. She scanned the hall and finally spied one empty seat at the end of a bench. Grateful for her luck, she quickly moved to the open space. The white gentleman occupying the seat next to the empty one, however, informed her that the seat was "engaged." A stubborn and independent woman, Davis simply ignored his comment and sat down. Within a few minutes, another man arrived and the first man explained that he had attempted to save the seat but "this lady thinks she has the best right." At this point, the second man plopped himself down on Davis's lap. Unnerved and uncomfortable, Davis attempted to extricate herself. Then "a colored man very politely rose and gave us a seat." While the white "gentlemen" humiliated her and violated the basic rules of decorum and respect, a kind and generous African American man inconvenienced himself (and perhaps put himself at risk by interfering with white men) to come to her rescue. This incident offered Davis further evidence that the color of one's skin was unrelated to one's character and that racial prejudice and slavery were a detriment to the nation.[2]

Davis's response to the insolent white male representatives of "galvanized aristocracy" she encountered at Chicago's City Hall well represented her outspoken support for the antislavery movement—she ignored opposition from those around her and forged an independent position that reflected her passion for the cause but that occasionally left her vulnerable to disparagement from the general public. A resident of Peoria, Illinois, throughout the 1840s, Davis became a zealous advocate of the Liberty Party and a skilled political recruiter among women. Like the Ohio women who organized female antislavery societies in the 1830s, Davis and her Liberty Party sisters carefully negotiated a cooperative and flexible position within the movement. But they crossed more boundaries and risked more opposition than their Ohio counterparts by entering the world of partisan politics.

The Liberty Party emerged among a small group of abolitionists frustrated with the failure of moral suasion. While the antislavery associates of William Lloyd Garrison disdained partisan politics as inherently corrupt and eschewed the Liberty Party, other abolitionists slowly came to see the new third party as a pragmatic method for achieving emancipation. Led initially by Alvan Stewart and Myron Holley, the party organized in Albany, New York, in April 1840, and nominated James G. Birney, ex-Kentucky slaveholder and former editor of the Cincinnati-based *Philanthropist*, for president. A one-issue party, Liberty called for the federal government to disassociate itself from slavery as much as possible—particularly by emancipating slaves in the District of Columbia and ensuring that the western territories excluded slavery. Liberty also opposed racial discrimination. Birney received less than 1 percent of the vote in 1840, and although the party experienced more electoral success four years later, its numbers remained small. Most Liberty voters came from the Whig Party, but some disgruntled Democrats also joined. In the Old Northwest, the party thrived primarily in small communities with substantial Quaker populations or strong abolitionist "come-outer" churches such as the Free Will Baptists, Free Presbyterians, and Wesleyan Methodists. In New Garden, Indiana, for example, where a large contingent of antislavery Quakers lived, "two of every three voters cast a third party ballot." By 1848, the Liberty Party was replaced by the more moderate Free-Soil Party, which emphasized the benefits of "free soil and free labor" for whites. The mid-1850s saw the development of the Republican

Party, a more traditional political organization that only loosely opposed slavery.[3]

Davis was among those who entered the Liberty Party camp with un-bridled enthusiasm. She and hundreds of other female abolitionists in the Old Northwest began actively and openly to support the Liberty Party throughout the 1840s. Until recently, historians have overlooked the partici-pation of these women because, as Julie Roy Jeffrey has suggested, they did not make headlines.[4] They did not write party policies or choose political candidates. Women were almost always absent from the published proceed-ings of Liberty Party conventions, save perhaps for a brief recognition of their efforts in a single resolution. Partisan women nonetheless attended Liberty meetings, raised money, "influenced" their men, petitioned state and national governments, and published their political opinions. Despite facing external opposition and occasionally internal conflict, they remained Liberty advocates throughout the party's existence. Their experiences changed their understanding of the world and paved the way for women's increasing role in partisan politics throughout the 1850s.[5] The Liberty Party also became an ave-nue for the continuing expansion of female abolitionism across the West.

The distinct personality of the Liberty Party—a cautiousness regarding the culture of politics—offered women an ideal entrance into the politi-cal sphere.[6] Most Liberty Party supporters had no illusions of widespread electoral victory. Liberty was designed to force the two major parties to pay attention to slavery.[7] Advocates prided themselves on their refusal to engage in traditional partisan politics. They sought not to acquire political power but rather the moral achievement of emancipation. They became a kind of antipolitical political party.[8] Liberty attracted the support of church-oriented abolitionists by highlighting the idea that abolitionists should "vote as they pray."[9] As the Illinois Liberty Party proudly declared in 1844, "Poli-tics properly considered is a branch of morals, and . . . every man is bound to exercise the elective franchise, under a deep sense of his moral obligation to his fellow man and his God."[10] Any party that linked itself to religion and boasted of its antipolitical character would welcome women.[11] Beginning with the efforts of early nineteenth-century charitable groups and continu-ing through women's abolitionist petitioning, female reformers had always recognized their role in politics as characterized by moral authority, so the Liberty Party offered a comfortable fit.[12]

Liberty also proved welcoming to women because of its local focus and particular gender dynamics. As long as the party emphasized the importance of small-town campaigns, with their church fund-raisers and local meetings, women found a niche for themselves.[13] With the rise of new more central-ized and nationally focused antislavery third parties in the 1850s, however, the focus shifted away from the local. Historian Nancy Hewitt has found that in western New York, as male abolitionists in the Free-Soil and Re-publican Parties changed their emphasis "from local and state to national electoral campaigns," they also moved from "the '*moral* effect of *numbers*' to their office-winning potential."[14] This concentration on political power and electoral success proved less welcoming to women, although many still carved out roles. The gender dynamics of the Liberty Party, characterized in the mid-1840s by what Michael Pierson has called "domestic feminism," also encouraged women's participation. Believing that women's public and political activism was justified if it was in defense of women—in this case, to protect slave women's sexual purity and their role as mothers—Liberty advocates encouraged women to employ their partisan voices. Although no absolute consensus emerged in favor of domestic feminism, Liberty sup-porters tapped into popular assumptions about virtuous femininity to entice female participation.[15]

Finally, abolitionist women of the Old Northwest were particularly re-ceptive to the Liberty Party because of regional distinctiveness. The West's cooperative, practical antislavery environment allowed women to become active in the party with less risk and more support than was the case in the East. Western abolitionists prided themselves on the harmony between moral and political abolitionism, opening the door for women to employ moral arguments as justification for their untraditional political activities.[16] Moreover, as other historians have shown, the West invited women's "cam-paign presence" in the early 1840s.[17] Hundreds of Whig and Democratic women participated in rallies, meetings, picnics, and processions. African American women, too, began participating at state colored conventions in the Old Northwest.[18] Liberty women joined and quickly surpassed this elec-toral activism.

Illinois Women and the Liberty Party

Davis and several of her abolitionist sisters in central Illinois catalyzed wom-en's participation in the state's Liberty Party in the early 1840s. Born and raised in a wealthy Virginia slaveholding family, Davis had extensive first-hand experience with slavery.[19] Much like South Carolina–born abolitionist Sarah Grimké, Davis employed anecdotes from her youth to construct a life story that emphasized her early distaste for slavery.[20] This distaste was rooted in a singularly moral framework. She credited her slave nanny, who watched over her "tottering infancy," with teaching her that slavery was marked by "great injustice, cruelty, and oppression"—particularly for females.[21] As Davis became more exposed to slavery during her youth, she wondered how the "curse" that "poisoned" the South could be removed. She admitted that she had considered immediate emancipation "perilous in the extreme" because of her prejudice against blacks: "I could not believe that the African . . . and the white man, could dwell together in the same land, and on the same footing, without murder, rapine, and every abomination." Davis also constructed her father as a vital antislavery influence, claiming that he was recognized locally for his "compassion" toward blacks.[22] More important, he lost his wife's entire fortune, ending up in debtor's prison, where his wife and two daughters joined him "to beguile his dreary hours." All of the family's fifty or so slaves were sold to pay his debt, a noxious scene Davis claimed to have witnessed from her prison window. This traumatic moment, which included the sale of her elderly nanny as well as a new mother, "scathed" her "young heart" and eventually marked Davis as a "friend of the down-trodden" who was committed to guiding her "oppressed brethren" toward "the land of freedom."[23]

Davis's interest in politics, much like her abolitionism, had southern roots. In the 1820s, Mary Brown married journalist Samuel Davis and began a family in Winchester, Virginia. By the early 1830s, she had begun her lifelong association with journalism, helping her husband edit and publish the *Winchester Republican*.[24] Her involvement in newspaper publishing exposed her to the latest political debates and controversies, including the unprecedented petition campaign initiated by some of her southern sisters. In 1831 and 1832, following the Nat Turner rebellion, hundreds of women in several Virginia counties petitioned the state legislature in support of gradual emancipation and colonization. Motivated by the "carnage" caused by the rebellion, they called on the state legislators' "manly reason" to obliterate slavery, the "bloody monster" that threatened to destroy hearth and home.[25] At least one of the petitions circulated in several newspapers, including the *Liberator*, and another reached nearby Fredericksburg.[26] Davis experienced the same fear and anxiety about a slave revolt and shared a sense of the "evil of slavery" that motivated these other Virginia women to push for colonization. This local example of women participating in the political process in support of emancipation laid the groundwork for Davis's decision less than a decade later to become a Liberty Party woman.[27] It also represented the growing connection between Davis's moral opposition to slavery and her eager interest in politics.

By the late 1830s, Samuel and Mary Davis had left the South in search of economic opportunity in the Old Northwest. The Davis family began publishing and editing the *Register and North-Western Gazetteer* in Peoria, Illinois, a river town that boasted a blend of southern, eastern, and immigrant populations.[28] This move raised Mary Davis's expectations—she hoped to find a more supportive antislavery community in the "free" North. Peoria, however, proved disappointing. Davis felt even more isolated as a consequence of the fierce influence of what she deemed "pro-slavery" southerners in her new community.[29] Only a few years earlier, an angry mob in neighboring Tazewell County had stoned a small group of slavery opponents who "met together to pray for the slave," quite seriously injuring a female abolitionist.[30] After a brief sojourn in Galesburg, a nearby antislavery oasis bursting with reformers and home to Knox College, Davis expressed regret at returning home: "When I drew near to Peoria," she wrote to an antislavery newspaper, "I could almost weep to think of the desolation that *sin*, and a subserviency to slaveocracy are making here."[31] Although some western women abolitionists lived in reform-minded communities such as Galesburg, many suffered from the hostility of the surrounding antiabolitionists and the scarcity of outspoken antislavery supporters.[32] As was the case for the Cincinnati sisters who taught in African American schools in the mid-1830s, the challenge of western isolation proved stultifying for some of Illinois's antislavery women. As one woman living on the lonely frontier complained to an urban friend, "You, who are surrounded with abolitionists, know nothing of the trials and difficulties that we have to encounter."[33] St. Louis resident Frances Dana Gage lived in a growing city, but abolitionism was absent: "You cannot know how alone I feel here," she groaned. "There is not one full reformer to take me by the hand."[34]

Although Davis could rely on at least one antislavery neighbor, Lucy Pettengill, for moral encouragement, few others were willing to stand up and be counted as advocates for emancipation in the Illinois river town.[35] The Reverend Jeremiah Porter and his wife, Eliza Chappell Porter, enthusiastic and outspoken abolitionists, had just left Peoria's Main Street Presbyterian Church for a more hospitable congregation in Farmington.[36] Even Davis's husband disapproved of and curtailed her antislavery activism. Samuel Davis still owned a few slaves in the South, so his aversion to Mary's abolitionism was grounded in both personal sentiment and economic interest.[37] While Samuel found the movement for immediate emancipation objectionable, his standpoint was moderated by his keen advocacy of freedom of speech, a position that occasionally led him into the antislavery camp.[38] His Peoria newspaper, for example, was one of the few in Illinois to condemn the 1837 murder of antislavery editor Elijah Lovejoy by an antiabolitionist mob.[39] In 1839, Samuel helped to form the Peoria Colonization Society.[40] Mary's espousal of immediate emancipation, however, was a far cry from colonization. Samuel refused to allow his wife to host a "prayer meeting for the oppressed" in their home, frustrating and irritating Mary.[41] Desperate for an abolitionist outlet, Davis began writing antislavery essays for the fleeting Illinois version of the *Genius of Universal Emancipation*.[42] By the early 1840s, she became a regular contributor to the Chicago-based Liberty Party newspaper, *Western Citizen*. The editor of the paper, Zebina Eastman, had worked with Samuel and Mary Davis on the *Peoria Register and North-Western Gazetteer* in 1839 and was a family friend.[43] Although Mary Davis's early letters to the *Citizen* fell squarely within the range of appropriate female concerns, describing the mental and physical abuse of slaves in her native state, she soon began writing about partisan politics and became an ardent supporter of the Liberty Party.

The addition of a single antislavery voice to their communities catapulted many isolated western women abolitionists into action. Betsey Mix Cowles's letters of encouragement to solitary abolitionists in nearby Western Reserve towns in the 1830s inspired many women to initiate antislavery action locally. Similarly, Davis's loneliness rapidly vanished when William T. Allan and his wife, Irene Ball Allan, moved to Peoria in 1842. William, an agent of the Illinois Anti-Slavery Society, became minister of the Main Street Presbyterian Church.[44] Irene Ball had been a student at the antislavery-leaning Oberlin College when she met and married Allan in 1837.[45] The Allans boarded with fellow abolitionists Moses and Lucy Pettengill, and despite experiencing opposition from the "leading influences in the church," the Allans challenged the antiabolitionist spirit that permeated Peoria.[46] The endeavor proved difficult because, as Irene Allan pointed out to an Oberlin relative, "It is a river town [and] there is much open rebellion against God."[47]

Davis, Allan, and Pettengill conferred about how to awaken their community's dormant antislavery sentiment. Peoria relied on the trade that moved up and down the Illinois River, and many of its citizens worried that a discussion of the slave question would alienate their lucrative southern contracts. "The nature of our population renders the work a difficult one," admitted Irene Allan in a letter to the *Western Citizen*, but "it is very important that anti-slavery principles should triumph in our State." She posed a rhetorical question: "What can the anti-slavery women of Illinois do for the cause?" Following Cowles's lead, Allan confidently responded that women needed to organize. "There are heart and talent and means in our rank, that might be made to bear with success upon the cause if they were only elicited and well directed."[48] Inspired and ready to act, Mary Davis and Lucy Pettengill joined Allan to become a commanding trio.

As Allan, Davis, and Pettengill mulled over the formation of a Peoria abolition society, they coordinated with local antislavery men. Like their Ohio abolitionist sisters in the 1830s, male and female reformers in Illinois worked closely together even when creating single-sex groups. Such cooperation proved especially important for the abolitionists of Peoria in February 1843, when they attempted to create an antislavery society. Less than a year earlier in nearby Washington, a small group of women and men were forcibly prevented from holding an antislavery meeting by a motley crew of "preachers and profane swearers, professors and infidels, men of property and standing, and ragged boys."[49] The Peoria abolitionists feared similar treatment but nonetheless published a notice in the *Register and North-Western Gazetteer* (Samuel Davis still edited but no longer owned) announcing the creation of a local abolitionist group.[50] On a chilly gray Monday evening, twenty hopeful and determined men and women met at William Allan's Presbyterian church. Similar to the unpleasant scene in Washington, the activists were confronted by a larger group of angry and threatening residents who broke up the meeting and warned the reformers that no such gathering would be tolerated in their city.[51] The fact that the small assemblage of abolitionists consisted mostly of women probably prevented a more dangerous physical confrontation. The proprietors of the *Register* refused to allow Samuel Davis, who was outraged by the event, to publish a critical account of the mob, leading him not only to resign as editor but to become a full-fledged abolitionist within a year.[52] Less than three years later, he would be beaten senseless on the streets of Peoria because of his antislavery reputation.[53]

As Samuel Davis reconsidered his position on slavery, the abolitionist women of Peoria wasted no time in making their sentiment quite clear. Undaunted by their rough treatment at their first meeting, Mary Davis, Irene Allen, Lucy Pettengill, and seventeen other local women gathered in the Main Street Presbyterian Church in July 1843 to organize the Peoria Female Anti-Slavery Society. Even as they anxiously watched the door for a return of their opponents, the women passed resolutions that crossed into the political realm. They vowed to write and distribute antislavery petitions to "the Legislative bodies of our country," appointing experienced activists Davis and Allen to prepare these political statements. They also declared their support for the Liberty Party.[54]

In her editorial about the inaugural meeting of the Peoria Female Anti-slavery Society, Mary Davis noted that the women, unlike the mixed-sex group, were left largely unmolested: "The *magnanimous heroes* of the 13th of February, have consented to permit an Anti-slavery Society to organize in this 'beautiful town,'" she sarcastically explained.[55] Although a few rowdies threatened William Allan, who spoke at the meeting, and dumped his carriage wheels into the Illinois River, the women of Peoria succeeded where the mixed-sex group had failed, institutionalizing abolition in central Illinois. The male abolitionists in the community were not completely excluded. They attended Allan's lecture at the beginning of the meeting, perhaps as a sign of chivalry, but withdrew after his talk, allowing the women to attend to the business of organizing.[56]

Constructing the Liberty Lady

Western female antislavery societies, especially those created in the 1840s, embraced the Liberty Party. While many eastern female antislavery societies, including those in Concord, Boston, Philadelphia, Rochester, and Rhode Island, remained caught up in the troublesome conflict of 1840 or struggled with other problems, support for Liberty in the West seemed natural and logical.[57] The Henry County Female Anti-Slavery became one of Indiana's most outspoken Liberty Party advocates.[58] In Michigan, women organized "ladies anti-slavery and benevolent associations" in support of Liberty Party lecturer Henry Bibb.[59] These groups raised vital funds to support local Liberty candidates and political publications. But Illinois boasted the most widespread advocacy of the party among female antislavery societies. "We know of no State in which the friends of Liberty are more busy than in Illinois," declared the *Cincinnati Weekly Herald and Philanthropist* in 1846, pointing specifically to "Liberty women."[60] As the most western of the Old Northwestern states, Illinois was both geographically and politically distant from the internecine divisiveness of eastern abolitionism. Garrisonians found little support anywhere from Alton to Chicago, and by 1844, Illinois abolitionism manifested itself primarily in the form of the Liberty Party.[61] Female groups in Bureau County, DuPage County, Galesburg, Princeton, and Union Grove cheered Liberty men, while the Putnam County Female Anti-Slavery Society praised the party for making "unchanging principles of truth and justice" its object and promised to help garner support.[62] A statewide female antislavery organization also coordinated its goals with those of the state's Liberty Party.

In April 1844, only a year after they organized their city's first antislavery group, the women of Peoria invited sister abolitionists from across Illinois to create a state female antislavery society.[63] Following a trend initiated by Ohio women, the Peoria ladies hoped that bringing together abolitionists from across the state would infuse them with strength and energy. Gathering in Peoria on a cool spring day, the women cautiously focused their meeting on such traditional female concerns as assistance, nurturance, and piety, thus creating a defense against accusations that they were violating the feminine sphere.[64] They pledged, for example, to provide financial aid to a local African American woman who sought to purchase her daughter out of slavery. The group thereby addressed the shameful separation of the slave family and highlighted women's "natural" concern with family. Members reminded each other that the "equality and brotherhood of man is the foundation of abolitionism" and that the poor needed to be treated with respect and servants had to receive fair wages. Participants also promised to "dissolve" any connection with churches that failed to acknowledge the sin of slavery, thus emphasizing Christian piety and the movement's religious nature.[65] Still worried that their resolutions would attract negative attention, Mary Davis wrote an article for the *Western Citizen* that depicted these Illinois abolitionists as feminine, motherly, and resolute. She described her sisters as "the most enlightened and lovely part of the female population of our state." Sensitive to their parental duties, they brought their "little responsibilities" with them to the meeting.[66] These angelic women, committed to a "heaven-born sacred cause," endured rowdy boys who threw eggs ("one of which found a resting-place in the lap of a young lady") and stole carriage wheels. Reports of the meeting included no discussion directly related to the Liberty Party.

Nonetheless, even the announcement of their intention to hold a meeting created a stir. The "call for a convention" invited both men and women to attend, thus creating a "promiscuous" mixed-sex gathering. It also "respectfully" requested the attendance of Liberty Party leaders James Dickey, Owen Lovejoy, and Ichabod Codding, thus making the assemblage seem political.[67] While antislavery men welcomed the development, opponents denounced the women in no uncertain terms. The editor of the *Chicago Daily Journal* reacted to the call for a statewide female antislavery society with vituperative scorn: "Shut up your 'little responsibilities,' ye mothers—initiate your husbands into the mysteries of your kitchens and larders, ye wives—and hasten to Peoria, to look after the concerns of the Nation." He concluded, "You are peculiarly fitted for the 'rough and tumble' scenes of life, and you certainly will shine more conspicuously in the forum than in the domestic circle!"[68] Assuming that the organization of a statewide female antislavery society would involve Illinois women in the "rough and tumble" masculine sphere of politics, the editor made clear his conviction that women were unsuited for such work and that the result would be the decline of the household as well as the statehouse. Men would be left home tending to children while women would be looking after the "concerns of the Nation." Gender roles would be catastrophically reversed.[69]

Mary Davis adroitly countered this editorial by presenting women's political activity as quite ordinary and common. She reminded her critic that nonabolitionist women—particularly Whigs—regularly engaged in politics with the encouragement of men: "Could this ladies' champion . . . visit Peoria just now, he would not only meet many Whig ladies at the Clay Club and public political exhibitions of oratory at the Court-Room, but he would find them patriotically assembling at one of the hotels of our place, making banners and other paraphernalia for the approaching Whig convention."[70] Women's enthusiastic participation in Whig politics represented a larger trend of which Davis was acutely aware. Women were becoming increasingly politicized through newspapers, sermons, education, and social interaction.[71] This politicization led to action, especially within the Whig Party.[72] Encouraged by male politicians, women began attending political conventions, and "feminine symbols" became "commonplace in the political rallies of both parties."[73] Whig women in Illinois gave several speeches in support of William Henry Harrison during the 1840 presidential campaign, and Samuel Davis's *Peoria Register and North-Western Gazetteer* published articles delineating women's increasingly visible support for the party.[74] African American women, especially in the Old Northwest, began participating more overtly in political gatherings. The 1848 Ohio State Convention of Colored Citizens at Cleveland witnessed a debate over women's right to be "speaking and voting as men did." After some heated discussion, the convention declared its belief in the "equality of the sexes" and invited women "to take part in our deliberations."[75] A year later, at another State Convention of Colored Citizens, held in Columbus, black women demanded that their voices be heard. They described the resistance to their participation as "shameful" and threatened to "attend no more" unless they were granted voting rights.[76] African American women continued their participation in colored conventions in Ohio into the 1850s. Sojourner Truth, for example, spoke at the 1852 convention in Cleveland, while women from the Cleveland Vigilance Committee and Oberlin Ladies Anti-Slavery Society presented a banner supporting education and denouncing colonization.[77]

After normalizing women's partisanship, Mary Davis also addressed the *Daily Journal*'s cries about gender chaos. She cleverly concurred with her opponent's gender definitions and used them to defend the femininity of abolitionist women: "The editor of the *Journal* forgets that women who have hearts to sympathize with the oppressed, the afflicted, the down-trodden, would be the last to . . . in any way disregard the domestic duties." Antislavery women, she confidently announced, "are the best wives, the best mothers, and the most useful part of the community."[78] Other Illinois women followed Davis's lead, rejecting the *Journal*'s unflattering depiction of female abolitionists. Southern Illinois activist Mrs. T. C. Hurlbut employed dry humor in her attempt to defend the honor of the Peoria women: "When I read of the dreadful fears of the poor Chicago editor lest Illinois women should turn politicians, and . . . leave him with no one to 'darn his hose or boil his porridge,' I could not but think that a slice of Phebe's nice pudding would have quite dispelled his fears."[79] Hurlbut also seconded Davis's contention that antislavery sentiment provided evidence of women's femininity: "Does not the man know that the more we value our own homes and all their household joys—the dearer our husbands or our children are to our hearts—the more must we feel for our poor sisters who are slaves, and whose husbands and children are slaves too?" Contradicting the *Daily Journal*'s argument, Hurlbut argued that abolition defended domestic bliss. Indeed, slavery's negative impact on the family—particularly women—was one of the most effective arguments employed by abolitionist women and fugitive slaves. Slavery desecrated domesticity, they argued.[80]

Male abolitionists also countered the *Daily Journal*'s critique. After all, any disparagement of antislavery women implied something about the masculinity of abolitionist men and thus required a response. Davis surely applauded when Eastman turned the tables and questioned the manhood of their opponents. He argued that the Chicago Whigs, unlike their Peoria counterparts, were simply resentful because they had failed to attract women to their events. The woefully small female representation at Chicago Whig gatherings, Eastman explained, meant that astute local women saw through the hypocritical "chivalry" of Whig men. "Perhaps, Mr. Journal, you had better make another effort to get the ladies to attend your Clay Clubs, and help you sing your 'Jim Crow' songs, or chant glorifications to 'that same old coon,'" Eastman sarcastically suggested. "It seems by the way your invitations are complied with, that your gallantry is already well appreciated."[81] Liberty men, conversely, had no difficulty attracting enthusiastic and virtuous women to their events. Green-eyed Whigs, argued Eastman, denounced abolitionist women's involvement in Liberty Party meetings simply because of their own feeble manhood.

Western male abolitionists such as Eastman not only defended their female colleagues but also advocated women's further activism in the Liberty Party. Owen Lovejoy, Liberty Party candidate from Princeton and brother of slain abolitionist Elijah Lovejoy, encouraged women in his community to sit down with neighbors and discuss Liberty Party policies and values. "Make them a social call," he instructed. "Let not the women be afraid of 'dabbling in politics,' so long at least as their sisters are imbruted by politics."[82] The sinful degradation of female slaves required the women of Princeton actively to support the Liberty Party. The western third-party movement in general proved relatively hospitable to women in part because it welcomed *both* evangelical and more politically oriented abolitionists. One historian has characterized the western Liberty Party as "predominantly religious."[83] In Illinois, clergymen dominated the Liberty Party leadership. Dickey, Codding, and Lovejoy, the three Liberty Party leaders invited to attend the inaugural meeting of the Illinois Female Anti-Slavery Society, were ministers.[84] Western antislavery activists often boasted about the congenial atmosphere that prevailed among Liberty abolitionists in their region. "Our third political party [and yours] in the East, they don't compare at all," declared Ohioan W. B. Irish in a letter to Garrison. Though not a Liberty man, Irish admired the amicable environment that permeated the western wing of the party: "Your new organized political parties are full of bitter invective against old organizations. Not so here."[85] Although Irish exaggerated the extent to which harmony predominated in the West, evidence suggests that the categories of "moral" and "political" antislavery overlapped significantly.[86] This tolerant atmosphere seemed to peak during the 1840s.

Western women abolitionists and female antislavery societies took advantage of this exposure to political debates as well as the relative harmony between moral and political abolitionism in the Old Northwest to vocalize their political convictions.[87] These convictions often were explicitly framed within a moral context, and this moral context was then linked to womanhood. The female abolitionists of Dundee, Illinois, for example, rationalized their interference in the political realm because "the rights of our sex are outraged." They demanded that local men vote for Lovejoy for Congress because he was "a living picture of the philanthropist and Christian."[88] In a letter extolling Lovejoy and Liberty Party advancement, Mary Davis concluded, "The mighty hand of God seems to be extended to aid the cause of Liberty."[89] A Michigan Liberty correspondent instructed local women that antislavery possessed "political as well as moral character" and therefore "has peculiar claims upon your sympathy, and may well demand the warm aspiration of your souls for its success. It is the cause of *suffering humanity*; and when has such a cause failed to touch a chord of sympathy in woman's heart?"[90]

Western Liberty women also connected their partisan involvement with domesticity and community.[91] In the West, both editors and women linked Liberty Party politics with the hearthstone. Emphasizing the intimacy of family and local community, Liberty organizers constructed the party as comfortable, familiar, and safe. Lovejoy gently prodded women to hold "neighborhood meetings" to chat with friends about Liberty.[92] The Michigan Liberty Party invited entire families to attend Liberty dinners and thanked Liberty women for providing attendees "with the richest of Michigan's bountiful dinners to cater for the body."[93] The editor of the Indiana-based Liberty paper *Free Labor Advocate and Anti-Slavery Chronicle* emphasized the importance of local organizing when he called on both men and women to create "Liberty associations" in "each township and school district."[94] Huldah Wickersham, the outspoken leader of the Henry County Female Anti-Slavery Society, referred to herself as a "humble and obscure country girl" in a letter to an esteemed male friend even as she confidently cited historical facts and religious motivations in a defense of the Liberty Party.[95] Davis concluded a letter to the *Western Citizen* praising the progress of the Liberty Party with a scene from the dining room: "As a proof that the principles of the Liberty Party are advancing, permit me to say I have the pleasure of sitting at table with from ten to fifteen gentlemen boarders at the house where I board, who are, with one or two exceptions, liberty men."[96] Blending the warm, comforting environment of the dining room with Liberty Party politics, Davis constructed a vision of partisan politics that was particularly inviting for women.

"Ladies, Will You Meet with Us?"

As Mary Davis and other leading abolitionist women carefully constructed a domesticated Liberty Party, they also negotiated an increasingly public space for themselves within the party. This public space first involved carefully timed female conventions that overlapped with Liberty Party gatherings. At the conclusion of Davis's description of the first Illinois Female Anti-Slavery Society Convention, held in 1844, she casually mentioned that the Liberty Party had met the following day. Her editorial comment about the gripping afternoon speaker revealed that she was present at the Liberty meeting.[97] The timing of these two assemblies was no coincidence. Illinois's antislavery families—including the Lewises, Kelloggs, Hurlbuts, Allans, Pettengills, Lovejoys, and Wrights—needed to make only one trip to enable both men and women to attend their abolitionist meetings. More surreptitiously, holding the two meetings at the same location during the same week also created an avenue for women to attend a "masculine" political meeting under the guise of a separate female organization. Indeed, when the female group adjourned at noon on May 24, many of the forty-five women in attendance followed Davis's lead and strolled from the Main Street Presbyterian Church down the street to the courthouse to watch the Liberty Party gathering.

The connections between these two Illinois groups were deep seated and important, as Davis recognized when she concluded her article about the women's gathering with a few words about the Liberty Party meeting. She expected that her readers would be interested in her description of both events. The Liberty Party's Codding provided the keynote addresses at both proceedings.[98] The groups addressed overlapping issues, including the controversial question of the need to leave a church if it failed to acknowledge the sin of slavery.[99] In highlighting a religious question (especially one that the women had just debated), Liberty Party advocates again made clear the moral foundation to their organization and its welcoming attitude toward women. Finally, the women made explicit the connections between their group and the Liberty Party by pledging to hold their next meeting at the "time and place agreed on" by the Liberty men.[100] Irene Allan suggested that scheduling the women's antislavery gathering at the same time as the men's would have the side benefit of swelling the numbers at the latter gathering. "If the sisters, wives and mothers want to go," she proclaimed, "the fathers, husbands and brothers *will* go."[101]

The Illinois Female Anti-Slavery Society met at the same time and location as the Liberty Party for three more years. At the 1845 meeting in Alton, the men gathered at a local Baptist church, while "the female convention met downstairs in the same building."[102] It was a simple act to close the women's meeting early and join the political debate upstairs. A female slave owner from Kentucky attended both the women's and men's meetings and became convinced of the need to emancipate her slaves.[103] One year later, the Illinois Female Anti-Slavery Society met in Chicago, coordinating its gathering with the North-Western Liberty Convention in late June. The two groups again shared both participants and topics of discussion. The call for the Liberty Convention, which included participants from across the Old Northwest, invited anyone interested in a "peaceable" overthrow of the "Slave Power" without "reference to sex, class, or condition."[104] Four of the document's eleven male signers were related to women who participated in the Illinois Female Anti-Slavery Society.[105] Eager to ensure women's presence, the organizers guaranteed housing for all out-of-town female participants: "Ladies, and gentlemen with their wives, will be provided with places in private families."[106] Lone men, however, would have to find lodging for themselves. Large numbers of women attended the meeting, where they were addressed directly by a few male speakers. Guy Beckley, a Michigan abolitionist, encouraged women to focus on "persuading pro-slavery husbands to act rightly." Lovejoy asked whether the great throng before him were all "Liberty men." After cries of, "Yes, yes!," he next asked, "Was every woman a Liberty *man*?"[107] In the heat of the moment and with the keen encouragement of the audience, Lovejoy walked a fine line in suggesting that Liberty women might identify themselves as Liberty men. Such passionate impromptu calls for women to find their inner masculinity were exactly what opponents feared. Where would these calls end? What other masculine activities or traits might women desire?

The Liberty women who attended both the political convention and the annual Illinois Female Anti-Slavery Society gathering recognized that they would be vulnerable to attack for violating feminine propriety. Prominent men's repeated acknowledgments and applause for women's presence gave them pride and strength, but it also highlighted their attendance. To contain any uproar their political activities might cause, the female group self-consciously and for the first time denoted officers by reference to their husbands' names in the published minutes of their meeting.[108] Moreover, the published account of their 1846 meeting was brief and vague, as if they preferred little attention. Similar to the Ohio female antislavery societies of the 1830s, Illinois Liberty women sensed the highly charged environment and responded with a sensible, practical change in tactics.[109]

Other women's groups in the West coordinated their meetings with the Liberty Party. Illinois's DuPage County Ladies Anti-Slavery Association met jointly with the Liberty Association to celebrate July 4. Hoping to attract entire families, the gathering involved a fund-raising fair, public addresses, and a "free public dinner."[110] In 1843, the Ohio Ladies Education

Society met at the same time as both the Ohio Anti-Slavery Society and the Ohio Liberty Party. Although *Philanthropist* editor Gamaliel Bailey claimed that keeping the conventions separate was important, the same people attended all the meetings.[111] In March 1844, Milwaukee's women abolitionists met to form a female antislavery society, and three days later, the Liberty Party invited the women to come to the party's meeting.[112]

By the mid-1840s, Liberty Party leaders in the West openly invited women to attend their local and state meetings. "The Liberty party relies with confidence on the co-operation of its female friends," declared the Illinois Liberty convention in 1844, "and deems it not only appropriate but highly desirable that they attend all its meetings."[113] Increasingly convinced that women could aid the party, many Liberty advocates no longer found it necessary for women to meet separately. After all, Whig women's Clay Clubs, parades, and attendance at political gatherings had set the stage for Liberty women. Most Liberty Party members in Illinois and elsewhere were former Whigs. As Davis had pointed out, "Whig ladies" were much more openly political than abolitionist women.[114] Liberty organizers continued to rationalize female participation by emphasizing their party's moral purpose and the domestic role that women might play. Women symbolized the purity of the Liberty Party, and their attendance at meetings brought the moral issue of slavery into clear focus.

Women from Peoria to Detroit to Cincinnati found themselves eagerly sought as public advocates of the Liberty Party. While organizers entreated women to attend the North-Western Liberty Convention in steamy Chicago during June 1845, the Southern and Western Liberty Convention in Cincinnati that same year upped the ante by allowing women (from the slaveholding state of Virginia, no less) to sign the call announcing the convention.[115] Male Liberty editors across the West began asking, "Ladies, will you meet with us?"[116] These invitations often were carefully phrased to connect female attendance to a moral imperative and thereby engender as little opposition as possible. "Come then to the meeting and cheer us on, and nerve our arms in assisting to bring back the country to a just sense of the necessity of purifying it of this Heaven-doomed curse of slavery," pleaded Liberty leaders in Oakland County, Michigan. "If you should hear its political aspect and hearings discussed, it will not harm you."[117] Bailey concurred: "The attendance of Ladies at great political meetings is proper enough," he declared in 1844. "Indeed, we think it beneficial to both sexes; quickening the mind of one, and restraining the violence of the other. . . . The presence of woman is a wholesome restraint."[118] Like Davis and her sister abolitionists,

Bailey creatively employed conservative notions of gender—male aggression and female passivity—to advocate women's political participation.[119] A strong female presence ensured that the convention would remain focused on the moral issue of emancipation. "No wonder that politics are corrupt and debased," wrote *Milwaukee Daily Free Democrat* editor Sherman Booth, "for woman's refining and purifying and elevating influence is divorced from them. Wherever woman meets man, in the church, the lecture room and at our social gatherings, the decencies and proprieties of life are observed."[120] A Michigan Liberty man assumed that females were hypersensitive when he asserted, "The ladies are especially invited to attend [the political gathering], they will hear the most interesting details ever presented to them, without a word to wound their feelings."[121] In this depiction, Liberty gatherings avoided the typical rough-and-tumble political environment that invited crude language and perhaps physical confrontations. Liberty organizers in Kendall County, Ohio, linked femininity to virtue by requesting that abolitionists bring their entire families: "Come *en masse* to the Convention with your wives and daughters, and let it be evinced to the world, that where the heart is in the work, all obstacles are easily surmounted."[122]

Some leading Liberty men in the Old Northwest keenly advocated women's participation in politics as healthy and natural. Codding, whose wife, Maria, was a leader in Illinois's female antislavery society, asserted that at an 1843 Liberty Party meeting in Lake County, "There were as many ladies present as gentleman. The cry of 'politics' possessed no terror to frighten them away. They believe in all kinds of appropriate Anti-slavery activities to destroy slavery, and especially in that which is the most effective, and why should they not give their approbation and presence to such meetings?"[123] Two years later, Eastman employed the example of Revolutionary War women to defend the participation of women in antislavery politics against male criticism. "The women of this country have as great an interest in its welfare as the other sex," he asserted. "Our grandmothers of the revolution... entered heart and soul into the strife.... When a brave matron took down her husband's rifle, and with eagle aim, sent a bullet through the head of some straggling Hessian... it was accounted to her patriotism.... But when the women of the present day, with motives equally pure and patriotic, raise their voices against evils which are preying upon the nation's vitals, why then, forsooth, they are out of their element, and talking about what is none of their business!"[124] Bailey declared, "If the discussions of a political meeting are unfit for a lady to hear, they are a disgrace to the gentlemen engaged in them."[125] These strong statements of support for women's role in politics did not necessarily translate into support for woman's rights—none of these men approved of feminism as advocated by Parker Pillsbury, Stephen Foster, and William Lloyd Garrison.[126]

Western women eagerly attended local Liberty meetings. Although they occasionally traveled great distances to attend large regional gatherings, most women participated in local Liberty events in connection with family and friends. A "great throng of Liberty men and women" attended the two-day Liberty meeting in Elgin that featured an Anti-Slavery Evening Tea Party sponsored by the "Ladies."[127] Acknowledging women's influence as "indispensable," the Elgin party organizers invited local women to "organize female associations in the different counties and precincts for the purpose of" employing their limitless "moral power in spreading our principles."[128] When the Crosby, Ohio, Presbyterian Church refused to house a Liberty meeting, one "spirited Liberty Lady . . . constructed an awning to shield the speakers from the sun." Her resourcefulness resulted in the "largest Liberty meeting ever held in the town."[129] Such gatherings occurred throughout the mid-1840s in small communities across the Old Northwest, allowing women to use their political voices with increasing confidence.

Women's participation in Liberty Party meetings served the needs of both political organizers and women abolitionists. The Liberty Party, like the Whigs, used female support as evidence of the party's virtue and integrity. Women symbolized the party's moral nature. Women, though willing to serve as proof of Liberty's righteousness, used their access to political gatherings to become literate in partisan politics and to emphasize their contributions to the movement. So successful was this effort that women found themselves sought by Liberty men as much more than symbols.

Female "Influence" and Liberty Men

Though some Liberty advocates envisioned an important role for women in their party, they clearly understood that popular opinion still equated politics with manhood. As the respected female educator Catharine Beecher argued in *A Treatise on Domestic Economy*, women had a critical role to play in the domestic arena. The public sphere, especially electoral politics, belonged to men.[130] By 1840, however, women had developed a number of tactics that allowed them to enter civic life without much public notice. The most effective of these tactics involved female "influence."[131] The idea of a powerful and morally bound feminine influence was a consistent thread in the gendered narrative of the early republic. Anne Boylan has illuminated how benevolent women throughout the antebellum period employed a deferential political style emphasizing feminine "influence" as they sought land grants, tax deferments, and public funds.[132] Rosemarie Zagarri has shown that male politicians in the early republic recognized the resonance of female influence: in 1787, one Federalist official encouraged women to use their "magic influence" over men in support of Federalist policies.[133] A few decades later, Whig politicians "celebrated the influence of wives and mothers and encouraged men to rely on women's moral guidance" as they showcased women in parades and public gatherings.[134] The Liberty Party slowly began to broaden this narrative to advocate female influence within the public sphere. Treading carefully, Liberty men and women began to encourage women to use their special female influence to affect "the tide of public opinion."[135]

Liberty advocates often began by focusing on the more traditional idea of women's influence over their families. "Who shall set bounds to the influence of an intelligent and virtuous female?," asked one correspondent to the Michigan-based *Signal of Liberty* in 1845. "You need not make a great public parade, but you can consistently, and without overstepping the bounds of etiquette, plead with your sons, husbands, brothers, and friends, the cause of the poor slave."[136] Illinois's Putnam County Female Anti-Slavery Society insisted that it was the "duty of all females to inform themselves on the political affairs of the country" and to "use their influence over their husbands, brothers, and associates . . . to vote for none but those who will . . . aid the cause of humanity."[137] Claiming that the freedom to "exert a moral influence . . . is our birthright," Indiana's Henry County Female Anti-Slavery Society resolved to "persuade our fathers, husbands and brothers" to vote for virtuous antislavery men.[138] Beckley encouraged women at the North-Western Liberty Convention to focus on "persuading pro-slavery husbands to act rightly."[139]

The *Western Citizen* offered an instructive example of the potential impact of this strategy. One eminent Liberty Party man, explained the editor, had first been introduced to antislavery principles when his astute wife asked him to read her antislavery newspaper aloud while she knitted. "He could not refuse so reasonable a request," and he now "reads, talks, and votes Liberty."[140] The clever employment of female influence, even through such seemingly benign means, could lead to more Liberty votes. This practical approach encouraged women to use whatever tools they had at hand to affect the political system, and some took the message very seriously.[141] Young Mary Sheldon, a student at Oberlin College in 1848, wrote in her composition book, "What has woman to do with *politics*? What can she do more than occasionally to attend a convention or mass meeting, and wave her handkerchief or hand to cheer the politician?" Sheldon answered her own question: "Let her become acquainted with government and the characters of the leading men of the nation. Let her influence be felt by her friends as on the side of justice and right. Hers it is to frown upon oppression and vice . . . and to strengthen the weak and vacillating mind to do the right."[142]

Liberty supporters soon broadened the potential impact of female influence beyond the domestic realm. As Mary Davis proclaimed, "Woman has influence, and directing that influence in the proper channel, she can effect mighty things."[143] A Wisconsin Liberty Party editor pleaded with women, "Organize for the purpose of making your influence decisive (we say it deliberately) . . . decisive upon the popular vote, and upon the legislation of the country."[144] The Henry County women announced in their constitution, "We feel bound as Christian women to exert all the influence we may possess in changing the current public sentiment."[145] A significant distinction existed between wives encouraging their husbands to consider the antislavery cause when they voted and "changing the current public sentiment." The avenue for affecting this political transformation quickly became persuading all "weak and vacillating" men to vote for the Liberty Party.[146] This tactic—women telling men how to vote—was actually more radical than it appears at first glance. After all, it implied that women understood the political system and knew better than men what was best for the nation. "What sort of consistency is there in talking about the political evils of slavery 364 days in the year, and the 365th go to the polls and give the lie direct to all their professions?," asked Wickersham. "Or in other words to go and vote into office those whom you know if elected, would be as dumb on the subject of the political aggressions and evils of slavery, as though they were utterly unable to speak?"[147] Wickersham's rhetorical questions certainly suggested that she understood the obvious inconsistency in such a vote. In the summer of 1844, Bureau County, Illinois, women interpreted "influence" broadly when they raised funds to hire a lecturer to encourage men to vote for Liberty Party candidates in the fall election. The women boasted that their effort "gave an additional impulse to the cause."[148]

In the process of instructing men in suitable political conduct, women abolitionists also made clear that true manhood was linked to the Liberty Party. In a published address encouraging local citizens to vote Liberty, the Ladies Anti-Slavery Society of Dundee, Illinois, suggested that only cowards would fail to support the Liberty Party. Northern men had heretofore "bowed the knee to, and kissed the feet of, the slave power" but now needed to reclaim their manhood: "We call upon you then to arise and shake off . . . this unmanly lethargy which has so long hung around you, if you lay any claim upon us to regard you as men."[149] Before the 1847 election, Davis wrote letters to the *Western Citizen* instructing male abolitionists on the importance of voting Liberty: "Liberty men of Illinois! Be true to your principles. Stand firm upon the platform of human freedom." After a very low Liberty Party turnout, Davis chastised Peoria abolitionists for their feeble and unmanly vote: "I rejoice that there are seven men [in Peoria] true to their principles under all circumstances."[150] The Henry County Female Anti-Slavery Society asserted, "We do not wish you to consider us dictatorial" even as they declared that wise, fearless, and independent men voted Liberty.[151] The Putnam County women abolitionists averred that if men lacked "firmness" or "vigilance," women had the duty of setting them straight.[152]

Some western women found other methods of employing their "influence" in favor of the Liberty Party. Davis's Illinois sisters proved especially skillful in using their influence to concoct friendly competitions that took advantage of masculine rivalries.[153] The "ladies of St. Charles" initiated this trend in February 1846 by publicly offering to bestow a beautiful banner at the upcoming Liberty Party convention to the precinct that furnished the most subscribers to the party newspaper, the *Western Citizen*.[154] The women noted that although they lacked the right to vote, "our country's destiny is our destiny"; it was thus imperative that voting "should be discharged with intelligence."[155] Reading the *Western Citizen* apparently would supply men with the necessary intelligence to vote Liberty. The competition triggered a fierce desire for victory among local abolitionists. McLean County took an early lead with 21 subscriptions.[156] A few weeks later, Eastman announced the competition had already resulted in 245 new subscribers. This number continued to rise, and the *Western Citizen* regularly reported on successes in various communities. Men began to boast that their county would win the banner. Bristol men, "desirous of obtaining the banner," asserted they would obtain one hundred subscribers.[157]

One month later, the Ladies Anti-Slavery Association of Dundee followed the lead of their St. Charles sisters by offering a "silk banner" to the precinct that gave the "greatest number of votes for Lovejoy and Liberty."[158] Lovejoy's commitment to honor the memory of his martyred abolitionist brother, Elijah, led to his leadership in the Liberty Party. His candidacy for Congress attracted the support of most northern Illinois abolitionists.[159] The Dundee women used the announcement of the competition as an opportunity to express publicly their political convictions. They published a lengthy address to the men of their district providing reasons for supporting the Liberty Party. Claiming the right to enter the political sphere wherever "the rights of our sex are outraged," they argued that slavery was a denial of Christianity and democracy. More than fifty women signed this bold call to their local men. The response was enthusiastic. One Liberty supporter in nearby Shabenah's Grove confidently announced that the banner "must belong to this precinct." Although, he explained, his small town had not received the benefit of antislavery lecturers, "our principles have taken deep root. Liberty men have learnt to act from principle in this precinct."[160]

The Liberty men of Shabenah's Grove would be disappointed. In May 1847, the Dundee women presented the Mill Creek Liberty men with the first-place banner after 66 percent of voters there selected "Lovejoy and Liberty."[161] Unable to resist another opportunity to articulate their political opinions, the Dundee women offered a statement during the presentation of the banner, though they bowed to expectations about appropriate female behavior by asking the Reverend Edwin E. Wells to read their testimonial. They did not, however, dilute their opinions. They claimed that the "ballot-box is the only effectual means, under God, of ridding our nation of that monster system of . . . American slavery." They rejected the idea that it was "impertinent" for women to "meddle with politics." As "*human beings* possessed of the feelings and sympathies of our common nature," women were compelled to applaud the growing number of "free and independent" men who made emancipation the primary focus of their votes.[162]

Although these Liberty women offered simple banners as evidence of their interest in local and national politics, they pragmatically and skillfully employed these symbols to have an impact on the system.[163] They expressed their political opinions with knowledge and passion. Their efforts resulted in more interest in the Liberty Party, perhaps more votes for Liberty candidates, and certainly more subscriptions to the *Western Citizen*. Energized by their engagement with the partisan world, western Liberty women began to focus their political efforts on combating the Black Laws.

Black Laws

Even as they used their influence in support of Liberty candidates such as Lovejoy, women also focused their attention on a more hands-on campaign to repeal the region's Black Laws.[164] Western antislavery societies, African Americans, and the Liberty Party campaigned relentlessly to eradicate these pernicious codes in the 1830s and 1840s.[165] The 1849 Convention of Colored

Citizens of Ohio, for example, focused entirely on eliminating the state's Black Laws.[166] The Ohio Liberty Party announced in January 1846, "The Black Laws of this State are unjust, oppressive and utterly repugnant to the liberal maxims of impartial democracy, and ought to be repealed."[167] A few months later, the North-Western Liberty Convention in Chicago unanimously passed a resolution declaring, "The laws of the several States marking an invidious distinction in political rights, on the ground of color, and thus injuriously affecting the colored portion of our fellow citizens, are not only oppressive and unjust, but in direct violation of the fundamental principles of republican governments."[168] Despite these efforts, only Ohio would repeal some of the laws in 1849.[169]

As early as Betsey Mix Cowles and her Ohio female antislavery societies in the 1830s, western women abolitionists had denounced the Black Laws. While these activists focused on creating educational opportunities for African Americans, Mary Davis and her Liberty women in the 1840s aimed more directly at eliminating the Black Laws. Ohioan Harriet N. Torrey wrote to the *Western Citizen* in 1846, "Were I the wife of one of those recreant Whigs who voted for the indefinite postponement of the bill for repealing the Black Laws, *my cheeks would be tinged with the burning blush of shame for him.*"[170] Not all abolitionists, however, considered the elimination of the Black Laws an appropriate focus for the movement. Many Garrisonians, particularly in the East, denounced racial inequality in the North but contended that demanding access to public education or voting rights for African Americans did not constitute a direct attack on slavery. As abhorrent as the Black Laws were, slavery was the more important sin.[171] When Cowles used funds from the Ashtabula County Female Anti-Slavery Society to publish her 1846 pamphlet, *Plea for the Oppressed*, which called for the repeal of the Ohio Black Laws, she earned the ire of some eastern radicals who considered this an inappropriate use of the group's finances.[172] Typical of western women abolitionists who embraced a pragmatic brand of abolitionism, Cowles ignored her Boston critics, persisted in her battle against the Black Laws, and developed a regional reputation for her thorough research and expertise.[173]

Western Liberty women employed the familiar and pragmatic methods of publishing and petitioning to campaign against the Black Laws. The first approach focused on presenting "evidence of black achievement" with the hope that such documentation would influence state legislatures to rescind race-based restrictive laws.[174] Liberty women wholeheartedly adopted this method, publishing their narratives in Liberty Party newspapers. Davis argued that the Black Laws offered unreasonable obstacles that kept African Americans from achieving success. She confidently asserted in an 1844 letter to the *Western Citizen*, "The colored man or woman, when thrown upon their own resources, are competent to take care of themselves, and become independent and good citizens."[175] Throughout the early 1840s, she used her memories of Virginia to pen real-life stories about slaves who proved themselves more full of humanity and determination than their owners. Davis supplemented these stories when she visited her family's home in Winchester in the summer of 1846, interacting with blacks and subsequently publishing her accounts in the *Western Citizen*. One such tale highlighted the remarkable achievements of Marcia, a native Virginian born into slavery who achieved her freedom by working for herself.[176] Marcia did not become a burden to society, as so many white Virginians expected, but instead through "economy and industry" built her own home. Despite the death of her recently freed husband, Marcia earned a "comfortable living for herself and her child" and, according to Davis, became "entirely independent, and has added house to house, until she now owns a block in the town of Winchester, occupied by some of the first families of the place." Marcia's narrative offered readers an alternative to the negative stereotypes about black women that prevailed in the northern and southern media. Davis also sought to reconstruct black manhood through the life story of Isaac Gray, another free black living in Virginia.[177] Although Davis had known Gray years earlier as a poor laboring "drayman," he had since purchased "several handsome buildings" and was now running a "splendid hack and horses for hire business." She claimed that he charged half the price of the competing white business, thus proving him more "honest" than his white competitors. "This man is quite intelligent, has a good library, and has sent his son to Pittsburgh to be educated."[178] These two examples provided Davis with evidence for her argument that even under the most difficult and challenging circumstances, blacks could and would become respectable citizens and community members.

Other women illuminated the harmful effects of the Black Laws. "Too long," wrote Cowles to her home state's *Anti-Slavery Bugle*, "have these statutes, infamous and black in character as the source from which they emanated, disgraced this nominally *free* State. Too long has the most fiendish iniquity triumphed, and humanity mourned in consequence of the vile outrages perpetrated under sanction of these 'Black Laws.'"[179] She offered as an example of the "fiendish iniquity" a Massillon, Ohio, case in which a public school was forced to expel all of its black students because of a petition raised by the local community. "The last who were driven from the house were two girls," explained Cowles, "who had walked a distance of two miles through mud and rain and had quietly taken their places as usual, when they were told to go. They lingered in the yard weeping most bitterly, then went away." Emphasizing the girls' sacrifices to gain an education and their emotional devastation when this basic right was denied, Cowles concluded, "It was a *most wicked outrage* and one which might justly mantle the cheek of the perpetrators with the deepest shame." In an irony, the Black Laws, which had been founded on the assumption of black inferiority, prevented African Americans acquiring the knowledge and skills to succeed. In Indiana, the Henry County Female Anti-Slavery Society contended that the Black Laws perpetuated racial bigotry. Encouraging members to labor tirelessly to see the laws "swept from out statute books," the society stressed the need for abolitionists to model racial respect: "We do not believe any person who is so prejudiced against color as to refuse to eat, to walk or sit with colored persons, can be a true Christian."[180]

Western Liberty women also began petitioning state legislatures to repeal the Black Laws.[181] This effort represented part of a larger trend in which African Americans and their advocates began to use state constitutional conventions to challenge legalized racism. Relying on petitions and lobbying, reformers took advantage of the reconsideration of state constitutions to try to convince lawmakers to extend suffrage to blacks and in some cases women. These efforts generally failed, with states refusing to grant basic educational, social, and political rights and sometimes even further curtailing the limited rights already afforded to blacks. Failure did not dampen the enthusiasm and persistence of equal rights proponents, however. Women in rural Upstate New York, for example, petitioned their state's constitutional convention for "equal, and civil and political rights with men" in 1846.[182]

Although abolitionists defined petitioning against slavery and racial inequality as a moral activity, their opponents recognized it as political.[183] Such increasingly became the case in the 1840s as abolitionism became linked to partisan politics with the rise of the Liberty Party. As a result, western Liberty women who petitioned against the Black Laws often found themselves excoriated and humiliated by opponents for violating the woman's sphere. The controversial topic of their petitions, as much as their supposed feminine violations, provoked this reaction. In late 1846, for example, Davis and a few other Peoria abolitionists circulated a petition calling for the repeal of "all laws now in force making a distinction between our people on account of color."[184] With more than three dozen signatures, including those of four women, the petition was forwarded to Springfield.[185] The document quickly became the subject of derision among politicians and the newspapers, particularly because of the participation of women.[186] Davis and her three antislavery sisters were singled out for attack. An anonymous correspondent to the *Peoria Democratic Press* summarized a local politician's theatrical presentation of the petition to the state legislature, characterizing the petition as an effort to legalize "amalgamation." The women who signed the petition, this antiabolitionist Democrat averred, clearly desired the "sweet enjoyment of holding in love's embrace the negro." He sarcastically agreed to support the petition if it would allow these four "ladies" the freedom to divorce their current "lords" and "to unite their destinies with those of the negro race for whom they seem to cherish such peculiar affection."[187] This race-baiting tactic was a favorite among opponents of abolition, perpetuating both racial prejudice and the stereotype of the debauched female abolitionist.

Davis and her male colleagues fought back. Eastman responded with a scathing editorial in the *Western Citizen* questioning the antiabolitionists' manhood. Of course, he cried, women would participate in a "good work" that challenged "our stupid, guzzling legislators to rise from the condition of animals, and infuse a little *humanity* ... into their acts."[188] Instead of denying that women abolitionists sought to marry African American men, Eastman brazenly asserted, "We should commend the taste and spirit of a woman who should give the preference to *any* respectable negro who has the heart of a *man* in his bosom, over the choicest selection from the prating demagogues who now control and disgrace the State." What woman would not prefer Frederick Douglass to "such poor specimens of humanity as are now upholding the infamous Black Code?"[189] Abolitionists usually defended the purity and piety of white womanhood in response to such tactics, contending that white antislavery women had no sexual or marital desire for black men. By asserting that a "respectable negro" was more of a man than a weak, corrupt, white politician in Springfield, Eastman challenged the popular association of manhood with whiteness. Amid Illinois's racist environment of the 1840s, this was an audacious strategy.

Davis also skillfully employed gender to skewer her opponent. She identified the anonymous correspondent to the *Peoria Democratic Press* as "the commander of the 'Peoria volunteers,'" who, presumably because of some manly failure, had been rejected for military duty by the governor.[190] In other words, any man who could not pass muster for the armed services could not be trusted to tell the truth. She highlighted his "unmanly, low, and vulgar allusion" to her and his "appeal to the worst prejudices of the community" as evidence of his lack of manliness. When the company commander publicly denied authorship of the letter, she accused him of cowardliness. "It is a maxim with the Colonel never to *appear* in these things; he sets his gulled agents to work, who are generally of the lowest order of humanity."[191] This man was not only rejected by the military but also too spineless to face the females he attacked. Davis concluded with an impudent promise: she would "send a petition next year with 200 names, 100 of which will be women."[192]

In 1847, Davis persuaded the Illinois Female Anti-Slavery Society to focus its efforts on repealing the Black Laws.[193] She offered to print and distribute free copies of the petition for women across the state.[194] Davis openly acknowledged that female abolitionists "may be derided by those who regard woman as designed by Providence to fill a subordinate sphere in life." But, she argued, "we must consent to be ridiculed and derided, and determine to permit our thoughts to stray beyond the narrow limits of the family circle. . . . *We have* an interest in the welfare of our country. . . . Sisters! be not startled, but come to the rescue."[195] This effort meant becoming knowledgeable about and involved in politics through the circulation of the anti–Black Law petition.

Davis and the Illinois Female Anti-Slavery Society were not the only western female abolitionists in the 1840s to engage in political activity in opposition to legalized racism. Young's Prairie, Michigan, abolitionists pledged to "remove the prejudice that has kept the free man of color from a participation in the rights of and privileges of citizens," and a mixed-sex antislavery group in Cleveland vowed to eliminate "all those laws and customs which deprive any portion of our fellow man of the enjoyment of equal rights."[196] The ladies of Ashtabula County worked with Liberty Party leaders to establish a newspaper "devoted to the repeal of certain odious Laws of Ohio, relative to the people of color in Indiana."[197] The Henry County Female Anti-Slavery Society promised to petition the state to repeal "all laws making a difference between man and his neighbor on account of color."[198] These outspoken Indiana women addressed the issue of racial discrimination as a political and moral issue at nearly every one of their meetings during the group's five-year existence.[199] Their sister abolitionists in Putnam County, Illinois, proved equally committed to eliminating prejudiced laws. The group's first action at its organizing meeting was to garner signatures on a "petition [to] our State Legislature, on the subject of the unjust and oppressive laws of our State with regard to colored persons."[200] Recognizing that knocking on neighbors' doors to discuss controversial political issues was a daunting task for women, the Putnam group assured supporters that persistence would make the task "less arduous" and that "our neighbors will be convinced of the safety and utility of this manner of expressing our sentiments, and will come into the measure."[201] Buoyed by "zeal and diligence," the women procured 163 signatures on this petition in just a few months.[202]

Women abolitionists involved with petitioning against their state's Black Laws understood their activism to be political in nature and clearly connected to the efforts of the Liberty Party. Even though many claimed to be motivated by morality or religion, they recognized that petitioning involved them in the governmental system. This involvement required them to understand the political process, from writing the petition to ensuring it was properly processed by local and state authorities. Davis appreciated the political nature of her petition and rejected the idea that women should remain outside this sphere: "I cannot but feel that the time has arrived when the co-operation of our sex is greatly needed."[203] Her use of the term "cooperation" is important here. Davis saw women as partners with men in the political system. Each brought different but critical insights to the table, and the combination could result in a solid and virtuous political system. In 1848, however, Illinois residents resoundingly approved a new state constitution that included a section prohibiting black emigration to the state.[204]

Conclusion

Though often subtly and in ways that were poorly documented, women participated in the Liberty Party as an expression of their antislavery convictions. Davis and many other western Liberty women became knowledgeable and skilled partisan players. They read newspapers, debated their neighbors, and listened to political speeches. They learned about the Black Laws and the constitutional debates over slavery, and they knew the local candidates' positions on these issues.[205] Their partisan knowledge and participation did not necessarily lead them to advocate woman's rights or woman's suffrage, but it did challenge the prevalent association of politics with masculinity.

Western women found that the "feminine" arena of morality overlapped with the "masculine" political domain in the context of third-party abolitionism. They did not abandon antislavery because it became increasingly associated with the Liberty Party, as historians have assumed; instead, they retooled and quietly entered the fray alongside their male colleagues. They did so with an understanding that their presence in the political system made the public uncomfortable and agitated male politicians. But they often justified this ripple in the status quo by arguing that the moral question of slavery demanded their untraditional activities.

As abolitionist women across the Old Northwest coordinated their activities with and in support of the Liberty Party, they simultaneously established other avenues for advancing the cause. While Mary Davis and Irene Allen canvassed their community for Liberty, the Quaker women of Michigan and Indiana initiated a campaign to boycott slave-made goods and thus destroy slavery's economic base.

CHAPTER 3

Free Produce in the Old Northwest

In March 1833, Michigan abolitionist Elizabeth Chandler shrewdly used her ladies' column in the *Genius of Universal Emancipation* to publish a letter from Ohio's Green Plain Free Produce Society. Hoping to highlight the compelling rationale for rejecting slave-made goods in favor of "pure" free-labor products, Chandler added an important western voice to the Pennsylvania-based free produce movement. The mixed-sex Green Plain group, nearly a year old, was responding to an offer from a Philadelphia free produce group to supply free-labor cotton. Pleased to receive this proposal "to procure the conveniences of life free from the stain of our brothers' blood," the central Ohio abolitionists placed a large order. They also took the opportunity to share with their eastern colleagues their high aspirations for the movement. While only a small number of locals were "willing to endure privations or to make sacrifices," they admitted, "it is consoling, however, that there are even a few, (and that number increasing,) to whom the sweets of the cane, cultivated amid sighs and tears, have become loathsome; and whom gorgeous apparel, purchased at the price of blood, hath become a burden too heavy to be borne." Pointing to the importance of free produce advocates modeling sacrifice, the group concluded, "Let your prayers ascend to Heaven, on our behalf,—that, by a consistent walking, we may be enabled to evince to those, who are looking on, that we have espoused a righteous cause, and to show to all around us that there is no necessity of strengthening the hand of the oppressor, by partaking of those *worse* than 'stolen goods.'"[1]

The free produce movement appealed to western women abolitionists because it offered a pragmatic and emotionally satisfying method for expressing their abolitionism. Like petitioning and Liberty Party activity, free produce allowed women to advocate antislavery within a moral framework and to see the results of their efforts. As one western free produce group proclaimed, "We are called to this abstinence by a twofold consideration—first to clear our hands and our consciences from a participation in the unrighteous gains of that system of oppression against which we profess to bear a religious testimony, and secondly, because it is a principle which as it is embraced must exert a patent influence on slavery itself, and ultimately remove this great crime with all its attendant evils and corruptions from the earth."[2] In refusing to purchase or use any products made by slaves—most commonly sugar, cotton, rice, and coffee—free produce advocates hoped to make slavery unprofitable. They contended that a widespread boycott of slave goods would economically devastate the plantation slave system, requiring slave owners to switch to free labor (the free produce movement was also called the free-labor movement). Confident in their approach, supporters believed free produce to be an aggressive attack against slavery. It also offered moral gratification. Plantation owners robbed slaves of their labor. By refusing to purchase this "bloodstained booty," women expressed their righteous objection to the sin of slavery.

The perceived benefits of free produce, however, came with some clear inconsistencies and even contradictions. The moral economy they created, in which the inhuman and unchristian treatment of laborers trumped profit and greed, proved more fluid than supporters admitted. While advocates adopted a self-righteous, often arrogant, and uncompromising position in relation to eschewing slave-made goods, they could not agree to employ the same standards to goods made by exploited English workers or women's home labor. The claim of moral purity and consistency lost some of its luster when the philosophy could not be applied outside of certain constructed boundaries. Advocacy of free produce often meant increasing women's unpaid "morally pure" labor in the home. So while boycotting slave-made produce might help immediate emancipation, it also reinforced the binary of women as moral domestics and men as paid players in the marketplace.

The Green Plain epistle illuminates the gendered themes of free produce. Following the tradition of women's participation in boycotts during the American Revolution, abolitionists constructed free produce as feminine and Christian movement.[3] With its focus on sacrifice, particularly the necessity of rejecting luxuries, free produce reflected common notions of wholesome womanhood. Down-to-earth, virtuous women of the West had no need for opulence, especially if supplied by the wicked institution of slavery. In calling on abolitionists to feel the "sighs and tears" woven into that "gorgeous apparel," free produce also emphasized the importance of identifying with slaves. Women, by their nature, felt deeply the pain of their slave sisters. Despite the movement's emphasis on "masculine" finance, business, and economics, free produce became linked to the "feminine" home through the modeling of virtuous consumption. Women made righteous purchasing decisions that kept their domain free from the immoral, stolen goods of slavery. Free produce advocates employed traditional gender notions to sell their unpopular movement.

The Green Plain letter also reveals the central role that western mixed-sex societies played in free produce. Men and women worked together, often in equitably balanced leadership roles, in this effort to undermine slavery. In focusing on how male and female abolitionists developed a truly collaborative approach to free produce, this chapter joins the literature that challenges a separate-spheres understanding of the early republic. Moreover, the collaboration between the Green Plain abolitionists and their Philadelphia colleagues demonstrates the importance of transregional and transnational connections. The East did not simply supply the West with its abolitionism. Ideas, people, petitions, finances, and publications flowed back and forth between regions. Finally, free produce allowed women to engage in local action and to visualize its global effects. The simple act of refusing to eat a slice of cake made from slave-produced sugar at a neighbor's tea party went beyond educating one's friends about the injustice of slavery. It became a brick in the worldwide economic wall that free produce advocates hoped would eventually isolate and destroy slavery.

The Launching of Free Produce

Quaker John Woolman gave voice to free produce in the 1770s, and Friends remained at the heart of the movement throughout its existence. Long Island Quaker Elias Hicks followed Woolman's lead in the antebellum period and preached against both slavery and the consumption of slave-made goods. Hicks's uncompromising 1811 essay, *Observations on the Slavery of the Africans and Their Descendants*, argued that the purchase of slave goods not only enriched slaveholders but also made consumers complicit in the sin of slavery. No one, he argued, could "plead the necessity" of indulging in the "luxuries raised by the labor of slaves." Within a few decades of Hicks's publication, Friends across the North were actively supporting the free produce movement.[4]

Among Quakers, women became early leaders. Pennsylvanian Alice Jackson Lewis began to advocate free produce around 1800 and offered a "forcible and impressive address" in support of the movement at the Philadelphia Yearly Meeting of Friends in the spring of 1806.[5] A little less than two decades later, British Quaker Elizabeth Heyrick published her testimony in favor of free produce, *Immediate Not Gradual Emancipation*, as well as two other pamphlets that discouraged women from using West Indian slave-produced sugar.[6] Heyrick's writings inspired a widespread boycott of West Indian sugar among British women. A few years later, a group of Quaker women in Pennsylvania organized the Female Association for Promoting the Manufacture and Use of Free Cotton, and Philadelphia's African American women created the Colored Female Free Produce Society.[7] In the Old Northwest, the mixed-sex Green Plain Quakers created the first free produce group in Ohio, but young Elizabeth Chandler, who moved to the frontier of Michigan in 1830, sparked the free produce movement in the West.[8]

Though only a resident of Michigan for four years, Chandler catalyzed western free produce by eulogizing female participation. Chandler used her column in Benjamin Lundy's *Genius of Universal Emancipation* to publish testimonies in favor of free produce, including the one from the Green Plain Free Produce Society. Poems such as "The Sugar-Plums" and "Oh Press Me Not to Taste Again" urged her sister abolitionists to find alternatives to sugar and cotton produced by suffering slaves.[9] Chandler did more than write about free produce—she organized the first female antislavery society in Michigan in 1832.[10] This twelve-member group instituted abstention from "slave raised articles" as a main goal.[11] Despite Chandler's death in 1834 at the age of twenty-seven, her advocacy of free produce and success in converting many in her rural neighborhood would set the standard for other female abolitionists in the Old Northwest.[12] She sought to establish free produce as an appropriately feminine endeavor, asking, "How can [women] reconcile it to themselves that they, christian mothers and wives and daughters, with all the kind and gentle sympathies of woman's nature playing about their hearts, should be accessories in supporting one of the most heinous systems of oppression ever known in the world?"[13] Her emphasis on identifying with and

Elizabeth Margaret Chandler, 1836. Courtesy of The Library Company of Philadelphia.

sacrificing for slave women would become the foundation for female free produce groups in the West.

Around the time Chandler made her way to Michigan, free produce began to attract more attention and support. William Lloyd Garrison copied Chandler's columns in the *Liberator* and editorialized about women's important role in the free produce movement.[14] When women abolitionists across the North gathered at their first national convention in 1837, they listened with interest as Philadelphia Quaker Lucretia Mott pleaded for support of free produce.[15] The following year, convention attendees passed an unyielding free produce resolution: "It is the duty of all those who call themselves abolitionists to make the *most vigorous efforts* to procure for the use of their families the products of *free labor*."[16] By the end of the 1830s, free produce had become firmly linked to female antislavery, both in and out of Quaker communities.[17]

But just as women gained a foothold in free produce, it fell into disfavor among many leading male abolitionists. Garrison stopped publishing supportive articles by 1840 and later in the decade attacked the movement as impractical and ineffective.[18] He became convinced that an economic boycott of slave produce by abolitionists would not affect the slave system at all. Slave products "are so mixed up with the commerce, manufactures, and agriculture of the world," he argued, "that, to attempt to seek the subversion of slavery by refusing to use them, or to attach moral guilt to the consumer of them, is, in our opinion, preposterous and unjust."[19] Garrison and his growing contingent of supporters also argued that the free produce movement distracted from the "real" work of abolition, which they increasingly defined as agitation in the North.[20] This attack frustrated many free produce supporters. Philadelphia Quakers defended free produce through the pages of the *Non-Slaveholder*, a new antislavery newspaper devoted primarily to boycotting slave produce.[21] African Americans also continued their support for free produce, though that backing peaked in the 1850s. Former slave Henry Highland Garnet lectured across Britain in 1850 as an agent of the Free Produce Association.[22] He highlighted the vital role of women in the movement, resulting in the formation of twenty-six female "free-labour" associations.[23] Back in the United States, African American poet and lecturer Frances Ellen Watkins advanced free produce in her antislavery speeches as well as her poetry. "Oh, how can we pamper our appetites upon luxuries drawn from reluctant fingers?," she asked.[24] In Ohio, the Cincinnati-based African American newspaper *The Crisis* implored "the friends of freedom" to "abstain entirely from the use of slavegrown cotton" as a way to "diminish" slavery and encourage "free-laboring farmers of the South."[25] Frederick Douglass also published articles on free produce in his *North Star*.[26]

Garrison's opposition to the movement had little effect in the independent Old Northwest: free produce experienced an upsurge in the early 1840s. In 1843, when a "large minority of radicals" left the orthodox Indiana Quaker organization to form the Indiana Yearly Meeting of Anti-Slavery Friends, its main focus was free produce: the group's newspaper was titled the *Free Labor Advocate and Anti-Slavery Chronicle*.[27] The Indiana organization would become the only Quaker society to make the boycott of slave products a "required article of discipline."[28] Even as visiting eastern Garrisonian Stephen S. Foster condemned the *Free Labor Advocate* for its impractical advocacy of free produce, westerners defended their position and accused the radical of hypocrisy.[29] Ignoring Garrisonians' blustering attacks, women, especially Huldah Wickersham, played pivotal roles in the Indiana Yearly Meeting of Anti-Slavery Friends.[30] Moreover, nearly a dozen female and mixed-sex free produce groups emerged in eastern Indiana and Ohio in the 1840s. Following the strategy employed by Betsy Mix Cowles in the 1830s in Ohio, free produce groups organized at both the county and state levels, thus creating a more unified and organized movement.

The Feminization of Free Produce

Although Indiana's Quaker-dominated Henry County Female Anti-Slavery Society emerged nearly a decade after Chandler's death, its members stood on the free produce foundation she constructed. At its inaugural meeting in the spring of 1841, the nearly one hundred female abolitionists who gathered in Spiceland, Indiana, declared that slavery "is undermining our civil and religious liberties and threatening the destruction of our country"; therefore, "we consider it to be our duty as professing Christian Females to exert all the influence in our power to remove so great an evil."[31] Initially focused on influencing their "fathers, husbands and brothers" to vote for Liberty Party candidates, the Henry County women quickly added free produce to their agenda.[32] In the fall of 1841, they passed their first free produce resolution, arguing that it was "in vain to plead for the liberation of the slaves and at the same time freely partake of the produce of their labor."[33]

Free produce appealed to western women in part because it seemed "righteous and unoffensive"—truly feminine.[34] The Henry County women had expected to be attacked for crossing gender boundaries since their inaugural meeting, when they had resolved "that tho' we are deprived of the privilege

*Free Produce Groups of the Old Northwest. Map created by Brian Powers
and William "Wes" Skidmore.*

of suffrage, yet as free American women we claim the right of being heard on this subject, and that we should be under no other restraints than that of truth and justice in promoting our opinions concerning it."[35] Like other female supporters of the Liberty Party, they understood their public partisanship made them vulnerable to gendered harassment, but they did not back down. At their fall meeting, the women responded to a speech in which North Carolina congressman Kenneth Rayner had assailed abolitionist women's meddling in politics and offered several historical examples of the results of such nefarious interference, including blaming women's influence for the "horrid butcheries" that occurred during the "Revolution of Paris."[36] The Indiana women chided Rayner's skewed representation of women as "the most dangerous part of creation" and offered to improve his memory by highlighting the more "noble and virtuous deeds of those of our sex in olden time." They established the superior virtue of northern abolitionist women by contrasting them with violent and even bloodthirsty plantation mistresses. Quoting from southern newspapers, the Henry County women identified examples of "ladies" beating, whipping, and mutilating female slaves. Having established their legitimate femininity, the members of the Indiana group went on to defend their desire to "shed a mellowing and softening influence" on men. "Women have no business to be interfering where men are contending for empire," they admitted, "but when violent men controvert the great principals of immutable justice," then it is women's "duty to give our influence to our brethren." They assured Rayner and others that "we shall . . . be very careful how we exercise [women's] authority" while commanding slave owners to "let their afflicted and oppressed brethren and sisters go free." Although these Indiana activists defended women's public voice in the antislavery movement, they did not embrace a Garrisonian vision of woman's rights that included property rights and suffrage. Instead, they pointed to women's instinctive moral nature as rationale for their public presence in the movement. Recognizing that men would and should dominate in the strife over "empire," the Henry County reformers pleaded with women to find a comfortable and natural place for themselves within the antislavery effort. Free produce, they believed, offered such a place.

Not long after the Henry County women passed their first free produce resolution, several other Indiana women's groups followed suit. The nearby Economy Female Anti-Slavery Society announced in the *Free Labor Advocate and Anti-Slavery Chronicle* that it was a mistake for abolitionists to act as "consenters with the thief" and "partakers with the oppressor" by purchasing slave-made goods. Such actions strengthened the foundation of slavery.

Members of this group also looked beyond the institutional impact of buying slave merchandise and emphasized the personal, moral effect. It was sinful and self-destructive to "partake of the fruits" of the iniquitous system they so deplored.[37] Three other eastern Indiana female antislavery groups immediately embraced free produce as an ideal form of women's antislavery activism.[38] Several Quaker-dominated mixed-sex antislavery groups in Indiana, Ohio, and Michigan also began supporting free produce.[39] Based in eastern Ohio, the Free Produce Association of the Friends of Ohio Yearly Meeting (known colloquially as the Ohio Free Produce Association) boasted a large female membership, and its leadership consistently included women.[40] Other non-Quaker female antislavery societies also expressed support for the boycott of slave goods.[41]

As support for free produce spread among women abolitionists in the West, the idea became increasingly linked to feminine characteristics, as Chandler had articulated a decade earlier.[42] At one of its first meetings, the Henry County Female Anti-Slavery Society asked free American women to identify with their slave sisters—"to place themselves in imagination in bondage"—and thereby personally feel the suffering of slave women.[43] In constructing the world of slavery, abolitionists pointed to the violation of womanhood—the utter disregard of true femininity—to engender support. Because "the system of American slavery is constantly separating wives from their husbands, daughters from their mothers, sisters from their brothers," asserted the Henry County women in 1843, "it is the duty of every female after remembering those in bonds as bound with them to be earnestly engaged in pleading their cause."[44] This demand that free American women identify with and aid slave women was followed immediately by the assertion that "those who (after due reflection) continue to purchase [slave-grown produce] whilst free labor may be had, exhibit little better principal than" slave owners.[45] The Indiana women were telling their audience that one of the most appropriate and effective methods for defending the honor of slave women was to refuse to purchase the goods that resulted from their labor. To ignore slave women's pain and buy slave cotton or sugar was, the activists argued, to become complicit in the horror of slavery and the violation of womanhood. "We should let the memory of the sufferings endured by the victims of oppression be so interwoven with the lines of our lives," explained the Ohio Free Produce Association, "that we shall be disposed to embrace every suitable opportunity to speak and act for their good."[46] At an 1846 meeting of the Western Free Produce Association, members of the mixed-sex Business Committee made clear the connection between identification with slaves and free produce: "It is our duty as antislavery men and women to abstain from the use of Slave labor produce as carefully as though our husbands, our wives, or our children were the victims of Slavery."[47] This group asked members to imagine themselves intimately connected to slavery to feel truly the impact of purchasing slave goods. The Henry County women similarly pleaded with southern white women to identify with slaves. In an "Address to the Women of Kentucky," the Henry County society asked women to use their influence to oppose the proposed state constitution that would forcibly colonize freed slaves, crying, "Mothers! What would your feelings be, did you know that your children must be forever exiled from the home of their fathers, and you left to wither in your chains?"[48]

After encouraging free women to identify with bondswomen, abolitionists then highlighted the torment endured by slaves in producing the goods consumed by carefree northerners. "It is a solemn thought to reflect that we should be living at ease, clothing ourselves with fine apparel, and faring sumptuously every day," mourned the Ohio Free Produce Association, "when a considerable portion of those things which we are apparently so pleasantly and unconcernedly enjoying are the fruits of the uncompensated toil of the poor slave, existing in a state of physical suffering and privation not easily to be conceived."[49] Free produce proponents also illuminated slave suffering by giving voice to the products of slavery.[50] If potential advocates of the free produce movement had any hesitation about the wrongfulness of purchasing slave-made goods, Quaker women enlivened the merchandise itself with powerful descriptors and sometimes even sad, pained voices. The Union County women lamented that even one of their sister abolitionists "should so far consent to strike hands with the oppressor, as lightly to purchase the goods in whose texture are seen the visible traces of oppression, cruelty and blood."[51] This powerful verbal evocation of a handshake between a woman abolitionist and a slave owner certainly produced just the feelings of horror and empathy that free produce advocates desired. Wondering why the western Garrisonian *Anti-Slavery Bugle* never published free produce articles, a female resident of Edinburgh, Indiana, asked, "Shall the friend of the slave then be found partaking of that which is dyed with the blood, and moistened with the tears of the slave?"[52] In this case, the slave-made product itself is injured and weeping, as if in response to the terrible system that led to its creation. By giving this wounded voice to the products of slavery and describing them as "blood-stained," free produce advocates hoped to evoke feelings of guilt and revulsion that would lead readers or listeners to avoid purchasing such merchandise. Proponents of free produce believed that women were by nature more emotional and empathetic than men and therefore more likely to be moved by such heartrending arguments.

Western Quaker abolitionists also pointed to noble feminine sacrifice to pull women into the movement and render the institution of slavery economically unfeasible. Chandler had modeled this type of argument a decade earlier in a series of fictional letters published in the *Liberator*. She accused "Isabel" of being a "willing partaker" in "all the luxuries" produced by slavery. Yes, Chandler admitted, it was "inconvenient" to forgo "poundcakes and ice cream," but antislavery demanded "a few sacrifices of inclination." When Isabel finally resolved to eschew slave goods, Chandler offered congratulations: "Your simple meal will be sweetened with the reflection that it is at least unpolluted."[53] In Indiana, the Newport Female Anti-Slavery Society expressed no toleration for the excuses of those who purchased slave-made goods: "Those abolitionists especially, who profess the doctrine of abstinence from the products of slave labor, and at the same time purchase such articles, without an absolute necessity to do so, or give them the preference on account of their superior quality, or because they please the fancy better, or are cheaper than similar articles of free labor produce, do in fact cast a stumbling block in the way of others, and bring reproach upon the truth."[54] Indiana Quaker Rebecca Beeson took the idea of sacrifice quite seriously. In the summer of 1843, as her health was declining, she used the time among her friends and family before her demise to "bear a faithful testimony against slavery." In control even during her final minutes on earth, Beeson "requested to be buried in free labor clothes" as she did not want to be surrounded by anything "that was stained with the blood of her brother." A zealous advocate of free produce, she used her death to draw attention to the economic war against slavery.[55] The all-female annual report committee of the Ohio Free Produce Association pleaded, "Let us lay aside considerations of individual comforts and pleasures, when they interfere with our duty to our less favored brethren and sisters, of whatever color or name."[56]

Female abolitionists reminded their sisters of the importance of sacrifice in part because they believed that western women in particular were familiar with the necessity of making do with less. Their region had not only fewer free-labor stores but also fewer stores of all types, especially in the countryside. Home manufacture offered a familiar solution for western free produce proponents who lived in rural Indiana. The free-labor Quakers of Marion County, Ohio, called on abolitionists "to manufacture their own clothing" and thus reject the "deplorable system of oppression."[57] Rural women in the antebellum period were quite adept at making their clothing, so this kind of sacrifice seemed natural and comfortable. Nonetheless, by constructing home produce as virtuous, these free produce advocates inadvertently furthered the contrast between women's unpaid work and men's paid labor. Women's work was seen as an appropriate sacrifice.

Western free produce women also compared their austere lifestyle and virtuous sacrifice to what they imagined to be the luxury-loving plantation mistresses who wore silk gowns and ate sumptuous meals while whipping slaves for the slightest infractions. In calling on women to shun basic comforts, abolitionists of the West pointed to their superior femininity. "Fancy" goods signified selfish indulgence—the antithesis of "true womanhood." Abolitionists consequently encouraged each other to take a simple approach to everything from dress to food. The Indiana women responded to grumbling about the high price and rough quality of free-labor goods by asking the complainers to adopt a "more self sacrificing spirit."[58] They also reminded one another that no matter what sacrifice had to be made for free produce, their lives were superior to those of even the best-treated slaves. "Our fellow men and women might abstain [from slave-labor products] and still retain a thousand fold the pleasures and enjoyment of life, of which the slave is deprived."[59] No free produce shirt or cake, no matter how scratchy or tasteless, could compare to the threadbare clothes and meager food that typically sustained southern slaves. Again, in glorifying women's sacrifice as normal and natural, women abolitionists reified gender norms.

In a broad sense, western abolitionists were rejecting the southern plantation economy with its wide disparity in wealth and eulogizing the northern free-labor system with its supposedly more equitable distribution of opportunity. Their vision of the northern economy was rooted more in an older agricultural model than in one driven by a burgeoning market. Their celebration of the northern free-labor system fit nicely with other modes of western abolition. Garrisonian organizers of fund-raising fairs in Ohio and Michigan often called for the contribution of simple basic goods that came from the handicrafts of individual abolitionists. "Let the farmer and his wife bring grain and wool, brooms and baskets, cloth and other manufactured articles," instructed the managers of the Western Anti-Slavery Society Fair in Salem in 1847. "Let the dairymaid come with her cheese and butter, and the miller with his flour—let the hatter and tinner, the saddler and shoemaker present such needful things as their several handicrafts can furnish."[60] Although most western Garrisonians had rejected free produce by the 1840s, their fairs emphasized "useful" goods that would appeal to housewives and farmers. Like free produce advocates, organizers of these events called for sacrifice and hard work. Editorials about the Salem fair often illustrated this theme by giving examples of the arduous labor of small-town abolitionists: "In one neighborhood in the county where the abolitionists are far from being numerous, the few there are laboring with a zeal highly creditable to them," explained one editorial in the *Bugle*. "They were making fifty yards of flannel, a considerable quantity of linen thread, some knitting work. Each dairy would contribute a cheese, and a cooper would furnish the boxes needed for the same. Some contribute butter, which will be exchanged for maple sugar, and in this way the value of these contributions will be swelled to a large amount."[61]

The popular notion of virtuous, hardworking, self-sacrificing westerners served free produce advocates nicely. Women unequivocally advanced the idea of female moral superiority to pull their sisters into the movement. They worked diligently to make their fellow Americans feel the pain of slaves and thereby convince consumers to boycott slave-made goods. While advancing basic gender stereotypes, however, these free produce women learned that their movement offered avenues for expressing themselves in less traditional ways.

Opportunities and Connections

Western women abolitionists did not use free produce as an opportunity forthrightly to advocate woman's rights, but they did find themselves confidently expounding on such "masculine" issues as international finance, labor conflict, and clerical failures. They discovered that their community struggles to access free-labor goods, sustain a store, and educate others about their movement led them directly into civic society. In the end, free produce taught the abolitionist women of the Old Northwest that antislavery was inherently a global effort and that their small contributions in rural Indiana, frontier Michigan, and central Ohio had larger meaning for both themselves and the movement.

In Indiana, free produce became linked to a larger battle within the Quaker community. Although the Society of Friends had a long history of opposing slavery, its members did so primarily within the context of Quaker meetings and individual decisions. Hoping to avoid larger conflicts that could further alienate them from the non-Quaker American public, Friends kept a low profile in relation to their opposition to slavery. Doing so proved increasingly difficult as the immediate emancipation movement challenged colonization in the 1830s, bringing abolitionism increasingly into the public eye. Many Quaker leaders opposed what they saw as the recklessness of immediate emancipation and quickly eschewed organized abolition. They closed their meetinghouses to abolitionist lecturers and threatened to disown members who participated in sectarian abolitionist groups. Many abolitionist Quakers battled their yearly meetings or left them to form separate meetings, as the Indiana Yearly Meeting did in the early 1840s.[62]

As Wickersham and other outspoken Quaker leaders in Henry County formulated plans to attract more support for free produce, they concentrated their attention on religious leaders. The timing of this focus was anything but random. The Quakers of Indiana in the early 1840s experienced a painful dispute that left the abolitionist contingent feeling rejected and abandoned. The powerful Indiana Yearly Meeting of Friends represented twenty-five thousand Quakers across the Old Northwest. While some, among them public activists Walter Edgerton, Charles Osborn, and Levi Coffin, advocated immediate emancipation and full racial equality, others, including Elijah Coffin, the influential clerk of the powerful Meeting for Sufferings, favored gradual emancipation through colonization and if necessary the forced expulsion of blacks.[63] In 1842, this underlying tension rose to the surface when Coffin and orthodox members of the Indiana Yearly Meeting arranged to oust a few outspoken abolitionists from positions of power. Although they had become increasingly uncomfortable with antislavery activists' vocal calls for Quaker support of the Liberty Party and the free produce movement, Coffin's supporters were probably moved to act when esteemed Whig politician Henry Clay attended the Quakers' annual meeting in October to drum up support for his 1844 presidential bid. Abolitionist Friends, who strongly opposed the slaveholding Clay, took the opportunity to read a petition asking Clay to free his bondsmen. While fifteen thousand Quakers earnestly listened, Clay responded that manumission would require time and compensation and, moreover, that his ownership of slaves was none of their business. Elijah Coffin and his supporters were appalled by what they perceived as a public humiliation of a leading politician and immediately expelled eight abolitionists from the Meeting for Sufferings. Orthodox Friends hoped that their action would send a clear warning to others, but the scheme backfired, infuriating the large group of Quaker abolitionists in eastern Indiana. Within a year, several thousand had abandoned the regular yearly meeting to form the

Indiana Yearly Meeting of Anti-Slavery Friends.[64] Like many Christians in other denominations, the Quakers reluctantly "came out" from their church because it would not tolerate their antislavery activism.[65]

The Quakers who dominated Indiana's female antislavery societies and provided the leadership for the free produce movement tended to side with the come-outers. The clerk of the women's meeting was among those expelled, an action that pushed other women toward the radicals.[66] Many of the most active female abolitionists, including Wickersham, Phebe Macy, and Rebecca Edgerton, also became leaders in the Indiana Yearly Meeting of Anti-Slavery Friends. It was no coincidence, therefore, that free produce advocates pointedly criticized the orthodox Quaker leadership for its failure to support the boycott against slave labor. Free produce offered an opportunity for Indiana's irate Quaker women to express their frustration with the established Friends leadership. In their 1842 annual report, the Henry County women accused the clergy of hypocrisy because these men boycotted alcohol but consumed slave goods: "There are religious professors who consider it criminal to furnish grain, vessels or other facilities for carrying on the distillation of ardent spirits, who at the same time purchase slave grown articles for their own consumption and apparently think themselves justifiable." These men plead "that it is right so to do, that it would be worldly policy in us to withdraw our support and thus force the slaveholder to quit the practice." The women argued that it was "inconsistent" to claim that boycotting alcohol was a moral necessity while boycotting slave products was too "worldly."[67] Carefully sidestepping the issue of their ousting from the yearly meeting, these women made public their disapproval and disappointment with the failures of male-dominated Indiana Quaker leadership.

The Wayne County women expressed their opinion even more explicitly in their address "to the Professors of Christianity in the United States."[68] How could Christian leaders fail to employ "every means in their power, to lessen the evils of slavery and to effect its total abolition?" More particularly, why did the clergy refuse to "abstain from commerce in the product of unrequited toil; and show to the world an example of Christian philanthropy?" In addressing their message to Christian clergy more broadly, the women avoided a direct attack against the leaders of the Indiana Yearly Meeting, but most observers understood the address as a response to the Indiana Quakers' rejection of abolitionists. The nearby Union County women publicly declared that those abolitionists who refused to cooperate with antislavery groups "for fear of censure" by antiabolition churches exhibited "a lamentable deficiency of moral courage."[69] The Quaker orthodox leadership, members of this group argued, should be ashamed at having frightened people away from abolition and free produce.

Emboldened by martyrdom and the perceived purity of their convictions, the women became increasingly assertive and uncompromising. Despite the high price of free goods and the difficulty of locating them, the Newport Female Anti-Slavery Society proclaimed in the fall of 1842, "Moderate degrees of reflection might convince any person that the purchase of slave labor is deeply implicated in the guilt of slaveholding."[70] Not missing a chance to incriminate orthodox leaders, the Newport women concluded by arguing that the conduct of "religious professors in general in regard to this subject very much retards the progressive of emancipation." In accusing religious authorities of being stubbornly ignorant and obstructionist, the women made clear their faith in the righteousness of their convictions. The Henry County women, always forthright in their resolutions, audaciously asserted in 1844 that "no person can be a true abolitionist and at the same time freely purchase and consume slave grown productions."[71] The free produce movement provided women abolitionists with the confidence to proclaim who was and who was not an abolitionist, to castigate the clergy, and to assert their moral leadership of the movement.

This confidence resulted not only from a sense that the movement was grounded in the feminine characteristics of sympathy and sacrifice but also from an understanding of women's role in the household economy.[72] Female domestic leadership had changed over the past half century; it now involved directing the household economy and purchasing goods for their families. Even western women, who a generation earlier had home-produced most food, clothes, and other goods, now found that the market offered them an increasing number of accessible and affordable manufactured products. While they publicly espoused the ideal of morally pure home manufacture, in reality, they needed to purchase many of their household goods. Women's expertise in choosing and purchasing goods helped them in the very tricky effort to rely exclusively on free produce.

The supply and distribution of free produce goods occupied much of the time and energy of its supporters. Free produce agents searched the South for nonslaveholding farmers who would provide cotton. The Philadelphia-based Female Society for the Encouragement of Free Labor proved unusually successful in this effort, obtaining several thousand pounds of free cotton from abolitionist Nathan Hunt Jr. and other farmers in Quaker-dominated Guilford County, North Carolina, and having the cotton manufactured into cloth. The Philadelphia society broke even in supplying this "free" fabric to abolitionists even though consumers often complained about its rough quality.[73] Small farmers in southern Illinois and southern Ohio grew cotton for home consumption, providing another source of free-labor cotton.[74] Abolitionists also sought to replace slave-produced sugar. Even the most self-sacrificing abolitionists tended to disdain maple sugar and beet sugar, thus forcing agents to look to Puerto Rico, Mexico, the Philippines, and China for "free" sugar.[75] The difficulty of obtaining the product inevitably made it more expensive. In addition to access, quality, and price, free produce consumers were concerned with the authenticity of the product. In London, Quaker Bessie Inglis set up "free-labor depots" to guarantee the quality and genuineness of goods.[76] From accessing to selling to authenticating, women abolitionists played key roles in the movement.

Free produce stores were few and far between. Chandler relied on her relatives in Philadelphia to purchase goods from Lydia White's free produce store and send them to the Michigan frontier. Chandler also used her column in the *Genius of Universal Emancipation* to promote White's store when it opened, boasting, "We are proud to know that the projector of so laudable a design is one of our own sex."[77] Nearly every mixed-sex free produce group in the Old Northwest attempted to create some type of store that carried free-labor goods. The Western Free Produce Association helped to support Seth Hinshaw's establishment in Greensboro, Indiana, in 1842.[78] The Free Labor Association in Young's Prairie, Michigan, was first formed to "consider the propriety of establishing a free labor Store" in the community.[79] After a brief period of inactivity, the Western Free Labor Association reorganized in 1846 and resolved, "It is important that a wholesale Free Labor Store be opened in Cincinnati in order that a due supply of free labor goods may be conveniently obtained throughout the western country."[80] The group attempted to sell six hundred shares in the store at five dollars each to raise three thousand dollars to open the establishment.[81] Only men were assigned as agents to sell shares for this store; perhaps as a result, they collected only four hundred dollars by the end of the first year. Despite the feminization of free produce, the business end of the movement was perceived as a male domain. Levi Coffin eventually opened a free produce establishment in Cincinnati, and the Western Free Produce Association encouraged abolitionists to sustain the store by making free-labor purchases exclusively through Coffin.[82] Quakers in Mount Pleasant, Ohio, proved unusually successful with their free produce store, which lasted from 1846 through 1863.[83] The central role of women in this organization and their passionate devotion to free produce may account for the store's success. By and large, however, western free-labor stores proved unreliable and short-lived, requiring western women to seek their products elsewhere. In the process of securing free produce, they helped to sustain the increasingly strong links between eastern and western abolitionists and to forge new ties between British and American reformers.

Links between East and West in the free produce movement were extensive. Information, publications, lecturers, petitions, and goods flowed in both directions between the regions. While historians have argued that Philadelphia was the heart of the free produce movement, western free produce supporters became increasingly vocal and powerful by the 1850s, with women leading the way.[84] The West's pragmatic and cooperative abolitionist culture helped the region to sustain its commitment to free produce as eastern activists found themselves mired in a public debate with Garrison about the relevancy of the movement.[85] The resuscitation of the Philadelphia-based *Non-Slaveholder* in the early 1850s offers a telling example of how the West tried to energize the lethargic free produce movement in the East.

First published in 1846, the reform-minded *Non-Slaveholder* offered extensive publicity and support for the free produce movement. Printed in the same building that housed Philadelphia's free-labor store, the paper consistently reported on new free produce organizations, the dilemma of finding free goods, and the activities of its supporters. The paper suffered when it became enmeshed in a squabble with Garrison about free produce in 1847 and ceased publication within three years as free produce lost support in the East.[86] Less than a year after the *Non-Slaveholder*'s demise, however, abolitionists in the mixed-sex Ohio Free Produce Association resolved to revive the paper.[87] Founded in 1846, this Quaker organization was based in abolitionist-friendly Mount Pleasant, Ohio. Within six years, its membership topped 130, and women and men truly collaborated as the group's leaders. Convinced that the continued growth of the free produce movement required an eloquent national publication, the energetic Ohio group debated tactics for reviving the Philadelphia paper at nearly every meeting of the board for two years.[88] At some meetings, the *Non-Slaveholder* was the only topic of discussion. After several New England free produce groups demurred at helping with the financing of the periodical, the Ohioans initially determined to replace the *Non-Slaveholder* with a new western publication, the *Remembrance*, under the editorial leadership of George Jenkins, owner of a local free produce store.[89] When Jenkins balked, the group returned to the resuscitation of the *Non-Slaveholder*. After months of negotiations, complicated financing, and subscription gathering, an agreement was reached. William T. Allinson, an experienced free produce activist, would edit the periodical in Philadelphia, while the Ohio group would provide at least two hundred dollars in financial support over its first year of existence, including fifty dollars guaranteed to Allinson as his salary. The Ohioans also appointed fifteen agents—seven of them women—to gather subscriptions. Convinced of their indispensable role in reviving the *Non-Slaveholder*, the westerners referred to it as "our proposed free labor paper."[90]

The relationship between the Ohio abolitionists and "their" Philadelphia-based newspaper, which debuted in January 1853, was troubled from the onset. The first issue of the new *Non-Slaveholder* failed to mention the Ohio Free Produce Association despite explicit instructions from the board to include in the "1st no. of the Paper some account of the origin, progress, and success of our association" as well as "some intelligence of our action in reference to the establishment of the paper."[91] The Mount Pleasant Quakers took pride in their institutional history and their critical role in the revival of the paper, but Allison apparently did not find the Ohio efforts newsworthy. The second issue of the *Non-Slaveholder* included a brief, indifferent history of the Ohio group, but the story of the restoration of the paper remained untold.[92] Even as their Philadelphia colleagues ignored them, the westerners continued to elicit support and financing for the paper. And they did not meekly give up control. In February 1853, as the second issue emerged, the Ohio group sent a notice to Allinson attaching conditions to the promised two hundred dollars. These conditions included requirements regarding the paper's size, quality, and price as well as a demand that "the expenses of publishing be as near as possible to those reported to this Board" in earlier communications.[93] In the Ohio Free Produce Association's 1853 annual report, published in the *Non-Slaveholder*, the association took credit for the paper's rebirth: "We have . . . labored much, in connection with others, for the establishment and support of a Periodical devoted specifically to the advocacy of the Free Labor question; and we are pleased to inform the Association of the resuscitation of the Non-Slaveholder."[94] Throughout the revived paper's two-year run, the Ohio group attempted to influence the content of the paper, providing the editor with articles and suggestions for improvement.[95] In November 1853, the westerners sent notice that although they would continue to solicit subscribers, they would not "make any definite pledge of money to support it another year."[96] When the paper merged with Elihu Burritt's *Citizen of the World* in 1855, the Ohioans continued to solicit subscriptions.[97]

Western free produce advocates understood that a national periodical could help to energize their movement and made extraordinary exertions to bring this goal to fruition. Although their relationship with eastern colleagues proved complicated and sometimes prickly, the Mount Pleasant Quakers remained focused on what they deemed to be in the best interest of the movement. Unintimidated by their Philadelphia friends, the men and women of the Ohio Free Produce Association used their finances, cohesiveness, negotiating skills, and dogged determination to initiate an eastern-based paper that reflected their vision of the movement. Even as they recognized that they could not entirely control the paper, they relentlessly offered advice and support.

Western free produce activists, particularly women, sought cooperative relations not only with their colleagues in the East but also with supporters across the Atlantic. Chandler gushed in 1830, "It is extremely gratifying to learn that our female friends, in Great Britian, are still actively engaged in exposing the manifold evils, and endeavouring to effect the final abolition, of British West-Indian Slavery."[98] She printed her personal correspondence with women's groups in Great Britain in her *Genius* ladies' column, hoping to inspire and motivate American women. In the spring of 1831, she informed her readers that the secretary of the Birmingham Female Anti-Slavery Society "states that, with one exception only, she knows of no ladies' society in England that has not resolved to reject the use of West Indian sugar."[99] Indiana's Economy Female Anti-Slavery Society expressed its conviction that the success of free produce depended on "the inhabitants of Europe" abstaining from slave products.[100] The Ohio Free Produce Association invited English abolitionist John Candler and his wife to participate in its annual meeting, thus bringing the British into its conversations.[101] The mixed-sex Western Free Produce Association declared, "If all the professed friends of the Slave in Europe and America, would abstain from the use of Slave Labor they would accomplish the Abolition of Slavery in less than two years."[102] In drawing attention to the economic relationship between the slave South and Europe, western women quietly entered the international world of business. While seeking "free" cotton for their sunbonnets, female free produce advocates comfortably discoursed about global economic ties.

Some western women abolitionists sought to convince their sisters in the British Empire to embrace free produce. British women needed little encouragement, since they had a long history of such activism. In addition to Heyrick's efforts, British women had canvassed door to door during the

1820s, "handing out pamphlets with such titles as *What Does Sugar Cost?* and *Reasons for Substituting West Indian Sugar.*"[103] Following emancipation in the West Indies in 1831, women's antislavery groups across Great Britain called for a boycott of slave-grown American cotton, an effort that peaked with the creation of Inglis's London store.[104]

Western women had an attentive audience, therefore, as they began to address their sister abolitionists across the Atlantic. When the *Free Labor Advocate* published an open letter from the abolitionist women of Scotland in 1847, the outspoken Henry County women responded with a strong call for free produce. "Much may be done," they assured their Scottish colleagues, "by refusing to partake of [slavery's] fruits." Advocacy of free produce would not only "greatly facilitate [slavery's] overthrow" but also provide evidence of practicing what one preached.[105] "Abstinence from articles produced by the unrequited labor of slaves," they knowingly declared, "certainly becomes those who profess to do all in their power to hasten the day of emancipation." Acknowledging that "the broad Atlantic" would forbid members of the two groups from working too closely together, the Indiana women nonetheless proclaimed, "We willingly unite heart & hand with you in this work of mercy & labor of love."[106] Pointing to sisterly ties and common interests, the Henry County women recognized the importance of international connections and support in their effort to end slavery by eliminating its economic foundation. Wickersham wrote several letters in which she pleaded with Elizabeth Pease, a wealthy English abolitionist, to side with the free produce radicals in the Indiana Quaker divide of the 1840s. Wickersham understood the importance of international pressure and used all her powers of persuasion to find support among influential British women.[107]

Such concern for the movement's Anglo-American implications spilled over into labor issues and allowed western women abolitionists to enter the masculine arena of labor relations. The mixed-sex Marion County Free Labor Association passed an 1842 resolution giving preference to "free labor goods of home manufacture, over foreign" whenever possible.[108] This action was related to abolitionists' concerns regarding worker exploitation in England. Labor sympathizers compared the position of English workers to that of American slaves. While the comparison proved controversial (no matter how exploited, English workers were not slaves), many American abolitionists worried about using the products of abusive English factories.[109] In 1846, the Western Free Produce Association debated a resolution that would have forbidden the sale of English goods in the association's proposed free-labor store because such goods were "produced by a monopoly of the soil and machinery from the free poor, thereby reducing them to a state of degradation and wretchedness but little better than that of the slaves of the South."[110] Although the resolution was eventually defeated, women abolitionists were confident enough to express their concerns.

The effort to eschew the products of slave labor and English factories caused the Marion County group to recommend that its members "as much as practicable . . . manufacture their own clothing."[111] In practice, this idea meant that *female* members should produce their family's clothing. Although a dubious honor, the labor involved in spinning and sewing the family garments brought Anglo-American economics into women's homes. In refusing to purchase "bloodstained" fabric or clothes produced through exploitation and suffering, women expressed a moral opinion in the context of a larger economy. By taking on the task of producing these goods, the Quaker women of rural Indiana and Ohio connected their local, familial experiences to events in factories across the Atlantic. By the late 1840s, the Henry County women moved increasingly toward this tactic, and "spinning and weaving" became a regular activity at their meetings.[112]

Free produce encouraged women to connect not only to abolitionists abroad but also to free and fugitive blacks in their neighborhoods. The Henry County Female Anti-Slavery Society from its inception organized a "vigilance" committee "to seek out such colored Females as are not suitably provided for [and] assist them in any way they may deem expedient."[113] As they negotiated with Scottish abolitionists to boycott American sugar, Indiana activists also sought out local women in need who suffered under the widespread racial inequalities that permeated both North and South. In the mid-1840s, the Henry County women devoted much of their time to sewing free produce clothes for fugitives as part of an interest in truly touching those whose lives had been damaged by slavery. Sewing with free-labor cotton seemed to offer such a connection. Needlework remained an appropriate feminine activity, making the reformers feel useful and important. Connecting with local blacks, however, proved more difficult. Henry County was not an especially active stop on the Underground Railroad, and the women eventually admitted that the clothes they were sewing for fugitives were not needed locally.[114]

Such attempts to connect with local fugitives and free blacks did not include inviting them to participate in their groups. Extant evidence suggests that the Indiana free produce groups included white female Quakers. The population of African Americans in this part of the country remained quite small, thus accounting in part for the lack of inclusion. The prevailing notion that blacks needed white abolitionists for "uplift" also accounts for the failure of free produce activists to court African Americans as equal participants.[115]

Conclusion

The free produce movement appealed to women abolitionists in the West because it drew on their domestic expertise and supposedly moral nature. It also encouraged them to contemplate cotton production, international tariffs, and labor conflict. Women such as Huldah Wickersham and Rebecca Beeson corresponded with free produce suppliers in the East and wrote addresses to abolitionists in Great Britain. Emphasizing the moral and practical aspects of the free-labor movement, these female abolitionists entered the "masculine" business and economic arena without raising the objections of their neighbors and fellow Americans. These women expressed their commitment to free produce with uncompromising personal and political assertiveness. They believed the future of the nation depended on the success of their movement.

As the Quaker women of the West negotiated a place for themselves in the free produce movement, the region's Garrisonian women advocated their vision of antislavery. A minority in the Old Northwest, Garrisonian abolitionists used traditional avenues, including sewing societies and fairs, to push their radical agenda in a region otherwise dominated by political and church abolitionists.

CHAPTER 4

Antislavery Fairs, Cooperation, and Community Building

They sent the box to Cincinnati. This infuriated the Salem, Ohio, Garrisonians. Sarah MacMillan made every effort to remain polite in her letter to Anne Warren Weston, but the exasperation behind her words burst through. Why, MacMillan inquired, had Weston's powerful Boston Female Anti-Slavery Society failed to send the Salem abolitionists the promised box of goods for their annual fair? Initially, MacMillan explained, the Salem organizers had assumed that the unpredictability of winter had prevented the box from arriving. However, she fumed, "we have now learned that a box of Boston goods has been forwarded to Cincinnati to the Society there." MacMillan rather sarcastically demanded confirmation of her assumption that the box had been intended for Salem but had gone to Cincinnati by mistake.[1] After all, the Salem women had faithfully responded to Weston's letter inquiring "what use would be made of the money, if a box of goods should be forwarded for their disposal," despite finding the tone of the missive patronizing.[2] Salem had a long history of "Old Organization" abolition, and slavery opponents there had worked closely with Weston and her Garrisonian colleagues for years. Why, they wondered, did they need to prove their worth to Weston?

MacMillan's frustration involved a regional competition between the two Ohio antislavery fairs and a complicated politics of abolitionist legitimacy in the Old Northwest. The Boston Female Anti-Slavery Society's famous winter fair provided the Garrisonians with thousands of necessary dollars every year. In distributing their much-coveted fair leftovers to various smaller bazaars, the Boston women made sure that the proceeds would benefit only Garrisonian auxiliaries.[3] MacMillan understood that the Boston women's decision to send the box of fair goods to Cincinnati meant that their sisters there had somehow been deemed superior in their Garrisonian legitimacy. This determination galled MacMillan, a passionate young woman who had honed her political skills at various radical antislavery and woman's rights conventions since the late 1840s. "They are freesoilers!," she exclaimed with disgust.[4] And she was right. Although Sarah Otis Ernst, the leader of the Cincinnati group, was a Garrisonian, the majority of the Cincinnati women were moderate political abolitionists. Weston may also have favored the Cincinnati women because of Ernst's elite Boston roots. The Boston women saw the movement from an eastern perspective. In 1846, their annual Massachusetts Anti-Slavery Fair had become the National Anti-Slavery Bazaar, with the new name signifying an inflated sense of importance.[5] Unlike the rural western fair hosted by the Salem women, the Boston bazaar boasted "a large assortment of fancy articles, imported from Paris," suggesting that class as well as region informed the arrogance of the eastern women.

The Cincinnati and Salem antislavery fairs illuminate the ways in which women such as MacMillan and Ernst negotiated the adaptable lines between different brands of abolitionism in the West to build a dynamic reform community. Except for a few small pockets of radicals, Garrisonians in the 1840s and 1850s were isolated from one another in the Old Northwest. They needed to establish contacts with each other and with non-Garrisonians to maintain their effectiveness and sustain their enthusiasm. The annual fair became a tool for becoming a viable influence in the state. But they did not surrender their radical identity. Ohio women used their fairs and the money they raised to sustain western unity even as they worked to maintain their relationship to eastern radicals.

Western women also used their fairs to bring respectability to abolitionism. Ernst carefully employed her wealth and connections to attract Cincinnati's leading ladies and gentlemen to her bazaar, thus reaching out to an unlikely audience. But she also ensured that the fair carried goods produced by local artisans and farmers, thus consciously creating a marketplace that adhered to her values. As Cincinnati became increasingly linked to the burgeoning market and consumer economy, Ernst highlighted and eulogized the declining production-based economy grounded in the honest, hard labor of good republican men and women. Unlike the famed and successful Boston fair, which was linked to opulent consumption, Ernst ensured that the Cincinnati bazaar remained deeply connected to the heartland. Ernst recognized that the city's elite could bring abolitionism power and influence, but she was not willing to sacrifice her sense of moral economy. She wanted to attract the elite and then helpfully instruct them in morality.

Cincinnati, a Burgeoning Borderland

Between 1800 and 1850, Cincinnati exploded with a diverse population and a strong economy that included manufacturing, commerce, property investment, and local banking. Strategically located along the Ohio River, the beautiful metropolis also boasted a rich, fertile countryside. By 1850, Cincinnati had become the nation's second-largest manufacturing city and had the fifth-largest population. Immigrants from Germany, Ireland, and England flooded to the Queen City, constituting 40 percent of the population by 1840. Its reputation as "Porkopolis"—the nation's pig center—attracted a steady stream of visitors seeking meat products as well as business opportunities. With nearly all of its fifty thousand inhabitants living within one square mile, Cincinnati was a walking city. Its busy streets were relatively clean, however, and included public gardens and parks. The citizens of the Athens of the West prided themselves on their thriving public educational system and wide variety of religious institutions.[6]

Cincinnati's African American population grew tremendously in this period, leading to the development of a lively black culture built on education, religion, reform, and employment opportunities.[7] In 1848, Martin Delany, a visiting African American abolitionist who wrote for Frederick Douglass's *North Star*, characterized the black community as "in as comfortable as condition as any place I have yet visited, East or West." He also highlighted the diversity of occupations among blacks—mechanics, carpenters, shoemakers, bricklayers, plasterers, saloon proprietors, and grocery store owners.[8] Excluded by Ohio's discriminatory Black Laws from the public school system, blacks prioritized education, resulting in an estimated literacy rate of between 60 and 70 percent.[9] Cincinnati housed one of the nation's two black high schools.[10] Reform efforts also took precedent. Delany found a variety of charitable organizations, including the United Colored American Association, the Sons of Temperance, and the Colored Orphan Asylum.[11] However, blacks in the Queen City also experienced oppression and violence, including at least four major racially motivated disturbances by the late 1840s.[12]

Perhaps because of this tension, the city maintained a wide-ranging public conversation about racial conflict and abolitionism throughout the 1830s, 1840s, and 1850s. The *Daily Cincinnati Republican and Commercial Register* warned in 1835 that antislavery agitation in the city would be dangerous because "the southern feeling is too strong in this city; the interests of her merchants, her capitalists, and her tradesmen, are too deeply interwoven with the Southern country."[13] Seven years later, the short-lived *Cincinnati Post and Anti-Abolitionist* published a list of the city's abolitionists and concluded, "Our friends in the South will know what use to make of it!"[14] The reform-minded *Cincinnati Gazette*, conversely, printed thoughtful editorials, letters, and articles about the Black Laws, the Liberty and Free-Soil Parties, the slave trade, fugitive slaves, and the sinfulness of slaveholding.[15]

Antislavery efforts began early in Cincinnati. The city's African Americans consistently aided fugitives. In 1831, a black agent promoted Garrison's *Liberator* in the city. Three years later, Cincinnati hosted the Lane debates, which featured evangelical students embracing the abolition movement.[16] A few Lane Seminary students subsequently went into the local black community, working to educate and "uplift" African Americans.[17] Cincinnati quickly became an important urban center for western antislavery. James G. Birney helped in this process by housing his antislavery newspaper the *Philanthropist* in the city in 1836.[18] The Ohio Anti-Slavery Society followed Birney to Cincinnati, making him the leader of Ohio abolition. By 1837, after the *Philanthropist* and its editor had developed a reputation by toughness for enduring several attacks by antiabolitionist mobs, Gamaliel Bailey took the reins of the paper and became a new leading voice in western antislavery.[19] Cincinnati abolitionism also benefited from the diligent efforts of free blacks and lawyers who worked together to challenge the state's Black Laws and defend against the kidnapping of free blacks and the forcible reenslavement of fugitives.[20] Salmon P. Chase and other Cincinnati abolitionists used the courts to institute Ohio's "law of freedom," which declared that slaves who were voluntarily brought into the state by their masters immediately became free.[21] These antislavery efforts brought forth vehement and often violent opposition directed at both outspoken abolitionists and free blacks. In 1836, when Birney refused to move the *Philanthropist* out of the city as critics demanded, the free black community experienced the wrath of a mob, which burned homes and attacked individuals.[22] In 1853, an antiabolitionist judge physically assaulted abolitionist attorney John Jolliffe in broad daylight as his wife and daughter watched. The judge, against whom Jolliffe had initiated an impeachment proceeding, was prosecuted and fined thirty dollars.[23]

Cincinnati abolitionism always remained moderate and supple. The city's location on the border of the South, its political and commercial ties with powerful southerners, its vibrant free black population and active Underground Railroad, and its large, diverse citizenry encouraged this flexible approach. As Delany explained, as long as black opponents of slavery "are conservative and time-serving," they could lecture in Cincinnati's white antislavery churches, "but a declaration of [abolitionist] truth, through the channel of liberal sentiments, is certain to meet with religious execration."[24] In 1840, when the eastern antislavery movement experienced its dramatic divide between the Old Organization Garrisonians and the New Organization reformers, Cincinnati abolitionists attempted to remain neutral, with Bailey acting as the leading voice of moderation. Cincinnati's antislavery movement remained largely focused on attacking slavery through education, the law, and judicious agitation.[25]

Cincinnati's agile abolitionism also made room for black and white women, though they worked mostly through separate organizations. The Colored Ladies Anti-Slavery Sewing Circle labored to provide goods and services for needy persons during the 1830s, while the white "Cincinnati sisters" joined the Lane students as educators in the black community.[26] Birney's *Address to the Ladies of Ohio* spurred the formation of the Cincinnati Female Anti-Slavery Society in 1836.[27] Two years later, when the Ohio Anti-Slavery Society met in Cincinnati, women for the first time enrolled as members. That year, the women even held a separate meeting at the home of activists Augustus and Susan Wattles, veteran teachers devoted to the local African American community.[28] This conscious effort to involve women in Cincinnati's antislavery movement continued throughout the next two decades.

Sarah Ernst and the Cincinnati Anti-Slavery Sewing Circle

Although Cincinnati abolitionism invited women's participation, the community discouraged Garrisonian immediatism because of its perceived disruptiveness. When the newly married radical Sarah Otis Ernst arrived in the Queen City with her husband in 1841, she instantly encountered this prejudice. An experienced Massachusetts Garrisonian, Ernst had low expectations for her new abolitionist associates. As she wrote to Weston, "I felt that no place needed the pure Anti Slavery influence more than Cincinnati."[29] With its focus on fugitive slaves, education, and the law, Cincinnati abolitionism embodied what Ernst and most Garrisonians deemed a false antislavery position. The radicals considered anything but a direct attack on the sinfulness of slavery a side issue that distracted from true abolitionism. As Ernst's neighbor and friend, Mary Donaldson, grumbled to Abby Kelley a few years later, "Antislavery proper [in Cincinnati] is asleep, & I fear must slumber on."[30]

Sarah Otis, born in Boston in 1809, grew up in an intellectual and reform-minded family whose genealogy traced back to the Mayflower. Her father, George Alexander Otis, was a well-known writer and translator, and her mother, Lucinda Smith Otis, was a reformer who hosted such abolitionist luminaries as William Lloyd Garrison, Wendell Phillips, and Charles Sumner. Her family attended King's Chapel Unitarian Church and became associated with Boston's radical Unitarians, including the Weston sisters, founders of the Boston Female Anti-Slavery Society. Sarah established a close friendship with Anne Weston that became increasingly important when Sarah left Boston for the West. At the age of thirty-two, Sarah married Andrew H. Ernst, a Cincinnati widower with six children. They likely became acquainted through their mutual friend, Adin Ballou, a Unitarian socialist and abolitionist, who conducted the couple's wedding ceremony at his church in Mendon, Massachusetts. Ernst had been a friend and correspondent of Ballou's since the early 1830s and visited the radical several times. Although Ernst was the son of poor German immigrants, he built a fortune through land speculation. He also manufactured candy and became locally famous for his horticultural knowledge and skill as a landscape architect. His home in Cincinnati, Spring Garden, certainly impressed even the well-heeled Sarah when she arrived in 1841. The large estate boasted a flourishing orchard, diverse gardens, and several houses. Bordered by a canal, Spring Garden inspired visitors with its beauty and tranquility. Sarah and Andrew remained at Spring Garden until his death in 1860, adding five more children to the already large family.[31]

Armed with wealth and boundless energy, Sarah Ernst was determined to agitate and radicalize Cincinnati. Understanding that the building of radical abolitionism in the city would require patience, she began slowly, infiltrating the moderate antislavery community. She immediately joined the Ohio Ladies Education Society for the Free People of Color, became acquainted with its membership and goals, and assumed the vice presidency within two years.[32] Working closely with the other leading ladies of Cincinnati abolitionism, including Mary Blanchard, the wife of evangelical abolitionist Jonathan Blanchard, and Margaret Bailey, who was married to the

Philanthropist editor, Ernst eventually created a new antislavery organization, the Cincinnati Anti-Slavery Sewing Circle. The Education Society, with its goal of teaching free blacks, simply did not challenge slavery in a way that satisfied Ernst. In 1846, she gathered together those women "who would labor for something besides politics and churches *as near to abolition*, as we might then reach" and organized a "sewing circle for the Fugitives of whom from 600 to a thousand passed through our city annually." Admitting that even this effort was tame—"I have never felt that by it we advanced real freedom"—she nonetheless defended her action as bringing "together Anti Slavery Spirits."[33]

Although other itinerant Garrisonians had attempted and failed to radicalize Cincinnati in 1845, Ernst felt that her residency and intimate knowledge of the city would allow her more success.[34] By 1849, this hope became centered on an annual antislavery fair, organized by the fifty-plus members of her Cincinnati Anti-Slavery Sewing Circle. Although the organization initially focused on raising funds to help fugitives, Ernst fully intended to move the group closer and closer to the Garrisonians, beginning with the fair.

The Cincinnati Antislavery Fair and Respectability

Fund-raising fairs had a long history associated with food, revelry, and trade but by the early nineteenth century had become closely linked to the serious work of women's charitable concerns.[35] In the complicated process of organizing "bazaars," women reformers solicited donations from supporters (both locally and abroad), arranged locations, publicized the events, and sold a variety of practical and luxury goods over the course of several days. By the mid-1830s abolitionist women, both black and white, began hosting fairs in cities and towns across the Northeast. African American women in Cincinnati and Columbus, for example, cooperated in a combined antislavery fair in 1848.[36] Because the antislavery movement encountered widespread disapproval, abolitionist women eagerly embraced this more traditional form of social activism as a way to legitimize their activities. Fairs allowed these women to raise funds, educate the public, and socialize within a traditional feminine framework. Fair organizers created a gorgeous, inviting setting that challenged their movement's negative popular cultural image.[37]

Antislavery fairs provided essential financial support to the movement. Disappointed with the paucity of African American bazaars, Delany may

have stepped on some toes when he reminded black women that white female abolitionists used fairs to sustain antislavery newspapers and instructed
"our ladies" to follow this fine example.[38] The most successful fair, sponsored
by the Boston Female Anti-Slavery Society, was held annually from 1834 until 1858 and is estimated to have raised more than $65,000.[39] The fair hosted
by the Philadelphia Female Anti-Slavery Society from 1836 until 1853 raised
a total of more than $16,500.[40] Dozens of smaller rural fairs raised money as
well, with nearly all profits going to support state antislavery societies and
newspapers.[41] The Philadelphia fair accounted for about 20 percent of the
Pennsylvania Anti-Slavery Society's budget in the late 1840s.[42] This financial
contribution in part explained women's prominent and long-term role in
the state society's leadership.[43] Sarah Ernst, intimately familiar with both
the Boston and Philadelphia bazaars, hoped that her Cincinnati fair would
replicate their success but proved more creative and independent in her use
of the funds raised.

When Ernst organized Cincinnati's first antislavery fair, she understood
the importance of constructing a more positive image of her beloved movement as well as of raising funds. She concluded that the fair could not only
make abolitionism more palatable but also serve as an effective tool to push
the city's moderate abolitionists toward an increasingly uncompromising
position, a very challenging and delicate task, as she knew.[44] Westerners' tendency to try to avoid or downplay the divisions that plagued eastern abolitionists obstructed the development of radical abolition in Cincinnati.

Ernst's effort to build a radical base in her hometown grew out of not
only her desire to see the expansion of "true" abolitionism but also her loneliness. "I am . . . almost lost for want of sympathy," she explained to an eastern
abolitionist in 1852.[45] Western Garrisonian women often relied on eastern
correspondents to sustain their enthusiasm and help them feel connected
to the movement. A short letter from a Boston leader might provide weeks
worth of emotional sustenance for a secluded Garrisonian.[46] "I often long for
dear New England," wrote Ernst to one of Boston's antislavery elites, "and
assure you I rejoice in a few lines from one of her own daughters like your-
self as over real treasure."[47] Ernst's Ohio neighbor, Clarissa Olds, explained
to Weston that the *Liberator* helped her to overcome her "loneliness and
sadness" by encouraging her to "look out upon the world, to feel that there
are still living, warm hearts, and that there are those in suffering who need
our aid."[48]

Ernst and other isolated western Garrisonian women found that anti-
slavery fairs offered them an opportunity to build a community with other

abolitionists—to talk with like-minded women, to share their struggles, and encourage one another.[49] Fairs were especially useful in the effort to establish community and reform respectability. Radicals such as Ernst walked a fine line between remaining true to their beliefs and maintaining respectability as Cincinnati reformers. Most of Ernst's fellow Queen City residents considered Garrisonianism inherently disrespectable.[50] Her sister sewing circle members shunned a public embrace of radical abolition in part because of the social costs—they would face public criticism from friends, neighbors, relatives, and even strangers. "Many more" would have joined the society, according to Ernst, did they not fear that their churches would object to their association with an Old Organizationist.[51] While Ernst claimed to have had a radicalizing influence on her sewing circle colleagues ("Many of them *now* seem to sympathize with me"), she understood the courage required publicly to declare oneself a Garrisonian. The antislavery fair allowed women to raise money for their cause while avoiding the ultraradical taint (though most Americans considered all abolitionists radical). The *Cincinnati Gazette* referred to the bazaar as a "creditable affair" on its front page and strongly encouraged its readers to attend: "We called in last evening, and were delighted with the tasteful display of useful and fancy articles—all sold at reasonable prices—a beautiful floral table, and, last in order but first in importance, the throng of fair ones that quite prepossess one in favor of at least one class of Anti-Slavery citizens. The Fair is worthy of universal patronage."[52] Such "fair ones" were just the sort of attractive young women Ernst hoped would bring respectability to Cincinnati's antislavery community. The *Gazette*'s endorsement suggested that Ernst's strategy had succeeded.

Perhaps because of her eagerness to appeal to moderates, Ernst's effort to build a strong antislavery fair met with resistance from some eastern radicals. Weston encouraged Ernst to join forces with the radical stronghold in Salem, Ohio, and have one large fair in the central part of the state. Ernst rejected this suggestion because she wanted to create a Garrisonian base in southern Ohio: "I am anxious to do something *here* in Cincinnati for there must be a beginning and if we send away all our influence it seems to me we shall never have a good one at home."[53] Ernst was partially motivated by the issue of respectability. As a member of the wealthy urban elite with New England roots, she could envision Cincinnati becoming the new Boston of the West and herself as its leader. She had carefully built her Cincinnati reform credentials with leadership in temperance and homelessness as well as antislavery.[54] Salem was a small, rural town in central Ohio that boasted a large crew of committed but socially disrespectable radicals. Ernst wanted to initiate a shift of power among Garrisonians in the West from the rural center of Salem to the urban center of Cincinnati. She wanted to transform Cincinnati from a "Dark and wicked city" into a morally pure radical headquarters.[55] "I have ever had this hope at heart that the true *would* come when we could raise the pure standard," she declared in 1850.[56] She even worked behind the scenes for several years to move the western Garrisonian newspaper, the *Anti-Slavery Bugle*, from Salem to Cincinnati.[57]

A brilliant and successful fair would offer just the method for building this Garrisonian base in Cincinnati. Ernst hoped that the fair would also provide uncompromising abolitionists in her city with a level of well-deserved respectability. One way to incorporate this respectability into the fair was to attract the support and aid of eastern and transatlantic abolitionists. Ernst attempted to make these connections by requesting donations from female antislavery groups in Boston; Philadelphia; Rochester, New York; and other locations as well. By the 1850s, many women abolitionists in Great Britain had formed groups with the specific goal of providing goods to antislavery fairs in the United States.[58] As historian Beth Salerno has argued, "The quality and novelty of the British goods helped the antislavery fairs . . . attract a wealthier and more powerful class of people" and establish a certain level of respectability. Some rural abolitionists, however, disapproved of the "exotic and upper-class fashions" included in these donations from Great Britain, seeing them as representing self-indulgence and materialism.[59] Ernst, who enjoyed an upper-class lifestyle, valued such contributions and used them to establish the superior quality of her fair. Her desire for foreign products, however, did not lessen her concern with issues of morality and materialism. Ernst tried to balance lavish goods with more affordable and pragmatic items. She described the harmonious blend of "the beautiful and utilitarian" at her 1852 fair, concluding, "There is scarcely a trade which was not represented in our collection, and yet nothing to jar the refined taste of the most fastidious." A year later, she proclaimed, "People are beginning to understand us, and are coming to our sales, expecting the homely and solid things there, which correspond with our stern estimate of right and wrong, justice and freedom, and we must try and meet the demand."[60] Following the tradition of pragmatic western abolitionism, Ernst balanced "beautiful and utilitarian" to please everyone.

Ernst also vehemently opposed holding raffles at antislavery fairs, explaining to Weston that this deplorable practice was "sin" because it had an "unhealthy influence on others." Never shy, Ernst instructed Weston, "*Do discard Raffling from your Bazaar. It is Gambling.*"[61] By the antebellum period, gambling had become gradually problematized because it contradicted the emphasis on frugal living and hard work.[62] While the market economy seemed to invite unregulated speculation (which looked a lot like gambling), a large literature emerged calling for good Christian men to earn their wealth by determination, fairness, and good old-fashioned toil. Moreover, making an easy dollar from luck seemed inherently unchristian amid the Second Great Awakening's rejection of predestination and its alternative call for perfecting the world through diligent, laborious effort. Ernst and other women reformers believed in the particular importance of distinguishing their "feminine" space in the market economy as morally driven. Gambling represented sinfulness and greed and could result in accusations that female-organized fairs promoted "masculine" self-indulgence and gluttony.

Ernst did not reject the market but instead sought to use it and sometimes to reframe it for her own purposes. Ernst built respectability into her fair by attracting the support of local businessmen who had succeeded in the market economy but still remained concerned with issues of morality, community, and reform. She had a very intimate connection to the Cincinnati elite: her husband, Andrew, could certainly be ranked among the city's more powerful businessmen. Reporting on the 1852 fair, Sarah Ernst thanked the "many prominent merchants of the city" who offered "liberal donations." She also highlighted the importance of the "Committee of Advisors," a group of "gentlemen" that included her husband, and the city's most powerful antislavery advocates.[63] A year later, Ernst cited businesses that had donated china and glass, shoes and books.[64] Aside from thanking a few women for the bouquets they provided for the hall, no one else was mentioned by name. The financial and moral support of the city's commercial leaders gave the ostracized antislavery group a remarkable public relations coup. By offering donations and the use of their names, these men encouraged others in their elite circles to do the same. Wealthy wives who might not have felt comfortable attending the fair now had motivation to participate as consumers.[65]

This appeal to Cincinnati's wealthy and powerful not only raised the status of the fair and the sewing circle but also made the fair more lucrative. And as the fair's financial success increased, so did the power that accrued to the women abolitionists. Between 1851 and 1855, the fair brought in nearly four thousand dollars. Although the Cincinnati women could not match the economic muscle of the Boston or Philadelphia fairs, the income offered the westerners a tool for establishing their reform credentials and dictating the type of antislavery work they wanted to see.[66] Unlike the large eastern fairs, the Cincinnati women did not donate most of their money to state societies or newspapers.[67] Instead, the Cincinnati group used its profits to hold an annual abolitionist convention designed to put the city on the antislavery map.

Cooperation and the Union Antislavery Convention

As Ernst negotiated the support of the city's leading businessmen and raised thousands of dollars, she also worked diligently to define her brand of abolitionism as virtuous and harmonious. The Cincinnati Anti-Slavery Sewing Circle had a long history of welcoming women from a variety of political perspectives. Ernst, though earnestly desiring to convince all her sister abolitionists of the superiority of the Garrisonian approach, recognized that a reputation for open-mindedness and cooperation would serve her well on a larger scale. Beginning with her first fair, Ernst used a portion of the bazaar proceeds to sponsor a three-day spring antislavery convention in Cincinnati. This convention was designed to symbolize collaborative western antislavery by welcoming abolitionists of all perspectives. Announcing the first convention in 1851, Ernst emphasized that the gathering would offer something for everyone—politics, religion, morality—and called for "one common platform" that centered on the basic idea that "slave-holding is a violation of God's law."[68] The 1852 call asked Cincinnati citizens to come together "without distinction of party" in the "spirit of fraternal love."[69] In an 1853 editorial about the convention, the *Anti-Slavery Bugle* asserted, "It is important we should not loose [*sic*] sight of what is in common between us if we would ever hope for agreement in the application of principles."[70]

These conventions, held every year between 1851 and 1855, proved very successful at a variety of levels but especially at building Cincinnati's reputation for antislavery nonpartisanship. In 1854, the Chicago-based *Free West* emphasized the "great harmony" that permeated the meetings and the "enthusiastic" response of the diverse audience.[71] The local Whig paper, *Cincinnati Gazette*, included full transcriptions of all three days of the convention. Acknowledging the wide-ranging debates, the diverse viewpoints of the speakers, and the general environment of respect and collaboration, the *Gazette* emphasized the good feeling that infused these meetings. Convention attendees were treated to an astonishingly wide variety of perspectives, arguments, methods, and approaches to antislavery.[72] As Garrisonian Joseph Treat explained after attending the first day's gathering in 1851, "Its design is to reorganize the Anti-Slavery sentiment of the country . . . on as catholic basis as possible."[73] He continued, "There were Liberty men, Free Soilers, Whigs, Democrats, Non-Resistants, Women, (For *they* are to be allowed their equal rights), and Come-Outers, all ready to act harmoniously against slavery."[74] This meeting proved cooperative and, from the perspective of the radical Treat, effective.[75] He gloated that Ernst had been appointed to the all-important Business Committee, a sure sign of radical influence. "When has a Free Soil Convention ever appointed *women* to all the responsible posts of Secretaries or members of the Business Committees? No, it is left for the Garrisonians and Gerrit Smith men to do that."[76] During the 1852 convention, according to Treat, a "spirit of fraternal kindness and harmony" again characterized the proceedings. "All sorts of Abolitionists occupied the platform together," he asserted, although "of course, [it] was not *radical* enough."[77] Treat complained that the gathering gave an "uncertain sound" on "the Church question" because the clergy were too fearful to "utter the whole truth."[78] Despite Treat's grumbling, the question of the relationship between the church and slavery received extensive attention during the convention, with at least seven speakers chiming in, resulting in just the type of com-promise resolution on which the convention prided itself: "*Resolved*, That slaveholding is in itself an act of immeasurable wickedness, and that for all the abominations connected with it, *a large portion* of the American Church and Clergy are pre-eminently responsible." The original resolution lacked the qualifier "a large portion," thus implicating the entire "American Church and Clergy" in the sin of slaveholding.[79]

Even in 1853, when Garrison himself attended the convention, the *Anti-Slavery Bugle* described the meeting as a "glorious occasion" where "all classes of Abolitionists" eagerly "mingled together with freedom and good will."[80] At the conclusion of this meeting, the gathering's president, Samuel Lewis, a political abolitionist, congratulated the attendees on their joyous coop-erative spirit. He began by emphasizing his commitment to working across differences: "Doubts were expressed whether I would be willing to attend this Convention if Wm. Lloyd Garrison were invited," he explained. "Now I want it understood that my feelings were hurt by the hint. . . . I love freedom of debate. Let no one think I lower my Christianity by entering into conven-tion with that man who has done more for liberty and right than hundreds of those who denounce him as infidel. You know I do not endorse him in all things, but in many I do, especially when he speaks of slavery." Lewis concluded by thanking the open-minded convention participants: "We have met here representing all the different aspects of anti-slavery sentiment to tell how we felt and for once it has been seen that all classes of Anti-slavery men can meet and discuss questions without attacking persons."[81]

In 1854, the convention continued its commitment to harmony. On the eve of the gathering, Frederick Douglass praised its cooperative tradition in his Rochester, New York, newspaper: "For several years past, a Convention has been regularly held in the city of Cincinnati, in the month of April," he explained. "In these Conventions all the bitter strifes of new and old organization, of moral suasionists, and of legal suasionists, have been shamed into silence by the over-shadowing influence of a common desire to regenerate the moral sentiment of the country, and to emancipate the slave." Moreover, he acknowledged, "The ladies especially . . . , by their bazaars, and their correspondence have been the instruments of this worthy assemblage of the friends of freedom. They have resisted all attempts against the liberty of their platform, and maintained successfully the spirit of anti-slavery brotherhood, without regard to sex or color, party or society."[82] After attending the gathering, Douglass more fervently applauded the conventioneers' energy, good spirit, and diversity: "Men and women, clergy and laity, black and white, stranger and citizen, christian and infidel, united here, in the name of common humanity, to utter one loud telling protest against slavery, the common enemy of all mankind."[83] He pointed specifically to his debate with radical Garrisonian Charles Burleigh regarding political antislavery as evidence of the meeting's truly open environment: "We had a fair opportunity of stating our views, and maintaining them before the same audience that listened to Mr. Burleigh. The whole debate on this subject was earnest and emphatic, and yet was conducted with entire decorum and apparent mutual respect and cordiality."[84]

Based on this reputation for community building, Ernst established the convention as a premier national reform gathering. In 1853, Douglass described these spring meetings as "the most influential Anti-Slavery conventions ever held in the United States."[85] To maintain this status, Ernst had to attract first-rate podium speakers and a large, reputable audience. As with her antislavery fairs, she brilliantly elicited the participation of some of the city's leading men. The 1851 announcement for the convention featured several men's names, including those of her husband, local Underground Railroad leader Levi Coffin, and attorneys John Jolliffe, William H. Brisbane, Edward Harwood, and Christian Donaldson.[86] The following year, the convention call included an official "Committee of Gentlemen," and last-minute advertisements for the meeting lacked women's names, leaving only a list of leading men.[87] This convention attracted nearly two thousand attendees, among them such antislavery luminaries as John G. Fee, George W. Julian, John Rankin, Henry Bibb, Douglass, and Burleigh. The 1855 convention announcement was signed by a man, Christian Donaldson.[88] According to abolitionist Josephine Griffing, the gathering included "several prominent Lawyers and Ministers."[89] Ernst understood that the participation of respected and prestigious men would bring her conventions both recognition and influence.

As Douglass's participation indicates, Ernst worked diligently to attract not only leading white male abolitionists but also the movement's most celebrated African American men. Samuel Ward, a renowned ex-slave and abolitionist orator, was the featured speaker at the first Cincinnati convention, and according to Treat, "Every body is crazy to hear him."[90] After Ward's two-hour evening speech, the hall "rang with tremendous cheering, and long shouts of applause went up." Even the many "worthless loafers" in the crowd who harbored "mean, low, heathenish prejudices against color" found themselves "sympathizing with black skin, thick lips, and wooly heads, against the government, laws, ministers, churches, and religion of the country, and even against themselves!"[91]

The following year, Ernst convinced two other nationally recognized ex-slaves and orators, Douglass and Bibb, to participate. The *Cincinnati Gazette* characterized Bibb as "a graceful and accomplished speaker" but reserved most of its praise for Douglass, whose eloquent, humorous, and charming speeches attracted large crowds.[92] Clearly enchanted with Douglass, the *Gazette* accounts of his lectures noted the "great laughter," "applause," and "sensation" he generated.[93] On the final evening of the meeting, Douglass again drew throngs of listeners: "For nearly an hour before the time of commencement, every seat on the main floor and in the galleries was occupied and before Douglass took the stand, every inch of standing room in the aisles, around the stage, and in the passage-ways, was occupied by an eager crowd."[94] When Douglass returned to the Cincinnati convention two years later, his reception proved equally enthusiastic. Although organizers charged a dime for admission to Douglass's talk as a way of keeping out the rowdies, hundreds of interested Cincinnatians were turned away at the door because people were packed into the aisles, along the stairways, and into every available corner.[95] For his part, Douglass lauded the efforts made by Ernst and the other organizers: "The Convention was one of the best we ever attended. We shall remember the Ernsts, Guilds, Donaldsons, Harwoods, and *other* kind friends who are mainly instrumental in assembling such Conventions, and in rendering them efficient instrumentalities for advancing the anti-slavery cause."[96]

Radicalizing Cincinnati

Ernst's success in creating a nationally acclaimed cooperative antislavery convention in Cincinnati encouraged her but did not satisfy her commitment to Garrisonian abolition. Toward this end, she initiated a local educational campaign designed to introduce uncompromising antislavery to Cincinnati. Recognizing that money could bring both respectability and power, she devoted a hefty portion of the funds raised by her annual antislavery fair to this goal—as she put it, for "the dissemination of Anti-Slavery truth by lecturers, agents, newspapers, conventions and tracts."[97] Ernst's particular understanding of the "anti-slavery truth" meant that much of this money supported the most uncompromising antislavery newspapers and lecturers.

The *Anti-Slavery Bugle* was *the* voice of Garrisonian abolition in the Old Northwest. Its sixteen-year run made it the West's only radical antislavery newspaper to last for any substantial length of time.[98] Beginning in 1845 and edited by experienced Garrisonians Benjamin Jones and Jane Elizabeth Hitchcock (who soon married), the *Bugle* consistently and wholeheartedly embraced disunionism (a controversial policy that called for the North to leave the Union to distance itself from slavery), nonresistance (the wholesale rejection of all forms of violence), woman's rights, and racial equality while passionately denouncing antislavery third parties as corrupt and dangerous. Because of its unyielding support for Garrisonian abolition, the paper struggled to remain financially viable. The consistent support it received from Ernst's Cincinnati bazaar helped the *Bugle* continue publishing. Between 1851 and 1856, Ernst and her sewing circle contributed at least one thousand dollars to sustain the *Bugle*.[99] In 1855, the *Bugle* noted the debt it owed to the Cincinnati "ladies for very opportune and indispensable aid in the publication of the Bugle."[100] Cincinnati's more conservative abolition community disapproved of the group's support for the *Bugle*, and Ernst wrote in 1852 that "the buzz against our appropriations to the Old Organization is loud."[101] She expected that buzz to increase because she intended to contribute even more to the Garrisonians: "We shall arouse the enmity of a share of the *community*, if not of the Society."[102] Ernst had prepared for this critique by supplementing her contributions to the *Bugle* with small donations to other non-Garrisonian newspapers. In 1851, she contributed a token twenty-five dollars to Henry Bibb's *Voice of the Fugitive*; the following year, she gave fifty dollars to the local, anti-Garrisonian *Christian Press*.[103] She also maintained five subscriptions to *Frederick Douglass' Paper*, which he had just begun publishing after leaving the Garrisonian fold, specifically "to prevent people from saying we did everything for the old organization."[104] One year later, Ernst again attempted to distract her opponents with the vague explanation that "donations have been made" to numerous non-Garrisonian as well as Garrisonian antislavery newspapers.[105] In return for these small donations, the *Voice of the Fugitive* and *Frederick Douglass' Paper* supported Ernst's fair and annual convention. In 1854, for example, Douglass praised Ernst's efforts and advised, "Let us all go to the Convention."[106]

Although Ernst occasionally used fair funds to subscribe to non-Garrisonian newspapers, the Cincinnati society continuously subscribed to the *Bugle*, the *Anti-Slavery Standard*, and the *Liberator*.[107] In 1853, Ernst asked Garrison to send six copies of the *Liberator* to the sewing circle. "We are encouraged in many ways about our prospects here [because] so many are willing to read the *Liberator*," she explained, although subscribing to this newspaper caused most of the community to label the group "Infidel," since many Garrisonians rejected the Sabbath and questioned the literal interpretation of the Bible. Ernst concluded by boasting that the society had unanimously decided to take so many copies of the *Liberator*.[108] As early as 1850, Ernst had described the *Liberator* as a "precious messenger" that she read to her husband and sons and then shared with her neighbors.[109]

Ernst's desire to see her adopted hometown become the center of western radicalism led to her attempt to move the *Bugle* from Salem to Cincinnati, since the paper's presence would attract both attention and support. "I wish the *Bugle* could be published in Cincinnati or some other paper of the right kind," she suggested to Weston in 1850. "What do you think of the *Bugle* locating here? Would it not do more good than in that part of the state where so many other good influences reach from New York?" Just in case Weston remained unconvinced, Ernst added, "I have heard several friends lately say 'they wished we had an *old* organized paper here for they were the only ones which did any real good' and if such a one *were* here perhaps our society would do something towards it which they might object to so far away."[110] Four years later, Ernst was still pressing for the *Bugle* to move south.[111]

Ernst never lured the *Bugle* to Cincinnati, but she did bring Garrisonian speakers to the city as often as possible. In 1850, she began complaining to her eastern correspondents about the paucity of radical lecturers in the Queen City: "We have no Speakers, of *the right kind*."[112] In the fall of 1852, she set aside two hundred dollars of the fair's proceeds to "defray the expenses" if Garrison and Wendell Phillips would attend the spring 1853 convention.[113] Andrew Ernst penned a short note explaining to Garrison that despite rumors to the contrary, Ernst would take the "greatest pleasure" in welcoming the famed abolitionist to his home and would work to ensure that his visit was filled with "pleasure and happiness."[114] The Ernsts' efforts worked. Garrison came to Cincinnati for the first time solely to attend the convention, staying at the Ernsts' "beautiful residence," where he was "most hospitably entertained." He described Sarah Ernst as the "soul of anti-slavery in that region."[115] In addition to Garrison and Burleigh, Ernst persuaded Lucy Stone and several other well known Garrisonians to make the long trek to southern Ohio.

In the fall of 1854 Ernst decided Cincinnati needed more than an annual spring abolition convention. A full-time Garrisonian lecturer should take a longer sojourn in Ohio, radicalizing Cincinnati and other communities across the state. To this end, she earmarked two hundred dollars from the 1854 fair to fund this radical speaker. "It is expected that Miss Sallie Holley will be the Lecturer," she stated in a letter to the *Bugle*.[116] "We feel that in no other way can the Anti-Slavery cause be so well served as by faithful Lecturers and an uncompromising Press." "Faithful" and "uncompromising" were code words for radical Garrisonians. Sallie Holley fit the bill quite nicely. The thirty-six-year-old New Yorker had excellent antislavery credentials as the daughter of Liberty Party founder Myron Holley. A graduate of Oberlin College, she had decided to become a full-time antislavery lecturer with the encouragement of woman's rights abolitionists Josephine Griffing and Abby Kelley. When Ernst requested Holley's services for southern Ohio, the radical had already developed a reputation as a persuasive orator.[117] Holley's support for woman's rights also appealed to Ernst, who hoped that Holley would not only convert more Ohioans to Garrisonianism but also model outspoken, intelligent womanhood.

Procuring Holley proved more difficult than expected. The Cincinnati Anti-Slavery Sewing Circle's secretary, Mary De Graw, wrote to Garrison in December 1854 complaining that the group had received no response to its request for Holley's services. De Graw warned that although the money was "on deposit," the "unsettled state of financial matters" could result in the loss of the funds.[118] Perhaps encouraged by the potential loss of money, the American Anti-Slavery Society arranged to have an agent devote a few months to lecturing in central and southern Ohio. Although Holley was unavailable, the Cincinnati women were probably pleased with the choice of William Wells Brown, another noted orator who had begun life as a slave. The sewing circle's public announcement of Brown's lectures included the instruction that anyone interested in meeting with him should contact De Graw, suggesting that the Cincinnati women controlled Brown's schedule.[119]

This effort to dictate Brown's itinerary may have been related to a few earlier incidents in which Ernst tried but failed to bring radical lecturers to Cincinnati. At the spring 1854 convention, for example, an Ernst-backed resolution proposing a sewing-circle-controlled fund-raising subscription for "sustaining Lecturers in the field" failed to win passage.[120] Ernst then attempted to arrange to have Garrison lecture in the Queen City. In August 1854, Henry Blackwell, a well-known Cincinnati political abolitionist who subsequently married Lucy Stone, wrote to Garrison on behalf of the sewing circle, offering a one-hundred-dollar honorarium for a November lecture in Cincinnati. A few months later, however, Ernst canceled Garrison's appearance because it was likely to interfere with the annual antislavery bazaar. Blackwell immediately wrote to Garrison to explain that that the women had been convinced of the need to change the fair's date to accommodate Garrison's lecture, but Garrison did not make the trip to Cincinnati.[121]

Ernst's attempt to influence the tone and content of the antislavery message in Cincinnati reflected her desire to challenge the moderate and male-dominated reformism that permeated the city. She recognized that Holley, who was widely admired for a lecturing style that blended ladylike modesty with moral passion, would connect with the members of the sewing circle and probably with a wider range of abolitionist women and men. Ernst's efforts to dictate when and where Brown would speak also spoke to her savvy regarding the politics of antislavery reform. Placing him at the most well attended and open-minded church would be more effective than assigning him to preach to the radical abolition choir. She wanted to make sure that her vision of true abolitionism received a fair hearing. Hiring itinerant Garrisonian lecturers to come to her community, assigning them speaking engagements, and controlling the purse strings earned Ernst respect and power in the Cincinnati reform community.

Obstacles

The effort required to build a foundation of respect and power among abolitionists in Cincinnati often exhausted and disheartened Ernst. The city had a long history of reluctantly accommodating very moderate forms of abolition and of violently rejecting more radical or outspoken efforts. Ernst understood this tradition in developing the Cincinnati Anti-Slavery Sewing Circle, building a successful and lucrative bazaar, and organizing the annual antislavery convention, endeavors that seemed to reflect a commitment to cooperation and compromise. But she also pushed the radical agenda while hoping that no one would notice. The effort to build an uncompromising antislavery sentiment in Cincinnati, however, led to feelings of loneliness, isolation, and failure in the woman Garrison called the soul of abolitionism in the Queen City. Radicals and moderates challenged her leadership and her authenticity as an abolitionist, and her tenuous relationship to church-based antislavery became an insurmountable obstacle.

Ironically, the Garrisonians expressed skepticism about Ernst's antislavery credentials. Some wondered if she was truly committed to disunionism and unsympathetic to antislavery third parties. Writing to Weston in February 1852 to request leftovers from the Boston fair, Ernst offered reassurance that "any thing you should send to me shall be religiously devoted to the principles we both believe to be the true ones."[122] She explained that political abolitionists dominated Cincinnati and that only her "determined principles" had ensured that half of the funds from the previous year's fair had gone to the Garrisonians. Ernst pointed to moderate abolitionists' rising opposition to her bazaar as evidence that it was truly radical. "They say we are Garrisonians and many who helped us a year ago never came near us this last year," she explained. Such efforts did not deter her from the radical course, however: "I *will not* labor for the political party, tho' I am willing to labor *with* it as long as by so doing, I can help our own." Later that spring, Salem's MacMillan wrote to Weston to express her shock and disapproval at the Boston Female Anti-Slavery's Society's decision to support the Cincinnati fair, which MacMillan characterized as dominated by political abolitionists.[123]

Ernst walked a tightrope, trying simultaneously to maintain her Garrisonian integrity and appeal to the moderate abolitionist community. Even as the Boston radicals demanded proof of her uncompromising abolitionism, her Cincinnati reform colleagues hesitated to cooperate with her because of her perceived radicalism. In the Cincinnati Anti-Slavery Sewing Circle's 1852 annual report, Ernst attempted to satisfy her conflicting constituencies, addressing the fact that many people intended to avoid the upcoming convention because of fears of Garrisonianism: "It ought to be understood by all that the Society is composed of almost every shade of Anti-Slavery interpretation, but there are not more than three or four among them all, who are of the old organization or Garrisonian principle; almost every one else is in favor of political action. Neither do I know of one member who does not belong to some religious denomination." She averred, "No undue advantage has been, or will be taken to present the views of Mr. Garrison, but all will in fairness present what they feel to be the best means of urging Emancipation." Ernst continued, "I feel sensitively the thrusts made against us for Garrisonian principles, for I know that my unshaken confidence in those principles as the only great and true ones, brings this criticism and distrust upon us." She encouraged her sister abolitionists to avoid becoming discouraged by this critique, suspecting that those who attacked the Garrisonians were probably not active in any type of antislavery.[124]

Ernst's attempts to cooperate with local antislavery churches proved especially challenging. Ernst understood that she would have to attract this powerful group of antislavery advocates to succeed in Cincinnati, and she recognized early on that one of the city's most influential antislavery ministers, the Reverend Charles Boynton, would not attend her fairs or conventions because of her perceived "infidelity."[125] Boynton established a reputation as an articulate, outspoken church abolitionist during the late 1840s and early 1850s. In 1848, for example, Boynton invited Delany to speak. Delany's lecture, which packed the church with a racially mixed crowd "of the most intelligent of both sexes and classes," offended the church trustees, who reversed Boynton's decision to allow Delany to speak again.[126] Boynton also helped organize two "Christian" antislavery conventions in Cincinnati in 1850 and 1851 and headlined an antislavery meeting in Chicago, offering an uncompromising report on "the connection of the churches with slavery through their communion and church fellowship."[127] Boynton coedited an antislavery newspaper, the *Christian Press*, in the early 1850s and became the sole editor in 1853.[128] Garrison's *Liberator* reprinted one of Boynton's more radical "come-outer" editorials calling on abolitionists to "unite in honesty of heart with those churches and that party which are *really* laboring for the freedom of the slave."[129] Boynton also earned the admiration of Cincinnati reformers and Whigs, helping to make his Vine Street Congregational Church one of the city's "most prosperous church organizations" by 1853.[130] Despite their common commitment to the abolition movement, however, Boynton and Ernst were initially distant and even hostile. Boynton disapproved of Ernst's outspoken radicalism and probably her Unitarian faith.[131] Ernst, for her part, resented Boynton's coldness. She wrote to her Boston colleagues in early 1852 that "jealousies have arisen [that] have been fomented by the Vine St. so called Anti Slavery church there, against our Bazaar and society because they say we are Garrisonians."[132] She responded to these rumors in March 1852, asserting in the sewing circle's annual report that "those who profess an interest in this cause" mistakenly assumed that her fair and convention represented only the interests of the radicals.[133]

Cognizant of Boynton's influence, Ernst decided to mend fences by making sure that moderate abolitionists were heard at the May 1852 convention.[134] More important, she devoted fifty dollars from the proceeds of the fall bazaar (which Boynton shunned) to the *Christian Press*. Ernst was very conscious that this was a compromise. "When we sent the money to the 'press' we knew how heartily Mr. Boynton hated and feared us, as Garrisonians, but we felt his was a good paper and being in our own city, and the only one too, and shunned by the pro slavery Christians of their own sect, we felt like giving them a little help."[135] The *Anti-Slavery Bugle*, perhaps encouraged by Ernst, published a short editorial praising the decision by the "Cincinnati Ladies" to "extend a helping hand to all classes of earnest laborers," including the *Christian Press*.[136] Ernst recognized that if she could convince Boynton that he had nothing to fear from her, others would follow his lead. Several members of the sewing circle had left the group because Boynton convinced them of her dangerous "infidel" influence.[137] Ernst's effort initially paid off: Boynton's Vine Street church opened its doors to the Anti-Slavery Sewing Circle, hosting its 1852 annual meeting. Boynton also publicly thanked Ernst for her donation, which "gave us the more pleasure because evincing great liberality of feeling upon the part of the donors, inasmuch as our course does not, in all respects, meet their entire approval." He concluded, "We tender the ladies of the Committee our hearty thanks, and wish them still greater success in similar efforts hereafter."[138] Ernst celebrated her victory by writing to Garrison in January 1853, "I really believe Mr. Boynton was melted by our returning him good for evil." She concluded, "Our donation to his paper was quite unexpected to him, for he has never been to our Bazaars and never as a participant to our Conventions."[139] Boynton also opened the pages of his newspaper to Ernst, publishing her speech before the Philadelphon Society on the "Rights and Wrongs of Women" and including a notice regarding her convention.[140] Considering Boynton's anti-Garrisonian, anti-woman's-rights sentiments and his past refusal to publicize her convention, these developments were astonishing.

The good feelings, however, were short-lived. Boynton's attendance at the spring convention coincided with Garrison's appearance, in which he offered numerous speeches in support of disunionism and come-outerism.[141] While several political and church abolitionists debated Garrison throughout the three-day gathering, Boynton did not participate. He dismissed the convention as failing to meet expectations and claimed that it "has made but slight impression on the public mind."[142] Boynton acceded to Ernst's request that he publish a notice about Garrison's postconvention lecture but took the opportunity to denounce Garrisonianism both in a sermon and in the *Christian Press*. He refused to publish Ernst's response to his assertions, which instead appeared in the *Anti-Slavery Bugle*.[143] The *Christian Press*, asserted the *Bugle*, was "ready to sacrifice the slave to its theological opinions."[144] Other Garrisonian antislavery newspapers, including the *National Anti-Slavery Standard* and the *Liberator*, entered the fray, with the *Standard* announcing that the *Christian Press* "has, for months, been employed in misrepresenting the Old Organized Abolitionists, with a view to convince the Anti-Slavery people of the West that they are all 'infidels,' whose object is not the overthrow of Slavery, but the destruction of the Bible, the Church, and all the institutions of religion."[145]

Boynton nevertheless participated in Ernst's convention the following year, along with a number of other Cincinnati ministers.[146] When Burleigh accused the *Christian Press* of administering a "theological test of admission to the Anti-Slavery platform," Boynton mounted a defense. "When the Bible, the only book of his hope, was rejected . . . such anti-Bible emancipators he did call Infidels." He also opposed the "demolition" of the church and the "dissolution of the American Union," instead favoring a "reformed" church and state.[147]

The tensions between Boynton and the radicals exhausted Ernst, who had continued to work with her sewing circle. Even this sturdy group experienced conflict in 1855. After a tempestuous twelve years, the thread that held together the Cincinnati Anti-Slavery Sewing Circle broke. Perhaps because of her conflict with Boynton or because of her rising sense of frustration at having to stifle her radical opinions, Ernst abandoned her longtime position as the society's president. Her departure was a great loss to the group, since she had brought not only unbounded enthusiasm and energy but also a good deal of financial support. She regularly opened her large, comfortable home for social gatherings and meetings. According to the sewing circle's 1854 annual report, the group held nearly fifty meetings for sewing as well as ten board meetings.[148] In a January 1855 public address to the group, Ernst reminded her antislavery sisters of the "physical effort" leadership required: "The meetings come so often that no one already overburdened should undertake it."[149] Ernst also asserted that financial issues motivated her to give up her position as president. While the group had initially united around the singular effort of helping fugitive slaves, now that "large sums of money are raised," the question of how to spend these funds led to "diversities of opinion." She understood that as a Garrisonian, she was outnumbered, and she felt the pressure of this reality. "As a *minority* here, I *may*, at any moment when you choose to exert your undoubted right as a *majority*, be forced into positions wholly against my convictions." She concluded by offering a veiled threat in regard to the annual fair: "If I ever act in a Bazaar again, it will be in full sympathy with a Committee not unwilling to be known as connected with the American Society." In other words, if the sewing circle wished to have Ernst continue organizing and leading the fair, members would have to agree to her terms. The *Anti-Slavery Bugle* acknowledged that the Cincinnati Society "has exhibited a rare spirit, not merely of toleration, but of cooperation in persons of conflicting views" but eulogized Ernst for the "courage to raise her voice singly, and alone in that pro-slavery city, against union with slaveholders, and fellowship with the sum of all villainy."[150]

Ernst kept her promise to devote the bazaar to the Garrisonians, creating the Anti-Slavery Bazaar Committee and populating it with women sympathetic to her position.[151] The *Bugle* editorialized more enthusiastically than usual about the need to support the Cincinnati bazaar, praising the "martyr-like self-denial" of the "ladies who direct its management." The fair raised more than eight hundred dollars in 1856, a stunning five hundred dollars of which they donated to the *Anti-Slavery Bugle*. The massive contribution led the Garrisonian newspaper's editor to exclaim, "We confess we feel painfully oppressed by the responsibility which this confidence of theirs, in the usefulness of the paper, imposes."[152] Ernst also arranged for well-known Garrisonians Lucy Stone and Lucretia Mott to speak at the fair and credited them with attracting most of the crowd.[153]

Despite finally having full control over the fair, Ernst began to experience exhaustion. She did not organize the annual convention in 1856 and claimed in January that she would not host another bazaar. Still nursing her youngest child, Ernst was completely worn out by her antislavery labors. "Sleepless nights and anxious distressed days are not calculated to give a healthy constitution to my body," she complained.[154] Still resentful that the *Bugle* remained in Salem, she announced to Weston, "Since the Bugle cannot be removed here [with] the workers it would have brought, the insinuations are that my work *must* be *suspended*." She reminded Weston that the few Garrisonian women in and near Cincinnati were married to more conservative husbands who disapproved of their politics. "Mrs. Thomas Donaldson, although a Disunionist herself, told me that her husband had become a Political Abolitionist," Ernst explained. She believed "that as husbands generally have *the say* as to which way a woman should work—in my own mind I feel that she will not do much for the future."[155]

Despite her gloomy predictions, Ernst held a fair in the fall of 1856. Ironically, she was motivated by a fugitive slave case, a topic that had for years caused some tension between her and her former sewing circle sisters. Even though Ernst saw individual fugitive slave cases as secondary to the larger issue of attacking the institution of slavery, the tale of Margaret Garner compelled Ernst to act. Garner had escaped from slavery with several of her children, and the group had made its way to Cincinnati. When slave catchers caught up with her, Garner killed one of her children and attempted to kill the others rather than let them be returned to slavery. Garner's actions brought national attention to the Underground Railroad in Cincinnati. As Ernst wrote in the bazaar committee's annual report, "We feel we *can not*, *dare not* relax in our endeavors . . . when a *mother* kills one child, and rejoices in the death of another."[156]

Despite Ernst's ultimate inability to bear the burdens of being a radical Garrisonian abolitionist in moderate Cincinnati, her success brought the city an international reputation for open-minded antislavery that became a role model for other groups. The Rochester Ladies Anti-Slavery Sewing Society's 1851 constitution announced, "Like the anti-slavery associations in Dublin, in Belfast, and in *Cincinnati*, they have taken their stand on independent ground, and are prepared to welcome straightforward antislavery advocacy without reference to its coming from Garrisonian or Liberty Party."[157]

A Garrisonian Fair in the Western Reserve

As Ernst struggled to negotiate the complex politics of antislavery in Cincinnati, the outspoken Garrisonians in Salem fought to maintain their numbers without diluting their uncompromising politics. The Garrisonian women, in particular, labored year-round to build a community that would sustain them personally as well as politically. Like their sisters in southern Ohio, the Salem women turned to the antislavery fair as a method of enlarging their numbers and providing much-needed emotional and financial sustenance for their organization.

By the mid-1840s, Salem had become the center of Garrisonian antislavery in the West. Located in Ohio's Western Reserve, about halfway between Pittsburgh and Cleveland, Salem's 1846 population numbered near fourteen hundred, including a large number of farmers. Though not a wealthy town, Salem boasted "twenty stores, six brick buildings, and a branch of the Ohio State Bank."[158] During the 1840s and 1850s, it supported two radical newspapers, the *Village Register* and the *Anti-Slavery Bugle*, though both suffered financially. The area's three hundred or so blacks included business owners, farmers, and day workers. Focused on economic success and self-improvement, African Americans supported an independent school, a church, and a temperance society.[159]

The region's Garrisonian women initially experimented with antislavery fairs outside of Salem. The first attempt in 1845 was a simple effort: they gathered a variety of useful goods ("toilet cushions and needle books, work bags and work boxes"), embellished some with antislavery mottos ("This for the sake of freedom"), and sold them at a "Fair Table" during the August 1 celebration in New Lisbon, ten miles from Salem.[160] A year later, Ashtabula's female antislavery society sponsored a fair at its annual meeting in Jefferson, sixty miles north of Salem.[161] Much like the Cincinnati Anti-Slavery Sewing Circle, the Ashtabula group boasted a radical leader but a more moderate membership. Betsy Mix Cowles had left the region in the late 1830s to work as a teacher but returned in the early 1840s and helped to revive the Ashtabula Female Anti-Slavery Society, which had become moribund since her departure. By 1846, she had embraced Garrisonian antislavery and worked diligently to push the women toward increasingly radical positions.[162]

Cowles, like Ernst, balanced uncompromising sentiments with the expectations of the more conservative abolitionists around her. Cowles advertised the Jefferson fair as open to all brands of antislavery: "All friends of the slave 'of every persuasion' are respectfully invited to attend," she wrote to the *Anti-Slavery Bugle*. "Come one, come all, friend and foe—come-outer and come-inner."[163] About one thousand people "of all sects, creeds and politics" attended the fair, and according to one correspondent, "every heart seemed joyous."[164] Abolitionist politician Joshua Giddings regaled attendees interested in antislavery politics with a lively speech. Those devoted to education and "uplift" for the black community enjoyed a musical performance and "speaking exercises" by "colored children and youth from Cincinnati."[165]

The fair's cooperative nature worried eastern Garrisonians, however. Just as Boston leaders required Ernst to prove her radical credentials, so too was Cowles expected to establish herself as an uncompromising abolitionist. "I have heard from various quarters, of your Fair," wrote eastern Garrisonian Abby Kelley to Cowles a few months after the event. "I rejoice it was held, because I see it was anti-slavery, not Lib[erty] party." Boston's Garrisonians, however, were not happy. According to Kelley, Maria Weston

Chapman (Anne Weston's sister) had recently expressed "the fear that your fair went to build up our worst foe and if so it had better never have been." Kelley promised to "undeceive" Chapman but nonetheless warned Cowles that future fairs should "commence operations with a definite understanding of the specific object you intend to promote and then let those help who will."[166] Cowles and other radicals attempting to establish an inclusive antislavery environment in the Old Northwest thus received the message that they should avoid compromise. But third-party and church abolitionists far outnumbered Garrisonians in Ohio, and Cowles recognized that compromise was necessary to work efficiently with others sympathetic to the movement. She, like Ernst, hoped to convert moderates to the Garrisonian position but was willing to work with all brands of abolitionists. Boston had other ideas about how to establish a radical stronghold.

Female Garrisonians in the West could not afford simply to follow Boston's dictates. Their minority status precluded such an exclusive approach. They had to cooperate with church and political abolitionists to have any hopes of succeeding in the West. The circular for the 1847 Western Anti-Slavery Fair clearly stated that the proceeds would go to the Garrisonian-dominated Western Anti-Slavery Society. But organizers also appealed to all "foes of oppression," to all those "who desire that our country shall be redeemed from the rule of tyrants—who wish to break the yoke of the captive."[167] On the long register of names appended to the circular, Cowles came first, a conscious effort to appeal to a broad cross-section of women. Although Cowles had been converted to Garrisonianism, she had a reputation for working with abolitionists of all brands. *Bugle* editors Benjamin Jones and Lizzie Hitchcock devoted several columns of their paper to why and how all abolitionists could contribute to the fair. But they also reminded readers that "clothing fugitives from slavery does not help those *in* slavery—educating the free colored people does not emancipate the bondmen." The Joneses concluded, "It has seemed sometimes that those who profess to be abolitionists, were willing to labor for almost any object that can be named, *except* the sundering of the slave fetters."[168]

Ernst and other Ohio abolitionists understood that one of the most important building blocks for successful antislavery fairs was the creation of sewing societies. These female-run organizations not only offered the assurance of a long-term commitment to the fair—sewing groups worked for months preparing goods for sale—but also created a safe space in which women could generate the energy needed to sustain their reform enthusiasm throughout the year.[169] Sewing societies, in fact, acted for women as political parties did for men.[170] The two settings offered people the opportunity to come together because of community, socioeconomic, and political concerns and to work in coordination to address perceived problems. Moreover, education and politicization were central components of the group experience. A typical sewing society gathering involved not only laboring together on a project but also reading aloud from antislavery newspapers or pamphlets. Education, gossip, food, and fun were central to these meetings. The blending of pleasure and work was important in encouraging women to attend regularly. As Deborah Bingham Van Broekhoven argues, both sewing societies and fairs served as "rites of community" that helped to sustain the larger antislavery family.[171]

In 1847, the Salem women labored to ensure that all Western Reserve sewing societies were devoted to the Western Anti-Slavery Fair. Lizzie Hitchcock published a "how to" guide for creating radical abolition sewing circles. She explained the uncompromising nature of Garrisonian abolition to anyone who might not fully understand its "character and design": "The Western Society advocates the Disunion doctrine. Its object is to effect a peaceable abolition of slavery [and] to secede from *churches, political parties, and governments that are pro-slavery*, believing that to be the only means by which we can wash our hands in innocency and benefit the bondman."[172] Hitchcock also highlighted the negative impact of supporting "false" antislavery. "If we use the money which was raised for anti-slavery purposes, to clothe and educate the few who have escaped, we do it at the expense of the many who are still groaning in the prisonhouse," she maintained. "Every dollar raised for the anti-slavery cause, and diverted from its legitimate purpose, prolongs the day of the slave's deliverance." Hitchcock's instructions met with some success. One Ashtabula County resident claimed that the local sewing group had quickly grown from six to more than seventeen, and the members eagerly embraced the radical banner: "We have given to our circle the name we love and honor—'Garrisonian Anti-Slavery Sewing Circle.'" Even the "little girls" of the community went to work "with great zeal" for the fair, "adopting for their motto 'No union with slaveholders.'"[173] The *Bugle* editorialized, "That little girls' circle pleases us. The slaveholder dreads such an organization with its bold hearted motto, far more than he does the namby pamby resolutions of political clique and ecclesiastical conclave whose members . . . intend to continue to hold fellowship with the oppressor."[174]

The 1847 Western Anti-Slavery Fair benefited from the devotion of many sewing societies as well as from the efforts of a broad cross-section of Western Reserve abolitionists. Despite the paper's initial discussion of the Garrisonian nature of the Western Anti-Slavery Society, later *Bugle* editorials failed to emphasize the doctrine. As a result, "quite a number of persons whose contributions helped to make up the Fair at New Lyme, and who participated in the sales, did not fully understand that it (the Fair) was designed exclusively to aid the Western Society." Some of these reformers apparently wanted to establish an "antislavery circulating library" or sustain a "school for colored children."[175] The fair's organizers, Cowles and Hitchcock, were frustrated by this confusion and made it clear that future fairs would be devoted to the radicals.[176] The call for the 1848 fair clearly stated, "The special object of the proposed Fair is to aid the Western Anti-Slavery Society."[177] The Ohio Garrisonians hoped to draw support from a wide spectrum of abolitionists but wanted to avoid any confusion about the purpose of their fund-raising event: "We labor not for the advancement of any political party [because] it is by the strength of moral power we would tear down the strong holds of oppression." This time, Lizzie Hitchcock's name appeared first on the list of names, followed by Betsey Cowles, an arrangement that sent a message about the event's nature. The decision to locate the fair in Salem also made it clear that it was a Garrisonian affair. Nevertheless, the organizers still sought to involve as many abolitionists as possible.[178]

This effort at creating a Garrisonian fair that would attract a broad community of abolitionists failed to meet expectations, raising less than $300. Organizers blamed this dismal performance on the distance between the meeting place and the fair room.[179] With so many leftover goods, the women decided to hold a second fair in nearby Massillon. Perhaps having learned from their mistakes, the women held the fair at the local Presbyterian church and worked with political and religious abolitionists to attract a large crowd. "The Free Soilers and their wives cheerfully lent their aid in getting up the Fair," explained the editors of the *Bugle*.[180] Baptist, Methodist, and Episcopalian churchgoers purchased bed quilts for each of their ministers. Although Massillon's elite snubbed the fair, it raised another $175 for the Western Anti-Slavery Society.[181]

Sensing incorrectly that they had finally found a recipe that worked, the western fair's organizers decided to hold a series of fairs throughout the late summer of 1849 in coordination with several antislavery conventions.[182] Probably because of the difficulty of moving fair goods from town to town and maintaining the discipline and organization required to hold a series of events in a short time, this effort failed. By 1850, the Salem women had decided to stabilize the western fair by hosting the event in their town once a year. The 1850 call did not list Cowles, who lived in Ashtabula, as an organizer;

all of the committee members resided in or around Salem.[183] This approach represented a significant shift in the fair's focus. Organizers ceased reaching out to non-Garrisonians and instead focused inward, on sustaining their own community. These Salem women took control of the fair and made it their own.

The Community of Salem Abolitionists

Salem's radical women sought to use the fair to build a community of committed abolitionists. The fair and its associated sewing society became the heart of Salem radicalism throughout the 1850s. The event encouraged men and women to come together on a year-round basis. It nourished them through difficult times, provided them with fellowship and sociability, and allowed them to aid the cause. Although the fair raised an average of only around three hundred dollars, the radicals were not deterred. "The results of our Salem Fair cannot be counted by thousands like those of Boston, Philadelphia, and Cincinnati," admitted bazaar organizers in 1854, "but considering the population of our village, the number of persons engaged in it and the comparative wealth of our community, we think it a highly successful effort."[184]

Salem's Garrisonian women had been involved with antislavery fairs for many years by the time they took over the leadership of the Western Anti-Slavery Fair in 1850. They understood that the event's success required long-term preparation and the committed participation of a large percentage of the local antislavery community. They also understood that men had to be included in all stages of preparation. Lecturer Joseph Treat proved especially sensitive to the need for men's participation. Hearing some local men instructing female abolitionists about the importance of immediately following a fair by beginning preparations for the next event, Treat issued a strongly worded critique of the men's laziness and selfishness: "You want to have these self-denying women, who have but just got through with the anxieties, and cares, and labors of one Fair, instantly engage in preparing for another, without even stopping to take a moment for break, while you *do nothing!*"[185] Treat pointed out that even if men could not aid in preparing for the fair, they should at least "hand over the money" more generously. "Give it to them. If you haven't got it, do as you tell them to do—go and *work* for it—*you* may as well work for the Fair, as they."[186]

Men were involved with eastern antislavery fairs and their associated sewing societies.[187] In the Western Reserve, however, men's participation went beyond simply making helpful business contacts or "speaking" for the women at public events. An 1842 editorial in the *Philanthropist* announced that fairs would be rendered "far more profitable, and efficient in the cause," if supported by men as well as women.[188] That same year, another Western Reserve antislavery society, this one in Cadiz, advised in regard to fair organization, "The brethren can give efficient aid, by assisting to furnish materials, or in preparing articles to be exhibited, of male manufacture."[189]

In Salem, men participated at every stage of fair preparation, including the creation and operation of sewing societies. In the summer of 1851, Sarah Macmillan, Sarah Bown, and her husband, Benjamin Bown, called on several local abolitionists of both sexes to encourage them to revive the local sewing society.[190] Several men opened their homes to sewing society meetings, which regularly moved from place to place.[191] Usually married to members of the group, the male hosts participated in the meetings by providing food, reading aloud from antislavery newspapers, and socializing with the participants. "The [sewing] circle met here today," wrote Salem abolitionist Daniel Hise in his diary, adding that "the circle had a pleasant time."[192] Men often accompanied their wives to the gatherings, thereby gaining an appreciation of the labor involved in the women's work. After attending a meeting at a neighbor's home, Hise mused, "They had quite a good turn out of the Ladies whose lives are devoted to the cause of universal emancipation. Heaven helps them, therefore they must succeed notwithstanding the obstacles thrown in their way by the Church & clergy of the land (Damn the toad eaters)."[193] Salem men also spent weeks in advance of the fair collecting goods, moving and building furniture, and running errands.[194] During the fair itself, scores of men worked around the clock in supporting roles. Treat and Hise spent several uncomfortable and cold nights sleeping in the hall to protect the fair goods.[195] Hise and others also remained on their feet for hours, cooking and serving food to the fairgoers.[196]

Salem fair organizers also called on the services of Garrisonians throughout the West, thus helping to build both the supply of fair goods and strong ties to other radicals. Though the Cincinnati women held their own bazaar, they regularly contributed to the Salem fair, as did other abolitionists from Ohio, Indiana, and Michigan.[197] The sewing society in Adrian, Michigan, became a passionate supporter beginning in 1851. Garrisonian lecturer James W. Walker encouraged Adrian's women to action. As he traveled across Michigan in the early 1850s spreading the message, "No compromise with slaveholders," Walker found a receptive audience among the group of nearly sixty women who met "regularly as clock work," even though some had to travel "five or eight miles" to attend circle gatherings. "I would not be surprised," Walker wrote in 1851, "if the Adrian Circle sent a hundred dollars worth of goods to the Fair."[198] As with the Salem circle, men regularly attended the Adrian gatherings. "The Adrian Sewing Circle met at Ephraim [Rulin's] and a fine time we had," explained Walker. Group members "spent the evening in social intercourse, much to the edification of all—our hearts were made glad by the presence of [Garrisonian abolitionist] Daniel Bonsall of Salem."[199] Henry C. Wright, another Garrisonian lecturer, also attended meetings of the Adrian circle and commented on members' willingness to sacrifice for the cause. Despite bad weather and difficult roads, he explained, participants had held their regularly scheduled meeting, working "to raise money to save this Nation from the fearful doom that awaits."[200] It is certainly no coincidence that the radical Michigan Anti-Slavery Society, created in 1853, was centered in Adrian. This mixed-sex group became the center of Garrisonian antislavery in the state, and its leaders included several female members of the sewing society.[201]

Despite the generous contributions of communities such as Adrian, the unity and commitment of locals made the Salem fair a success. In addition to its financial accomplishments, the fair rejuvenated radicals at a time of year when their spirits needed uplifting and provided them with a sense of "group loyalty."[202] As the women asserted in 1851, the fair allowed them "to lay their hands upon each other's hearts and feel that they were beating for liberty; to look into each other's eyes and see that the fire of freedom still burned in their souls."[203] The fair encouraged interpersonal and casual interactions among the participants. "The social intercourse connected with" fairs, asserted the editors of the *Bugle*, "serves to keep alive the zeal and energy of those engaged in them."[204] Organizer Sallie Gove was more emphatic: the fair "quickens into life the spirit of Anti-Slavery, rubs from the soul the rust of lethargy, [and] enlarges and gratifies the social feelings."[205]

Held every year around the New Year's holiday, the Salem fair became a highlight of radical reformers' social calendar during a time of rest and relaxation. With scores of nearby abolitionists visiting for the fair, the women arranged a variety of social gatherings, including dances, dinners, and concerts.[206] Blending work and play for a few weeks, the abolitionists baked pies, transported fair goods, sang antislavery songs, shared the latest news, and developed such intense and intimate ties with one another they became like family. A few days before the 1852 fair, Hise recapped a joyous evening in his diary: "At night went down to Joel McMillan's, took supper, sang and danced (not I) but the rest of the company. Got home at ½ past 10 oclock. Jane E.

Jones was there and took part in the Dance. She is a good dancer."[207] Hise also described the intense and endless labor involved with the fair, ranging from baking cakes to building "table legs." He and his wife had devoted the final weeks of December wholly to preparing for the fair, but the evening of fellowship was clearly a highlight. His comment about Hitchcock's talents on the dance floor reveals that the interpersonal relationships between these radical abolitionists were more complicated and intimate than their public writings and uncompromising positions would suggest. Hitchcock had developed a reputation for fearless advocacy of the cause in both her writings and her public lectures. Among her radical companions, however, she felt free to explore a more physical and sensual side that certainly offered a sense of freedom as well as relief from the challenges of being a Garrisonian.

The Salem fair gave Ohio radicals an opportunity to unwind and reconnect even as they raised much-needed funds for their movement. It also allowed them to build support for their particular brand of abolitionism. As Gove explained, the fair "presents to the world an evidence of the faithfulness of those who are laboring for redemption of the bondman from his chains, of our country from its curse."[208] The Salem women worked hard to reconstruct the popular vision of the Garrisonian movement through a focus on virtue and down-to-earth respect for society's disempowered, a goal that affected the type of goods the organizers desired to sell.

In their calls for contributions to the Western Anti-Slavery Society Fair, the Garrisonians consciously emphasized the need for practical items, as in 1852, when they wrote, "We wish that articles of *real utility*, such as must be purchased somewhere by every family, may preponderate."[209] Organizers recognized that many of the rural abolitionists who would attend were not interested in expensive fancy imported goods but rather in items that would help to improve and simplify their daily lives. "We want not only the products of the needle, in every variety, but the products of the farm also."[210] Although the Salem women, like their counterparts in Cincinnati, always included "beautiful" items that "please the eye, adorn the body, and gratify the taste," they highlighted the need for homespun products: "Let the farmer and his wife bring grain and wool, brooms and baskets, cloth and other manufactured articles—let the dairymaid come with her cheese and butter, and the miller with his flour—let the hatter and tinner, the saddler and shoe-maker present such needful things as their several handicrafts can furnish."[211] The labor involved in creating baskets, shoes, clothes, and food products imbued these goods with virtue and thus gave the fair a certain sense of moral purity that spilled over into the cause. Organizers believed that the honest work of free-labor mechanics, manufacturers, and farmers contrasted with the indolent, useless lives of the southern slaveholders. This assumption allowed also the Salem women and their abolitionist supporters to emphasize the simplicity and virtue of their fair, as opposed to the materialism that predominated among the South's luxury-loving white women. As one western abolitionist explained, the money obtained from fairs was "of far less value than the moral influence exercised, first, upon those engaged in the preparation and sale of articles, and then upon the minds of those not yet imbibed with anti-slavery, who come in contact with them through this agency, and who cannot fail to be benefited by the impression such an exhibition of benevolence, diligence, and devotion to principle, is calculated to produce."[212]

Among those useful goods that rural abolitionists sought and fair organizers provided was food. Unlike the Boston fair, where elite organizers asked farm women to contribute raw ingredients, which a "Boston confectioner" would "transform... into fancy treats for the dessert table," the Salem women simply made the basics available for attendees.[213] "There is an especial demand for the products of the farm, particularly poultry, eggs, butter, cheese and fruit," advised fair managers in 1853.[214] Food played a dual role for the radical women, not only providing real nourishment to antislavery families across the state but also symbolizing the nurturing and nourishment of the larger antislavery family. Nearly every call for fair contributions included specific requests for cheese, grain, flour, fruit, butter, eggs, pickles, and coffee. Although organizers at times requested cakes, they generally emphasized the basics, products that rural farming abolitionists were likely to have produced themselves. This approach allowed even those who struggled financially to contribute to the movement. The fair typically included a "supper" for attendees for which local farmers were asked to donate "sugar, fruit, flour, butter, cheese, eggs, poultry and whatever else of country produce can be conveniently bestowed."[215] A very successful public meal resulted: "The supper, which was handsomely got up, was superintended by Annie Wilson, and Margaret and Howell Hise, whose labors in the department assigned them were arduous and unceasing. Our farming friends in the neighborhood, as well as those more remote, contributed liberally to the tables; a fine fat buck, a small drove of turkeys, a large flock of chickens, vegetables, fruit, cakes, butter, &c., constituted a supply fully equal to the demand, though the latter was large. William A. Lease, a Free Soiler of this place, volunteered to cook the meats, and by the admirable manner in which he did it, gave entire satisfaction to those who partook of them, and saved the Committee considerable labor and some expense."[216] Food thus unified the antislavery movement by bringing together radical and political abolitionists to converse while tending the barbecue and showed that wholesome, free-labor meals were possible.

By emphasizing the virtue of contributing homemade food, Garrisonian fairs also supported the free produce movement. As fair organizers in 1842 asked, "To carry forward a work of mercy, shall we stain our hands with the blood, in which cruelty has steeped every particle of those products the bondman has created?"[217] Food products from small farms symbolized the superiority of free labor. "Will not the sugar maker whose labor in the camp is but as play to the toil of the slave in the cane field, put aside a portion of what he has made, and bring the luscious gift to the Anti-Slavery Fair?," asked fair leaders in 1847.[218] Organizers openly congratulated the free produce Quakers who contributed goods to the bazaar: "The contribution of the Green Plain Friends has already arrived. The articles are all useful, and such as will doubtless find a ready sale; consisting of straw satchels, band boxes, *free labor* cotton shirts, collars, and bosoms," explained the *Bugle*. "This donation is valuable, not only for the funds it will place in the Treasury of the Society, and the amount of good that will be effected by their expenditure, but as evidences of the sympathy of those members of the Society of Friends, who, unlike the great mass, are not afraid to unite with the world in deeds of benevolence and philanthropy."[219]

The Salem fair offered local abolitionists an opportunity to come together in fellowship, labor, nurturance, and joy to reenergize and share their commitment to the movement. By 1850, organizers had abandoned the effort to raise large sums of money, instead focusing on the purity of their effort, the small financial benefits it offered, and the concrete testimony it provided to their cause.

Conclusion

Sarah Ernst and Lizzie Hitchcock adapted their uncompromising abolitionism to their region. Cincinnati was not Boston, and Salem was an exceptional small town welcoming to the radicals. Sewing societies and antislavery fairs fit nicely within the traditional female sphere. The radicals used these feminine arenas to their advantage. Ernst's conventional fair allowed her to host an annual antislavery convention that received national recognition for its cooperative spirit and open environment. For radicals such as Ernst, success meant simply bringing more people to the table for discussion and debate. When William Lloyd Garrison and Charles Boynton joined together on the Cincinnati podium to discuss central issues before large audiences, Ernst had achieved her goal. For five years in the 1850s, she attracted the nation's leading abolitionists to the Queen City, educating thousands of locals and awakening antislavery sentiment in a key border city. Day-to-day life for this brilliant organizer, however, involved enormous labor and anxiety, and the unending obstacles and pressure eventually forced her to scale back her abolitionism. The Salem Garrisonians experienced many of the same difficulties and similarly negotiated a solution that allowed them to remain true to their ideals despite opposition. The Salem fair served the radicals well. Purity remained the central focus for Hitchcock and her Salem family, offering emotional sustenance if not financial success.

The Salem women also took the lead in antislavery lecturing, another arena of western abolitionism during the 1840s and 1850s. Inspired by eastern orator Abby Kelley, a small cadre of outspoken women took to the podium to promote abolition. These women more directly violated the boundary between the public and private spheres and thus endured more public criticism than did fair organizers or free produce advocates. Hitchcock and others created an oratorical style that worked well in the western environment.

CHAPTER 5

Women Lecturers and Radical Antislavery

The Quakers accosted her. An experienced and road-weary Garrisonian lecturer from Massachusetts, Abby Kelley had encountered hostile audiences across the Northeast for nearly a decade. She had come to the Old Northwest in June 1845 at the invitation of the Ohio Anti-Slavery Society. By the time she arrived at the Orthodox Yearly Meeting of Quakers in Mount Pleasant, she had been lecturing across the state for four months. The usually nonviolent Quakers reacted surprisingly fiercely to her, however. Only a few minutes after she rose to offer an unsolicited antislavery speech, she was asked to sit down and be quiet. She replied that she "must speak whether men would hear, or whether they would forbear." While the congregation watched in some confusion, "she was seized by one or two elderly men and dragged out of the house, with, perhaps two or three women pulling at her dress."[1] Many of the younger Quakers followed Kelley out of the meeting house "to defend her from injury" and to hear what she had to say. Determined to satisfy her audience, Kelley walked down the street, stopped at the front step of abolitionist Aquilla Hurford's door, and "spoke to those who assembled to hear." Despite the inconvenient location, "the street was crowded for a considerable distance, all eager to catch the sound of her voice as it rung through their midst in behalf of the suffering and bleeding slave."[2]

Eight years later, Mount Pleasant would again host a female antislavery lecturer, though the audience and the reaction were different. When Josephine Griffing, a friend and protégé of Kelley, arrived at the abolitionist meeting in a grove outside Mount Pleasant, she found an eager crowd despite bleak rainy conditions. All of the "thrilling" speakers who preceded her were "colored men" who had offered bold, intelligent, and articulate speeches. Griffing and her husband, Charles, spoke at the close of the meeting, and the mostly African American audience responded with exuberance. "I have never witnessed more patience, earnestness and delight," wrote Josephine, "than was manifested in those countenances, crowded together under umbrellas and carriages, for a little shelter, and that they might hear amid the roaring thunder and the storm, which tossed the trees above them, words which they received as prophetic and sentiments to which their glad hearts often responded."[3]

The "glad hearts" across the Old Northwest that listened to Griffing and the other abolitionist speakers in 1853 had become increasingly comfortable with women taking to the pulpit to preach the "gospel of liberty." African American audiences such as the one in Mount Pleasant welcomed Griffing and other female speakers because the women addressed issues of concern to free blacks. But not all audiences were so convivial. As Kelley's violent ejection from the Quaker meetinghouse in Mount Pleasant suggests, Ohioans were sometimes inhospitable. The Orthodox Friends had many reasons besides Kelley's sex to disapprove of her uninvited discourse.[4] Her standing as an eastern Garrisonian proved particularly galling. Westerners had little patience with the controversies of the eastern abolitionist movement and were especially intolerant of Kelley and other women lecturers who tried to import these conflicts into the region.

While Kelley irked some orthodox Quakers, she had a stimulating effect on Ohio's Garrisonians. In particular, women found her to be a source of inspiration. After Kelley visited Betsey Mix Cowles at her home in Austinburg, Cowles converted to Garrisonianism and employed her charm to proselytize for the radicals. Josephine Griffing, Lizzie Jones, and several others decided to take to the lecturing stand, preaching the Garrisonians' uncompromising position. These speakers attacked the members of the clergy for their failure to condemn slavery and pleaded with abolitionists to eschew party politics and focus on moral suasion. They worked in coordination with male lecturers, often traveling and speaking in pairs or mixed-sex and mixed-race groups. Even as they were inspired to take the podium by an eastern Garrisonian, however, women such as Griffing and Jones established a western approach to lecturing characterized by cooperation and negotiation and including a distinctly non-Garrisonian focus on challenging racial inequality in the law and social settings. Though Ohio, Michigan, and Indiana abolitionists in the 1840s and 1850s preferred third-party politics, Griffing, Jones, and other radical women abolitionists worked effectively within this context. They also understood that as women orators, they were vulnerable to accusations of violating the "woman's sphere" and that they consequently had to walk a fine line. They eventually came to see the "public" sphere as a place to be negotiated. Western women learned that by "domesticating" the lecture podium through both demeanor and message content, they could create a civic space for themselves. As several scholars have revealed, antebellum "separate spheres" was a contested, shifting concept. Western women proved adept at negotiating this unstable terrain.[5]

Women at the Podium

The first American-born woman to take to the platform was Maria Stewart. A young, African American widow, Stewart condemned slavery and encouraged her fellow Boston blacks to challenge racial inequality and support temperance and education for their community. Ruthlessly criticized for speaking to a mixed-sex audience in 1833, Stewart left the lecturing field, though she maintained her commitment to antislavery for the rest of her life.[6] The few women who followed in Stewart's footsteps in the 1830s experienced similarly censorious reactions. Angelina and Sarah Grimké, the daughters of a South Carolina slaveholder, moved to Philadelphia, became Quaker abolitionists, and began speaking to small female-only audiences in the fall of 1836. Their compelling lectures soon attracted men. These "promiscuous" mixed-sex gatherings disturbed Presbyterian ministers in Massachusetts as well as famed female reformer Catharine Beecher. The clergy and Beecher argued that the Grimké sisters had violated the "woman's sphere" by entering the public domain and adopting the role of men, thus bringing "shame and dishonor" to womanhood.[7] Not everyone concurred with the self-appointed guardians of appropriate feminine behavior. Abby Kelley witnessed the Grimkés' first "promiscuous" lecture in her hometown of Lynn, Massachusetts, in 1837. Inspired by the sisters' courageous rejection of restrictive gender roles, Kelley decided to copy them. She gave her first public speech to a mixed-sex audience in 1838, at the second national antislavery women's convention in Philadelphia, one day after she had attended Angelina Grimké's marriage to abolitionist Theodore Weld. Despite a mob shouting threats and throwing rocks outside the building throughout her speech, Kelley continued to "plead the cause of God's perishing poor."[8] Thus baptized into the world of antislavery lecturing, Kelley continued speaking on the podium for nearly three decades. She became the symbol of female public speaking, radicalism, and eventually woman's rights. An accusation that one was an "Abby Kelleyite" meant that one had violated both social norms and gender roles.[9]

Western women abolitionists stepped up on the podium in the 1840s. Most entered the field of public speaking as a part of their commitment to Garrisonian abolitionism, which advocated a broader range of equal rights than most other forms of opposition to slavery. Fighting an uphill battle as radicals in a region dominated by moderate political antislavery, their status as women made the task even more challenging. As late as 1849, Oberlin clergyman James Fairchild declared female public speaking a "misfortune."[10] Although the western public became more accepting of female lecturers by the 1850s, such a career remained untraditional and grueling.

Radical Antislavery in Ohio

Garrisonian abolition in the Old Northwest proved most successful in Ohio, though it spread slowly and unevenly. When the abolition movement splintered in 1840, the Ohio Anti-Slavery Society refused to take sides. It ended its relationship with the "Old Organization," the Garrisonian-led American Anti-Slavery Society, but declined to become an auxiliary to the "New Organization," the moderate American and Foreign Society.[11] Not everyone was happy with this neutrality. Some Ohioans wanted to align with the Garrisonians, but most favored the Liberty Party.[12] Even Gamaliel Bailey, who had previously opposed the creation of an antislavery third party, helped form the Ohio Liberty Party. As this trend became apparent, a group of anti-third-party abolitionists fought back, encouraging eastern Garrisonians to send reinforcements in the form of lecturers.[13] The East responded by dispatching Oliver Johnson and Charles G. Burleigh to Ohio in 1842. These lecturers influenced some wavering abolitionists to embrace the Old Organization; as a result, the Ohio Anti-Slavery Society experienced a divide at its 1842 state gathering. The Old Organizationists, led by Joseph Dugdale and Abram and James Brooke, called for a debate on the issue of realigning with the American Society. The majority of delegates declined to debate the issue, leading the Garrisonians to withdraw and create their own group, the

Ohio American Anti-Slavery Society, which immediately became an auxiliary to the American Anti-Slavery Society.[14]

Over the next several years, the two groups developed a cooperative relationship. Some abolitionists participated in both organizations, helping to create a community that remained cordial because members agreed to disagree. One of the issues that clearly differentiated the two associations, however, was the role of women. The Ohio Society tacitly excluded women from leadership positions, while the Ohio American group was led by Hicksite Quakers and included a number of outspoken and experienced women leaders.[15] Despite the strong guidance of talented women, however, the radicals lost ground to the Liberty Party in the mid-1840s. The situation worsened by 1844, when eastern Garrisonians had begun calling for disunion, arguing that the federal government's continuing support for slavery meant that the Union could no longer be supported. Many westerners were also appalled by the radicals' tendency to demonize the Liberty Party, and some moderates in the Ohio American group began to question their relationship to the Garrisonians. At the organization's 1844 annual meeting, several moderate members supported a resolution to withdraw from the American Anti-Slavery Society. Although the convention passed a substitute resolution that simply criticized the society for narrowing "the original platform" with "tests of Abolitionism," radicals worried that moderates were gaining influence and again called for eastern support.[16] This time, help arrived in the form of Kelley, one of the group's most experienced and controversial public speakers.[17]

Abby Kelleyism

Kelley had an immediate and explosive impact on Ohio abolitionism. Although the reform-minded *New Lisbon Aurora* enthusiastically welcomed Kelley and her lecturing partner, Lizzie Hitchcock, "whose match-less eloquence and soul-stirring appeals stand unrivaled in the Antislavery annals," others were less happy.[18] The Orthodox Quakers who physically ejected Kelley from their meetinghouse in September certainly felt threatened by her message. Many third-party moderates also expressed concern about her presence in Ohio, denouncing her as an irritating representative of the troublesome William Lloyd Garrison. Liberty Party supporters had good reason to be wary of Kelley. She influenced the Ohio American Anti-Slavery Society to become more outspoken and uncompromising, disrupting the tentative cooperation that existed among abolitionists in the state. At the society's 1845 annual meeting in New Lisbon, for example, she initiated the passage of a variety of radical resolutions, including one that outright rejected the Liberty Party: "The formation of a distinct political party based upon *one idea*, that shall become sufficiently numerous to sway the political action of the nation, and yet retain the unity and firm basis of moral principles necessary to bring about a great *moral change* . . . is in the *very nature of things impossible*."[19] The *New Lisbon Aurora* reported that Kelley publicly "avowed that their object in coming to this state *was the destruction of the Liberty party*." The editor doubted that Kelley would effect this goal and concluded with a call for cooperation: "The result of the meeting, it is hoped, will be for the best; and every true-hearted Abolitionist will rejoice at the overthrow of slavery whether it is effected by moral, political or religious power."[20] Some members of the Ohio American Anti-Slavery Society were dismayed by Kelley's influence because they recognized that it would alienate the Liberty Party supporters. Eastern Garrisonian Giles Stebbins admitted that many westerners found "our view" rather "startling," and Kelley averred, "Our positions were astounding to most of the abolitionists."[21] Cyrus McNeely, one of those who voted Liberty and still agreed with Garrison on most other issues, resigned as chair of the society's 1845 meeting even though "he sees no incongruity whatever, in an advocate of the liberty party acting as President of a Society, which adopts the constitution of the American Anti Slavery Society as its bond of union."[22] The attendees overwhelmingly reelected him after his resignation, expressing their confidence in his leadership, but the Ohio American Anti-Slavery Society leaned increasingly toward uncompromising positions.[23] Within a year, McNeely abandoned the third party, to the disbelief of Liberty Party leaders.[24] Kelley "has stated in this county that Cyrus McNeely has left the Liberty party and joined the dissolutionists," pouted the Liberty Party *New Lisbon Aurora*. "It is true?—rather doubtful."[25]

Anti-Garrisonian political abolitionists immediately attacked Kelley. One Liberty Party paper described her speeches at the annual meeting of the Ohio American Anti-Slavery Society as "treasonable."[26] Another Liberty advocate sarcastically proclaimed in a party newspaper, "Abby Kelley, that sweet sister of 'the MAN whose reputation is world-wide,' is now canvassing the Reserve, in her *peculiar* manner, to cheer on the '*Indomitables*,' to make another bold push for power." He concluded, "She preaches, uniformly, DISUNION, and a cutting loose from all known forms of national, state, and parental government. It seems to be the chief end of the 'woman's rights, No Government Party' of which Miss Abby is a bright examplar [*sic*]."[27]

Abby Kelley Foster, 1846. Courtesy of the American Antiquarian Society.

In response to this assault, local Garrisonians censured the Ohio Liberty Party for falling into the trap of engaging in bitter invectives, just like eastern abolitionists. It was no surprise that the eastern Liberty party would cruelly scorn lecturers such as Kelley, the Ohioans proclaimed, "but, in Ohio, the party *did* bear a different character, and we expected better things of its adherents—we looked for candor, fairness, and gentlemanly treatment." Constructing an alternative vision of Kelley as a self-sacrificing and morally superior woman, the editor of the *Anti-Slavery Bugle* concluded, "Is it the province of the Ohio Liberty partyism to sneer at the efforts of woman, to disparage her labors in the cause of humanity, and to strive to crush the efforts she is making for her enslaved sisters?"[28] In the region for only a few months, Kelley had already initiated a whirlwind of conflict that would follow her throughout her time in the West.

Other Liberty Party advocates and non-Garrisonian moral suasionists in Ohio initially expressed a more tempered wariness about Kelley's presence in the state. Bailey encouraged his colleagues to listen respectfully to Kelley: "We hope our Liberty friends will bear complacently her attacks upon them, for the sake of the many wholesome truths she utters on the general subject."[29] But Bailey also worried that Kelley intended to introduce the conflicts of the East to the West: "Let those who come among us from the East receive our hospitalities, and our co-operation, so far as they devote themselves to the cause itself; but when they attempt, if they ever do, to introduce other matters, in which *Persons*, rather than *Principles*, figure, let us advise them that in Ohio, such things are not to our taste."[30] Constructing the West as a virtuous region unsullied by the vicious intrigues of the East, Bailey made it clear that he considered Kelley an unwelcome interloper.[31]

By November 1845, Bailey and others became increasingly frustrated with Kelley. When she and her fiancé, anticlerical abolitionist Stephen Foster, lectured in Cincinnati, Bailey's hometown, he penned a public message to the two Garrisonians. After criticizing them for "inflicting" upon their listeners an excruciatingly long description of "the divisions in the ranks of Abolitionists at the East," Bailey advised Kelley and Foster to reassess their patronizing assumptions about the West. "If the speakers to whom we have referred could live in the West long enough, they would learn that the strife between certain anti-slavery gentlemen in Boston, is of the least possible concern to us." Bailey concluded with a defense of western independence: "The West is a world within itself. . . . We are very much bent upon thinking our own thoughts, speaking our own words, and going our own ways."[32]

The same month, Benjamin Stanton, the editor of the Indiana-based *Free Labor Advocate and Anti-Slavery Chronicle*, accused Kelley and Foster of disrupting a meeting of the Indiana Anti-Slavery Society with their eastern conflict. "No one, perhaps doubts the . . . conventional right of our friends from the East to introduce their views as to the best method of operating against slavery, but the exercise of that right, can have no other effect, if it has any, than to introduce those contentions among us." Stanton, like Bailey, encouraged his readers to continue to eschew the tribulations of the East and to stay focused on the destruction of slavery: "We of the West have labored in a good degree of harmony, directing our arrows at our inveterate foe, instead of shooting them into each others hearts."[33] In the summer of 1846, the *New Lisbon Aurora* pronounced with some irritation, "It has been stated more than once that the business, and the principal business of the eastern agents to this region was the destruction of the Liberty movement in it: they were *sent for* to accomplish this end. Like other foreigners, they thought themselves about smart enough to lead all the Ohio Abolitionists by the nose wherever they saw proper, but still more like other foreigners they found we were not quite so green as at a distance we might have seemed."[34]

Liberty Party abolitionists were dismayed to learn that Kelley not only ignored their criticism but created an alternative antislavery newspaper to challenge their dominance. Recognizing that Garrisonians in the West had no public voice with which to counter the Liberty Party, Kelley insisted that it was essential to have a Garrisonian newspaper located in Ohio. She lobbied, cajoled, and financed the *Anti-Slavery Bugle* into existence. After failing to recruit a leading eastern Garrisonian to edit the *Bugle*, she finally convinced her friends Benjamin Jones and Lizzie Hitchcock to guide the paper.[35] Although new to Ohio and inexperienced in the business of newspapers, Jones and Hitchcock enthusiastically embraced their editorial responsibilities.[36] Jones quickly advised Kelley that the paper required a substantial base of reliable subscribers to stay financially viable. He also warned Kelley that several members of the executive committee of the Ohio American Anti-Slavery Society, which had initially sponsored the paper, "will be shocked to learn what ground the Bugle will take." He feared that these moderates would shut down the paper. Jones also reminded Kelley that the *Bugle* "was undertaken under the influence of temporary excitement" caused when she raised "the mercury by blowing upon the bulb of the thermometer." He concluded, "It *will* fall in obedience to the laws of calorie, unless we can build up a hotter Anti-Slavery fire."[37] Kelley responded by hitting the lecturing circuit, singlehandedly building a subscriber list that topped one thousand by April 1846, less than a year after the paper's inauguration.[38] She would remain the *Bugle*'s most dedicated financial supporter and cheerleader for the next fifteen years.[39] The *Bugle* became the most important media outlet for Garrisonians in the West and a consistently outspoken advocate of women public speakers. By the early 1850s, the *Bugle*'s subscribers included abolitionists from twelve states, among them Virginia, Michigan, and Pennsylvania. The radical paper was mailed to eager readers in nearly every Ohio county.[40]

Kelley used the pages of the *Bugle* as well as her private correspondence to publicize and highlight the importance of Ohio and the West in the antislavery movement. "My present belief is that Ohio is the place for us," she explained to Foster.[41] Although she sometimes took a patronizing attitude regarding the West, she also made sure that her eastern colleagues recognized that the region would be a critical battleground in the war against slavery.[42] "I write mainly to you at this time to draw your attention to the western field," she explained to Maria Weston Chapman. "I fear you (I mean our eastern friends) do not feel the importance of this section. And I fear again that you do not realize what a great work we are doing here."[43] Kelley delineated the achievements of Ohio's radicals, especially in regard to challenging the dominance of the Liberty Party in the region, despite intimidating obstacles. "The Liberty party priests and Demagogues have left no stone unturned to destroy the influence of the disunionists," she bitterly complained. "No scandal is too mean for them to resort to."[44] Nonetheless, Kelley boasted, Ohio Garrisonians had developed clever methods for converting political abolitionists: "As a stroke of policy we have kept pretty quiet, seldom reporting progress for fear Liberty party could head us. We go in and catch the demagogues napping and so carry off the soldiers. We sometimes sweep a whole town in this way. For instance, in one town some twenty miles from this there have been for some two years, between eighty and ninety Liberty votes. This year there were six only."[45] Depicting the western antislavery community as a battleground, Kelley saw herself as the general who guided the radicals in each skirmish.

Kelley also ensured that eastern leaders knew about the efforts and accomplishments of individual abolitionists in Ohio. She wrote several times to Chapman to praise Hitchcock's self-sacrificing efforts, requesting that Chapman make sure that Hitchcock receive a salary.[46] Kelley's efforts paid off. Chapman sent Hitchcock one hundred dollars from the American Anti-Slavery Society and found a sponsor to donate fifty dollars to support Kelley's western activities.[47] Encouraged by the recognition from the east, the Ohio American Anti-Slavery Society changed its name in 1846 to distinguish itself from the more moderate Ohio Anti-Slavery Society. The new Western Anti-Slavery Society openly embraced Garrisonian abolition.[48]

Kelley not only publicized the West to Boston leaders but inspired and radicalized hundreds of western abolitionists, especially women. Some came to regard Kelley as a saint, glorifying her presence. "She has been among us; we have seen her with our own eyes, and have heard her with our own ears," rhapsodized Harriet N. Torrey after listening to Kelley lecture. "That she possesses a strong, original, comprehensive and truth loving mind and that her opinions are the result of long, patient and vigorous investigation, none but those who have cringed beneath her withering sarcasm, or who are tinged with the chameleon edge of moral cowardice will have the temerity to deny."[49] Cincinnati resident Mary Donaldson groused that local abolitionism had fallen asleep since Kelley's departure and would continue to "slumber on" until Kelley returned to "wake it up."[50] Even moderate women abolitionists had difficulty resisting Kelley's charisma and oratory. "When Abby was here, I felt convinced that God was in his providence sending her through the country to proclaim the truths of his words, against the sin of slavery," gushed the wife of a Presbyterian minister in Lake County, Ohio. Considering that Kelley devoted a good portion of her lectures to denouncing the failures of the clergy, it is especially revealing that the spouse of a preacher was deeply moved by her rhetoric: "Though she may say some things, which we may think incorrect or injudicious, yet she advances such Bible Anti Slavery truth, so reprovingly, so fearlessly as I have heard no Anti-Slavery lecturer before." Kelley awoke in women a passionate abhorrence of slavery that motivated action. Kelley's Lake County admirer concluded her letter by announcing, "A Female Antislavery Co. Society has been formed and we hope to have sewing circles in every town; for in that we pledge ourselves to do *all that we can*."[51]

Kelley initiated all types of abolitionist activity in the Old Northwest. "O! How I wish I could spend all my time in organizing women's societies, getting up fairs, and in time, bringing the most effective power of the state into activity," she reported to Cowles. "I would evangelize it in short space."[52] The women of Ohio who experienced Kelley's personal charm and powerful persuasive abilities found themselves believing in their ability to make a difference. Some spoke with their pocketbooks. During the two days of the June 1846 Western Anti-Slavery Society annual meeting, Kelley collected donations from more than fifty women from ten different communities.[53] Many felt empowered by Kelley's uncompromising message and applied it to their lives in a variety of ways, choosing to leave their churches or publicly embrace woman's rights. Only a few weeks before Kelley's ejection from the Mount Pleasant Quaker meetinghouse in the fall of 1845, forty-three-year-old abolitionist Rachel T. Hurford announced her decision to leave the same Quaker Monthly Meeting. Employing the "come-outer" language of most Garrisonians, Hurford explained, "It is absolutely necessary that I should withdraw from *all* sectarian corporations, which assume authority over the minds and consciences of their members."[54] A few months after Kelley began her Ohio tour, abolitionist Harriet Smith published a letter praising women orators: "I rejoice that females can be found, who are willing to sacrifice themselves on the altar of humanity, and go forth as the champions of universal rights." She expressed frustration that members of her sex were "declaiming against women speaking in public" even as these same critics "would have no repugnance to attending a circus, or they could witness a public execution."[55] Public denunciation of Kelley and other women lecturers caused Smith to ponder the limited nature of the female sphere. "I marvel not that the Lords of Creation, consider woman out of her appropriate sphere, when she leaves the kitchen or parlor to go forth on her mission of mercy and love," she explained. "Their opposition arises from a convicted conscience, or a jealous spirit."[56] Smith, in contrast, believed that the public sphere should be a gender-neutral space where concerned citizens acted for the general good.

The Ashtabula Activist: Betsey Mix Cowles

Kelley's years as an organizer and activist provided her with the skills to awaken and inspire women such as Rachel Hurford and Harriet Smith. She also acquired the savvy necessary to recognize potential leaders and encourage their radical activism. Betsy Mix Cowles, a woman of "uncommon intellect" and a "playful disposition," was one such leader.[57] By the time Kelley arrived in Ohio, Cowles had earned a widespread reputation as a skilled reformer. Her educational goals and teaching responsibilities had taken her away from Ashtabula County, but she returned in 1843 to become the head of the female department at the Grand River Institute in her hometown of Austinburg. Kelley quickly learned of Cowles's organizing skills and requested a meeting. "I want to be acquainted with you," she explained. "There are many points on which I wish to converse with you."[58] Kelley and her new husband, Stephen Foster, arrived in Austinburg in January 1846. She and Cowles then spent several days together, building the foundation of what would become a lasting friendship. They found comfort in each other's intelligence, generosity, and passion for the cause. Kelley immediately recognized Cowles's potential as a leader of Ohio's radicals. Cowles was equally impressed: "Abby & Foster are all that is noble and excellent; I love them very much."[59]

Cowles's loyalty to the radicals was tested immediately. Knowing that Cowles was well loved in northern Ohio reform communities, Kelley asked her new friend to write a letter of support for Kelley's upcoming trip to Oberlin. While Oberlin was known for its antislavery sympathies, most reformers in this small community preferred to work through political parties and religious institutions. They spurned Garrisonian radicalism and disliked the confrontational style of disunionists and come-outers.[60] The Fosters did not expect a generous welcome and believed that a letter from Cowles, who was related by marriage to Oberlin faculty member Henry Cowles, might help to open doors and minds. Betsey Cowles penned the requested letter to her in-law. "I know the tide of prejudice is strong against them," she admitted. But she implored him to hear the radicals without prejudice. "I believe them to be the untiring zealous friends of humanity & when they are understood [they] are appreciated as such by those who sympathize with the slave."[61] Oberlin reformers should feel free to challenge Kelley and Foster if they were "propagating error," Betsey Cowles admitted, but they should do so through "free discussion." Henry Cowles's wife, Alice Welch Cowles, had provided him with a positive evaluation of Kelley in 1840, when the two women met in Connecticut. Despite the fact that Kelley "was compared to Fanny Wright [and] called a *man woman*," Alice Cowles liked her and thought her "a thorough going reformer [and] a lady of manners. Simple and unaffected."[62]

However, the Fosters' Oberlin visit provided a lesson in the cost of being a Garrisonian in Ohio and the censorious public attitude toward women speakers. Henry Cowles published a critique of the radicals' lectures in the *Oberlin Evangelist*, but he thoughtfully engaged with their central arguments and respectfully disagreed.[63] Others were less generous. Helen Cowles, Betsey's cousin and an Oberlin resident, described Foster and Kelley in physically unflattering terms: Foster was "an inferior looking man," and although Kelley had a "noble forehead," she wore a "look of contempt and scorn upon her countenance" and had a voice that was "so strained as to be disagreeable."[64] So disgusted with Kelley's unfeminine appearance was Helen Cowles that she left in the middle of the lecture, sending a message to the speaker and the rest of the audience. Kelley's public performance in front of a mixed-sex audience fueled Helen Cowles's unfavorable reaction: "When she arose to speak, breathless silence prevailed. She said she was surprised that any one should be opposed to having a woman speak here in Oberlin as they heard young ladies read compositions every year and she thought that they admired extemporary speeches much more than written discourses. This created quite a laugh." Helen Cowles found Kelley less amusing. Three years later, Oberlin faculty member James Fairchild denounced Kelley's public oratory as a violation of feminine propriety, assailing her for the "sharpness of her words and the bitterness of her denunciations."[65]

Other Oberlin residents also criticized the radicals' visit. Betsy Hudson, a Liberty abolitionist, liked her former neighbor, Betsey Mix Cowles, "a little less" for contracting a serious case of "Abbyism."[66] Hoping to undermine Cowles's infatuation with the notorious eastern Garrisonian, Hudson disparaged Kelley and Foster for critiquing certain antislavery methods but offering no viable alternative: "They entirely failed to point out that more excellent way, and *I* for one have yet to be convinced that the Liberty Party is not the heaven-appointed means for the overthrow of that most vile and heaven-insulting system of slavery." Hudson concluded with a personal attack, accusing Kelley of intentionally spreading false rumors about Betsy Hudson's husband, Timothy Hudson, also a close acquaintance of Cowles, and alluded to some of Kelley's "vulgarities." Even Hudson's carefully constructed critique of Kelley's antislavery message also highlighted the radical's failures as a respectable woman. Spreading gossip and engaging in "vulgarities" suggests at best a lack of virtue and piety and therefore an unforgivable collapse as a lady.[67] Hudson hoped that if Cowles continued to support Garrisonian methods of abolitionism, she would at least distance herself from the disreputable Abby Kelley.

A few weeks later, Timothy Hudson wrote to Betsey Cowles about Kelley. An experienced antislavery lecturer, Hudson began by admitting Kelley's strengths: "She is a person of powerful mind & of deep devotion to the cause of the bleeding slave." He then switched course, questioning Kelley's antislavery politics and her feminine virtues. "That she is an accurate reasoner, that her positions are all sound, that she is charitable, kind, fair, & at all times truthful," he asserted, "I do not at all believe." Hudson suggested that Cowles was taken in by Kelley's crafty ways: "She is doubtless a charming woman, when she pleases to be so in the social circle. But I have the testimony of one who has long known her that she is at times vulgar enough." Following the lead of his wife, Hudson referred to some perceived violations of femininity without elucidating. Hudson designed such insinuations to plant seeds of doubt in Cowles's mind. In case Cowles was completely mesmerized by the cunning Kelley, Hudson concluded by schooling his friend in the virtues of womanhood and further questioning the radical's integrity: he had heard that Kelley "told the Oberlin people in one of her public speeches 'that our own Betsey Cowles *had taken the stand.*' You endorse her truthfulness so earnestly that we are not quite at liberty to disbelieve her. Well, then, Betsey, welcome to the toils & perils of a speaker's life." Assuming that Cowles had no intention of becoming a lecturer, Hudson hoped to highlight what he perceived to be Kelley's dishonesty. "On the *propriety* of the course, I have nothing to say, because you know all I would say. But if you feel it to be your duty to 'cry aloud & spare not' God forbid that I should lay a straw in your way." Even as he purported to adopt a tolerant position, Hudson warned Cowles that true women did not become public speakers. "If you seriously think of speaking much don't think of ever marrying," he cautioned. "The wife & mother can not very well add to her numerous duties, that of the public orator. Always excepting this, that she have a rich husband."[68] Only a selfish seeker of glory would consider a career that would prevent a woman's true mission, that of mother and wife. Cowles did eschew a career as an abolitionist lecturer, but she never married.

These various critiques of Kelley highlight the instability of gender notions in the antebellum North.[69] Despite the pervasiveness of the "woman's sphere" discourse, Oberlin had become familiar, if not completely comfortable, with women's public oratory. Oberlin's young female students, as Kelley pointed out, regularly spoke in front of audiences. But Kelley's oratory differed in significant ways. She was not fulfilling a class project created by male educators. She was speaking her mind and engaged in a career of public lecturing. As Timothy Hudson made abundantly clear, the role of "wife and mother" precluded such an occupation for respectable women. Her topic, more importantly, offended much of her audience, especially male professors such as Fairchild. In calling for true abolitionists to withdraw from their churches and abandon the "proslavery" Constitution, Kelley questioned the nation's foundation. Who did this modestly clad Quaker woman think she was? In describing Kelley as "strident" and "bitter," Fairchild denounced her as both a woman and a reformer. Kelley's speech violated feminine norms because of its content as much as its tone.

Kelley kept in close contact with Betsey Cowles, encouraging and sustaining her radicalism in the face of widespread disapproval. Ten days after Cowles received Timothy Hudson's disparaging letter, she opened a missive in which Kelley offered a very different construction of the Oberlin visit, highlighting the closed-mindedness of the local religious leadership. "Bigotry there is as thick as the darkness of Egypt," she complained. "You can cut it with a knife."[70] Because Oberlin was in the throes of a revival during their visit, the radicals encountered difficulty in finding a venue for speaking as well as an audience.[71] Only the "loving and kind" Lucy Stone, who "was sound" before Kelley's arrival, provided hope for Oberlin.[72] After describing Oberlin, Kelley effusively thanked Cowles for sustaining their friendship despite the opposition of others and explained that she cherished open-minded and generous spirits such as Cowles: "You cannot, my dear friend, appreciate my feelings, because you have never been situated as I am. You have never known what it was to be looked upon with distrust and suspicion by the honest common people, and hunted and persecuted by the 'chief priests and rulers of these people.' Hence you have never known how sweet, how *very sweet* it is to find, occasionally, in this world's desert of . . .

brutality a bright oasis that sends up its sparkling [pints] of pure water to refresh the thirsty traveller whose lips are parched by the scorching heat of the desert."[73] In depicting Cowles as a lifesaving and exceptional friend, Kelley made the Austinburg teacher feel connected to a small, intimate circle of virtuous and self-sacrificing reformers. "You comprehend our aim," she happily proclaimed. "You know we want to bless and not curse mankind."[74]

Nurtured and nourished by Kelley's correspondence, Cowles increased her dedication to Garrisonianism. She did not, however, join Kelley in the lecturing field, though not because of a lack of effort on Kelley's part. Although it is unclear whether Timothy Hudson was correct in claiming that Kelley exposed Cowles as a public speaker, Kelley certainly pressured Cowles to use her persuasive skills more publicly.[75] A year into their friendship, Kelley was still attempting to cajole Cowles into pursuing a lecturing career. Kelley became pregnant in the fall of 1846 but only reluctantly stopped lecturing in January 1847 because there was "already too much gossip."[76] Nevertheless, Kelley had difficulty "quit[ting] the battle field when we see such an army of opposition on every side." She remained, "full of anxiety that the cause of liberty, our country's salvation and the world's redemption should move onward at an accelerated rate." After implying that every radical lecturer was needed to ensure nothing less than "the world's redemption," Kelley commented that Lizzie Jones had reported that Cowles said she would "never lecture." The juxtaposition of Kelley's regret at leaving public speaking and Cowles's refusal to lecture was no coincidence. Kelley hoped that her sacrifice would compel Cowles to reconsider her position: "I am glad there is room for retraction as well as time for repentance," Kelley preached. "May the cry of the bleeding hearted and down trodden fill your ear by the glare of the day [and] stir your conscience to duty that you will be *obliged* to cry aloud for the shame, the sin, the curse, the humiliation of your and my wicked nation." Kelley concluded by sharing her motivations for becoming a public speaker: "I felt that woe was me if I preached not the gospel."[77] Cowles resisted this intense lobbying, perhaps feeling the opposition of the Hudsons and other friends as well as the continuing social disrepute of lecturing as a career for women.

Despite Kelley's disappointment that Cowles refused to enter the lecturing field, the two women sustained a warm relationship. Cowles's enthusiastic support for Garrisonianism despite widespread opposition was critical. "A hard campaign is to be maintained," Kelley warned Cowles after returning to the East. "I am saddened that I have left so few unyielding warriors on the battlefield."[78] Cowles's leadership among abolitionists on the Western

Reserve was unsurpassed during the late 1840s and 1850s, and her reputation soon spread even further. In 1847, eastern abolitionist Sarah Hallowell asked Cowles to become the general agent in charge of "getting up sewing circles" in western New York.[79] Frederick Douglass, a friend of Cowles, had recommended her for the position.

Kelley recognized her friend's leadership and further developed their relationship by rewarding Cowles with information, advice, encouragement, and personal intimacy. Kelley, for example, expressed concern with and interest in Cowles's personal life: "Perhaps I have told you of Stephen's bachelor brother, a *reformed* lawyer of this place," she casually remarked. "So reformed that he can't continue in the degrading twaddle of the law. He is a glorious soul and if he [should] go into partnership with Stephen will be a grand acquisition to our little circle." Such remarks allowed Kelley to offer reassurance not only that Cowles would be a desirable sister-in-law but also that she was already part of "our little circle." Kelley also shared her delight at the possibility of acquiring a home and promised to describe the structure as soon as it was chosen. Never far removed from thoughts of abolition, however, Kelley fretted about "mocking the agony" of slaves, who could never own homes, and feared "grow[ing] too selfish."[80] Kelley thus modeled all-consuming abolitionism.

Cowles admired Kelley but nevertheless established a personal style and philosophy of abolitionism. Cowles was determined to find a position that allowed her to be true to her Garrisonian beliefs while appealing to both Liberty Party and church abolitionists. She, like many others in the Old Northwest, reached across boundaries and sought to broaden her audience. One such method involved a focus on racial inequality in the North. Cowles worked closely with black abolitionists on issues such as education and legal discrimination. She created a Sabbath school for African American girls excluded from white institutions and included blacks in meetings and conventions, as when she invited a group of Cincinnati students to sing at the 1846 annual gathering of her ladies' society.[81] This commitment to racial equality as an expression of her abolitionism began with her first female antislavery society in the mid-1830s and continued throughout her reforming career. Although the Garrisonians advocated racial equality, they also vociferously argued that battling Black Laws, working on the Underground Railroad, creating schools for blacks, and aiding fugitives in Canada did not directly challenge slavery. "We condemn none of these benevolent enterprises—they are all good—Heaven speed them, but they never can redeem the slave," explained Benjamin and Lizzie Jones in a *Bugle* editorial. "Enlist as many persons in them as you choose, prosecute them with as much vigor as you please, yet not a slave chain will be broken thereby."[82] Cowles found herself more in line with Liberty Party abolitionists on this issue, allowing her to coordinate her efforts with non-Garrisonians.

Cowles also influenced radicals, who softened their stance and expressed interest in her efforts. She praised the *Anti-Slavery Bugle* when it followed her lead and began condemning expansive racial discrimination in Ohio. "I am glad to see that you are publishing articles on the unconstitutionality of the 'Black Laws of Ohio,'" she wrote to the paper in 1849. "You seem to be looking that way, and certainly it is time for some one to look."[83] Cowles had written and published a three-part pamphlet, *Plea for the Oppressed*, meticulously critiquing Ohio's Black Laws of Ohio and attracting the interest of many lecturers. Although Garrisonian Parker Pillsbury had condemned Cowles and her Ashtabula ladies' group for devoting money to such a publication—"It has no more to do with Anti-Slavery, than with the man in the moon"—the *Plea* incorporated disunionism.[84] Cowles's writings on the Black Laws proved very helpful to abolitionists, suggesting that radicals could at times ignore official policy in response to local issues. As Lizzie Hitchcock commented, audiences across Ohio appreciated the *Plea for the Oppressed*.[85] Even Kelley, who once complained to Cowles that Ohio women's sewing societies aided "fugitives and schools and asylums for the free" instead of "*real*" abolitionist efforts, asked to receive a copy of *Plea for the Oppressed*.[86] In ignoring official Garrisonian policy and following her beliefs and passions, Cowles bridged the gap between the political abolitionists and radicals and opened the door for others to enter.

Lizzie Hitchcock

Kelley never convinced Cowles to stand before the podium but did inspire a group of outspoken women radicals who followed her into lecturing. With Kelley as their role model, these women spread out across Ohio, Indiana, Michigan, and Illinois to promulgate the Garrisonian message to anyone who would listen. Like Kelley, they endured social opprobrium and sometimes mob opposition. But although Kelley inspired them, they followed Cowles in developing a western style that was rooted in compromise, negotiation, and the primacy of local issues. The most important of these orators, Jane Elizabeth "Lizzie" Hitchcock, accompanied Kelley to the West in 1845, became a friend of Cowles, and aroused Ohio with the radical antislavery message.

The year before Kelley toured Ohio, she convinced Lizzie Hitchcock, an unmarried thirty-year-old from Vernon, New York, to become her lecturing companion in New Hampshire and Pennsylvania.[87] Hitchcock's decision to join the infamous Garrisonian met with disapproval from family and friends.[88] Kelley recognized the strength of character that enabled Hitchcock to ignore the counsel of her loved ones. The enthusiastic New Yorker proved to be a talented public speaker and a reliable partner for Kelley. After a few months in the field, Hitchcock could also ignore hecklers, organize antislavery meetings on a moment's notice, and sleep comfortably in a crowded bed.[89] One admirer effused to Kelley, "Tell Jane Elizabeth . . . that some of our friends who heard her at Centerville, say that her speech there cannot be surpassed even by *Abby Kelley*."[90] Hitchcock established herself as a Garrisonian insider, gossiping with colleagues, knowledgably describing the lecture tour to movement leaders, and asserting her authority with Kelley.[91] "Lizzie says I may tell you she has been cultivating her will ever since she saw you," Kelley joked to Foster, "and I can testify that she has a sufficiency for my comfort, to say the least—*won't* is the word frequently in her mouth."[92] Several male lecturers joined the two women throughout the tour, including Philadelphia Quaker Benjamin Jones. Like so many other young abolitionists thrown together on the road, Hitchcock and Jones developed a romantic attachment, and they married within two years.[93]

By March 1845, Hitchcock and Kelley had developed a reputation for converting their opponents. As a result, the Ohio American Anti-Slavery Society asked the women to attend its annual meeting in New Lisbon and spend the summer promoting Garrisonianism in the West.[94] Immediately before their departure, the two women electrified the attendees of the American Anti-Slavery Society annual meeting in New York with brilliant lectures. Riding the wave of their New York success, the women arrived in Ohio with confidence and determination.[95]

Hitchcock endured a variety of obstacles and inconveniences upon her arrival. In addition to her lecturing duties, she reluctantly agreed to assist Jones, who followed her to Ohio, in editing the newly created *Anti-Slavery Bugle*, a task she found very frustrating because of the *Bugle*'s controversial and divisive nature: "I am willing to work where I can, it is true," she assured Kelley in July, "but I am very confident it is not in writing for a paper like the Bugle."[96] Editing the *Bugle* was time-consuming, stressful, and thankless. Even the members of the executive committee of the Ohio American Anti-Slavery Society, which founded the *Bugle*, immediately began to quarrel over its content. Within a few months, the *Bugle* would lose its funding.

Even as Hitchcock reluctantly settled into the coeditorship, she, Jones, and Kelley began holding meetings in New Lisbon and nearby communities.[97] A miserable case of the measles prevented her from speaking for a time, but she quickly regained her health and hit the lecturing circuit with her radical colleagues.[98] She experienced an inauspicious return to antislavery fieldwork when New Lisbon locals threatened to tar and feather her.[99] After more than a year as a radical abolitionist lecturer, however, she was not easily intimidated. She was more amused than frightened, for example, when an angry antiabolitionist man returned an antiwar pledge she had accidentally sent him with a list of signatures creatively constructed out of obscene words and concluding with the threat, "If you ever show you selfe in this county you will be tard and featherd."[100] By the fall, Hitchcock and Jones had moved with the *Bugle* to Salem and were speaking to audiences three to six times a week.[101]

The West elicited in Hitchcock a new vigor and independence that she had lacked in the East. "She was reared in the most delicate and tender manner," explained Kelley to Chapman, "wished and was gratified—spoke and was obeyed. She had no iron constitution of body and I thought not of mind. But since she has laid herself on the slave's altar she has become another being."[102] Her career as an abolitionist lecturer and editor strengthened her sense of self, and she began to make decisions that reflected this newfound identity. Although she and Jones had quickly become engaged, they postponed their marriage because their first priority was antislavery lecturing. When they settled down as coeditors of the *Bugle*, however, they decided it would be more convenient to marry so that they could live together and think about starting a family.[103] They wed in early 1846, and within a year, Hitchcock became pregnant, soon giving birth to the couple's only daughter.[104] Like several other abolitionist couples, Jones and Hitchcock attempted to establish an egalitarian relationship that allowed both partners to fulfill their responsibilities to the movement while maintaining their commitment to one another, apparently constructing a long-term, healthy, and happy marriage.

Hitchcock and Jones also became increasingly comfortable amid the generous community of kindhearted progressive farmers and abolitionists in their new home of Salem.[105] Boasting a "thoroughly antislavery atmosphere" that was "feared and hated by the South," Salem welcomed all reformers.[106] While Hitchcock and Jones initially boarded with other abolitionists, they eventually purchased a small home, which became the social center for Salem's reformers.[107] The gregarious couple hosted gatherings that ensured that local reformers felt connected to one another.[108] Serious about their activism but willing to loosen up and have a good time, the Joneses offered their home as a kind of salon for reformers. "I am well, & intensely enjoying our own home, & the fine intelligent friends we have around us," wrote Hitchcock to Kelley in 1856.[109] Cowles often stayed with the Joneses, sharing holidays and birthdays with lively conversation and delicious food.[110] Visiting abolitionists who boarded with the Joneses included William Lloyd Garrison in 1847 and 1858.[111] "A very large and choice company of anti-slavery friends assembled in the spacious parlor of our friends Benjamin and Elizabeth Jones, for social interchange of thought and feeling; a very pleasant time we had of it," enthused Garrison.[112] Easterners Margaret Burleigh and Mary Grew sojourned for several weeks at the Joneses' home, describing it as "pleasantly located" amid beautiful fields and woods.[113] Pillsbury considered the Joneses' Salem home his primary residence during his months in the West and had his mail sent there.[114] "It is one of the most delicious little homes I ever saw," he explained. "It is the abode of fidelity, truth, and generous love."[115]

Lecturing and writing about disunionism and racial oppression was exhausting, unprofitable, and sometimes dispiriting. Throughout its existence, the *Bugle* remained underfunded, undersubscribed, and the source of political intrigue.[116] Year after year, both western and eastern abolitionists whispered to one another about possible changes in the *Bugle*'s editorial leadership and location. In addition to Sarah Otis Ernst, who wanted the paper moved to Cincinnati, northern Ohioans reportedly were conniving to move it to Cleveland. Kelley heard a rumor that the *Bugle* was to be absorbed by Douglass's *North Star*, based in Rochester, New York.[117] When Pillsbury heard the same rumor, he quipped, "It is the Star, not of Hope, but of Despair to the *Bugle*."[118] The Joneses not only weathered these false reports but maintained a grueling public speaking schedule. Their five-week lecturing tour during the winter of 1847–48, for example, was characterized by difficult travel, small audiences, and terrible weather.[119] Although they sold thirty dollars worth of books and obtained nearly two dozen subscribers to the *Bugle*, Hitchcock was "disheartened at the prospects of the cause here in the West." She angrily sputtered to Kelley that people in the region were "*mean, destitute of principle, unstable, [and] worth very little in any moral enterprise*."[120] Hitchcock's uncharacteristic outburst was probably influenced by her financial worries. The Joneses struggled with money issues throughout the antebellum years. Unlike many other radical abolitionists in the West, Benjamin Jones and Lizzie Hitchcock did not own a farm or engage in a trade.[121] After nearly three years in Ohio, Hitchcock complained that she and Jones could no longer expect to live on "the promise of $400 from a Soc[iety] that has not a copper in its Treas[ury]. We have this winter been living on money that I have made in selling books."[122] Expecting a baby, Hitchcock attempted to supplement their income by writing an antislavery children's book, *The Young Abolitionists; or, Conversations on Slavery*. She shared the manuscript with Kelley, hoping to improve the book and induce her to help publish it. Although Hitchcock chafed at the critical feedback her friend offered, she was grateful when the antislavery office in Boston published the narrative.[123]

Being a Garrisonian public speaker involved many personal challenges as well. Hitchcock drew hostility because of her decision to lecture before mixed audiences on a very controversial topic. When she became pregnant she, like Kelley, recognized that social expectations required her to take a hiatus from the field. Hitchcock struggled with her beliefs about motherhood and in so doing imposed typical nineteenth-century ideas about gender on Kelley. After learning that Kelley would be returning to Ohio to lecture only months after giving birth, Hitchcock accused her friend of joining those thoughtless mothers who had "thrown off [their] duties and responsibilities." She continued, "Your influence on the cause of human freedom will be good, but your influence on home duties & home virtues will be bad. If you would wait till your child is old enough to wean it would be less reprehensible."[124] Hitchcock then announced that she too was expecting a "little stranger" in six months but averred, "I think I shall not feel like leaving it, to lecture, in 10 months." Hitchcock's comments reveal the fluidity and complexity of gender. Even as she consciously engaged in a public career that violated the "woman's sphere," she impressed certain elements of this sphere on herself and her public-speaking sisters. Hitchcock soon rethought her notions of motherhood, however. A few months later, when she wrote to Kelley to express some concerns about a controversial fellow abolitionist, Hitchcock worried that her thoughts would be dismissed as having been caused by pregnancy-induced irrationality: "Don't attribute any thing I have written to my situation, for I am altogether sure & of sound judgement. I have not exaggerated."[125] Learning through experience about the negative stereotypes associated with pregnancy, Hitchcock developed a more complicated understanding of motherhood. In the fall of 1848, a few months after the birth of her daughter, she attended the annual meeting of the Western Anti-Slavery Society, where she participated in the executive committee's grueling meetings.[126] She organized the Western Anti-Slavery Society fair six months later and reentered the lecturing circuit soon thereafter.[127]

Just as she creatively managed an exhausting schedule, problematic home finances, and family growth, Hitchcock negotiated the complicated politics of western abolitionism. Like Cowles and Ernst, Hitchcock developed a grassroots style that proved very adaptable, enhancing her popularity. After hearing Hitchcock lecture, one man professed, "I never listened to anything from bar or pulpit that afforded me more delight," even though he was a "Liberty party man."[128] Hitchcock found that lecturing offered her the opportunity to listen as well as speak, and she learned to adapt her message to local concerns and situations. She found that paying attention to her audiences also allowed her to improve her editorial skills. "We are glad that we have been" lecturing, she wrote after a five-week tour. "Now we know the position of affairs on the Reserve much better than we did. I wish we were personally acquainted with all our subscribers, & then we should better understand all their wants."[129] She often worked with women in the villages she visited to initiate sewing groups or female societies, establishing a local connection that allowed her to keep in touch with the abolitionists who constituted the heart of the movement. She did not dilute her radical message for the comfort of her sister abolitionists. Her editorial in the *Bugle* urging Ohio women to create disunion sewing societies focused on discouraging them from giving money to Canada missions, Underground Railroad efforts, or schools for blacks.[130] Despite this uncompromising position, Hitchcock and other western Garrisonians were forced to negotiate with those abolitionists who rejected disunionism or wanted to vote.

Hitchcock and Jones preached the Garrisonian message from the editorial chair of the *Bugle* and in the field through 1849, when Hitchcock began in earnest a new career as a hygiene lecturer, a more stable and lucrative vocation than antislavery editing and lecturing.[131] Hitchcock spent the next five years traveling across the West and even the South, speaking to women about their bodies and health concerns.[132] "Lizzie continues quite successful," wrote Kelley in 1850, "the first month she cleared $110."[133] In limiting her message to more comfortable health issues and in speaking to women only, Hitchcock attracted large and generous audiences. When Foster asked Kelley why Hitchcock was "so much more successful, pecuniarily, in lecturing on Physiology than on Anti-Slavery," Kelley responded, "Don't you know people will pay you for scientific knowledge when they will kill you for showing them their sins?" Frustrated with the constant struggle of making ends meet, Hitchcock had decided to use her public speaking skills to increase her family income. While remaining active in reform, she self-consciously adopted a less controversial message. "I am before the public as a lecturer on science, & of my private opinions in relation to any other question, in regard to Theology, politics, or reform, I feel that the public have nothing to do," she explained to someone who inquired about her position on woman's rights. "I confine myself strictly to my subject, & do not ever in private advance any views that can be used to injure the cause, in wh[ich] I am now so much engaged, & wh[ich] I flatter myself is doing much good."[134] Hitchcock understood that as soon as her radical antislavery or feminist politics entered the conversation, her appeal to large audiences of women would decline.

This career as a hygiene lecturer proved intellectually and personally satisfying but exhausting. "Jane E. Jones started to Illinois [and] expects to be gone until Oct. next," wrote her Salem neighbor and friend Daniel Hise in his diary in March 1854. "She sacrifices a great deal in leaving home. But in the [end] she hopes to make her home the more desirable."[135] The process of organizing lectures in new cities proved challenging, especially for a woman alone. In Chicago, she relied on a male colleague to take care of her public business. "Mr. Brass kindly offered to get my advertising done," she explained. "He advised me not to go to any of the Offices myself, so I obeyed, & was as prudish as the most fastidious soul desire. He settled my bills & did every thing in that line."[136] Despite her strong support for woman's rights, Hitchcock engaged in "prudish" behavior for the sake of public acceptance.

Hitchcock did not permanently abandon abolitionism. In 1857, she spoke at the disunion convention in Cleveland and lectured on abolition in New York.[137] While in the Empire State, she wrote a third-person letter describing the difficulties she experienced as a Garrisonian lecturer: "She is no longer Mrs. J. Elizabeth Jones, 'the distinguished physiological lecturer' whom hundreds and thousands of ladies flock to hear. She is now 'J. E. Jones Esq.,' a woman straying around the country with a man she calls her husband, to talk about the 'niggers.'"[138] The tour brought Hitchcock small audiences, mob opposition, and financial disaster.[139]

During her hygiene tours, when she spoke to female-only audiences about a suitable topic, Hitchcock's lecturing career did not represent a violation of the woman's sphere. She could enter such civic spaces as meetinghouses, churches, and public buildings and attract large, prosperous audiences. The woman's sphere was not, in fact, a carefully prescribed space, but a shifting set of ideas. Even though her hygiene career took her away from her home and her daughter and made her the family's primary breadwinner, certainly a stark violation of the woman's sphere, Hitchcock's efforts won her accolades from admiring audiences. Only when she returned to Garrisonian abolitionism did she endure social ostracism and personal attacks. The radical content of her public message suddenly caused the woman's sphere to narrow significantly.

Josephine Griffing

While Lizzie Hitchcock was regaling large audiences with health lectures, Josephine Griffing became a leading Garrisonian speaker in the West. Josephine and her husband, Charles, moved from Connecticut to Ohio's Western Reserve in 1842 and became active in local antislavery efforts. Much like Cowles, they were converted to Garrisonianism by Kelley during her Ohio tours. In 1850, the Griffings hosted Kelley in their home. Kelley recognized in Josephine Griffing a kindred spirit and encouraged the Litchfield mother to consider public speaking in support of her antislavery beliefs. Within a year, the Griffings became paid agents of the Western Anti-Slavery Society, picking up where Hitchcock had left off.[140]

Josephine Griffing became a brilliant antislavery advocate during the 1850s, despite enduring the death of her teenage daughter.[141] "I have never been so impressed with the talent and capacity of Mrs. Griffing, for a public missionary in the work of Reform, as during our recent tour in Michigan," testified Pillsbury. "The Society has never had an agent in its employ, whose labors commenced with greater efficiency and usefulness, than those of Mrs. Griffing."[142] Griffing spoke more often than almost any other Garrisonian in the West during the mid-1850s, and she served as vice president of the Western Anti-Slavery Society from 1852 to 1858. Usually lecturing with her husband and one or two other male Garrisonians, Griffing traveled across Ohio, Indiana, and Michigan for four years. Like Kelley and Hitchcock, she appealed especially to women, encouraging them to initiate local groups to raise money for the cause. "In every place we visit to a considerable extent, we found an interest in the Anti-Slavery cause awakened and increased in women, by Josephine's presence and addresses," confirmed Charles Griffing. "And now, surely, the time has come when women may plead for the oppressed without opposition from the 'world' in the sense the church uses that word."[143] Despite her husband's praise, however, Josephine Griffing occasionally encountered opposition as a female public speaker. One woman in Deersville, Ohio, claimed that she would rather see a local church "burned" to the ground than opened to the "monstrous" Griffing.[144] Like Frances Wright, who was also denounced as a "monster," and Kelley, who was censured as a "Jezebel," Griffing raised worries about female virtue. As historian Sylvia Hoffert has noted, women lecturers were perceived as having more opportunity for promiscuous sexual behavior, and even such a perception was enough to fuel opposition.[145] Traveling alone or with men, lodging with strangers, and speaking before mixed audiences, these women had a peripatetic lifestyle that invited suspicion. Griffing and Kelley protected themselves to some degree by traveling with their spouses, but this protection only went so far. After the Griffings lectured in Linesville, Pennsylvania, one local editor advised Charles to "take Mrs. Griffing home and introduce her to the kitchen, and learn her to mind her own business."[146]

In spite of such occasional hostility, however, Griffing, like her friends Cowles and Hitchcock, negotiated a cooperative reputation that allowed her to appeal to as wide an audience as possible. Often speaking in locations dominated by Free-Soil abolitionists, the Griffings found common ground whenever possible. Describing a meeting in Brecksville, Ohio, Charles explained, "After we had spoken several Free Soilers present, responded to most of our positions, and in a truly catholic spirit avowed their willingness and determination to co-operate with any and all who were laboring for the overthrow of Slavery. To us such assurances were truly encouraging." A few days later, the radical couple spoke in nearby Bennetts Corners and again created a cooperative spirit among political abolitionists: "A good Free Soiler came forward to apologize for his party, who he admitted were not what he desired, but had hope that they might hereafter attain to a respectable Anti-Slavery position."[147] Josephine also regularly acknowledged political abolitionists who exhibited integrity and honesty, as in Georgetown, Ohio, where she met with "an honest anti-slavery sentiment in the form of Free Soil, that is set to do its utmost to [destroy] Slavery."[148]

The Griffings did not feel bound by the dictates of eastern Garrisonianism. They worked closely with African Americans and supported the Underground Railroad. Their home served as a way station for slaves heading north, allowing the Griffings to develop an understanding of slavery and its horrors. Josephine compared one group of slaves—"sixteen heroic men and women from Kentucky"—to American revolutionaries: the fugitives had made their way "thro' a land of enemies more formidable and 'ferocious' than British soldiers at Bunker Hill or Brandywine."[149] The Griffings also ignored the Garrisonian policy of discouraging aid to Canadian settlements of ex-slaves. Recognizing that many western abolitionists wanted to aid these communities, the Griffings visited Canada in 1854 and wrote public letters detailing former slaves' tragic personal histories and highlighting the breakup of slave families. The Griffings also investigated the various fugitive aid organizations and suggested that interested abolitionists should finance the Refugee Home Society run by Charles C. Foote of Detroit. "He is not a sectarian, but forms Union Religious Societies among them, and encourages them to serve God in love and kindness to each other," explained Charles.[150] The Griffings developed a flexible position on Canadian fugitive aid that reflected their own anticlericalism and their commitment to helping blacks.

Less than a year after traveling to Canada, Josephine Griffing found herself in the same difficult position that confronted Hitchcock and Kelley. Pregnancy would force Griffing out of lecturing and into the domestic sphere, at least for a time.[151] Remaining at home would eventually frustrate Griffing, who was back in front of the podium in less than five years. She returned to public speaking in the summer of 1860, a time of anxiety and tension. Still reeling from John Brown's raid at Harpers Ferry, the North buzzed with the presidential campaign that resulted in Abraham Lincoln's election. Even some radical abolitionists had toned down their uncompromising positions and united with the "Wide Awake" Republicans. Griffing, in contrast, became increasingly uncompromising and rejected the Republicans' moderate antislavery.[152] She and the equally uncompromising Pillsbury hit the road and shared their radical message with audiences across Michigan and Ohio.[153] For the next two years, Griffing, Pillsbury, and other radicals encountered hostile audiences and sometimes mobs.[154]

Josephine Griffing's decision to return to the lecturing field proved painful in personal ways as well. She decided to end her marriage at the same time she left home to lecture. Charles Griffing was shocked and devastated by this decision and blamed Pillsbury, whom Charles accused of seducing Josephine into a "free love" philosophy that caused her to leave him: "He first sowed in Josephine's mind these seeds of death, which he has since assiduously cultivated, that has resulted in the destruction of my family and influenced my wife to procure by fraudulent representations in Indiana, a bill of divorce from me."[155]

Bostonian abolitionist Loring Moody witnessed an 1853 lecture by Hitchcock and Josephine Griffing in Columbus, Ohio, and commented that their speeches possessed a "scope of thought, depth of reasoning, and power of appeal [that] I have seldom heard equaled, never surpassed."[156] Skilled debaters and persuasive lecturers, these women stood on the podium alongside such male luminaries as Garrison, Joshua Giddings, and Douglass. Hitchcock and Griffing occasionally outshone the movement's stars but spent most of their time in small towns speaking to men and women who had basic questions about disunionism, come-outerism, and racial equality. The two women worked diligently to answer those questions, allay fears, and instigate the creation of antislavery societies. Recognizing that grassroots networks were necessary to sustain the movement over time, the itinerant speakers nourished local leadership, especially among women. On occasion, Hitchcock and Griffing inspired other women to follow in their footsteps. Dozens of Ohio, Indiana, and Michigan women emulated these radicals and become speakers for the cause. Some became comfortable at the lecturing podium, spending years delivering speeches to eager crowds across the Old Northwest. Others found the mobs, social isolation, and public disapproval too much to bear for any length of time. But all of these passionate radicals proved adept at promoting Garrisonian abolition in an environment that demanded flexibility and patience.

Other Women Lecturers

Parkman, Ohio, resident Harriet N. Torrey was one such woman. After attending Kelley's first lectures in Ohio in 1845, Torrey proclaimed it a "fearful thing for a woman to question the wisdom of men, and break through the conventionalisms which confine her physical and intellectual energies within a limited and subordinate sphere." Many women abolitionists in Ohio shared Torrey's irritation. But they also accepted Torrey's conclusion: "If man would prove his own humanity, by pleading the cause of the oppressed, there would be no necessity for woman to diverge from her own legitimate sphere."[157] Torrey not only applauded Kelley but eventually followed down the same path, publicly vocalizing uncompromising political opinions and advice. Embracing the Garrisonians' anti-third-party position, Torrey initially employed the pages of the *Bugle* to highlight the hypocrisy of politicians. Dismissing antislavery Whigs as ineffective and dishonorable— as failed men—Torrey used the Ohio party's record to expose local politicians and prod the voters who supported these officials.[158] She relentlessly needled the Liberty Party as well, finally deciding in January 1847 to take her message to the public through a lecturing tour.[159] Continuing to battle third-party politicians, Torrey also exchanged verbal blows with the clergy. Speaking in Troy, a small Ohio village, she "took up the Churches—exposed their hypocrisy and consummate knavery with decided truthfulness and ability," in the words of her lecturing partner, H. W. Curtis. Confronted by a local clergyman who "undertook to set her right," Torrey refused to back down.[160] Because neither Torrey nor Curtis would yield to his argument, the minister "abruptly left, muttering away at us while going." Troy locals followed the lead of their religious leadership. Incensed by the radicals' denunciation of

"Church and State" and probably by the fact that Torrey was a young single woman who was violating feminine decorum, antiabolitionists disrupted the next meeting. Led by "the church," according to Curtis, and supported by "hair-brained ninnies," Troy citizens prevented the abolitionists from speaking and drove them from the meeting.[161]

Although Torrey's lecturing career seems to have concluded with this short tour of eastern Ohio, she did not abandon the radical antislavery movement. A few months later, she organized her neighbors and friends into the disunionist Geauga Female Anti-Slavery Society, which operated as an auxiliary to the Western Anti-Slavery Society. Torrey then assumed the group's presidency.[162] She continued writing letters to the *Bugle* condemning third-party politics, participated at annual meetings of the Western Anti-Slavery Society, and served on a committee at the 1850 Salem Woman's Rights Convention.[163] Public speaking proved too difficult for Torrey, so she found other more comfortable and socially acceptable methods of battling slavery.

Meigs County, Ohio, abolitionist Hannah Thomas, conversely, remained in the lecturing field for several years, motivated in part by the isolation of her community. "Liberty party has the entire ascendancy and gives character to abolitionism here," she grumbled in 1847. "There are but a handful of Disunionists in this section, and they are persons unused to public speaking; but we are doing what we can, though we have to contend against powerful odds."[164] Thomas adapted to a lecturing career by finding common ground with the political abolitionists who surrounded her. One year after stepping up to the podium, Thomas wrote enthusiastically to the *Bugle*, "The friends of the slave in this part principally adhere to the Liberty party; but they are the whole material and many of them are just such spirits as we love and admire in the ranks of those whose motto is 'no union with slaveholders.'"[165] Although many of the farming families that made up her Meigs County audiences were "attracted perhaps more by the novelty of a woman lecturing than by any great desire of hearing the subject of anti-slavery discussed," they respectfully listened nonetheless. Thomas certainly encountered obstacles, including locked meetinghouse doors, but she remained persistent and confident.[166] Thomas admitted that "we might almost as well solicit subscribers for a new edition of Paine's *Age of Reason* among the Orthodox professors, as to try to get subscribers for the *Bugle*," but, she assured her readers, if "these very men (for among Liberty party generally women, are an non-entity) could have the principles of Disunion laid before them in the right manner, many of them would embrace them."[167] Suggesting that women knew better than to fall prey to the Liberty Party's false promises, Thomas pointed to men as the potential converts for thoughtful Garrisonian lecturers.

To the north, in Michigan, Mary Philleo and her husband, John H. Philleo, joined the ranks of Garrisonian lecturing couples. Radicals organized the Michigan Anti-Slavery Society and officially associated with the Garrisonians in 1853, although women had previously played an important role in radical antislavery across the state. Several women regularly attended the important monthly state central organizing committee meetings, and in 1852 attendees at the convention of the Michigan Anti-Slavery Society requested Kelley and Sallie Holley as lecturers.[168] When the Philleos began planting seeds with their lectures in 1855, the ground had already been tilled.[169] Like Hitchcock and Griffing, Philleo inspired other women to become more active in the movement. While in Grand Rapids, for example, Philleo's female host was so electrified by her guest that she initiated a daring push into a nearby town. She proposed taking Philleo "to Plainfield, a distance of ten miles, for the purpose of getting up a meeting the following night." And they went, "although the extreme coldness and inclemency of the weather made such an undertaking seem rather forbidding, yet screwing up our courage and jocously [sic] saying that our abolition would defy the external elements." The two women arrived in the "little village of strangers" after dark but nonetheless organized an antislavery gathering. They were greeted "with a large respectable, and apparently interested audience." Philleo and her partner violated nearly every dictate of "true" womanhood by traveling alone at night, lecturing to a mixed-sex audience, and advocating an unpopular and radical message but nevertheless garnered a "liberal contribution" and "a cordial invitation" to return.[170]

By the mid-1850s, female public speaking had become less scandalous than it had been ten years earlier, when Kelley arrived in Ohio. "Women lecturers are becoming so common as almost to cease to excite curiosity in most places north of the Mississippi," Missouri abolitionist Frances D. Gage happily declared in 1855.[171] Ohio resident Celestia Rice Colby recorded how her attitude toward female public speaking had changed from the 1840s to the 1850s: "Looking through the glass of prejudice which my early training had inspired, I thought Abby Kelley was entirely 'out of her sphere' but it seems not thus now. Long may she live to fill the sphere which she now occupies, and which she fills so well and so fearlessly." Colby concluded with a hope for more female lecturers: "The world needs her labors in this sphere, and I would that there were many women fitted for the same task."[172] In a *Bugle* editorial regarding a woman's rights lecture, Marius Robinson articulated one of the key reasons such public lecturing had become less contentious: the domestication of the public sphere. "Heretofore, whatever has been peculiarly woman's influence, has been excluded from its operation through the public audience. It has been a 'shame for a woman to speak.' All know the magic of that influence in the private social circle. It will not be less in public, if freely admitted."[173] Alluding to woman's natural benevolence and virtue, Robinson suggested that conservative ideas about female difference might have influenced the increasing acceptance of woman's public role. Women simply brought their "natural" moral sensibility into public spaces.

Such changes should not be exaggerated, however. A self-declared abolitionist Baptist minister in Milford, Michigan, refused to open his church to the Philleos because he was too "shocked to see a *woman* in the pulpit."[174] When African American orator Frances Ellen Watkins lectured in Ohio during the late 1850s, she found herself occasionally subject to protests and mob opposition. A well-educated and articulate woman, Watkins had developed a reputation as a thoughtful and persuasive abolitionist orator.[175] In Fairfield, Ohio, a group of rowdies surrounded the lecture hall as Watkins spoke, yelling obscenities and breaking windows. Local citizens were so appalled by this behavior that they made sure that the "ruffians" were brought to justice. At trial, the mob's leader revealed his intolerance by referring to abolitionists as "maggoty-brained friends of the slave," and he was convicted of disturbing the peace.[176] The fact that the violent antiabolitionists were prosecuted and that most of Watkins's lectures in Ohio were peaceful suggests that the western environment had become less tolerant of mob action. After hearing Watkins speak, Salem's Hise declared, "*Miss Watkins*, a collored lady made as good a speech as I ever listened to."[177]

Watkins's status as an outspoken African American female accounted for the intensity of the opposition she engendered. When Sojourner Truth spoke in Indiana in June 1861, she also met a mob. Truth had encountered racism in Indiana a few years earlier, when the "mouthpiece of the slave democracy" in Silver Lake accused her of being a man disguised as a woman. Truth "disrobed her bosom" to the audience, averred that her "breasts had suckled many a white babe," and asked her accuser if he, too, "wished to suck."[178] Truth returned to the state in the summer of 1861 simply to visit friends in the town of Angola. Two months after the Civil War had begun at Fort Sumter, local abolitionists requested that Truth speak about the conflict.[179] Truth began her lecture with the confession that she wished she could join the brave troops on the battlefield, at which point, according to Josephine Griffing, a mob "rushed up the stairs, and like a pack of hounds,

Frances Ellen Watkins Harper. From Frances Ellen Watkins Harper,
Iola Leroy; or, Shadows Uplifted *(Philadelphia: Garrigues, 1892).*
Courtesy of the Library Company of Philadelphia.

with ears well rubbed, set upon this patriotic, noble woman, and with insolent threats and yells choked her down."[180] The following night, the mob
surrounded the home of Truth's host, "one of the oldest and wealthiest men
in the county," failing to carry through on their "hellish plan" of violence only
because "they were soon too drunk for a riot." Still determined to run Truth
out of the state, the leaders of the mob prosecuted her for violation of the
Black Laws. Truth was first arrested for "coming into the State, being black;
next, as a mulatto; then, for coming in; then, for remaining in the State!"[181]
Four different trials were held, with Truth acquitted at all of them. "The most
influential and noble-hearted women" of the county attended the proceedings and "produced a marked impression." Griffing, who had encountered
violent opponents during her years as a Garrisonian lecturer, concluded, "In
my experience with mobs, I have never seen such determination. No dog
ever hung to a bone as have these hungry hounds to Sojourner."[182]

The passionate mobbing of both Truth and Watkins is evidence not
only of continuing deep racism in the North but also of ambivalence about
women's intrusions into civic spaces. The questioning of Truth's femininity
reveals that many people still equated public oratory with manhood, assuming that any woman who excelled in this arena was either a disguised man or
a promiscuous female. This discomfort with women's public role centered on
sexuality because it was the issue of greatest tension. Griffing's divorce and
the consequent gossip about her relationship with Pillsbury simply added
fuel to an already roaring fire. Moreover, public women defied stereotypes
about what historian Nancy Cott has deemed female "passionlessness," an
idea that permeated popular literature in the antebellum period.[183] Offering
vibrant and ardent speeches, these women were anything but passionless.
Garrisonian women in particular endured accusations of sexual misconduct,
as much because of their status as women as their advocacy of what was considered an extreme political position. Hitchcock's success as a hygiene lecturer and her condemnation as an abolitionist activist highlights this point.

Conclusion

Isolated, outnumbered, and underfinanced, Garrisonians fought simply to
keep their movement viable through most of the 1840s and 1850s. Women
radicals helped sustain and advance Garrisonianism in Ohio, Michigan,
and Indiana despite the disadvantages they faced. As public speakers and
behind-the-scenes leaders, they effectively negotiated with more moderate

abolitionists. Hoping to effect change among third-party and church abolitionists, women such as Betsey Mix Cowles, Lizzie Hitchcock, and Josephine Griffing sometimes set aside the hard-line Garrisonian position they had learned from Abby Kelley to attract supporters. They worked on local issues with community residents to battle slavery in all its forms. They flattered local ministers into opening church doors and sponsoring antislavery fairs, raised money to fund anti–Black Law publications, and cooperated with third-party abolitionists on mutually beneficial projects. Though sometimes censured by their East Coast colleagues, Cowles, Hitchcock, and Griffing refused simply to follow the party line. Their undeniable commitment and sacrifice sometimes persuaded eastern leaders of the effectiveness of more cooperative approaches.

One such cooperative approach involved the issue of aid to fugitives. While Garrisonians publicly argued that true abolition did not involve aid to escaped slaves, many reformers privately participated in the Underground Railroad. In the West, abolitionists of all shades worked in coordination with African Americans to ensure that the hundreds of fugitives who sought safety in their region would be aided and protected. While women's role in this realm of the abolition movement has been underrecognized, it was both critical and wide ranging.

CHAPTER 6

Abolitionists and Fugitive Slaves

I n the late summer of 1854, as the nation confronted the growing controversy around the Kansas-Nebraska Act, which reaffirmed the West
as a battleground between slavery and freedom, abolitionists met in Salem,
Ohio, for the twelfth annual meeting of the Western Anti-Slavery Society.[1]
Most of the region's leading Garrisonian women were there, including Josephine Griffing and fellow lecturer Lizzie Hitchcock, who would serve as
vice presidents, as well as Cincinnati powerhouse Sarah Otis Ernst, who
participated on the Business Committee. The issue of fugitive slaves making
their way north to freedom through Ohio dominated discussions. Several
resolutions proclaimed the moral necessity of aiding these men, women, and
children in their dangerous travels. On the afternoon of the conference's
third day, attendees heard a startling announcement: a telegraph had warned
Salem citizens that a "Southern family with a slave girl would arrive on the
Express train (then nearly due) in Salem." The audience voted immediately
to adjourn, head to the depot, and give "a practical illustration" of their commitment to abolition.[2]

While several hundred curious and excited Ohioans, black and white,
young and old, waited outside, a carefully chosen "committee of four" entered the train and discovered the young slave girl with her owners.[3] An
African American man on the committee asked the girl if she desired her

freedom. "The child expressed her wish to be free," and she was picked up "and hurried out of the Car" as the slave master "hollered murder" and the crowd cheered.[4] *Bugle* editor Marius Robinson, who watched the scene, reported that the owner, Memphis resident J. J. Robinson, appeared "sad, and terribly scared," bemoaning the fact that the girl's mother, also a slave, would "waste away with sorrow" when she learned of the fate of her daughter.[5] "A lady present suggested that these broken hearts might be mended by sending the mother to Ohio to live in freedom with her daughter." The slave owner declined, leading Marius Robinson to conclude that he was "quite below our par estimate of Southern chivalry." Later that night, "a large jubilant meeting was convened," the young girl was renamed Abby Kelley Salem, and nearly fifty dollars was raised to provide her with a home, education, and support.[6]

The Salem Rescue (or the Salem Robbery, as southern newspapers dubbed it) would play itself out in the media over the next several months.[7] Both southern and northern newspapers generally condemned the "fanatics" who carried out the "rash and illegal" act. The man who grabbed the girl was initially depicted as a "black ruffian" who "violently tore her away" from her mistress, injuring the woman in the process.[8] Although an African American man carried the young girl off the train, white Cincinnatian Henry Blackwell had lifted the girl out of her mistress's arms.[9] When Blackwell's role was revealed, he became the focus of public outrage in the South. As Blackwell explained to Lucy Stone, whom he married soon thereafter, "It is written . . . that I assaulted the lady, scratched her neck, and tumbled the baby on the floor." This libelous account, he complained, could not be further from the truth. When he picked up the slave girl, he was immediately accosted, requiring him to "let go of the child, who was instantly caught up by the other members of the committee and passed out, and carried swiftly off into the town in the arms of a colored man."[10] When Blackwell returned to Cincinnati, the city was "buzzing like a hornets' nest," and some residents joined with J. J. Robinson to threaten to ruin Blackwell's wholesale hardware business through bad publicity. Blackwell admitted to Stone, "The odium which attaches to me from the Salem affair has been, to a certain extent, injurious to our business."[11] Even though a public letter from a group of eyewitnesses describing Blackwell's conduct as "calm, peaceable and gentlemanly" was circulated in Ohio newspapers, several southern cities held public meetings to denounce the Salem Rescue and Blackwell in particular. Robinson's hometown, Memphis, threatened to cease business transactions with the entire city of Cincinnati if its leadership failed to denounce the incident.[12] In response, the Cincinnati Chamber of Commerce considered a resolution repudiating the Salem Rescue but eventually decided to remain neutral by arguing that the issue was not relevant to the chamber.[13] At least one southern businessman ceased patronizing Blackwell's company because the owners were "abolitionists and robbers of other people's property."[14] Macon, Tennessee, offered a one-thousand-dollar reward for the deliverance of Blackwell.[15] But Blackwell, "not the man to be intimidated," according to Marius Robinson, continued to defend his actions.[16]

The Salem Rescue highlights how cooperation across race, party, and gender lines characterized the abolitionist effort to aid fugitive slaves in the Old Northwest. Black and white abolitionists worked together to gain the girl's release. Although the false stories about the violent "black ruffian" who roughed up a white woman to steal a child reveal the predominance of racial stereotypes in the public discourse surrounding fugitives, the diversity of the crowd that applauded the rescue points to the interracial character of this method of abolitionism.[17] Such interracial cooperation also helps to explain the virulent racism employed by opponents; the idea of African American and white abolitionists harmoniously cooperating raised the specter of miscegenation, a familiar bogeyman used by antiabolitionists.

The mixed assemblage, including Garrisonians and third-party supporters, also makes clear the way in which aid to fugitives encouraged abolitionists to cross ideological dividing lines. Blackwell, a political abolitionist who served on the conference's Business Committee, had spent the first two days of the convention debating the radicals over nonvoting and disunionism, only to join hands with his opponents and hurry to the train station to rescue a slave girl.[18] "It is charged that the rescuers were fanatical Disunionists," huffed the *Bugle*. "They were of all parties. Whigs, Democrats, Free Soilers, Disunionists, Bible men, and Infidels. An honorable common sympathy animated all—a regard for liberty and a determination to vindicate it. A noble example which should be imitated everywhere."[19] Though some historians have found more evidence of Underground Railroad activity among political abolitionists, at least in the Old Northwest, all brands of abolitionists participated in helping fugitives.[20]

Finally, the Salem Rescue reveals how gendered assumptions permeated discussions about fugitives. In depicting Blackwell as an honorable and courageous gentleman who stood up to the threats of proslavery bullies, the abolitionist press used ideas about Christian manhood to defend the rescue. (Blackwell would use the rescue to convince the reluctant Stone to marry him.)[21] Moreover, the invisibility of women in this rescue is emblematic of their behind-the-scenes critical but underrecognized role. While the committee of four "was made up of our most respectable men," Josephine Griffing, Lizzie Hitchcock, Sarah Otis Ernst, and other local women certainly participated in the rescue and were left to care for and ensure the girl's safety.[22] As men claimed the headlines in controversial rescues, women and their antislavery societies focused on practical issues such as raising funds, sewing clothes, providing food, and offering education to fugitives. Moreover, western women boldly applauded, advocated, and even employed violence to protect fugitives.

Fugitive Slaves and Cooperation

The Old Northwest served as a route toward free Canada for thousands of fugitive slaves.[23] Moving quickly and quietly toward northern river towns, freedom seekers employed ingenious methods for eluding slave catchers and reaching the Ohio River.[24] The well-networked black community in Cincinnati and Ripley worked in coordination with local white abolitionists such as John Rankin and Levi Coffin to aid exhausted and hungry escapees who reached Ohio. Although the Underground Railroad of popular imagination is more myth than reality, Coffin, Rankin, John Parker, Laura Smith Haviland, and many others across the Old Northwest developed an organized system for aiding fugitives.[25] Coffin claimed in his *Reminiscences* that as far as he knew, not a single escapee he aided was captured. Not all fugitives were as fortunate, however, so abolitionists occasionally organized "rescues" of slaves being held in local jails or traveling through the region, as was the case in Salem.[26] More commonly, white and black abolitionists aided fugitives by providing housing, food, clothing, money, information, transportation, and legal advice and support.[27] Freedom seekers were not simply passive victims, however. They continued to direct the course of their escape. They also had a tremendous impact on their hosts and collaborators.[28] Interacting with fugitives and listening to their life narratives influenced abolitionists' identity and behavior in both subtle and significant ways, breaking down barriers and changing the movement.

The process of helping fugitives unified western abolitionists, bringing together Garrisonians and third-party activists, men and women, blacks and whites. At the celebratory meeting following the Salem Rescue, an eminent local Whig offered an animated speech, admitting that "he had heretofore opposed such operations, but late events had opened his eyes."[29] As the embodiment of slavery, escapees reminded advocates of the purpose of the movement. Interacting with a malnourished, exhausted, determined young slave woman, for example, made political or philosophical conflicts among the abolitionists seem unimportant. Those Salem residents who might shiver at the idea of Abby Kelley lecturing before a "promiscuous" audience would nonetheless work willingly with Josephine Griffing to find wagons to carry a group of fugitives to the next town.[30]

Overcoming such conflicts between different brands of abolition was important. When Scotland's Glasgow Female Anti-Slavery Society chose to give financial support to the New York Vigilance Committee, which focused on aid to escapees, instead of to the Garrisonians, Maria Weston Chapman retorted that fighting to free two and a half million slaves was more important than aiding two and a half thousand fugitives.[31] Ernst believed that lending a helping hand to disadvantaged escapees was not an appropriate job for an abolitionist group.[32] Hitchcock took this argument a step further, asserting that aid to fugitives impaired legitimate antislavery efforts.[33]

Despite the forcefulness of such declarations, however, the party line on aid to escapees among western Garrisonians proved fluid. Groups often publicly eschewed aid to fugitives but found other methods of helping. The Michigan Anti-Slavery Society expressed its support for fugitives by denouncing the 1850 Fugitive Slave Law, boldly proclaiming, "We will allow no fugitive slave law nor any law in support of slavery to be executed within the State jurisdiction of Michigan."[34] This kind of public excoriation of the inhumane laws that upheld slavery, they believed, constituted appropriate activity for an antislavery organization. Private support for fugitives was the responsibility of individual abolitionists. So when, in October 1854, one of their local agents gave three dollars from the organization's coffers "for the benefit of a fugitive family on their way to Canada," the society's executive committee expressed its disapproval.[35] Yet that same month, Garrisonian lecturers Josephine and Charles Griffing, who were closely linked to the Michigan group, visited Canadian fugitive settlements.[36] Knowing that many western female antislavery societies organized exclusively to support Canadian settlements, Josephine Griffing credited abolitionist aid for helping to create a "comfortable and prosperous" escapee community in Canada.[37] The Griffings directed abolitionists to send financial support to the more Garrisonian-minded Refugee Home Society.[38]

The Griffings and many other Garrisonians found ways to support fugitives in coordination with all brands of abolitionists. At a memorial gathering to honor John B. Mahan, a leader of the Underground Railroad, Salem abolitionists declared, "Whether we are *Liberty men*, *come-outers* or *stay-inners* we will not aid the *slave claimant* to recover the fugitive slave, but we pledge ourselves to assist him in his flight, or protect him while among us."[39] While this diverse group managed to find consensus regarding the importance of aiding escapees, members could not agree on other key issues. According to the minutes of the meeting, seven other resolutions, among them a condemnation of all political parties and a denunciation of proslavery churches, were "offered but not passed." Aid to fugitive slaves brought abolitionists together but could not eliminate all their differences.

Interracial Networks

Working in support of escaped slaves not only bridged the gap between differing abolitionist groups but facilitated the development of interracial networks.[40] Women in particular proved willing and eager to transcend racial boundaries in support of fugitive aid. White abolitionists quickly learned that local free and fugitive blacks were knowledgeable and daring advocates of the Underground Railroad.[41] African Americans in Cincinnati and Cleveland as well as in small rural enclaves such as Pokepatch, Ohio, and Lick Creek, Indiana, were well prepared to aid escapees in their effort to remain free.[42] In the summer of 1833, a fugitive couple in Detroit, Ruthy and Thornton Blackburn, were legally apprehended and imprisoned before being returned to their Kentucky owner. The local African American community, particularly women, immediately initiated a clever plan to rescue the Blackburns, who had resided in Detroit for more than two years. Two of Ruthy's friends visited her in jail; one exchanged clothes with the prisoner, allowing her to walk out a free woman. While Ruthy immediately crossed into Canada, her rescuer languished in jail until her husband found a sympathetic judge who "secured a writ of *habeas corpus*" and forced the authorities to release her. Soon thereafter, a large crowd of blacks distracted the sheriff, enabling Thornton to secure a gun and attempt to escape. While the sheriff tried to hold off the crowd, an "old colored woman named 'Sleepy Polly'" guided the shackled prisoner to a cart and quickly drove away.[43] These rescues resulted in mass arrests of local blacks, the declaration of martial law, and the arrival of a detachment of federal troops in the city.[44] The mayor ordered all blacks who could not post a five-hundred-dollar bond to leave Detroit, and most fled to Canada, depriving the city of "all but the most entrenched of its black citizenry."[45] The Blackburns moved to Toronto and eventually gained financial success through a thriving cab company.[46]

The Blackburn Rescue was planned and implemented by local African Americans, but whites also participated.[47] Many white women abolitionists began working both formally and informally with African Americans to aid fugitives across the Old Northwest. This interracial network resulted in a flexible and effective method for helping slaves to escape.[48] Laura Smith Haviland, a white Michigan abolitionist who honed her activist skills working with young Elizabeth Chandler during the 1830s, interacted closely with the black community that lived near Adrian. Haviland and her husband, Charles, who died in 1845, owned a farm, where they employed escapees and free blacks; the Havilands also leased blacks land and invited them to attend the couple's interracial school, the Raisin Institute.[49] In many instances, Haviland cooperated with her African American neighbors and friends to house and hide fugitives as well as to ensure their long-term safety.[50] Other Michigan abolitionist women also participated in a lively interracial community focused on helping escaped slaves during the 1840s and 1850s. When Henry Bibb, a celebrated fugitive, began lecturing for the Liberty Party in Michigan in the mid-1840s, women organized to raise funds to support his tour. The abolitionist movement embraced eloquent fugitives as lecturing agents throughout the antebellum years, and Bibb was a particularly popular and effective public speaker.[51] Encouraged by the Michigan Liberty Party newspaper, *Signal of Liberty*, women organized "ladies benevolent and antislavery societies" solely for the purpose of financing Bibb's lecturing tour and the publication of his memoir.[52] Women found Bibb's heartrending life story compelling in part because after his initial escape, he returned south several times in failed attempts to rescue his family and was recaptured twice before making his final getaway.[53] The tragic breakup of slave families had long been a special concern for women abolitionists, who hoped that Bibb's distressing history would convert more women to the movement. The *Signal of Liberty* happily reported that ladies benevolent and antislavery societies emerged in a variety of locales, including Lenawee, Cass, Highland, Salem, Washtenaw, Dundee, Franklin, Van Buren, and Jackson.[54]

As Michigan women gathered in homes and churches to raise funds for Bibb, other women across the Old Northwest interacted more intimately with escapees. White women abolitionists found that contact with slave men, women, and children was a transformative experience. Housing, feeding, and communicating with those who had experienced chattel slavery awakened women to the real-life horror of the institution. Michigan resident Pamela Thomas attributed her conversion to abolitionism to an elderly fugitive woman who had "made her way [north] on foot and alone from Missouri" to Michigan. Thomas portrayed her houseguest as "an eloquent talker" who vividly described what female slaves "had to endure from cruel,

Laura Smith Haviland with slave irons, n.d. Laura Smith Haviland Collection, Box 1, Photographs Folder, File HS 1511, Bentley Historical Library, University of Michigan, Ann Arbor.

licentious masters." This interaction convinced Thomas that she had a "duty" to make every effort to aid "those attempting to escape from bondage."[55] Western Reserve activist Lovina Bissell, whose home served as a comfortable and safe stop for fugitives, described the stay of "a female slave with a little son eleven months old." Bissell was impressed with the intelligence and skillfulness of her guest despite the machinations of the woman's master to prevent her from learning. Bissell also noted that the young woman was in search of her husband, "who passed through here last fall," though she had resigned herself to the fact that he might have married again. Intensely affected by this resilient mother, Bissell concluded, "There must be untiring self-denying labor" in support of such freedom seekers.[56] Bissell's friend, Betsey Mix Cowles, who worked closely with free and fugitive blacks throughout her career as a reformer and educator, was so stirred by a free black woman's story of being kidnapped and sold into slavery that she spent a day traipsing through mud to "purchase materials for a cloak" for the woman. Cowles noted with no little measure of sympathy and passion that this fearless woman was now "so full of fight that she could kill the whole nation."[57]

Many other African American women appealed directly to abolitionists such as Cowles for funds and support, sharing stories of dangerous and dramatic escapes. Mrs. Wiltslow, a fugitive mother, attended the 1844 meeting of the Illinois Female Anti-Slavery Society in Peoria to request financial aid to purchase her daughter, who remained enslaved in Louisiana. Wiltslow undoubtedly hoped to find compassion among the women abolitionists, many of whom attended the meeting with their daughters, sisters, and mothers. She was not disappointed. After collecting funds to help reunite this slave family, the conventioneers unanimously resolved, "We deeply sympathize with our colored sisters in bonds, as bound with them, and . . . we pledge ourselves, mutually and severally, to use every means in our power for their emancipation and elevation."[58]

White women abolitionists found that interaction with escapees not only motivated action but also challenged ideas about race. Mary Davis grew up in a slaveholding household, but her interaction with free blacks and escapees passing through Peoria reminded her to applaud their achievements. Local incidents of racial oppression or stories of bold escapees became opportunities to highlight the intelligence and ingenuity of African Americans. She initiated a series of articles celebrating the heroics of escaping slaves for the *Western Citizen* in the mid-1840s.[59] In 1845, for example, Davis described how one brilliant fugitive outwitted the slave catchers who had apprehended him near Springfield, Illinois. After fooling his captors into thinking he was wholly passive and submissive, he was momentarily left alone and "availed himself of the opportunity to escape." After running for several miles, he broke off his front teeth while removing his handcuffs. He then met up with several other fugitives, and together they made their way to "a sweet, sequestered" cottage near Peoria that "has often been shelter to the care-worn liberty-seeking pilgrim."[60] Davis understood the importance of publicizing the accomplishments of escaped slaves as a means of breaking down racial stereotypes.

Working with and in support of African Americans did not always result in conquering racial stereotypes. Many white women abolitionists remained patronizing and paternalistic toward escaping slaves. Anne Thomas of New Garden, Ohio, emphasized passivity in escapees when she explained to abolitionist Nathan Thomas of Michigan that "Coloured People were Conveyed from one place to another by the Abolitionists." She also highlighted the traitorous behavior of a black man in the area who was spying for slave catchers, referring to him as a "notorious villain" and concluding, "If execution was justifiable or requisite it was in his case though his degraded Ignorance Called loudly for Simpathy [sic]."[61] Passivity, unreliability, and "degraded Ignorance" represented very common racial stereotypes. Haviland represented herself as a heroic savior for naive and childlike slaves.[62] The Salem Rescue group that dashed onto the train to "save" the young slave girl disregarded any familial ties that might complicate her situation. Their decision to rename her further revealed their assumptions about her passive position as a victim.[63]

The Work of the Underground Railroad

Haviland, Anne Thomas, and many other western women abolitionists imbibed racial stereotypes but also labored tirelessly in support of escapees.[64] Exhausting domestic responsibilities defined most western women's lives, forcing them to become skilled in a variety of different arenas. These skills proved valuable for their work on the Underground Railroad. Pamela Thomas described a typical encounter with fugitives during her decades-long work with freedom seekers: "They soon began to arrive in loads of from six to twelve. This brought much hard work to me and great expense to my husband. Often after my little ones were asleep [and] I thought the labor of the day over, friend [Zachariah] Shugart would drive up with a load of hungry people to be fed and housed for the night."[65] Cincinnati abolitionist Levi Coffin boasted, "It was never too cold or stormy, or the hour of night too late for my wife to rise from sleep, and provide food and comfortable lodging for the fugitives. Her sympathy for those in distress never tired, and her efforts in their behalf never abated."[66] Although Coffin offered his wife this small token of acknowledgment, he rarely emphasized women's participation in the more than seven hundred pages of his *Reminiscences* of the Underground Railroad. Because women's work was considered natural and mundane, it did not receive the same accolades that men's more public and presumably risky work did. As escapees must have recognized, however, the domestic labor of women was critical to their survival. Pamela Thomas recalled one incident in 1847 in which slave hunters were hot on the trail of a large group of escapees. A courier sent a message asking her quickly to prepare food. "I hastened to prepare what I could and asked a loan from a kind neighbor, who often so accommodated me. They soon arrived, took the provisions without alighting, and passed in safety to Canada."[67] Because some leading male abolitionists had obstructed authorities' efforts to recover these slaves, the men's actions became the headline news, while the behind-the-scenes labor of the women was ignored.[68]

Thomas and other women who labored on the Underground Railroad sometimes allowed their frustration with this lack of appreciation to simmer to the surface. One Saturday evening, Shugart showed up at the Thomas home with yet another "lumber wagon filled with colored people." Despite the fact that she was already hosting three clergymen, Pamela Thomas immediately fed the hungry group and made them comfortable for the night. When her husband left to arrange "a man and team" to take the fugitives to their next stop the following morning, she found herself criticized by the youngest visiting minister. He "turned a censorious glance" toward her because she dared to send the fugitives away on the Sabbath: "'It does seem,' he explained, 'when the Lord has protected them thus far on their road to freedom, that they ought to be allowed to rest on the Sabbath day.'" Frustrated at the man's arrogance and ignorance, Thomas highlighted her unappreciated labor. "'Sir,' I said, 'how would my Sabbath be passed if I had all these colored folks to cook for?'" She concluded, "Long before the clergyman had risen the next morning, the fugitives had eaten their breakfast and were on their way."[69] Of course, she had provided the escapees with their sustenance. Simply ignored as part of the natural terrain of women's everyday activity, women's contribution to sustaining fugitives has been written out of the literature.

Bissell understood Thomas's frustration and recognized that housing fugitives required a willingness to accept very different, sometimes frightened and reticent people into one's home. "To receive them and their children into our families for any length of time would need a much greater amount of sympathy than to attend an Anti-Slavery prayer meeting once a month or give to them of our substance," she thoughtfully noted. "I am more and more convinced that the giving of our names and pronouncing the wordage a few times will never effect much. There must be untiring self-denying labor."[70] Emphasizing the importance of action and sacrifice, Bissell saw her work on the Underground Railroad as more effective than speeches or pamphlets. In direct opposition to the Garrisonians, Bissell came to believe that whatever she might do to personally to aid a single escaping slave had significant meaning for her, for the slave, and for the abolition movement overall.

Haviland enthusiastically concurred with Bissell's call for "untiring self-denying labor," opening a Canadian school for refugees geared toward providing blacks with education and skills.[71] This educational labor remained relatively unappreciated by the public. Garrisonian Charles Griffing, who visited Haviland's classroom in 1854, extolled the Michigan activist—"She has made more sacrifices than most whose names are honored for their devotion to liberty"—but recognized the invisibility of her work: "The world knows her not; but the blessings of many a fugitive slave rest upon her and the God of the oppressed knows her as one who loves his suffering poor."[72]

Female Antislavery Societies and Freedom Seekers

While Haviland tended to operate on her own, supremely confident that she knew best, female antislavery societies across the Northwest focused their collective attention on aid to fugitives. Beginning in the 1840s and continuing through the 1850s, women's abolitionist groups in Ohio, Indiana, Illinois, and Michigan officially embraced the illegal work of the Underground Railroad.[73] They passed resolutions, initiated funding efforts, applauded rescues, and boldly declared their intention to disobey unrighteous laws. While some individual women abolitionists in the East aided escaping slaves, evidence suggests that eastern female antislavery societies generally did not participate at the organizational level.[74] The Northwest afforded increased opportunity for female involvement because its Underground Railroad was more active. The more rural and isolated location of many northwestern towns created space for women's participation. Their wide range of experiences, from farming to building homes, supplied them with the skills and confidence to participate more widely and boldly.[75] Moreover, the region's Black Laws created a hostile and dangerous environment and encouraged black and white women abolitionists to confront racism in whatever way they could, including aid to fugitives.

Many western female antislavery societies passed resolutions that called on abolitionists to aid escapees and resist slave catchers.[76] Some groups adopted subtle approaches, hoping to avoid direct confrontation with local authorities yet still express support for the Underground Railroad. Indiana's Union County Female Anti-Slavery Society resolved in 1842, "When we obey the promptings of humanity and tender pity, by endeavouring to relieve the oppressed, we are acting the part intended by our beneficent Creator when he gave us hearts to feel for the sufferings of our species."[77] A year later, group members remained opaque: "It is the duty of every christian to plead for the poor and oppressed, to help the needy, to clothe the naked, feed the hungry, visit the sick, & receive the stranger."[78] These references to clothing, feeding, and receiving "the stranger" certainly included aiding fugitive slaves seeking safety and shelter.

While their Union County sisters carefully whispered their support for the Underground Railroad, the Henry County women adopted a more slap-dash and thunderous approach. Empowered and encouraged by the county's large contingent of abolitionist Quakers and Methodists, these women con-sistently passed resolution after resolution, year after year, celebrating slave rescues and escapes.[79] They consciously connected their support for fugitives with the goal of eliminating racism and racist laws in their region. As the women stated at their 1841 organizational meeting, "We deeply deplore . . . prejudice against the colored race in our own section of the country," espe-cially "the various legislative enactments [that] have a direct tendency to in-crease and strengthen that prejudice thereby rendering the fetters of slavery more firm and secure."[80] One method of challenging these racist laws was willingly and knowingly to aid fugitives. "It is our duty to assist the way-worn traveler on his journey from the land of oppression to a land of liberty," they asserted in the spring of 1843.[81] By December, the group members were ready to make their command more specific: "We should feed, clothe, pro-tect and assist the flying fugitive from slavery to a land of liberty."[82] Later that month, the Henry County women became more aggressive in their injunction to their fellow Indianans. Speaking directly to the men of their state, they declared, "Behold yon poor lacerated and houseless sister as she is flying from the blood hounds of her brutal pursuers, and calling on you to give her shelter from her tyrant master, behold her, unprotected, and suf-fering as she is, and then turn your eyes on the pages of your law books and read there to your shame the penalty annexed to the act, which the promptings of humanity urge you to do, and which the wild untutored savage of the wilderness would scorn to leave undone." The women concluded with a question: "Dare you turn away from the famishing strangers, and tell them that the laws of your state forbid your administering to their wants?"[83] Constructing adherence to the law as a shameful and feeble response, the women hoped to connect Christian manhood to protecting innocent and vulnerable slave women and children. The juxtaposition of law and morality mirrors the 1850s "higher law" debate about the constitutionality of slavery. For many people, especially women, even the highest law of the land—the Constitution—must come second to the law of God. This idea also predates the compelling scene in Harriet Beecher Stowe's *Uncle Tom's Cabin* in which a northern antislavery-leaning state legislator who has just voted for a restrictive fugitive slave law cannot help but break this law when a fugitive slave mother and child show up at his door.[84]

Other female antislavery societies openly supported aid to fugitives. Wayne County's women abolitionists declared in their 1843 annual report, "During the past year our feelings have been engaged in relation to the situation of those fleeing from the land of bondage [and we] have done somewhat towards providing and placing clothing for them, where it may be available." They called on other women to support the Underground Railroad: "We would earnestly call the attention of our sisters to the important duty of relieving their tried and gloomy passage through our state, in every way we can."[85] The April 1843 constitution of Illinois's Putnam County Female Anti-Slavery Society audaciously declared the group's intention to "befriend the outcast who flies from oppression," a vow that was repeated in virtually every report or address the society published.[86] In September 1843, the Putnam County women announced, "Regardless of the consequences to ourselves we will lose no opportunity of assisting, supporting, and encouraging the 'star-led' pilgrim in his struggle after freedom."[87] At the group's next meeting, attendees devised a plan "for the establishment of a depository, where the star-led pilgrim, in case of need, may replenish his scanty wardrobe."[88] The Putnam women were led by Lydia S. Lewis, whose willingness to house and clothe escapees probably influenced other women in the group to embrace the Underground Railroad as a formal policy. The enthusiasm of a single woman often could influence a group.[89]

While individual leaders such as Lewis inspired female antislavery societies to endorse the Underground Railroad, local issues and incidents also had a tremendous impact on these groups. Lewis and her sister activists often alluded to specific episodes as motivating their public support for the Underground Railroad. When several Illinois abolitionists were temporarily incarcerated for violating the state's Black Laws, the outraged Putnam Female Anti-Slavery Society declared, "Should our husbands or brothers in the same way be prevented from acting their part in relieving the poor fugitive we pledge ourselves to do all in our power to *keep the cars running*."[90] Local rescues motivated other groups to pass resolutions in support of the Underground Railroad. The Henry County women applauded local abolitionist "friends" who helped a fugitive who was "torn from his quiet home" by slave catchers. This middle-aged man had finally found "peace and plenty" and was "rejoicing in the labor of his own hands" when his world was violently disrupted. Thanks to the efforts of those "friends," however, the "cruel task master" was thwarted in his goal of capturing the man as well as his wife and children and returning them to "the doleful prison house of slavery."[91] Only a few months after passing a vague resolution in support of the Underground Railroad, the Union County Female Anti-Slavery Society openly pronounced the freeing of captured fugitive George Latimer in Boston "a cheering indication of the blessed results of anti-slavery action."[92] Though black Bostonians had failed in their attempt to rescue Latimer after his October 1842 arrest, extensive protests and petitions eventually led to the purchasing of his freedom.[93] The Female Anti-Slavery Society of Princeton, in Bureau County, Illinois, declared at its organizing meeting that the recent failed prosecution of local abolitionist Owen Lovejoy for his Underground Railroad work was a "cause of rejoicing"; the society went on to declare aiding escapees as the group's primary objective.[94] In May 1843, Lovejoy had been indicted by the Bureau County Court for harboring slaves, but his attorney persuaded a jury that the two slaves Lovejoy aided had been voluntarily brought into Illinois by their owner and therefore were legally free.[95]

Many northwestern female antislavery groups did more for escaping slaves than simply pass resolutions. These organizations began to produce clothing for local escapees and those who relocated to Canada. Peoria activist Irene Ball Allan advised the Illinois Female Anti-Slavery Society in 1844 to "assist in furnishing 'ready made clothing for those travelers of the night-line'" and occasionally to send a box of clothes "for the fugitives in Canada, and the self-denying missionaries who are laboring with them."[96] Sewing not only fell clearly within the purview of women's domestic activity but also resulted in a product that could make a significant difference in the lives of former slaves who had little access to employment, funds, and quality clothing.

"Often the slaves were shoeless and almost naked," explained one early anti-slavery historian in his praise for the sewing society of Newport, Indiana.[97] In other words, sewing allowed Rebecca Wickersham, Sarah Edgerton, and the other members of the Henry County Female Anti-Slavery Society to feel meaningfully connected to the work of the Underground Railroad. Even though they rarely interacted with escapees, "spinning and weaving" for African Americans offered a sense of accomplishment and sacrifice.[98]

These groups were industrious. A few months after the Henry County women began to make clothing for escapees, they noted the results of their efforts: 127 yards of fabric, and many individual garments—vests, coats, shirts, dresses, and socks. The fabric and garments were sent to Salem and Westfield, heavily trafficked stops on the Underground Railroad. The Henry County women saw "minister[ing] to the wants of these outcasts from common society" as their "imperious duty."[99] Constructing their labor as necessary and generous, they made it clear that sewing for the slave was a womanly activity. Ohio's Orwell Female Anti-Slavery Society produced "various articles of clothing" for the relief of "the down-trodden & oppressed" and proclaimed that "happy hours" spent sewing were "a cause in which every female should feel proud of having the privilege of contributing."[100] A male columnist for the *Western Citizen* extolled the Female Anti-Slavery Dorcas Society of Jerseyville in southern Illinois for their four-year history of monthly meetings to "ply the thimble and knitting needle." Devoted to "assisting those persons in Canada who have escaped hither from the land of Republican oppression and tyranny," these women accumulated nearly two hundred dollars worth of "goods and money" for former slaves. Clearly very pleased with this appropriately feminine method of abolitionist activism, the columnist concluded by insisting that all "females, like Dorcas of old, are 'full of good works and alms-deeds'" and wondered why women's anti-slavery societies in northern Illinois failed to follow the lead of the "zealously engaged" Jerseyville women.[101] When Allan visited Jerseyville, she too emphasized the productivity of the women abolitionists: "I have been much gratified since I have been here, to find *active* anti-slavery women—practical abolitionists—women who are *attempting* something for the cause." She noted that the seamstresses made garments both for fugitives in Canada and "for the passengers of the abolition 'night line,' which runs through this place towards Canada."[102] Even some southern women who lived close to border towns chose to participate in this feminine form of antislavery. In 1857, Kentucky's *Newport News* happily reported that several local women had crossed the river to join a meeting of the Cincinnati Anti-Slavery Sewing Circle "in preparing clothing for the fugitive slaves." Describing these women as "pure and noble" and the "embodiment of humanity," the editor proclaimed that such an "organization of ladies" deserved the "respect and adoration of all the nations of the earth."[103]

Ernst, the Garrisonian leader of the Cincinnati Anti-Slavery Sewing Circle, did not consider Underground Railroad work the appropriate focus for antislavery organizations but recognized its appeal to local women abolitionists.[104] Both "Aunt Katy" Coffin, Levi Coffin's wife, and Ernst opened their large, comfortable, well-furnished homes to the Cincinnati sewing circle, and at least a dozen determined women attended each week.[105] Chatting about local politics and the latest abolitionist news, the women eagerly consumed the delicacies provided by their hostesses and plied their needles. Because Cincinnati served as a gateway to freedom for many escaping slaves, the women knew that their labor was important. As Ernst told a Boston friend, "We make up coarse clothes for fugitives who pass through here in large numbers and use all, and more than we can furnish."[106] Levi Coffin believed that the members of the sewing circle "wrought much practical good by their labors."[107] Cincinnati abolitionists praised the antislavery seamstresses, while one columnist for the *Philanthropist* even chastised less active women for failing to contribute to the sewing group's efforts. Pointing to the "strength of *Woman's energy*," this critic wondered why only a dozen abolitionists participated when there should be "forty or fifty" at least. "Will you not come and meet with us, with warm hearts and ready hands, to do what we can to put down this great sin?," she asked.[108] In the group's 1852 annual report, Ernst announced that "one hundred and forty two new garments have been distributed." Like the *Philanthropist* columnist, Ernst called for more support: "It seems strange to me, when I look round and see so much energy and benevolent effort in exercise, that so little is devoted to" fugitives.[109]

During her tenure as leader of the sewing circle, the astute Ernst portrayed the group's purpose and activity as domestic as well as religious, hoping to construct the Underground Railroad as wholly appropriate for women. She compared Cincinnati's popular charity organizations with the more consecrated and important sewing societies that aided escapees. Referring to fugitives as "God's poor," she decried Cincinnati women's tendency to give "their money and time, their energy and intellect" to benevolent causes and "sectarian organizations" instead of to the sewing circle. This misappropriation of labor left nothing for the "languishing cause of the perishing slave."[110] Many other abolitionists linked religion with female antislavery societies' work in support of the Underground Railroad. Edgerton and her Henry County sisters declared in December 1845, "The injunction of our Savior 'to do unto others as we would that they should to unto us,' requires that we should feed, clothe, protect, and assist the flying fugitive from Southern slavery."[111] A few years later, these Indiana women asserted, "It is in perfect accordance with religion professed by people generally" to assist "the houseless stranger" in "obtaining liberty."[112] Group members even resolved to instruct the "representatives of Congress and the State Legislature" to repeal all laws that conflicted with "the following statute given to the Israelites, namely: 'Thou shalt not return to his master the servant that has escaped from his master to thee. He shall dwell with thee even among you in that place which he shall choose, even one of thy gates where it liketh him best.'"[113] The Putnam Female Anti-Slavery Society's constitution asserted, "As the disciples of Jesus took their believed brother Paul by night and let him down by the wall in a basket . . . so will we, openly or by stratagem, use every imminent means to secure the fugitive slave from the hand of his pursuer."[114] In declaring their intention to violate the law, these women prioritized their adherence to Christianity over their respect for man-made laws, a common tactic among abolitionists.[115] The Putnam women also pointed out the religious rewards that would accrue to women who followed their lead: "First we receive the blessings of heaven, the reward of a good conscience for fulfilling the Divine law by taking in and cherishing the stranger. . . . [T]hen we are paid double in the relief of sympathetic suffering in ourselves; and lastly, in our leisure moments we have the exalted reflection that we have performed these offices to Jesus Christ himself."[116]

While both the Putnam and Henry County women linked their Underground Railroad work to Christian benevolence, they also understood that it was deeply political. They depicted their labor as inherently democratic, a true manifestation of the Declaration of Independence. They also vocally opposed all laws that curtailed northerners' ability to aid escaping slaves. Maria Coffin, Phebe Willits, and Susannah Gordon proposed a resolution at a meeting of the Henry County Female Anti-Slavery Society declaring that both Christian benevolence and the "republican form of government" required their organization—and all other compassionate patriotic Americans—to "shelter the houseless stranger and assist him in obtaining liberty, the dearest of all rights." Doing so represented "no violation either of the fundamental principals of our government or the precepts of the Gospel."[117]

Gender, Rescues, and Violence

Other women, both as individuals and in groups, engaged in more untradi-tional kinds of behaviors in their determination to aid escaping slaves. These transgressive actions ranged from participating in violent rescues to slipping into border states with the intention of initiating escapes. Such efforts often built bonds between black and white abolitionists. As early as 1836, women participated in the rescue of two African American females from a Boston courtroom. The two women had been arrested onboard a ship on suspicion of being fugitives. In court, however, the judge determined they had been illegally held and granted them their freedom. As a representative for a slave catcher attempted to arrest the women again, the mixed-sex, mixed-race crowd forcibly grabbed the women and spirited them away.[118] While news-papers denounced the mob, intense outrage was directed toward the "inde-cent conduct" of the women in the crowd. One newspaper editor "urged the husbands of the culprits to chastise them properly."[119] While such incidents were fairly uncommon in the 1830s, more and more confrontations between abolitionists and authorities occurred after the passage of the 1850 Fugitive Slave Law.[120] These moments of conflict occurred throughout the North, but the Old Northwest was the site of countless small bursts of tension that often involved African American and white women.

Most of the encounters between slave catchers, escapees, and their abet-tors in the West occurred quietly and with little media attention. However, the number of people involved or the drama of the confrontation occasion-ally brought nationwide attention. But for each of these well-publicized rescues, dozens of unpublicized fierce and frightening encounters occurred across the Old Northwest. While women's participation in these incidents was often ignored or downplayed, women were unquestionably present and involved. Teasing out the intensity and nature of women's roles certainly poses a challenge, as extant evidence at best only vaguely mentions women. Either by design or by default, black and white women occasionally found themselves in confrontational situations involving escapees. These incidents frequently occurred in small, rural, frontier communities where the actions of a single person might have a significant impact on the success or failure of a slave escape.

In several volatile episodes involving slave catchers, the daughters of Un-derground Railroad operators saved the day through their physical prowess, courage, and ingenuity. These young women had witnessed the late-night ar-rivals of malnourished but determined escapees and understood the danger involved in hiding them. Youth and sex often allowed these women to engage in helpful activities under the radar of watchful authorities. Many of these young women considered their parents models of Christian and republican stewardship and attempted to follow in their footsteps. In Medina County, Ohio, a girl named Julia secretly guided several slaves out of her home to a nearby swamp while her father distracted the U.S. marshals who had arrived at the door.[121] In rural Champaign County, Ohio, another bold girl, Amanda Hyde, risked her life to help Addison White, a fugitive from Kentucky who lived and worked with her father, Underground Railroad operator Udney H. Hyde. When White's letters to his still-enslaved wife found their way into the hands of his old master, a slave catcher turned up on Hyde's doorstep with U.S. marshals and demanded that White return to Kentucky with them. While White held off the authorities with a firearm, Hyde, who was bedridden with a broken ankle, had fourteen-year-old Amanda run to her brother's house to get help. "As the young girl was passing out of the gate, the marshals divining her mission, called to her to come back, one threatening to put shackles on her and another to shoot her if she did not do so. She did not obey." Amanda, who was "swift of foot" and who felt "responsible for the delivery of the message . . . outran her pursuer, reached her brother's house, roused him from his morning slumbers, and stated her mission."[122]

While some white females encountered intimidating slave catchers, free black women risked much more in aiding fugitives. The Fugitive Slave Law of 1850, which deprived accused fugitives of the right to testify in their own defense, caused free African Americans to fear kidnapping and forced enslavement.[123] Many followed Bibb's advice and immigrated to Canada.[124] One historian estimates that more than two thousand free blacks escaped to Canada within a few weeks of the law's passage.[125] African Americans living in border cities such as Cincinnati felt particularly vulnerable, with slave catchers often prowling the streets in search of escapees. Despite the combined efforts of Cincinnati's white and black abolitionist community, many incidents took place in which African Americans were kidnapped there.[126]

With tensions high and free blacks extremely vigilant, women often found themselves defending and protecting fugitives. Indiana's Milly Wilkerson used a corn knife to hold off several men looking for her fugitive granddaughters. "Described as 'large and stout,' and 'able to handle an axe or rifle equal to any man,'" Wilkerson stood her ground against the southerners as her granddaughters escaped.[127] On another occasion, an elderly African American woman forced some slave catchers "into a corn crib by threatening them with a knife, thus allowing two fugitives to flee."[128]

Few women abolitionists, whether white or African American, risked more than did Haviland. Her widespread and diverse activism on the Underground Railroad earned her the right to boast that the State of Kentucky offered a three-thousand-dollar reward for her capture. She often traveled across the Old Northwest to help fugitives on their way north and made several daring trips into the South to garner information, deliver messages, or aid in escapes. Many of the episodes she described in her autobiography involved threats of violence, but Haviland always managed to escape unharmed, usually as a result of her willingness to stand up to slaveholders, whom she depicted as bullies. In 1846, for example, two of Haviland's Michigan neighbors, Elsie and Willis Hamilton, came to her for advice and help. Willis had been a slave but was legally freed by a repentant owner. Elsie was a fugitive. Although they had lived in Michigan for several years, they constantly feared that Elsie's owners would find her. They consequently were suspicious when they received a letter purporting to be from Willis's former owner offering information about their two children, who remained enslaved. The writer asked the Hamiltons to meet him in Toledo, Ohio. Curious but also dubious, the Hamiltons asked Haviland for advice. Haviland shared their suspicions and offered to go to Toledo with a friend who resembled Willis Hamilton to find out if the letter was a trap designed to recapture Elsie. Haviland and her friend quickly confirmed their fears; for their part, the slave catchers recognized Haviland as an abolitionist and threatened her with revolvers as she attempted to return to Michigan. According to Haviland's account, she calmly responded, "I fear neither your weapons nor your threats; they are powerless. . . . You are not in Tennessee." She and her accomplice returned home safely and encouraged the Hamiltons to seek refuge in Canada. Haviland also noted with some satisfaction that both slave catchers died soon after the encounter—one was shot by a free black man, while the other contracted a fatal—and extremely painful—disease.[129]

Conclusion

Western women's labor in support of freedom seekers was both critical and undervalued. Late nights of cooking, cleaning, organizing, and sewing were common for many western women, whether in support of escaping slaves or for their own families. This labor was key to the success of the Underground Railroad. Ironically, women's less traditional activities in support of fugitives were also invisible because they contradicted stereotypes about female passivity and timidity. Laura Smith Haviland forced the public to recognize her role when she published her autobiography. Without this effort at memorializing her activity, she would probably now be long forgotten.

Women abolitionists nonetheless developed a variety of methods for aiding fugitives. Many of these women worked in interracial groups and cooperated with all stripes of abolitionists. Aiding fugitives infused their abolitionism with a sense of meaningfulness that other methods lacked. While Maria Weston Chapman and other eastern Garrisonians chastised their western sisters for wasting time and energy on the futile task of aiding escapees, western women understood their work with fugitives as deeply fulfilling and sometimes life changing.

When western women crossed gender boundaries in their Underground Railroad efforts, they often garnered public chastisement for violating the rules of womanhood. While such scolding usually failed to change these women's behavior, it did occasionally lead some women to question the logic of the rules themselves. Abolitionism politicized and complicated many western activists' understanding of the world and led them directly into the woman's rights movement.

CHAPTER 7

Woman's Rights and Abolition in the West

Eliza T. Frantz wrote to the *Anti-Slavery Bugle* in March 1856 to update readers on the reform environment in her small northern Indiana town, Warsaw, which she characterized as "dark and benighted." She confessed that she had spent much of her two years there "sunk in hopeless despair thinking, that no good could come out of Sodom." Her spirits lifted, however, when she initiated a "series of debates on Woman's rights" that resulted in "quite a victory." She, "two sisters," and "a young Baptist who dared to declare the rights of woman" organized several meetings that attracted large, enthusiastic audiences. "We have been listened to with deep interest, astonishment, and wonder," she boasted, "more perhaps of the latter than the former because the personal appearance of a woman in public is unusual in this place." Their opponents consisted of several local men, "some of them professors and Divines as they term themselves," who "insisted that Mother Eve's fall, was sufficient to seal our damnation." At the end of the debates, a panel of neutral judges decided unanimously in favor of the women. Although Frantz was encouraged by this small step for woman's rights, she concluded with a complaint about the town's moribund abolition movement, requesting that "workmen in the field of reform" visit Indiana to confront the state's appalling Black Laws: "Indiana has the blackest and most inhuman laws that disgrace any of the Statutes of the pretended free States of the North!"[1]

Historians have long since documented the close relationship between antislavery and woman's rights that Frantz's letter illuminates.[2] Relying an on inclusive human rights philosophy and a network of experienced reformers, abolitionists of all stripes advocated on behalf of woman's rights. Some antislavery supporters favored equal educational opportunities for their daughters, others desired access to male-dominated professions, and still others called for women's right to their own property and earnings. Some demanded suffrage. Though these reformers did not always agree on goals or tactics, their basic belief in equality held them together. In the 1840s, abolitionists supported equal rights primarily through example. Mary Davis, Sarah Otis Ernst, Lizzie Hitchcock, and countless other abolitionists engaged in activities that most people considered to be reserved for men, including political partisanship, community organizing, and public speaking. By their public presence, leadership, articulateness, and intelligence, these women defied common stereotypes about womanhood. Criticized for both their abolitionism and their intrusion into the masculine arena, many began to question the logic and fairness of the prescriptions of their gender. Some, like the Grimké sisters, began to speak out against the limiting boundaries of womanhood. By the late 1840s, on the heels of the first woman's rights convention in Seneca Falls, New York, antislavery and woman's rights converged. For many, woman's rights seemed to be a natural extension of the fight for emancipation.

When turning to woman's rights, western abolitionists continued to employ the cooperative tactics that served them so well in antislavery. They recognized that many of their neighbors were cautious about if not openly opposed to woman's rights. The fact that a panel of local men in Frantz's small town favored woman's rights suggests that the movement worked to appeal to a broad cross-section of the public. Moreover, western reformers tended to emphasize the practicality of woman's rights, focusing on issues such as education and dress reform that could be linked to pragmatic improvement in family and community life. Supporters of woman's rights also worked hard to appeal to men as well as women, pointing to the movement's benefits for everyone.

"The Meeting Struck by Its Novelty"

Although western abolitionists knew about the 1848 Seneca Falls woman's rights convention, a last-minute local meeting in the spring of 1850 sparked an organized woman's rights movement in the Old Northwest. With Ohio on the verge of amending its state constitution, a small cadre of abolitionists recognized the remarkable opportunity to make legal advances toward women's equality in the Buckeye State. Whenever a state chose to revise or replace its constitution, various advocacy groups had a chance to lobby for changes that would advance their goals.[3] When New York debated its constitution in 1846, supporters of racial equality vigorously lobbied state representatives for a law that would enfranchise blacks, and woman's rights supporters labored to persuade legislators to include a married women's property provision. A small group of women in Upstate New York even offered a petition demanding their right to vote.[4] This articulate petition preceded the Seneca Falls convention, suggesting that some women and men took seriously women's natural right to vote earlier than has been believed. The constitutional convention did not extend the vote to women or blacks but passed a married women's property act.[5]

When several hundred westerners met in Salem, Ohio, in 1850, they firmly believed in their ability to influence the Ohio constitution. They sought to "agitate" the subject, making representatives aware of key woman's rights issues and arguments.[6] Like the Seneca Falls convention, Salem was first advertised only a few weeks in advance. The gathering nonetheless attracted at least two hundred attendees.[7] Also like Seneca Falls, the Salem convention debated what role men would have at the gathering. While the Seneca Falls conventiongoers allowed men to sign the constitution and participate fully, Salem became the first and last antebellum woman's rights meeting to exclude men from holding office or speaking during the convention. Salem's abolitionist organizers prided themselves on this novel decision: "As the convention has been called distinctively as a *Women's* Convention, we hope it will be such in fact, and that no patronizing *male* orators will be called in to . . . in any way control its proceedings. Let it not be said of the Women of Ohio that, having called a convention, they were unable to carry it on, and were obliged to cry to the 'Lords' for help."[8] Men were encouraged to attend and listen, and organizers arranged for a meeting immediately following the convention "composed of both sexes, in which men can find abundant opportunities for display of their superior eloquence and wisdom."[9] A convention in which only women held office and spoke required both a strong contingent of self-confident, skilled women and a vibrant, generous crew of men willing to play supporting roles. It is no surprise that these conditions occurred in a western location where men and women worked cooperatively and women already played a leading role in the movement. In fact, the mixed-sex nature of western antislavery enabled the emergence of the policy against male speakers. Men worked intimately with their female colleagues, recognizing their abilities and supporting their leadership. These male abolitionists were invested in the success of woman's rights. They perceived women's increased access to basic legal and political rights as a victory for abolition as well. The empowerment of women would strengthen antislavery, giving it a larger and more influential base of support.

The decision to exclude men might also be seen as pragmatic. Beginning with the organization of separate female antislavery groups in the 1830s, women recognized that laboring apart from men would engender less criticism. To join a female sewing society or a free produce group seemed very familiar—like participating in more traditional women's charitable and reform groups. It did not easily lead to accusations of "promiscuous" mixed-race and mixed-sex gatherings. Although the Salem women constructed their decision to exclude men as a way to empower women, it may also have been a way to dampen opposition. Lizzie Hitchcock, Betsey Mix Cowles, and Josephine Griffing had the experience and acumen to recognize the impact of such a decision, which may have quietly become an unspoken secondary rationale for excluding men. Hitchcock's keynote speech emphasized that both men and women were responsible for woman's "wrongs" and that men had a role in the movement.

The Salem meeting also prided itself on the leadership of local women: "Its proceedings will do honor to the Women of Ohio," they boasted. "True we are not able to promise the attendance of any distinguished speakers from abroad, but we think that among the intelligent and earnest minds which will compose the Convention there will be many who will prove themselves fully capable of pleading the cause with credit to themselves and to their sex."[10] While the group read aloud letters from such eastern antislavery luminaries as Elizabeth Cady Stanton and Lucretia Mott, local women offered speeches, developed policy, debated resolutions, and simply absorbed the uplifting environment. As was the case in Seneca Falls, many attendees had grown up on farms and had learned their radicalism from their churches, family, and friends. All of the leading participants hailed from rural communities, including Salem, Marlborough, New Lisbon, Randolph, New Garden, and Litchfield. The convention's satisfaction in its Ohio roots speaks to the nature of western antislavery. Rejecting the notion of anti-slavery as an eastern import, westerners took pleasure in their homegrown reform movement.

Although a distinctly western affair, the two-day Salem meeting had significant regional and national influence. "The Women's Convention lately held in this place has excited a great deal of discussion upon the subject of Woman's Rights and Wrongs, in all parts of the country," bragged the *Bugle*. "In the City of Lowell, Mass., for example, we perceive that a voluntary association called 'The Senate,' and composed of some of the foremost citizens of the place . . . has taken the subject up for discussion."[11] After attending the Worcester woman's rights convention, held seven months after the Salem gathering, Parker Pillsbury proclaimed, that the proceedings there had "not awakened half the public interest and attention that [Salem] did some months since in Ohio. That meeting struck by its novelty. It jogged the wheels of society considerably. It seemed like an Insurrection among slaves. Every body was astonished at its audacity. That woman *had* rights, was something new and startling enough. That she should *demand* them, was monstrous indeed."[12] Worcester organizers advertised their gathering as the second national woman's rights convention, after Seneca Falls, but Salem set the stage. Well attended and bold, the Salem meeting addressed all of the key issues that woman's rights conventions would tackle for the next several decades and particularly those that would come to dominate western woman's rights meetings. Salem's participants immediately established that "all rights are *human* rights" and denounced all "distinctions between men and women" as "unjust" and "contrary to the laws of Nature." They called on women to "secure to themselves the elective franchise" to participate in developing the laws that affected them. They deplored the sexual double standard and unwarranted limitations on female employment and educational opportunities. They called on women to prove themselves, to reject an "idle, aimless life," to endure the "sneers of the public," and actively to enlarge women's "spheres of labor."[13]

Salem also attracted its share of ridicule and opposition. The *Saturday Evening Post* pointed out that even some woman's rights supporters considered the Salem convention full of "nonsensical extremes." Jane Swisshelm rejected the "ridiculous language" in one of the Salem resolutions that proclaimed "all distinctions based upon a difference of sex should be abolished." The *Post* accurately depicted Swisshelm's more moderate woman's rights position as envisioning men and women as different but equal.[14] The *Home Journal* took a different approach, editorializing that women were already physically, morally, intellectually, and religiously superior to men and that organizing to pressure and bully men would enable women to "influence the motives and conduct of any public man."[15] In other words, women simply did not need any more rights.

The Salem meeting led to a series of western woman's rights conventions throughout the 1850s, making the topic a constant source of debate and discussion in the region.[16] Ohio hosted at least three additional state conventions. The first, in Akron in June 1851, attracted leading feminists Jane Swisshelm and Amanda Coe as well as abolitionist lecturer Sojourner Truth, who gave the impromptu discourse later immortalized as the "And Ar'n't I a Woman?" address.[17] The 1852 Massillon meeting and the 1853 Ravenna gathering attracted large and enthusiastic audiences.[18] National woman's rights conventions also occurred in Cleveland in 1853 and in Cincinnati in 1855.[19] Indiana also regularly hosted statewide woman's rights conventions between 1851 and 1857.[20]

Abolitionists from various camps initiated, led, and dominated these woman's rights meetings.[21] The Salem meeting paved the way. Nearly every officer, committee member, participant, and speaker there had some connection to antislavery. Cowles served as president, while Hitchcock offered the keynote address.[22] The entire thirty-member executive committee had antislavery experience, ranging from public lecturing to sewing societies to Liberty Party activism. The same recipe held true for all of the Ohio and Indiana woman's rights meetings. Experienced abolitionist Hannah Cutler served as president of the Ohio Woman's Rights Association and received national publicity for her articulate participation at the national woman's rights convention in Philadelphia in 1854.[23] Immediately thereafter, Cutler became a corresponding editor for a Chicago-based antislavery newspaper, the *Free West*.[24] She used this position to publicize the woman's rights cause as much as possible. The *Free West* began featuring leading woman's rights activists in its front-page "People's Portrait Gallery," with Mott the first to appear.[25]

As historians have long since pointed out, many reformers believed that antislavery and woman's rights were mutually beneficial.[26] The call for the 1851 woman's rights meeting in Indiana clearly linked woman's suffrage to the elimination of the Black Laws—only virtuous voting women would repeal these horrendous laws.[27] The convention itself devoted half a day to a discussion of antislavery.[28] In an editorial about another woman's rights convention, Marius Robinson announced in the *Anti-Slavery Bugle*, "The Woman's Rights movement as presented by the principles and action of that convention, is no 'extraneous topic' to an anti-slavery newspaper. It is anti-slavery itself, in one of its purest, most comprehensive and effective forms."[29] Recognizing the connection between the two movements, abolitionist editors and lecturers increased their support for woman's rights following the Salem gathering. The *Anti-Slavery Bugle* consistently publicized woman's rights lectures and meetings throughout the 1850s. When Coe embarked on an 1851 lecture tour of Ohio, for example, the *Bugle* enthused, "She has come forward to do battle, against law and popular sentiment, in behalf of justice and humanity. This is true heroism."[30] Speeches by abolitionist lecturer Joseph Treat regularly blended woman's rights with abolition and other reforms: in one lecture, he wrote, "I was led to speak of Sunday, Slavery, War, Woman's Rights, Land Reform, the Bible, &c, &c."[31] Fellow lecturers Robinson, James Walker, Hitchcock, Griffing, and Harriet N. Torrey also consistently supported woman's rights during their antislavery tours.

"Are You a Woman's Rights Man?"

As with the advocacy of antislavery, woman's rights supporters approached their topic with sensitivity to their audience. Recognizing that many westerners might find only one or two aspects of the movement appealing, proponents began with the most palatable aspects of woman's rights. This pragmatic approach included focusing on women's difference, women's education, men's support, dress reform, and the distinct appropriateness of woman's equality on the western frontier.

Gamaliel Bailey's 1838 contention that even if some women decided to step up to the podium, natural differences between the sexes would prevent women from becoming "public actors" was characteristic of this moderate approach. There should be "no fear of the two sexes changing places," he preached. "God has made this an impossibility."[32] This argument made potential constituencies more comfortable and allowed supporters to manipulate common notions of womanhood and manhood for particular purposes. Many moderate abolitionists concurred with Bailey. Davis, who had become increasingly critical of the Garrisonians by the 1850s, believed that women's moral nature gave them a special and different societal role than men. "We are an advocate of the rights of women in a certain sense," she admitted, "and believe that our laws do not regard her as she should be regarded." However, "we do feel that our sex should not aspire to the pulpit, the public platform or the polls. She may *edit* and *print* a newspaper—may pursue, at least among their own sex, the practice of medicine—but she was not intended 'in senates or in courts to shine.'"[33] In advocating women's access to the media and medicine, Davis focused on female influence. She argued that women's voice needed to be heard (through proper channels) and that the silencing of that voice was detrimental to society. The fact that Davis had to earn her living after the death of her husband probably influenced her support for women's increased access to professional occupations. "Your correspondent begins to realize some of the discomforts of the position of her sex. Not that she wishes to be numbered with the 'strong minded,' but she does feel that woman should be permitted to get her living in some other way, if capable, than by 'taking in sewing,' teaching for a paltry sum, or keeping boarders." Davis's frustrations at her inability to find professional employment as a writer motivated her final comments: "Here in this enlightened city a woman may *starve* before the editor of a paper will employ her to do that which she can perform as well as any man. For instance to take charge of the 'local column' of some daily at a reasonable salary. Your correspondent knows this from experience. Could she obtain press and type she would advocate the rights of women in this city and set the editors an example which it would be to their advantage to follow."[34] Refusing to be associated with the "strong-minded" (code for a woman's rights activist) but nonetheless recognizing that many women needed to support themselves, Davis sought a middle ground that allowed women access to "feminine" jobs that paid living wages.

Western woman's rights activists often emphasized the least controversial aspects of their call for equality. Education, for example, proved very popular among the citizens of the Old Northwest. Although a few private colleges, including Oberlin, had opened their doors to women by the 1850s, women were largely excluded from advanced education and all the opportunities it afforded. Western women found this situation particularly frustrating as the number of male colleges in the region grew. By 1860, the West boasted 60 percent of the nation's colleges.[35] Eastern women certainly emphasized the importance of access to education, but in the West it was a top priority. Attendees at the Salem woman's rights meeting proclaimed that female education would allow women to acquire "self reliance and true Dignity" and thus better fulfill their "proper" duties.[36] Following the lead of reformers such as Catharine Beecher, western feminists argued that education made women better mothers and wives. All of the Indiana woman's rights conventions in this era focused on access to improved education for women. "The great stress and peculiar force of the resolutions" at the 1853 Indiana woman's rights gathering, explained Griffing, "was aimed at the universal education of woman."[37] This concern for education was also in evidence at most of the

Ohio woman's rights gatherings.[38] In 1851, several Akron speakers, including Truth, Emily Rakestraw Robinson, Coe, and Hannah M. Tracy, passionately advocated female education.[39]

This prioritization of education was in keeping with western women abolitionists' long history of supporting African American education. Men and women of both races collaborated to eliminate the Black Laws, which restricted access to public education and built, funded, and sustained schools for blacks. That this group would turn to the expansion of female education makes perfect sense. Abolitionists had great faith in the power of education to undermine inequality and build an increasingly sensitive, smart, open-minded population of men and women in the West. This educated citizenry would then work together to create a more perfect society by eliminating such sinful institutions as slavery. A key to this process was the cooperation and collaboration of both men and women.

Woman's rights, like western abolition, emphasized a mixed-sex approach to reform. Even the Salem meeting that disallowed male participation sparked such interest among abolitionist men that several wrote public letters in response. Micajah T. Johnson of Short Creek, Ohio, "read with much interest the proceedings of the late Woman's Convention at Salem, and the reading thereof bro't up a few ideas that I should like to communicate." He offered a spirited support for women's full political, legal, and social equality and encouraged women to demand their rights: "Women can have as much influence in regulating the affairs as men, and if they do not, it is because they wish to shrink from responsibility."[40] In Akron in 1851, men participated with such vehemence and dominance that one man "inquired whether this was not designed to be a Woman's Convention and urged [that] the gentlemen should be silent." A woman then defended the men, arguing that the call for the meeting invited "all who felt friendly to the cause" to participate. The loquacious men, including Robinson, Jacob Heaton, and Joseph Barker, had been defending an uncompromising resolution that condemned the "criminal injustice and gross tyranny" of men when they were accused of talking too much. The idiosyncratic Swisshelm opposed the resolution because she believed it was too harsh on men. A fierce combatant, Swisshelm eventually tamed the amendment.[41] This type of collaboratively developed moderation made western woman's rights more palatable.

Abolitionist papers also highlighted the diversity and respectability of male supporters as proof of the movement's legitimacy. In 1850, the *Bugle* elaborated on the background of some of the more prominent names attached to the call for the Salem meeting: "We append this week a large number of names," explained the editor, "among them are those of Mrs. Tilden, wife of the former member of Congress, [and] Mrs. Swift, wife of the State Senator." Such names made the Salem meeting seem reputable because of their association with powerful and influential men. "We mention these, not invidiously, but to show that the movement has the hearty concurrence and co-operation not only of those who are known as ultra Abolitionists and Reformers, but of many others, who agree with them in believing that the time has come for Woman to assume her true position as the equal companion of MAN, not less in matters of Government than in the relations of domestic life."[42] Both Martha Tilden and Adeline Swift were experienced activists with impressive antislavery credentials as well as significant social cache through their prestigious husbands. Tilden, "well known for her devotedness to the anti-slavery cause," had organized the young girls of Ravenna into an antislavery sewing society in 1847, served as vice president of the Western Anti-Slavery Society in 1852 and 1860, and helped coordinate abolitionist fairs with Cowles, Torrey, Hitchcock, and Maria Giddings.[43] Tilden's husband, Daniel, was also a well-known abolitionist and woman's rights supporter who served two terms in Congress as an antislavery Whig, working in coordination with Joshua Giddings.[44] Indeed, the *Bugle* also eagerly underscored the cooperation of Tilden and other local politicians. Only a few weeks after the Salem woman's rights meeting, Tilden and Akron mayor Lucius V. Bierce participated in a woman's rights meeting at the city's Presbyterian church. Only forty miles from Salem, Akron boasted a strong contingent of woman's right supporters. The two politicians "took a manly stand on the right side" at the meeting, according to the *Bugle*.[45] Bierce had also written a public letter encouraging the organizers of the Salem woman's rights meeting: "Let the ladies hold their Convention and set forth their wants, and rights, and be determined in asserting them." He denounced opponents of women's equality as "shallow biped[s]" who "disgraced a pair of breeches."[46] The support of outspoken and successful male politicians such as Tilden, who would serve as a probate judge in the region for decades, was invaluable to the movement.

Tilden's local ties were important because, as the Salem convention revealed, the woman's rights movement in the West was characterized by regional pride. Pleased with their "frontier" image and eager to distinguish themselves from the stuffy, fleshy East, westerners connected woman's rights to certain popular ideas about physicality. The West supposedly created natural, strong, hardworking bodies, both male and female, that contrasted to the weak and frail bodies engendered by crowded, unhealthy, polluted eastern cities. As the Henry County Female Anti-Slavery Society preached in an address to the "men of Indiana" about the importance of women's public activism, "Why cannot a beacon fire be kindled up by the females of the western wilds, that will serve to light and invite, the geniuses of the eastern world from their pent up city garrets, to breathe the free unchained breezes that sweep over the wide and extensive forests, and broad prairies."[47] The women of the West understood the importance of healthy bodies, nurtured by access to the outdoors and strengthened by virtuous hard labor in support of their families and communities. Woman's rights activists cleverly employed these notions of virtuous western physicality to advocate closely related feminist issues such as dress reform and independence.

Abolitionists often linked woman's rights to nature and respect for the "western wilds." Robinson used the pages of his *Anti-Slavery Bugle* to remind residents of the Old Northwest that simple, good-hearted, hardworking farmers—men in touch with the earth—recognized the logic and righteousness of the woman's rights movement. After attending the Cleveland woman's rights convention, Robinson journeyed back home to Salem with a "countryman who was passing in his buggy." This farmer immediately asked Robinson, "Are you a Woman's Rights man?" When Robinson answered in the affirmative, the man waxed eloquent about the convention: "Them women can speak some, can't they? I attended the whole of it. The women are right. They ought to have all they ask for." He concluded with a slavery analogy to highlight his belief that "priests" were the most vehement opponents to equality: "Woman's Rights is to the priests, just what abolition is to the slaveholder. It proposes to take away their power and authority, and they will do anything to prevent it." Robinson agreed with his "sensible farmer friend" but suspected that the man underestimated women's determination.[48] Robinson's depiction of this salt-of-the-earth farmer emphasized the man's simple but insightful approach to life. The fact that a farmer would attend a woman's rights convention in and of itself suggested something naturally appealing about the movement. His articulate and logical support for the women's demands also brought a certain backwoods legitimacy to female equality. In highlighting the feminism of a rustic man who made his living through the physical labor of growing the crops that sustained western bodies, Robinson linked woman's rights to the virtuous earth. The representation of woman's rights opponents as "priests" jealously defending their power also suggested that men who did not engage in physical labor were less generous and intelligent.

The association of woman's rights with strong natural bodies led to a focus on dress reform. Westerners idolized hard work in part because much of the population lived in rural areas that required physical strength and endurance. While cities such as Cincinnati, Cleveland, and Chicago boasted more diverse job opportunities, most westerners lived in small towns, and many continued to work on farms. Women often helped build homes, gardened, and engaged in various types of physically challenging household labor. As a result, many women sought comfortable, reliable clothing. In rejecting uncomfortable and expensive fashionable apparel, the dress reform movement appealed to western women. Celia R. Colby, a rural Ohio abolitionist and reformer, argued in favor of a practical approach to shoes for girls: "It seems a little strange that while good thick boots are thought necessary for the health and comfort of boys, during the severe cold of this inclement season, yet their companions of the weaker sex are seldom seen with them on, even though exposed to the same vicissitudes of wind and weather. Why this unwise distinction?" She continued, "A neat, well fitting pair of boots is an essential article which should be found in the wardrobe of every country dame or damsel, who has an eye to her own comfort or convenience, nor should she hesitate to wear them whenever and wherever health and prudence may dictate."[49] Focusing particularly on "country" women and girls, Colby emphasized both the inequity of the situation and the benefits to physical well-being that boots offered. Silly fashionable expectations must not be allowed to weaken girls and threaten their health.

The 1851 Indiana woman's rights convention passed a dress reform resolution that mirrored the concerns Colby expressed: "We believe the present style of female dress is highly inconvenient, unnatural, and destructive of health, and a mark of the degradation of woman. Therefore, *resolved*, that the women of this convention pledge themselves before our common families, to throw off the bondage imposed upon us by Parisian milliners and adopt a style of dress more in accordance with reason."[50] Suggesting that imported French fashions were a form of slavery that threatened women's health and demeaned them, western feminists again revealed the extent to which abolitionism infiltrated their movement. This allusion to fashion enslavement raised the image of the poorly clad slave, who had no choice in her garments and whose meager apparel certainly proved detrimental to good health. Like slaves, women's bodies were owned by others—in the case of free women, foreign designers.

Dress reform appealed to rural Indianans who needed thick boots and warm, comfortable clothing to fulfill their household responsibilities. Abolitionists and woman's rights activists recognized that a farmer's wife might enthusiastically support practical clothing for women but fear any suggestion of woman's suffrage or other political rights. In calling for a rejection of "inconvenient, unnatural" apparel, feminists hoped to appeal to a broader spectrum of women. This emphasis on practical clothing eventually began to center on the newly designed "Bloomer" outfit, named for Amelia Bloomer, the woman who publicized it. It featured a Turkish-style pantaloon combined with a loose fitting dress that reached halfway down the calf. Although generally ridiculed by the public, the comfortable outfit helped initiate a loud call for a change in women's clothing.[51]

Abolitionism and the Bloomer outfit became linked because women known for antislavery activism were the most likely to don the new apparel. As a result, the new garb was perceived as tainted by radicalism. Even in western abolitionist strongholds such as Galesburg, Illinois; and Salem, Ohio; the Bloomer costume led to mockery. Visiting Galesburg in 1851, Davis cheerfully noted that several local women were not "afraid of the ridicule of those who look upon a change in the style of dress as an unwarrantable innovation." Though founded by abolitionists and the home to an ambitious antislavery society, Galesburg citizens considered the Bloomer outfit lacking in femininity and unbecoming. Dismissing such critics, Davis concluded, "The new costume is neither unwomanly or in any degree a usurpation of man's habiliments."[52] A moderate woman's rights supporter, Davis understood dress reform as an effort toward comfort and practicality, not an attempt to become more like men. She considered such unwarranted assumptions about dress reform frustrating and infuriating. When Margaret Hise wore the Bloomer dress in Salem in the summer of 1851, she created "quite a sensation" and felt self-conscious despite being surrounded by dozens of supporters, family, and friends.[53] Only a few months later, the *Bugle* reported that the First Baptist Church of Salem had excommunicated two female members "for no other crime than that of listening to the Gospel of Anti-Slavery righteousness, and being arrayed in such temporal habiliments, as convenience and comfort happen to require." The *Bugle* concluded, "Who can tell why it is that the modern Church manifests more zeal in opposition to the late style of dress, the Bloomer Costume, than in the advancement of pure and undefiled religion? Rather let me ask, who cannot plainly see that its hatred of the unbecoming costume, as it is sometimes religiously named, is only another demonstration of enmity to the Anti-Slavery cause?"[54] Echoing the argument of the farmer with whom Robinson had conversed, the *Bugle* depicted the church as the enemy to both abolition and woman's rights.

Most woman's rights supporters in both the East and the West abandoned Bloomers by the mid-1850s as a consequence of the persistent ridicule and harassment they endured.

The Bloomer outfit engendered opposition not only because of its association with antislavery and radicalism but also because of issues of sexuality. With the rise of the free love movement in the 1850s and its linkage to woman's rights, the Bloomer costume became a symbol of women's larger attempt to claim the same social, political, and even physical rights as men. Free love, which called for the equalization of standards in relation to sexuality, appealed to many feminists. It advocated not that women adopt the unrestrained sexuality popularly associated with manhood but rather that both men and women embrace a respectful, love-based sexuality. The idea also advocated women's control over their bodies, an alternative to popular notions of female passionlessness that encouraged sensual pleasure between consenting (and preferably married) adults.[55] More comfortable clothing for women was a first step down the road to demanding other kinds of bodily privileges afforded to men. James Walker inadvertently alluded to this progression when he praised the mixed-sex school in Bedford, Michigan, where the young women not only talked of "health and life" but also "dressed as though they meant to be healthy, nearly all having on loose Bloomer dresses."[56] While Walker emphasized the health benefits of the comfortable dress, others worried that young women attending a mixed-sex school and attired in pantaloons and shorter dresses might be prone to promiscuous behavior . The *Western Citizen and Chicago Weekly* more self-consciously connected the new apparel and women's sexuality in its review of Bloomer's 1853 woman's rights lecture in Chicago. While the *Citizen* approved of the Bloomer outfit as worn by the speaker, the paper bemoaned the fact that the "matronly" Bloomer "is not so well calculated to exhibit the real beauty of this style as the belle just blooming into full womanhood."[57] Such a description of the sexual potency of the new apparel further provoked those who worried about the effect of dress reform on both men and women. Although the Bloomer costume proved much less sexual than many of the new fashions featured in well-circulated magazines, its connection to radicalism made it a source of greater concern. After all, fashionable clothes proved constraining, expensive, and uncomfortable, limiting women both physically and financially. Dress reform sought to challenge these constraints.

Dress reform in the West quickly moved beyond the controversial Bloomers and focused on access to comfortable clothes that promoted good health. As Bloomer introduced her practical outfit to westerners in 1853, Hitchcock also promoted dress reform to audiences at her hygiene lectures. Hitchcock believed that her switch from lecturing on abolition to lecturing on hygiene enabled her to do "more for the elevation of woman than I could in any other way."[58] Women were considered natural caretakers (of families and friends) and therefore increasingly sought general knowledge about physiology.[59] Moreover, advocates argued that healthy bodies improved moral and spiritual life. Because women's upbringing did not include regular exercise and biological knowledge, audiences were eager to learn from itinerant health reformers.[60] Hitchcock's lectures involved not only good hygiene practices and basic information about how the female body functioned but also a smart, practical approach to female dress. Though Hitchcock did not don the Bloomer costume, she modeled pragmatism by eschewing uncomfortable fashions and accessories. Western audiences, especially in urban areas, were intrigued by her lectures. She found that influential women in particular flocked to her gatherings. When she lectured in Detroit, more than one hundred women bought tickets, and most of the patrons were of the "elite" stamp and were certainly vulnerable to the attraction and pressure of fashionable apparel.[61] Her audience in Chicago was also well-heeled: "I was told that a more respectable class could not be formed" and "that I was patronized by the very first ladies in the city."[62] Rural women proved more cautious about attending Hitchcock's gatherings, especially in locations with no antislavery community. "In these small out-of-the-way places, the people do not really know whether they ought to come out," she admitted to a friend. "Some have not the money & others fear it will not be genteel."[63] Just as antislavery experienced opposition and hostility in certain areas of the West, so too did dress reform and woman's rights.

The link between woman's rights and abolition in the West as manifested through issues of the body can be illustrated through no better example than that of Kansas.[64] With the passage of the 1854 Kansas-Nebraska Act, which abrogated the sacred Missouri Compromise and determined that popular sovereignty would determine whether Kansas was admitted to the Union as a slave state, both abolitionists (including many women) and slavery supporters flocked to the territory to attempt to create a majority population.[65] Kansas proved an incredibly dangerous environment, and women were forced to adapt to the potential of violence at all times. Moreover, with few well-developed urban areas, most Kansas settlers had to construct homes, farms, and communities from scratch. As one resident wrote in 1855, "It is the newest country that I ever saw. People living in tents, and shanties, and wagons and sod houses—just staying till they can get something planted. No mills, no shops, no fields, no nothing to remind one of old countries."[66] Physical strength, skill, and courage were the minimum characteristics necessary for even the most basic hope of success in this battleground environment.

The *Bugle* and other newspapers highlighted stories of physical bravery among the women of Kansas, thereby furthering both woman's rights and abolition. Under the headline "The Ladies of Lawrence," the *Bugle* reprinted an article about the critical role played by "Free State ladies" in the defense of Lawrence against antiabolitionist "invaders." In contrast to the proslavery women who abandoned the town when violence began, the abolitionist women refused to leave. "Forty ladies of Lawrence enrolled their names secretly, with the determination of fighting by the sides of their husbands and sons as soon as the fighting commenced!"[67] Many of the women practiced shooting with pistols, and one "young girl (a beauty of nineteen years)" reported that she "dreampt last night of shooting three invaders." This emphasis on the youth and beauty of female abolitionist warriors was designed to reassure readers that although these women had adopted such manly characteristics as strength, courage, and determination, they remained feminine. The article concluded by telling the story of two women who risked their lives to sneak gunpowder and rifle cartridges into the town, using their femininity to fool the opposition. When an enemy scout stopped their wagon, he "saw only a work-basket, which had purposely been filled with sewing materials." He did he not notice the enormous gunpowder-filled pillows beneath their skirts and allowed them to continue on.[68] Combining masculine and feminine traits, the women embodied a new vision of womanhood that was bold, independent, and clever. The women were strengthened by their commitment to the virtue of the abolitionist cause, and the moral foundations of their untraditional activity were consistently highlighted.

Kansas offered women not only the opportunity for displays of courage but also the prospect of independence. Susan Wattles, who had honed her antislavery skills among Cincinnati's antiabolitionists when she taught African Americans there during the mid-1830s, wrote a public letter calling for women to charge off to Kansas in pursuit of both antislavery and liberty: "Are you not acquainted with some young women who desire to come to Kansas to take claims and make themselves independent? I know three who have taken claims. One of them frequently reconnoitered on horseback when advancing border ruffians were expected, and also stood on guard nights when her tired brothers were sleeping." Wattles offered specific instructions about how to go about achieving liberty in Kansas, including how much money would be needed, what to purchase, what to build, and how to garden. She admitted that it would take a woman "not afraid of some privations and hardships," willing to be isolated, endangered, and subject to illness. Girded by "the consciousness of their own integrity and purity," such women "must know how to be happy without society, and spiritual minded without a church." Wattles concluded, "Let those who are tired of sewing, tired of teaching, and tired of doing nothing come to Kansas, and arouse to action those dormant powers of body and mind which are necessary to the perfection of their being."[69] Wattles saw womanhood as grounded in action, strength, integrity, and determination. Kansas offered the chance to prove one's commitment not only to liberty for slaves but also to liberty for oneself. Woman's rights supporters across the nation found Wattles's message encouraging. Sarah Grimké wrote to Susan Wattles's daughter, Sarah Grimké Wattles, "Have any women been induced to your mother's stirring letter to go & take claims in Kansas, if we could rouse a spirit of independence in women; our work as to her Rights would be accomplished." Associating liberty and spiritedness with woman's rights, Grimké concluded, "Freedom brings with it great responsibilities, heavy burdens & imperative duties & it must necessarily be long before those accustomed to the helplessness & dependence of childhood & slavery can throw off the emasculating influences which have surrounded them & gird themselves for the battle of life."[70]

Susan Wattles knew whereof she spoke in regard to Kansas. Not only did she and her husband, longtime abolitionist Augustus Wattles, move to Kansas to help the cause, but daughter Sarah Wattles owned land and built a home in the battleground state.[71] "I am rejoiced to find that you are mistress of 100 acres of land," Sarah Grimké wrote to her namesake. "I am still more rejoiced to find that you are living out a glorious independence seeing to the building of your own house & preparing a habitation for your parents & family."[72] Fifteen-year-old Sarah Wattles proved independent well beyond her years, and Grimké envisioned the girl as the future of young womanhood: "I have a hope that you may ere long thrill the soul of Kansas with vocal pleading for the rights of women as well as by calmly using the rights which nature gives you." In using her strength, intelligence, and courage to carve out a home for herself in the dangerous backwoods of Kansas, Sarah Wattles exemplified independent womanhood. She remained in Kansas through 1859, when she accepted Grimké's suggestion that she travel east and pursue a college education with the help of her eastern mentor.[73]

Young Sarah and her mother simultaneously pursued abolition and woman's rights in their Kansas adventure. Their presence in the risky territory offered a clear defiance of the supposed "woman's sphere," and their advocacy of free-state politics further pushed them outside "normal" female behavior. But the Wattles women were not alone. Hundreds of other women put their bodies in the line of fire in Kansas. This expression of bravery and boldness found a certain comfort in the context of the western frontier.

Conclusion

Although not every western woman abolitionist embraced feminism, many eventually found a comfortable path toward woman's equality. Whether the motivator was the inspiration of a public lecture by Abby Kelley or Lizzie Hitchcock; a sewing society gathering with a dozen witty, articulate women plying their needles for a better world; or a union antislavery convention organized by Sarah Otis Ernst, the end result was the same. Women and men began to question basic inequities that prevented women from access to equal education, careers, property rights, and suffrage. They wondered why girls did not wear warm boots and were expected to don restrictive, impractical clothing. Western abolitionists helped to initiate a woman's rights movement that began slowly in the 1840s and burst forward in the 1850s with dozens of feminist meetings across the region. These meetings followed the same traditions developed by western abolitionists—cooperation and practicality combined with energy and a focus on goals. These women would build a foundation for the woman's suffrage campaign that developed after the Civil War.

Afterword

In reply to a request from Susan B. Anthony to write down her memories of woman's rights activism in the antebellum West, Emily Rakestraw Robinson included a brief antislavery reminiscence. In "Our Old Anti-Slavery Tent," Robinson described the life span of a canvas tent, a piece of which she included in the letter. After hosting revival meetings in western New York, the tent housed the 1843 Liberty Party convention in Buffalo that nominated James G. Birney for president. The shelter soon found its way to Ohio, providing cover as young abolitionist students graduated from Oberlin College in the 1840s before the Western Anti-Slavery Society bought the tent for five hundred dollars. "Under its sheltering roof all the noted anti-slavery orators and advocates have been heard in their pleadings and appeals to God," Robinson recalled. And it continued to serve the cause even as it aged. "In 1863, the tent was in a dilapidated condition—its . . . work done and the abolition of slavery assured—we decided to economize the wreck." Selling its best parts for one hundred dollars and repairing the rest, western abolitionists donated the proceeds to "terrified fugitives" who had escaped the ravages of war. Like many western women abolitionists who continued their activism in the postwar period, the tent proved its worth long after the official end of U.S. slavery.[1]

This tent, with its simplicity, rustic nature, and solid construction, symbolized the most important characteristics of western women's antislavery, according to Robinson. It served as a home for abolition meetings, providing shelter and warmth—"feminine" characteristics—to eager crowds. It accommodated all brands of abolitionists, including Liberty Party politicos, religious activists, and Garrisonians. And it remained useful to fugitives, offering protection and aid throughout its history.

Western women abolitionists used common assumptions about femininity, including morality, nurturance, domesticity, and sacrifice—qualities they genuinely embraced—to serve the cause of emancipation. But these activists experimented with womanhood, too, pushing at its edges. They walked boldly into the civic arena alongside their brothers and fathers and husbands. They offered political advice to the men of their communities. They negotiated the antislavery political environment of big cities such as Cincinnati. They took to the podium and spoke to "promiscuous" audiences with confidence and authority. Some questioned the limits of their sphere and moved seamlessly into the woman's rights movement.

Like Robinson's canvas tent, western antislavery embraced all types of abolitionists. Though many women had very strong loyalties to their particular brand of antislavery, they crossed the boundaries between those brands to ensure that the movement benefited from a united constituency. More than their eastern sisters, western women built bridges and interacted with each other. Sometimes they bickered. Sometimes they failed. But mostly they welcomed difference. They focused on the larger goals of emancipation and racial equality. They wanted to make a difference. And they did. They allowed the West's distinctiveness to guide their activism and give them pride.

Like the tent, many women continued their reform work after the Civil War. Laura Smith Haviland, Ruth Dugdale, Sojourner Truth, Betsey Mix Cowles, Emily Rakestraw Robinson, Frances Ellen Watkins, and innumerable other western women remained committed to racial equality and social reform well into old age. This reform work continued in the pragmatic tradition of western abolition. These women remained focused on empowerment through education, aid, and opportunity. Haviland, for example, worked diligently to support her House of Refuge, a home for black southern orphans in Adrian, Michigan. She cajoled, bullied, and manipulated the American Missionary Association into financing the institution despite the hesitancy of its board of directors. Ignoring the opposition of radical abolitionists, who abhorred the association for its former acceptance of slavery and criticized Haviland for working with the group, she recognized that the increasingly conservative and racist political environment required compromise. Haviland understood that the House of Refuge's success would offer compelling evidence of the need for egalitarian racial policies and continued humanitarian and educational support for freed slaves.[2] Despite her declining health, Cowles worked with the Freedman's Aid Society in Cleveland to raise money to for the education and support of newly freed slaves.[3] Sallie Holley, an Oberlin graduate and abolitionist feminist, devoted twenty years to teaching ex-slaves at a school in Virginia.[4]

African American women such as Truth and Harper focused on issues that resembled those that engaged Haviland, Cowles, and Holley but also emphasized the federal government's responsibility to provide land to former slaves as well as the importance of a universal suffrage amendment. Truth toured the North in 1870 and 1871 to gather signatures on a petition that reminded Congress of its debt to slaves for their service to the nation before and during the Civil War and called for the distribution of land to these new freedmen and -women. Harper traveled across the South during Reconstruction and called on middle-class black women to join the effort to educate free slaves. She also focused on suffrage as a basic right that should be granted to all regardless of race or sex.[5]

Perhaps more than any other western woman abolitionist, Josephine Griffing continued her activism well into the postwar period, becoming a radical voice in the Freedmen's Bureau in Washington, D.C. While the bureau's free-labor-touting male leaders demanded that ex-slaves immediately and independently find work, Griffing recognized the problems of finding jobs for decent pay, child care, and expensive fuel and food. Griffing also continued to call for woman's suffrage, often connecting the rights of women with those of former slaves.[6]

The fact that many western women continued to agitate for the rights of society's disempowered demonstrates the persistence of the original impulses that had led these women to join the unpopular abolitionist movement. They grounded their activism in a pragmatism that allowed them to negotiate with their more moderate neighbors even as they followed their impulse to reform the world around them.

Notes

ABBREVIATIONS

AK
Abby Kelley

ASB
Anti-Slavery Bugle

AWW
Anne Warren Weston

Ball-Curtis Genealogy
Ball-Curtis Genealogy, Oberlin
College Library, Oberlin, Ohio

BJ
Benjamin Jones

Blanchard Papers
Jonathan Blanchard Papers, RG 2.1,
Wheaton College, Wheaton, Illinois

BMC
Betsey Mix Cowles

BMC Papers
Betsey Mix Cowles Papers, Kent State
University Libraries, Special Collec-
tions and Archives, Kent, Ohio

BPL
Boston Public Library, Department of Rare Books and Manuscripts, Boston, Massachusetts

CG
Cincinnati Gazette

FDP
Frederick Douglass' Paper

FLAASC
*Free Labor Advocate and
Anti-Slavery Chronicle*

Fletcher Papers
Robert S. Fletcher Papers, Oberlin
College Library, Oberlin, Ohio

Foster Papers
Abby Kelley Foster–Stephen S. Foster Papers, American Antiquarian Society, Worcester, Massachusetts

GUE
Genius of Universal Emancipation

Henry FASS
Records of the Henry County Female Anti-Slavery Society, Indiana State Library, Indiana Division, Manuscripts Collection, Indianapolis

Hise Diaries
Daniel Howell Hise Diaries, Ohio Historical Society, Columbus

JEH
Jane Elizabeth Hitchcock

LMW
Lucy M. Wright

MBD
Mary B. Davis

MRR Papers
Marius R. Robinson Papers, MSS 1660, Western Reserve Historical Society, Cleveland, Ohio

MWC
Maria Weston Chapman

NLA
New Lisbon Aurora

Norris Papers
Norris Family Papers, Bentley Historical Library, University of Michigan, Ann Arbor

NS
North Star

Ohio FPA
George E. Jenkins Papers, Ohio Free Produce Association Papers, MSS 100, Western Reserve Historical Society, Cleveland, Ohio

Portage LASS
Portage County Ladies Anti-Slavery Society Papers, MSS v.f. L, Western Reserve Historical Society, Cleveland, Ohio

PRNWG
Peoria Register and North-Western Gazetteer

SOE
Sarah Otis Ernst

SSF
Stephen S. Foster

TDW
Theodore Dwight Weld

WC
Western Citizen

WLG
William Lloyd Garrison

INTRODUCTION

1 Maria Giddings mentioned the speakers at the fair in her letter to BMC, January 3, 1847, BMC Papers, Box 1, Folder 14. The other items are mentioned in the advertisement for the fair: "The Thirteenth National Anti-Slavery Bazaar," *Liberator*, December 25, 1846.

2   JEH to BMC, January 4, 1847, BMC Papers, Box 1, Folder 14.

3   Maria Giddings to BMC, January 3, 1847, BMC Papers, Box 1, Folder 14.

4   JEH to BMC, January 4, 1847, BMC Papers, Box 1, Folder 14.

5   On cheese production in the Western Reserve, see the following articles in the *Ohio Cultivator*: "Ohio Cheese," December 1, 1847; "Dairy Products of Ohio," May 15, 1848; "Notes of Our Trip North," July 15, 1848. For the comment about the cheese attracting attention, see Maria Giddings to BMC, January 3, 1847, BMC Papers, Box 1, Folder 14. For another example of cheese as symbol and politics, see Pasley, "Cheese and the Words." For more on dairy farming, see McMurry, *Transforming Rural Life*.

6   JEH to BMC, January 4, 1847, BMC Papers, Box 1, Folder 14.

7   Lovina Bissell to Francis Jackson, October 7, 1848, BPL, MS A.4, 6A, vol. 3, no. 27.

8   See Winch, *Gentleman of Color*; Richard S. Newman, *Transformation*.

9   The many scholarly works on WLG include Merrill, *Against Wind and Tide*; Nye, *William Lloyd Garrison*; Thomas, *Liberator*; Mayer, *All on Fire*.

10 Berlin, *Slaves without Masters*.

11 See Grimsted, *American Mobbing*; Richards, *"Gentleman of Property and Standing."*

12 Several of the classics of abolitionist scholarship remain important sources. For a basic history of the movement, see Stewart, *Holy Warriors*. On political abolitionism, see Sewell, *Ballots for Freedom*. On black abolitionism, see Quarles, *Black Abolitionists*.

13 Jeffrey, *Great Silent Army*.

14 For an excellent discussion of early women's reform groups, see Boylan, *Origins of Women's Activism*.

15 "The Liberty Party in Northern Ohio," *Philanthropist*, July 17, 1845.

16 "Annals of Women's Anti-Slavery Societies," *Liberator*, January 15, 1864. The article, written by Philadelphia Female Anti-Slavery Society leader Mary Grew, mentions only one western group, in Massillon, Ohio.

17 See, for example, Earle's award-winning *Jacksonian Antislavery*; McCarthy and Stauffer's highly regarded edited collection, *Prophets of Protest*; Richard S. Newman's excellent *Transformation*; Laurie, *Beyond Garrison*; Petrulionis, *To Set This World Right*. Some exceptions exist. See, for example, Harrold's works on southern abolitionism, *Abolitionists and the South* and *Subversives*. Blue, *No Taint of Compromise*, highlights several western abolitionists, including one woman, Jane Swisshelm, who spent part of her career in Minnesota. Quist, *Restless Visionaries*, discusses abolitionism in Michigan. For a discussion of the "Massa-centric" focus of abolitionist studies, see the H-SHEAR discussion logs for July 2007 at <www.h-net.msu.edu>.

18 See, for example, Abzug, *Passionate Liberator*; Harrold, *Gamaliel Bailey*; Stewart, *Joshua R. Giddings*. For more recent examples, see Lovejoy, *His Brother's Blood*;

H. Robert Baker, *Rescue*. Some exceptions exist. See Gamble, "Garrisonian Abolitionists"; Muelder, *Fighters for Freedom*. In addition, many unpublished theses and dissertations focus on western abolition.

19 The scholarship on women's abolitionism is too extensive to list here. The most thorough and important recent study is Jeffrey, *Great Silent Army*.

20 Van Broekhoven, *Devotion of These Women*.

21 Salerno, *Sister Societies*, 142–48.

22 Pierson, *Free Hearts*.

23 Etcheson, *Emerging Midwest*, 2.

24 WLG to Helen Garrison, November 10, 1855, BPL, MS A.1.1, vol. 6, no. 138.

25 Lesick, *Lane Rebels*.

26 See, for example, the discussion of a sermon on the "Alton mob" in Cincinnati: Emily Rakestraw Robinson to Marius Robinson, November 12, 1837, n.d., MRR Papers.

27 "To the Anti-Slavery Women of Illinois," *WC*, October 6, 1846.

28 "Ladies Benevolent and Antislavery Association of the County of Jackson," *Signal of Liberty*, July 11, 1846.

29 See Berwanger, *Frontier against Slavery*, 7–29; Finkelman, "Evading the Ordinance"; Middleton, *Black Laws: Race and the Legal Process*.

30 See, for example, Quarles, *Black Abolitionists*; Yee, *Black Women Abolitionists*.

31 Etcheson, *Emerging Midwest*, 2.

CHAPTER 1

1 LMW's entire family embraced immediate abolitionism. See Goodheart, *Abolitionist, Actuary, Atheist*, 45. On Wright's experience teaching in Cincinnati, see Weld, Weld, and Grimké, I *Letters*, 178–79, 194, 216–17.

2 There are two biographies of BMC: Geary, *Balanced in the Wind*; DeBlasio, "Her Own Society." On the Ashtabula Female Anti-Slavery society, see Padgett, "Abolitionists of All Classes."

3 LMW to BMC, March 5, 1836, BMC Papers, Box 1, Folder 3.

4 See the Ashtabula County Female Anti-Slavery Society Records, Western Reserve Historical Society, Cleveland, Ohio; BMC Papers. TDW mentioned helping to organize the Ashtabula County Female Anti-Slavery Society during a visit to Austinburg in September 1835 (TDW to Elizur Wright Jr., October 6, 1835, in Weld, Weld, and Grimké, I *Letters*, 240). Ashtabula congressman Joshua Giddings, a committed abolitionist, declared in 1845, "I probably live in the strongest abolition county in the United States" (Joshua Giddings to David Lee Child, November 13, 1845, BPL, MS A.4.1, 103).

5 LMW for the Portage County Female Anti-Slavery Society to the Boston Female Anti-Slavery Society, August 11, 1836, Boston Female Anti-Slavery Society Letterbook, Massachusetts Historical Society, Boston; Portage LASS.

6 Soderlund, "Priorities and Power," 70; AWW for the Boston Female Anti-Slavery Society to the Putnam Female Anti-Slavery Society, July 22, 1836, Boston Female Anti-Slavery Society Letterbook. Debra Gold Hansen writes that the Boston group had two hundred members in 1836 (*Strained Sisterhood*, 17). The Ladies' New-York City Anti-Slavery Society consisted of 33 officers and managers, and chapters in most smaller communities had only a few dozen members (*First Annual Report*).

7 "Ladies' Anti-Slavery Societies," *Anti-Slavery Record*, April 1836.

8 Extant membership rolls suggest that white women predominated in Ohio's female antislavery societies of the 1830s. By the 1840s and 1850s, a few African American women had begun to participate in these organizations. I have been unable to find the records of any black female antislavery groups in the Old Northwest, though black women certainly participated in all types of abolitionist activities.

9 Myers, "Antislavery Activities," 95.

10 In the early 1830s, northern Ohio also experienced some abolitionist growth centered at Western Reserve College in Hudson. This growth was linked to the brief tenure of Charles Storr, Beriah Green, and Elizur Wright Jr. at the college (Wyatt-Brown, "Abolition and Antislavery").

11 Cheek and Cheek, "John Mercer Langston."

12 Fladeland, *James Gillespie Birney*.

13 Myers, "Antislavery Activities." See also Lesick, *Lane Rebels*. On TDW, see Abzug, *Passionate Liberator*.

14 In 1836, three different abolitionists published appeals to Ohio women to join the movement. Lane rebels wrote two of these. Birney, a former Kentucky slaveholder and editor of the Cincinnati-based *Philanthropist*, published *Address to the Ladies of Ohio*, arguing that the moral foundation of abolition made it appropriate and in fact critical for women to participate (Fladeland, *James Gillespie Birney*, 148). James Thome read his *Address to the Females of Ohio* at the annual meeting of the Ohio Anti-Slavery Society in Granville, declaring, "We need *your* aid—your sanction—your interests and prayers—your wakeful concern—your heart-beating sympathies—the encouragement of your unwavering faith" (Thome, *Address*, 1). Within a few months, Muskingum County Female Anti-Slavery Society leader Maria Sturges saw her "Address to the Females in the State of Ohio" published in the *Philanthropist*. "We have fallen upon troublous times," worried Sturges, and "God holds us accountable" (Maria Sturges, "Address to the Females in the State of Ohio," *Philanthropist*, June 24, 1836).

15 TDW to Lewis Tappan, March 18, 1834, in Weld, Weld, and Grimké, I *Letters*, 132–35.

16 Samuel Wells to TDW, December 15, 1834, in ibid., 179. Many male and female reformers moved to the West to Christianize and otherwise "civilize" the untamed territories. Harriet Beecher Stowe's father, Lyman Beecher, moved his family to

Cincinnati in 1832 to ensure the dominance of Protestant Christianity in the West (Hedrick, *Harriet Beecher Stowe*, 67–70). I thank Michael Pierson for pointing out the Beecher connection.

17 Phebe Mathews to TDW, January 9, 1836, in Weld, Weld, and Grimké, I *Letters*, 251. Mathews explains that the sisters are "in debt about two hundred dollars."

18 Marius Robinson to Emily Rakestraw Robinson, January 29, 1837, MRR Papers.

19 Emeline Bishop to TDW, May 6, 1835, in Weld, Weld, and Grimké, I *Letters*, 219–20.

20 Ardath Hagaman argues that most of the Ohio female antislavery societies "were either formed by Weld himself, or by some of the Lane Seminar rebels" ("Women of the Old Northwest in the Antislavery Movement," 431–32, May 1941, Box 1, History 431, 432, Student Papers, Department of History, University of Michigan, Bentley Historical Library, Ann Arbor). While I agree that the Lane rebels helped catalyze many female groups, the women did the organizing and most of the grassroots work.

21 See Salerno, *Sister Societies*, table A, 165–74.

22 On BMC's background, see Geary, *Balanced in the Wind*; DeBlasio, "Her Own Society." See also Padgett, "Abolitionists of All Classes." On the rapid growth and economic development of Ohio, see the essays in Cayton and Hobbs, *Center of a Great Empire*.

23 Cayton, "Significance of Ohio," 5.

24 See BMC Papers; Ashtabula County Female Anti-Slavery Society Records.

25 The Oberlin Female Anti-Slavery Society was founded in December 1835 (Fletcher, *History*, 237).

26 LMW to BMC, March 5, 1836, BMC Papers, Box 1, Folder 3.

27 Sarah Carpenter to TDW, October 2, 1835, Weld-Grimké Papers, William L. Clements Library, University of Michigan, Ann Arbor.

28 Proceedings of the Portage County Ladies Anti-Slavery Society, February 1836, Portage LASS.

29 James Alvord to TDW, February 9, 1836, in Weld, Weld, and Grimké, I *Letters*, 260.

30 Proceedings of the Portage County Ladies Anti-Slavery Society, February 1836, Portage LASS.

31 Meeting of the Portage County Ladies Anti-Slavery Society, March 12, 1836, Portage LASS.

32 For more on Thome, see Myers, "Antislavery Activities," 105–7.

33 James Thome to TDW, March 31, 1836, in Weld, Weld, and Grimké, I *Letters*, 283.

34 Ibid.

35 Thome mentions the antiabolition meeting in James Thome to TDW, March 31, 1836, in Weld, Weld, and Grimké, I *Letters*, 284. See also "List of Anti-Slavery Societies in Ohio," *Philanthropist*, September 4, 1838.

36 Preamble and Constitution of the Canton Ladies Anti-Slavery Society, Canton Ladies Anti-Slavery Society Records, MSS 26, Western Reserve Historical Society, Cleveland, Ohio.

37 Augustus Wattles to BMC, April 9, 1836, BMC Papers, Box 1, Folder 3.

38 Ibid.

39 Ibid.

40 Thome estimated that "70 or 80" women were present on the first day (James Thome to TDW, May 2, 1836, in Weld, Weld, and Grimké, I *Letters*, 299). Only 18 women enrolled their names in the minutes of the meeting, however (Price, "Ohio Anti-Slavery Convention").

41 Howe, "Granville Riot," 80.

42 Price, "Ohio Anti-Slavery Convention," 185.

43 James Thome to TDW, March 31, 1836, in Weld, Weld, and Grimké, I *Letters*, 286. I thank Carol Lasser for sharing her excellent analysis of Thome's writings, "Abolitionist Appeals to Women."

44 Thome, *Address*, 2.

45 James Thome to TDW, May 2, 1836, in Weld, Weld, and Grimké, I *Letters*, 301.

46 Howe, "Granville Riot," 80.

47 James Thome to TDW, May 2, 1836, in Weld, Weld, and Grimké, I *Letters*, 301.

48 Ibid.

49 Their meeting had not been announced at the state gathering because the "lawless mob" that was "perambulating the peaceful village of Granville, threatening with insult and outrage, every friend of the slave," had caused the participants and attendees to be anxious and hurried ("Proceedings of the Female Delegates at Mount Pleasant," *Philanthropist*, May 12, 1837).

50 "Preamble and Resolutions of the Ohio Female A.S. Society," *Philanthropist*, May 27, 1836.

51 LMW to BMC, May 20, 1836, BMC Papers, Box 1, Folder 3.

52 "Petition of the Ladies Resident in the State of Ohio," *Philanthropist*, June 24, 1836.

53 "Proceedings of the Female Delegates at Mount Pleasant," *Philanthropist*, May 12, 1837; "Proceedings of the Convention of Women," *Philanthropist*, June 19, 1838.

54 "Proceedings of the Convention of Women," *Philanthropist*, June 19, 1838.

55 Isenberg, *Sex and Citizenship*, xviii.

56 Price, "Ohio Anti-Slavery Convention," 176–88.

57 Women attendees, however, often failed to register as delegates, thus suggesting that the meeting was much larger and included a higher percentage of women.

58 The Oberlin Anti-Slavery Society boasted three hundred members by 1835. Two women's groups, the Young Ladies' Anti-Slavery Society and the Female Anti-Slavery Society, organized in 1835 (Fletcher, *History*, 237).

59 On family ties in the Western Reserve, see also Padgett, "Abolitionists of All Classes."

60 See the Ashtabula County Female Anti-Slavery Society Records.

61 On Leonard Beardsley, see Weld, Weld, and Grimké, I *Letters*, 324. Salerno, *Sister Societies*, 36, refers to this agent as "Mrs. Beardslee." For confirmation that "Beardslee" is male, see Maria Mills to BMC, January 19, 1836, BMC Papers, Box 1, Folder 3: "Mr. Beardsley would undoubtedly be kindly received should he be disposed at any time to favour us with a lecture."

62 Eunice A. Ensign to BMC, June 1, 1836, BMC Papers, Box 1, Folder 3.

63 Marius Robinson to Emily Rakestraw Robinson, February 7, 1837, MRR Papers.

64 "Abolition Proceedings," *Philanthropist*, July 7, 1837.

65 Portage LASS; *Philanthropist*, July 24, 1838, June 24, 1836.

66 On abolitionist couples in general, see Hersh, *Slavery of Sex*, 218–51. See also Padgett, "Abolitionists of All Classes." On Augustus and Susan Wattles, see Getz, "Partners in Motion."

67 Phebe Mathews to TDW, May 6, 1835, in Weld, Weld, and Grimké, I *Letters*, 220.

68 On the importance of family and community among abolitionists, see Friedman, *Gregarious Saints*.

69 Emily Rakestraw Robinson to Marius Robinson, January 23, 1837, MRR Papers.

70 Ibid., January 13, 1837.

71 Ibid., February 4, 1837.

72 Marius Robinson to Emily Rakestraw Robinson, February 16, 1837, MRR Papers.

73 Edward Weed to Emily Rakestraw Robinson, January 25, 1837, MRR Papers.

74 Emily Rakestraw Robinson to Marius Robinson, January 13, 1837, MRR Papers.

75 Marius Robinson to Emily Rakestraw Robinson, January 29, 1837, MRR Papers.

76 Marius Robinson, handwritten description of the attack, n.d., MRR Papers.

77 "Great Convention in the West," *Liberator*, October 5, 1849.

78 "Important Suggestions," *WC*, December 30, 1842.

79 Sophia Arnold to BMC, April 5, [1836], BMC Papers, Box 2, Folder 9.

80 "Preamble and Resolutions of the Ohio Female A.S. Society," *Philanthropist*, May 27, 1836.

81 Thome, *Address*, 2.

82 Maria Sturges, "Address to Christian Females in the Slaveholding States," *Philanthropist*, March 25, 1836.

83 "The Third Quarterly Meeting of the Chicago Female Anti-Slavery Society," *WC*, July 25, 1844; "Address to the Men of Indiana," and "Address to the Females of Indiana," *FLAASC*, December 22, 1844; "Address to Females," *WC*, April 6, 1843; "Address to the Females," *FLAASC*, July 11, 1843.

84 "Proceedings of the Convention of Women," *Philanthropist*, June 18, 1838. Ohio's Cadiz Female Anti-Slavery Society proclaimed the "wicked prejudice which is cherished against the people of color" to be the "offspring of slavery and no less wicked" ("Abolition Proceedings," *Philanthropist*, July 7, 1837).

85 "Female Anti-Slavery Meeting," *Philanthropist*, August 28, 1838.

86 SOE to AWW, February 1, 1852, November 14, 1852, BPL, MS A.9.2, vol. 26, nos. 8, 70.

87 Mary Bent Blanchard, "Report of the Society for the Education of Colored People," n.d., Blanchard Papers.

88 For more on Black Laws and the Liberty Party, see Middleton, *Black Laws: Race and the Legal Process*; Volpe, *Forlorn Hope*, 104. See also Berwanger, *Frontier against Slavery*; Harrold, *Gamaliel Bailey*, 60; Litwack, *North of Slavery*.

89 By the 1840s, western women focused more directly on eliminating the Black Laws. See chap. 2.

90 In addition to supporting schools and teachers, Ohio women abolitionists also supported individual students in need. See H. W. Cobb to Mary Blanchard, June 21, 1842, Blanchard Papers.

91 "Abolition Proceedings," *Philanthropist*, July 7, 1837.

92 Soderlund, "Priorities and Power," 76–77.

93 Debra Gold Hansen, *Strained Sisterhood*; Van Broekhoven, *Devotion of These Women*.

94 *First Annual Report*, 18.

95 Strane, *Whole-Souled Woman*; Martha S. Jones, *All Bound Up Together*, 34–35.

96 On blacks and education, see Quarles, *Black Abolitionists*, 106–12; Pease and Pease, *They Who Would Be Free*, 144–70; Winch, "'You Have Talents'"; Yee, *Black Women Abolitionists*, 47–51, 60–74.

97 *Liberator*, November 17, 1832.

98 Pease and Pease, *They Who Would Be Free*, 147. See also "School Fund Institute," *Philanthropist*, April 9, 1839, October 22, 1839.

99 "Colored Schools in Ohio," *Philanthropist*, September 15, 1837.

100 "Convention of the Colored Inhabitants of Butler County, Ohio," *Colored American*, July 11, 1840.

101 "Communications," *FDP*, October 1, 1852.

102 "To the Female Anti-Slavery Societies in the State of Ohio," *Philanthropist*, January 20, 1837.

103 "Proceedings of the Female Delegates at Mount Pleasant," *Philanthropist*, May 12, 1837.

104 "Anti-Slavery Society," *Philanthropist*, February 13, 1838. See also "Women's Anti-Slavery Society of Cincinnati," *Philanthropist*, October 22, 1839.

105 "Proceedings of the Convention of Women," *Philanthropist*, June 18, 1838.

106 The group gave financial support to schools in Cabin Creek, Richmond, Mercer County, Cincinnati, Mount Pleasant, Beach Creek, Dayton, Ross County, Shelby County, and Oberlin (ibid.).

107 "The Fourth Annual Report of the Ladies Education Society for the Education of the Free People of Color," *Philanthropist*, July 30, 1845.

108 "Colored Schools in Ohio," *Philanthropist*, September 15, 1837.

109 "A Plain Statement of Facts," *Philanthropist*, November 14, 1837.

110 Ibid.

111 "To the Female Anti-Slavery Societies in the State of Ohio," *Philanthropist*, January 20, 1837.

112 "Colored Schools in Ohio," *Philanthropist*, September 15, 1837. On the Wattleses' agency, see "Proceedings of the Female Delegates at Mount Pleasant," *Philanthropist*, May 12, 1837. See also Getz, "Partners in Motion."

113 "Proceedings of the Female Delegates at Mount Pleasant," *Philanthropist*, May 12, 1837.

114 "Proceedings of the Convention of Women," *Philanthropist*, June 19, 1838.

115 Women abolitionists in Illinois also emphasized the importance of becoming acquainted with those whom they hoped to assist. This relationship would encourage African Americans to send their children to school. "The colored people are so unused to any thing like [the opening of schools], that they will hardly know how to understand us at first," explained Irene B. Allan. "You must get into your wagon, and go out on the prairie to that colored family you may know out there, and see if there is not one that can be spared and induced to go [to school]; then you must go down to ——— street, where there are several families, and do what you can do there: then, perhaps you know of some living in white families; visit them" ("To the Managers of the Illinois Female Anti-Slavery Society," *WC*, September 5, 1844).

116 See Susan E. Wattles's report for the Ohio Female Anti-Slavery Society delineating the experiences of female teachers in a variety of locations: "Education among Colored People—Report," *Philanthropist*, November 26, 1839.

117 "Heroism," *Philanthropist*, May 10, 1843.

118 See the following articles in the *Philanthropist*: "Education of Colored People," June 23, 1840; "The Call of the Ladies' Committee," October 6, 1840; "Notice," April 21, 1841; "Education Society," June 9, 1841; "Education Society," June 29, 1842; "Anti-Slavery in Sharon," February 15, 1843; May 3, 1843; "The Anniversary," May 31, 1843; "Education Society," July 5, 1843; "Education Society," August 2, 1843; "The Fourth Annual Report of the Ladies' Education Society for the Education of the Free People of Color," July 30, 1845. According to Dorothy B. Porter, "The reports of the Ohio Ladies Education Society . . . probably did more towards the establishment of schools for the education of colored people at this time in Ohio than any other organized group" ("Organized Educational Activities," 572).

119 Sarah B. Eustis to Mary Blanchard, March 9, 1847, Blanchard Papers.

120 Sturges was supposed to write an address to the state's African Americans in 1843, but she died that year ("Education Society," *Philanthropist*, August 2, 1843).

121 "Education of Colored People," *Philanthropist*, June 23, 1840.

122 Ibid. Both Bailey and Blanchard served for several years in official positions within the group. See "Education Society," *Philanthropist*, August 9, 1843; "To the Friends of Education," *Philanthropist*, February 18, 1846; "The Fourth Annual Report of the 'Ladies' Education Society for the Education of the Free People of

Color,'" *Philanthropist*, July 30, 1845; "To the Friends of Education," *Philanthropist*, February 18, 1846.

123 For more on petitioning, see Carwardine, *Evangelicals and Politics*; Jeffrey, *Great Silent Army*, 87–92; Lerner, "Political Activities"; Van Broekhoven, "'Let Your Names Be Enrolled'"; Zaeske, *Signatures of Citizenship*.

124 Zaeske, *Signatures of Citizenship*, 69–74.

125 Laura M. Wright to BMC, April 1, 1835, BMC Papers, Box 1, Folder 1.

126 See McKivigan, *War against Proslavery Religion*.

127 See Jordan, "Quakers, 'Comeouters,' and the Meaning of Abolitionism"; Padgett, "Comeouterism and Antislavery Violence."

128 Salerno, *Sister Societies*, 64.

129 LMW to BMC, March 5, 1836, BMC Papers, Box 1, Folder 3.

130 Sarah Coleman to BMC, April 11, 1836, BMC Papers, Box 1, Folder 3.

131 Maria Kellogg to BMC, April 9, 1836, BMC Papers, Box 1, Folder 3.

132 "Proceedings of the Female Delegates at Mount Pleasant," *Philanthropist*, May 12, 1837.

133 Sophia Arnold to BMC, April 5, [1836], BMC Papers, Box 2, Folder 9. See also Padgett, "Abolitionists of All Classes."

134 Zaeske, *Signatures of Citizenship*, 55. See also Van Broekhoven, "'Let Your Names Be Enrolled.'"

135 "Petition of the Ladies Resident in the State of Ohio," *Philanthropist*, June 24, 1836. A slightly different version of appears in Weld, Weld, and Grimké, I *Letters*, 175–76.

136 Zaeske, *Signatures of Citizenship*, 55. Though Sturges was born in Connecticut, she was the likely author. I thank Patricia Cline Cohen for her dogged ancestry research on Sturges. See <http://www.ysearch.org/gedcom_show.asp?uid=&viewuid=KRXTF> (September 12, 2007).

137 "Preamble and Resolutions of the Ohio Female A.S. Society," *Philanthropist*, May 27, 1836.

138 LMW to BMC, May 20, 1836, BMC Papers, Box 1, Folder 3.

139 "Address to the Females in the State of Ohio," *Philanthropist*, June 24, 1836.

140 Ibid.

141 LMW to BMC, May 20, 1836, BMC Papers, Box 1, Folder 3.

142 Portage LASS, May 17, 1836.

143 LMW to BMC, May 20, 1836, BMC Papers. Sturges reported only 423 signatures on the Portage petition ("Proceedings of the Female Delegates at Mount Pleasant," *Philanthropist*, May 12, 1837).

144 "To the Females of Ohio," *Philanthropist*, December 9, 1836.

145 "Proceedings of the Female Delegates at Mount Pleasant," *Philanthropist*, May 12, 1837.

146 According to Padgett, the Ohio women garnered 575, 265, 545, and 441 signatures on this petition following the Granville meeting in 1836. Sturges also explained

that "due to the delinquency of our co-operators abroad," the gag rule was passed before the petitions could be sent to the House of Representatives. "It was therefore thought best to forward our memorial to the Senate." Not being acquainted with or trusting Ohio's senators, Sturges sent the petitions to Senator Daniel Webster of Massachusetts, but "of the fate of this Memorial, we are altogether ignorant." See Padgett, "Abolitionists of All Classes," 253.

147 Van Broekhoven, "'Let Your Names Be Enrolled.'"

148 Portage County Female Anti-Slavery Society to Boston Female Anti-Slavery Society, August 11, 1836, Boston Female Anti-Slavery Society Letterbook.

149 AWW for the Boston Female Anti-Slavery Society to the Portage County Female Anti-Slavery Society, August 27, 1836, Boston Female Anti-Slavery Society Letterbook.

150 Augustus Wattles to BMC, April 9, 1836, BMC Papers, Box 1, Folder 3.

CHAPTER 2

1 See "Frederick Douglass in Chicago," *Liberator*, November 18, 1853; "Speech of Fred Douglass at the Jerry Rescue Celebration," *Chicago Daily Tribune*, October 19, 1853; "Speech of Frederick Douglas [*sic*]," *Chicago Daily Tribune*, October 24, 1853.

2 MBD letter, *Oquakwa (Illinois) Spectator*, November 9, 1853. MBD had also just attended a convention "of the colored people of the state" whose attendees she characterized as knowledgeable, respectful, intelligent and cultivated. See MBD letter, *Oquakwa Spectator*, October 19, 1853.

3 Volpe, *Forlorn Hope*, 64. For more on the development of the Liberty Party, see Johnson, *Liberty Party*; Sewell, *Ballots for Freedom*. See also Harrold, *Gamaliel Bailey*.

4 Jeffrey, *Great Silent Army*, 136–37. Antislavery historians have until recently assumed that third-party abolitionism in Old Northwest precluded women's participation. See, for example, Blue, *Free Soilers*; Gienapp, *Origins of the Republican Party*; Volpe, *Forlorn Hope*. A recent resurgence of interest in antislavery third parties has, by and large, continued to disregard women. Although Blue's *No Taint of Compromise* devotes two chapters to women, Earle's *Jacksonian Antislavery* ignores women, and Laurie's *Beyond Garrison* pays scant attention to them. The women who receive attention often are related to male politicians (Jessie Benton Frémont) or are outspoken leaders (Jane Swisshelm), not the rank and file. Some scholarship that more thoroughly explores women's participation includes Evans, "Abolitionism"; Gamble, "Moral Suasion"; Quist, "'Great Majority'"; Pierson, *Free Hearts*; Schwalm, "Antislavery and Reform Activities"; Alice Taylor, "From Petitions to Partyism." See also Zaeske, *Signatures of Citizenship*.

5 Maine women abolitionists, for example, increasingly entered partisan politics in the 1850s. See Alice Taylor, "From Petitions to Partyism."

6 Gustafson argues that antislavery third parties "were broad entities that fused the civic world of benevolent and reform organizations with the electoral world of voting and legislating. As such, they provided women with a new path into partisan politics, as antislavery activism moved from moral suasion to practical politics" (*Women and the Republican Party*, 7). Schwalm asserts, "In Wisconsin's first territory-wide antislavery association, political and moral goals were merged as they were in nearly all western antislavery societies" ("Antislavery and Reform Activities," 18). Volpe argues, "Third party voters remained committed to the duty of a righteous minority to regenerate politics" (*Forlorn Hope*, xvi).

7 Gamaliel Bailey, an important leader in the Ohio Liberty Party, "conceived the role of an independent political organization to be one of influencing the old parties" (Harrold, "Forging an Antislavery Instrument," 379).

8 Kraut, "Partisanship and Principles."

9 McKivigan, "Vote as You Pray."

10 "State Convention of the Liberty Party of Illinois," *WC*, February 1, 1844.

11 Although Volpe, *Forlorn Hope*, highlights the strong connection between abolitionist churches and the Liberty Party in the Old Northwest, he does not discuss how such ties also opened the door for women to participate in politics.

12 On the difference in the approaches to politics favored by women's charitable groups and by female abolitionists, see Boylan, "Women and Politics."

13 On Liberty Party organizing at the local level, see Laurie, *Beyond Garrison*, 63; Johnson, "Liberty Party," 246.

14 Hewitt, "Social Origins," 218.

15 Pierson, *Free Hearts*, 33–37.

16 Although some leading western abolitionists, including Gamaliel Bailey, stressed the distinctions between moral and political action (Harrold, *Gamaliel Bailey*, 20–24), the overwhelming consensus among the rank-and-file women abolitionists was that westerners did not distinguish as clearly between the two as did easterners.

17 Rebecca Edwards, *Angels in the Machinery*, 18.

18 Martha S. Jones, *All Bound Up Together*, 78–82.

19 Many other prominent western women abolitionists hailed from southern states, including at least two from Virginia: Margaret Lucy Shands Bailey, wife of Gamaliel Bailey, was born in Sussex County, and Indiana abolitionist Rebecca Updegraff hailed from Loudoun County. See Harrold, *Gamaliel Bailey*, 13; Josiah Parker Papers, Earlham College, Earlham, Indiana.

20 Lerner, *Grimké Sisters*, 19.

21 MBD, "The Cause of the Oppressed," *WC*, February 23, 1842.

22 MBD, "A Tale of Truth," *WC*, September 5, 1844.

23 MBD, "Early Impressions of Slavery," *WC*, September 2, 1842.

24 MBD had covertly penned pieces for the *Alexandria Kaleidoscope* during her youth. She increased her journalistic output after the death of her husband in 1849,

writing for several different newspapers through the 1860s (Jeanne Humphreys, "Mary Brown Davis, Journalist, Feminist, and Social Reformer," May 1939, unpublished Honors Project, KO H927m, Knox College, Special Collections and Archives, Galesburg, Illinois).

25 Quoted in Breen, "Female Antislavery Petition Campaign." See also Zaeske, *Signatures of Citizenship*, 36.

26 Zaeske, *Signatures of Citizenship*, 190 n. 16.

27 The women of Virginia would continue with their political activism into the early 1840s through the Whig Party (Varon, "'Tippecanoe"). Tennessee women would also participate in partisan politics during the 1840s (DeFiore, "'COME, *and Bring the Ladies'"*).

28 MBD regularly wrote articles for the *PRNWG*. See "Monticello Female Seminary," February 19, 1841; "Retrospection," July 16, 1841; "A Tale of Truth," August 6, 1841; "Woman," October 15, 1841; "Clemency," November 5, 1841; "The Singing School," December 10, 1841; "Fate of Genius," February 25, 1842; "A Scrap," April 15, 1842; "The Revival of Letters—No. 1," October 14, 1842; "The Revival of Letters—No. 2," October 28, 1842; "The Revival of Letters—No. 3," November 25, 1842; "The Revival of Letters—No. 4," December 20, 1842.

29 On antislavery opposition in Peoria, see MBD, "The Progress of Truth in Peoria," *WC*, February 9, 1843; Irene Ball Allan to Lucinda Ball, January 17, 1842, May 15, 1842, Ball-Curtis Genealogy.

30 William T. Allan, "Mobocracy in Tazewell County," *WC*, July 26, 1842.

31 MBD, "A Trip to Galesburg, Knox Co.," *WC*, June 22, 1843.

32 For more on the history of Galesburg and the abolition movement, see Dillon, "Antislavery Movement in Illinois, 1809–1844"; Muelder, *Fighters for Freedom*.

33 "State Female Anti-Slavery Society," *WC*, March 25, 1846.

34 Frances D. Gage to Ruth and Joseph Dugdale, April 23, [1855], Joseph Dugdale Papers, Friends Historical Library, Swarthmore College, Swarthmore, Pennsylvania.

35 Lucy Pettengill preceded her husband, wealthy merchant Moses Pettengill, into abolitionism. By the mid-1840s, the Pettengills became the financial foundation of Peoria abolitionism (Muelder, *Fighters for Freedom*, 174; *Moses Pettengill*).

36 Muelder, *Fighters for Freedom*, 130–31.

37 *PRNWG*, December 16, 1837. See also Muelder, *Fighters for Freedom*, 174; Weiner, "Anti-Abolition Violence."

38 Samuel Davis occasionally printed articles that touched on abolition. See "Anniversary of the Illinois State Anti-Slavery Society," *PRNWG*, August 14, 1840; "Interesting Reminiscences" and "The Right of Petition," *PRNWG*, January 22, 1841. For more on Davis, see Weiner, "Anti-Abolition Violence."

39 For Davis's response to the Lovejoy murder, see *PRNWG*, December 16, 1837. On Lovejoy, see Dillon, *Elijah P. Lovejoy*.

40 See *PRNWG*, August 31, 1839. For more on the history of colonization in Illinois, see Dillon, "Antislavery Movement in Illinois, 1824–1835."

41 MBD, "The Progress of Truth in Peoria," *WC*, February 9, 1843. Although MBD does not openly identify herself as the female abolitionist whose husband refused to allow her to hold the prayer meeting, it is implied.

42 *GUE*, July 26, 1839. See also Muelder, *Fighters for Freedom*, 177.

43 Muelder, *Fighters for Freedom*, 177.

44 MBD, "The Progress of Truth." See also Irene Ball Allan to Lucinda Ball, January 17, 1842, Ball-Curtis Genealogy. Volpe has pointed out the importance of churches, especially in small midwestern communities, in sustaining and encouraging abolitionists and the Liberty Party: "Centered in small, sometimes stagnant, self-conscious village communities, the Liberty party often drew the bulk of its strength from members of one local religious body. More than any other factor, identification with a particular church community motivated individuals to cast Liberty party ballots. In a symbolic yet meaningful way, the commitment to Liberty helped reaffirm and unify the community while further insulating it from society's woes" (*Forlorn Hope*, xiii).

45 For more on Irene Ball Allan, see her letters in Ball-Curtis Genealogy.

46 Irene Ball Allan to Lucinda Ball, May 15, 1842, Ball-Curtis Genealogy. The Pettengills were also recovering from the death of their oldest child, 3½-year-old Hannah, in March 1841. See *PRNWG*, March 26, 1841.

47 Irene Ball Allan to Lucinda Ball, May 15, 1842, Ball-Curtis Genealogy.

48 "Important Suggestions," *WC*, December 30, 1842. Although this letter to the editor is signed only "I . . .," the writer is likely Irene Ball Allan because the author says she is a woman and the style of the letter resembles that of Allan's other published writings.

49 "Doings in Washington, Tazwell County," *PRNWG*, May 13, 1842.

50 By 1842, Samuel Davis had become slightly more sympathetic to antislavery. See "Abolition Movements," *PRNWG*, May 13, 1842; "Abolition Movements," *PRNWG*, May 30, 1842; "Liberty Nominations," *PRNWG*, June 17, 1842. On Davis's decision to sell the newspaper, see his editorials in the *PRNWG* on September 23, 1842, and February 17, 1843.

51 See "Mob in Peoria" and "Freedom of Speech Suppressed," *WC*, February 23, 1843. See also Muelder, *Fighters for Freedom*, 147–48; Humphreys, "Mary Brown Davis."

52 See Samuel Davis's editorial, *PRNWG*, February 17, 1843. For the antiabolitionist editorial that followed Davis's departure, see *PRNWG*, March 3, 1843. See also Muelder, *Fighters for Freedom*, 178–79; Weiner, "Anti-Abolitionist Violence," 5–6.

53 Samuel Davis, "Another Outrage in Peoria," *WC*, July 7, 1846; Weiner, "Anti-Abolitionist Violence," 13.

54 MBD, "Female Anti-Slavery Society of Peoria," *WC*, August 17, 1843.

55 MBD, "Character of Peoria in Some Degree Retrieved," *WC*, August 17, 1843.

56 MBD, "Female-Anti Slavery Society of Peoria," *WC*, August 17, 1843.

57 The Massachusetts Female Emancipation Society, for example, temporarily backed the Liberty Party but by 1843 "would withdraw their support from partisan politics and turn their attention to moral reform movements that were less contentious than antislavery" (Salerno, *Sister Societies*, 104). Rhode Island women abolitionists in the 1840s were caught up in a sex scandal and paid little attention to Liberty (Van Broekhoven, *Devotion of These Women*, 27–35). Rochester women abolitionists either joined the anti-third-party Garrisonians or moved on to other reform activities, though many would join the Free-Soilers and Republicans in the 1850s (Hewitt, "Social Origins," 210). The Liberty Party is only once referenced in Debra Gold Hansen's *Strained Sisterhood*, a study of the Boston Female Anti-Slavery Society, thus suggesting the group's lack of concern with Liberty (which is no surprise considering their association with the Garrisonians). There is no reference to the Liberty Party in the index of Petrulionis's study of Concord abolitionists, *To Set This World Right*.

58 See Henry FASS.

59 "The Central Committee at Detroit to the Ladies of the State of Michigan," *Signal of Liberty*, April 27, 1846; Gara, *Liberty Line*, 115–42. See also Quist, "Great Majority.'"

60 "The Movement," *Cincinnati Weekly Herald and Philanthropist*, March 18, 1846.

61 See Dillon, "Antislavery Movement in Illinois: 1809–1844"; Evans, "Abolitionism."

62 "Putnam Co.," *WC*, October 3, 1844.

63 "A Call for a Convention to Form a State Female Anti-Slavery Society," *WC*, April 18, 1844.

64 On the weather, see [Laura B. Coleman] letter, *WC*, June 6, 1844. For a discussion of the meeting, see "Female Anti-Slavery State Society," *WC*, June 20, 1844.

65 Many western men and women "came out" of their churches because of the institution's failure to oppose slavery. Volpe has pointed out the synchronicity between religious and political come-outerism in the Old Northwest: "Northwestern Liberty voters were typically members of separatist religious groups who denounced slaveholding as grievous sin. . . . Voting for the abolition third party was often the political equivalent of religious 'comeouterism'" (*Forlorn Hope*, xii).

66 MBD, "Female Anti-Slavery Convention at Peoria," *WC*, June 6, 1844.

67 "A Call for a Convention to Form a State Female Anti-Slavery Society," *WC*, April 18, 1844.

68 "More from the 'More Favorable Party'—Gallantry," *WC*, May 2, 1844.

69 For a discussion of the relationship between gender and partisan politics in the antebellum period, see Ryan, *Women in Public*; Varon, *We Mean to Be Counted*.

70 MBD, "Explanation," *WC*, May 23, 1844. Henry Clay was the Whig presidential nominee in 1844. He lost the election to Democrat James Polk. For more on women's Clay Clubs, see Van Broekhoven, "'Better Than a Clay Club.'"

71 Padgett, "Abolitionists of All Classes," 225. See also Boylan, "Women and Politics"; Carwardine, *Evangelicals and Politics*, 32–34.

72 Varon argues that "historians have underestimated the extent and significance of women's partisanship in the antebellum period.... Whig womanhood embodied the notion that women could—and should—make vital contributions to party politics by serving as both partisans and mediators in the public sphere" ("Tippecanoe," 495).

73 Ryan, *Women in Public*, 136. See also DeFiore, "COME, *and Bring the Ladies*"; Varon, "Tippecanoe"; Zboray and Zboray, "Whig Women."

74 Gunderson, *Log-Cabin Campaign*, 136–37. See, for example, "Patriotism of the Ladies: All for Harrison!!," *PRNWG*, September 18, 1840. Abolitionist Hannah Bent declared in 1844, "Though I am a Whig I do not feel very sorry Polk is elected. Indeed I am quite easy on the subject. I hope it will teach them not to put up a slaveholding candidate again" (Hannah Bent to Mary Blanchard, November 15, 1844, Blanchard Papers). Hannah Bent married Moses Pettengill in 1866. It was a second marriage for both. See "Memorial Notice of Mrs. H. W. Pettengill," n.d., Blanchard Papers.

75 Martha S. Jones, *All Bound Up Together*, 59–61. See also "Proceedings of the Colored Convention," *NS*, September 29, 1848.

76 Philip A. Foner and Walker, *Proceedings*, 227.

77 "Communications," *FDP*, October 1, 1852.

78 MBD, "Explanation," *WC*, May 23, 1844.

79 Mrs. T. C. Hurlbut to Irene B. Allan, *WC*, August 8, 1844. Although this letter is not signed, a reference to "Mr. Hurlbut" signified the author as Mrs. Hurlbut, who would go on to become the vice president of the Illinois Female Anti-Slavery Society in 1848.

80 Nearly all the literature on female antislavery efforts discusses the importance of domesticity. For an example of fugitive slave literature, see Jacobs, *Incidents*.

81 "More from the 'More Favorable Party'—Gallantry," *WC*, May 2, 1844.

82 "Notice," *WC*, March 21, 1844.

83 Volpe, *Forlorn Hope*, xi.

84 Ibid., 69, 76.

85 W. B. Irish to WLG, April 25, 1845, BPL, MS A.1.2, vol. 15, no. 28.

86 "Ohio Anti Slavery men have more of harmony and unity among them," an editorial in the *Colored American* asserted ("The Aspects of Our Cause," *Colored American*, March 21, 1840). "The midwestern antislavery movement was," according to Schwalm, "relatively free of the hostility which existed in the East between moral and political factions of the national movement" ("Antislavery and Reform Activities," 1). Seigel, "Moral Champions," argues that Indiana reformers linked moral and political antislavery. Gamble, however, asserts that the harmony among western abolitionists was short-lived: "Their unity was also temporary, though, and when abolitionists in the West did divide, it was over basically the same issues

which split the eastern movement" ("Moral Suasion," 118). Gamble's research focuses primarily on Garrisonians in the West.

87 MBD's friends and neighbors in the Putnam County Female Anti-Slavery Society expressed their political opinion when they resolved that "as the *Liberty party* makes the unchanging principles of truth and justice their object, we will use our influence to further their progress." Perhaps fearing that this statement might appear too openly political for a female group, the Putnam women established their moderate credentials by explicitly distancing themselves from woman's rights: "Ambition for office with anti-slavery females," they declared, "is incompatible with their purity of motives." Six months later, this group of women became increasingly bold, passing a sarcastic resolution praising the state legislature for finding the time "amidst the pressure of business, to manifest their zeal in the anti-slavery cause, by forming themselves into a Colonization Society." The women cleverly redefined colonization to suit their purpose, concluding, "Whereas, we have long been agents for the Underground Railroad, designed, as all know, for the colonizing of the slaves with their own consent, therefore . . . we rejoice in [the politicians'] benevolent design, and . . . we cordially invite them to cooperate with us" ("Putnam Co.," *WC*, October 3, 1844; "Putnam County Female A.S. Society," *WC*, April 8, 1845).

88 "Address of the Ladies' Anti-Slavery Association of Dundee," *WC*, March 25, 1846. Lovejoy lost the 1846 election. He was elected to Congress as a Republican in 1856 (Lovejoy, *His Brother's Blood*, xxix).

89 MBD, "For the Western Citizen," *WC*, May 9, 1848. ·

90 "Extract from an Address to the Liberty Association of Detroit, by Horace Hallock," *Signal of Liberty*, May 20, 1844.

91 Pierson, *Free Hearts*, 33–37. Alice Taylor argues that in the 1850s, Maine abolitionist women's partisan activism "served to domesticate the political sphere" ("From Petitions to Partyism," 85).

92 "Notice," *WC*, March 21, 1844.

93 "The Ladies of Michigan," *Signal of Liberty*, September 26, 1846.

94 "Political Convention," *FLAASC*, May 20, 1843.

95 Huldah Wickersham to Charles H. Test, n.d., Charles H. Test Letters, 1840–43, S1296, Indiana State Library, Indiana Division, Manuscripts Collection, Indianapolis, reprinted in Hamm, *Antislavery Movement*, 62–65.

96 MBD, "For the Western Citizen," *WC*, May 9, 1848.

97 "Female Anti-Slavery Convention at Peoria," *WC*, June 6, 1844.

98 Ibid.

99 Liberty conventions often debated the issue of the relationship between the church and the abolition movement. See McKivigan, "Vote as You Pray," 183.

100 "Female Anti-Slavery State Society," *WC*, June 20, 1844.

101 Irene B. Allan, "To the Managers of the Illinois Anti-Slavery Society," *WC*, August 15, 1844.

102 Evans, "Abolitionism," 66.

103 "State Female Anti-Slavery Society," *WC*, March 26, 1846.

104 "A Call for a North-Western Liberty Convention at Chicago," *WC*, March 18, 1846.

105 Ibid. The four men were Charles V. Dyer, Luther Rossiter, Codding, and Lovejoy.

106 "North-Western Convention," *WC*, June 30, 1846.

107 Ibid.

108 "Female Anti-Slavery State Society," *WC*, June 20, 1844; "State Female A.S. Society," *WC*, August 11, 1846.

109 This cautious trend continued amid increasing concerns about women stepping out of their sphere. With the 1845 death of Irene Allen, one of the group's more outspoken political advocates, the women became more concerned about public opprobrium. As members noted in a public address to the antislavery women of Illinois later that year, "It is . . . objected, that as we meet at the same time our brethren do, we shall love much of the pleasure of those meetings which embrace the talents, learning, &c of the other sex." The women clearly felt pressured to distance themselves from the male sphere of partisan politics. Trying to put a positive spin on this development, the address concluded by pointing out that separate meetings allowed for more female agency: "Which confers the greatest benefit, to become ourselves, thinking, originating agents, or mere passive listeners to addresses, however eloquent and excellent they may be? In short, it is to be entertained, or is it to be useful that we number ourselves in the Anti-Slavery Host?" The women also strengthened their ties with religious abolitionists. Five months after the Chicago Liberty Convention, the group met in conjunction with the Christian Anti-Slavery Society at Granville. The call for the convention asserted that "all that can touch the heart of the Christian or philanthropist" required women to attend. Hoping that this coordination with the Christian Anti-Slavery Society would engender less opposition, the women met at a church and invited the Reverend Levi Spencer to lecture. See Ball-Curtis Genealogy; "To the Anti-Slavery Women of Illinois," *WC*, October 6, 1846; "Illinois State Female Anti-Slavery Society," *WC*, September 29, 1846; "Ill. State Female A.S. Society," *WC*, November 14, 1846.

110 "Notice," *WC*, June 13, 1844.

111 "Our Eighth Anniversary," *Philanthropist*, July 5, 1843.

112 Schwalm, "Antislavery and Reform Activities," 25.

113 "State Convention of the Liberty Party of Illinois," *WC*, February 1, 1844.

114 MBD, "Explanation," *WC*, May 23, 1844.

115 "Southern and Western Liberty Convention," *Philanthropist*, April 23, 1845.

116 "To the People of Oakland County," *Signal of Liberty*, July 18, 1842. For other examples of published calls for women's attendance at Liberty meetings, see the following in the *Signal of Liberty*: "Public Discussion" and "Oakland County Convention," April 8, 1844; "Extract from an Address," May 20, 1844; "State Liberty

Convention," September 16, 1844. In the *WC*, see "Bureau County," June 22, 1843; "Northern Indiana Liberty Convention—Ninth Congressional District," September 21, 1843; "Liberty Convention," November 30, 1843; "State Convention of the Liberty Party of Illinois," February 1, 1844; "Kendall County" and "Notice," February 8, 1844; "Notices," February 22, 1844; "Notice," March 21, 1844; "Annual Meeting of the De Kalb County Anti-Slavery Society," April 1, 1844; "Attend Those Conventions!," April 18, 1844; "Remember," May 2, 1844; "Notice," May 23, 1844; "Cook County Convention," July 11, 1844; "Wood Up the Fires!" and "Boone County," March 11, 1846; "A Call for a North-Western Liberty Convention at Chicago," March 18, 1846; "McHenry County," April 15, 1846; "Mass Meeting of the Friends of Liberty in Lake County," May 13, 1846; "Present at the North-Western Convention," June 3, 1846. In the *American Freeman*, see March 27, 1844; January 22, 1845 (in Schwalm, "Antislavery and Reform Activities," 22–27). In the *Philanthropist*, see "Mass Meeting—Attention!!," March 13, 1844; "Make Way for Liberty!—Liberty Mass Meeting at Harrison," August 16, 1844.

117 "To the People of Oakland County," *Signal of Liberty*, July 18, 1842.

118 "Shameful," *Philanthropist*, September 4, 1844.

119 Varon, "Tippecanoe," finds that in 1840 and 1844, Whig women too were expected to have a "civilizing" influence on politics.

120 "Remarks," *Daily Free Democrat*, March 27, 1855.

121 "Antislavery Lectures," *Signal of Liberty*, April 28, 1845.

122 "Kendall County," *WC*, February 8, 1844.

123 "Mr. Codding's Report," *WC*, November 18, 1843.

124 "Political Influence of Women," *WC*, March 4, 1846.

125 "Politics and Ladies," *Philanthropist*, August 23, 1844.

126 Booth, editor of the Wisconsin-based *American Freeman* and *Daily Free Democrat*, eventually supported woman suffrage: "Why not also, should woman meet man at the ballot-box?" ("Remarks," *Daily Free Democrat*, March 27, 1855).

127 "Great Liberty Convention at Elgin, Kane County," *WC*, January 26, 1847.

128 "Liberty Convention," *WC*, February 23, 1847.

129 "Meetings in Crosby, &c," *Cincinnati Weekly Herald and Philanthropist*, August 16, 1844.

130 See Paula Baker, "Domestication of Politics."

131 Van Broekhoven notes that "before 1837 American antislavery leaders more commonly advised women to influence family members" ("'Let Your Names Be Enrolled,'" 181).

132 Boylan, "Women and Politics," 370–78.

133 Zagarri, "Gender and the First Party System," 123.

134 Rebecca Edwards, *Angels in the Machinery*, 17.

135 MBD, "For the Western Citizen," *WC*, August 24, 1847. There are many examples of western abolitionists calling for women to use their "influence." See, for ex-

ample, "Address to Females," *WC*, April 3, 1843; Emily S. Colton, "Constitution of the Female A.S. Society of Princeton, Bureau Co., Ill.," *WC*, November 9, 1843; "Political Convention," *FLAASC*, May 20, 1843; "Notice," *WC*, March 21, 1844; "The Akron Convention," *Philanthropist*, June 26, 1844. Alice Taylor reveals that Maine women abolitionists a decade later also emphasized female influence ("From Petitions to Partyism," 72).

136 "A Chapter for the Ladies," *Signal of Liberty*, August 11, 1845.

137 "Putnam Co.," *WC*, October 3, 1844. For other examples of the Putnam County Female Anti-Slavery Society, see *WC*, September 7, 1843, April 8, 1845.

138 Henry FASS, September 20, 1841, April 3, 1841.

139 "North-Western Liberty Convention," *WC*, June 30, 1846.

140 "What the Women Do," *WC*, April 2, 1845.

141 Some historians interpret this traditional appeal to women through "moral" avenues as evidence that women's participation was seen as ancillary. See Quist, "'Great Majority,'" 336.

142 "Women and Politics," September 20, 1848, Composition Book, 1842–53, Mary Sheldon Papers, Box 1, Folder 2, Oberlin College Library, Oberlin, Ohio.

143 MBD, "For the Western Citizen," *WC*, August 24, 1847.

144 "Our Best Respects to the Ladies of Wisconsin," *American Freeman*, January 22, 1845, cited in Schwalm, "Antislavery and Reform Activities," 28.

145 Henry FASS, April 3, 1841.

146 MBD, "For the Western Citizen," *WC*, August 24, 1847.

147 Huldah Wickersham to C. H. and E. W. Text, n.d., in Hamm, *Antislavery Movement*, 62–65.

148 "Putnam County Female A.S. Society," *WC*, April 8, 1845.

149 "Address of the Ladies' Anti-Slavery Association of Dundee," *WC*, March 25, 1846.

150 MBD, "For the Western Citizen," *WC*, August 24, 1847.

151 Henry FASS, July 1, 1842.

152 "Putnam County Female A.S. Society," *WC*, April 8, 1845.

153 Jeffrey briefly discusses women's symbolic political activity, including banner presentations (*Great Silent Army*, 165–66). For another reference to Liberty banners, see "State Liberty Conventions," *Signal of Liberty*, September 23, 1844.

154 Anti-Slavery Women of St. Charles letter, *WC*, February 11, 1846. The presentation of banners was not unprecedented in the early republic. The Massachusetts Female Emancipation Society, for example, sewed "liberty banners" for districts that voted for Liberty candidates (Van Broekhoven, "'Let Your Names Be Enrolled,'" 194). Maine women abolitionists also used banners to express their political opinions. These banners became increasingly partisan in the 1850s (Alice Taylor, "From Petitions to Partyism," 76–77).

155 Anti-Slavery Women of St. Charles letter, *WC*, February 11, 1846.

156 "The Ladies of St. Charles," *WC*, February 25, 1846.

157 "The Banner," *WC*, March 4, 1846. More than 50 percent of Bristol's 177 voters chose the Liberty candidate in the 1846 election (Volpe, *Forlorn Hope*, 65).

158 "Address of the Ladies' Anti-Slavery Association of Dundee," *WC*, March 25, 1846.

159 Lovejoy, *His Brother's Blood*.

160 "De Kalb County," *WC*, April 15, 1846.

161 "Presentation of the Banner," *WC*, May 11, 1847.

162 Ibid.

163 Varon, "Tippecanoe," finds that Whig women's participation in the 1840 campaign, like that of Liberty women a bit later, involved much more than a passive presence and represented a shift in women's political identities.

164 For more on Black Laws and the Liberty Party, see Middleton, *Black Laws: Race and the Legal Process*; Volpe, *Forlorn Hope*, 104. See also Berwanger, *Frontier against Slavery*; Harrold, *Gamaliel Bailey*, 60; Litwack, *North of Slavery*.

165 Middleton, *Black Laws: Race and the Legal Process*, 101; Middleton, *Black Laws in the Old Northwest*, 274; *Proceedings of the First Annual Meeting of the Ohio State Anti-Slavery Society*; Yee, *Black Women Abolitionists*, 132.

166 Philip A. Foner and Walker, *Proceedings*, 214. See also "Ohio Black Laws," *NS*, March 10, 1848; "Legislative Wisdom," *NS*, March 31, 1848; "To the Friends of Liberty and Justice in Ohio and Indiana," *NS*, November 24, 1848.

167 "Liberty State Convention," *Cincinnati Weekly Herald and Philanthropist*, January 7, 1846.

168 "North-Western Liberty Convention," *WC*, June 30, 1846.

169 Middleton, *Black Laws in the Old Northwest*, 6, 161, 274.

170 Harriet N. Torrey letter, *WC*, April 17, 1846.

171 See Kraditor, *Means and Ends*.

172 "Plea for the Oppressed and Enslaved," *ASB*, November 20, 1846. See also Padgett, "Abolitionists of All Classes," 326.

173 An eastern male abolitionist collecting data on the topic asked BMC to share her research: "Remembering that in the fall of 1846 you . . . collected many facts bearing on the object of the proposed work, I beg you to forward me copies of whatever you may have or can honestly lay your hands on that will aid me in the collection of facts" (Timothy B. Hudson to BMC, January 20, 1848, BMC Papers).

174 Middleton, *Black Laws: Race and the Legal Process*, 89.

175 MBD, "On Immediate Emancipation," *WC*, January 25, 1844.

176 MBD, "Slavery in Virginia," *WC*, September 29, 1846.

177 Ibid.

178 Ibid.

179 "Outrage upon Human Rights," *ASB*, February 2, 1849.

180 Henry FASS, July 23, 1843.

181 By the 1840s, the antislavery petition campaign had slowed down, with many eastern women turning to other antislavery activities and Liberty men focused on partisan politics. Western women, however, continued to employ petitioning to push for emancipation. Zaeske notes, "There was a noticeable increase during the early 1840s in petitioning activity among women of the western states and territories" (*Signatures of Citizenship*, 156). See also Van Broekhoven, "'Let Your Names Be Enrolled,'" 193.

182 Ginzberg, *Untidy Origins*, 132; Keyssar, *Right to Vote*, 55.

183 Zaeske argues that petitioning became a method for women to express their political authority (*Signatures of Citizenship*, 1–2).

184 "Letter from Springfield," *Peoria Democratic Press*, February 17, 1847.

185 The mixing of male and female names on petitions was unusual in the 1830s but had become more commonplace by the 1840s (Zaeske, *Signatures of Citizenship*, 156).

186 See the following letters and editorials in the *WC*: "The Black Laws," February 16, 1847; "The Peoria Petition," March 2, 1847; "Mr. Eastman," March 23, 1847; MBD, June 1, 1847, June 15, 1847. See also "Letter from Springfield," *Peoria Democratic Press*, February 17, 1847.

187 "Letter from Springfield," *Peoria Democratic Press*, February 17, 1847.

188 "The Black Laws," *WC*, February 16, 1847.

189 Ibid.

190 "The Peoria Petition," *WC*, March 2, 1847.

191 MBD, *WC*, March 23, 1847.

192 "The Peoria Petition," *WC*, March 2, 1847.

193 "Farmington Convention," *WC*, July 27, 1847.

194 "Petitions—Female Anti-Slavery Meeting," *WC*, August 3, 1847; "For the Western Citizen," *WC*, August 24, 1847. Van Broekhoven argues that women's petitions after 1840 became less deferential and placed more emphasis on "the responsibilities of female citizenship" ("'Let Your Names Be Enrolled,'" 193).

195 MBD, "For the Western Citizen," *WC*, August 24, 1847.

196 "Anti-Slavery Meeting at Youngs Prairie," *Signal of Liberty*, July 3, 1843; Cleveland Anti-Slavery Society Papers, MSS v.f. C, Western Reserve Historical Society, Cleveland, Ohio.

197 Parker Pillsbury, "Annual Meeting of the Lake and Ashtabula Counties Ladies' Anti-Slavery Society," *ASB*, July 31, 1846.

198 "Female A.S. Meeting," *Free Labor Advocate*, August 8, 1843.

199 See Henry FASS.

200 "Constitution and Proceedings," *WC*, April 6, 1843.

201 "Address to Females," *WC*, April 6, 1843.

202 "Constitution and Proceedings," *WC*, April 6, 1843.

203 MBD, "For the Western Citizen," *WC*, August 24, 1847.

204 Volpe, *Forlorn Hope*, 151 n. 3.

205 See, for example, Huldah Wickersham to Elizabeth Pease, November 26, 1844, BPL, MS A.1.2, vol. 14, no. 25; Betsy Hudson to BMC, February 27, 1846, Fletcher Papers, Box 5, Folder 9; Sarah to Joel McMillan, October 10, 1847, Alice McMillan Papers, Ohio Historical Society, Columbus; Harriet N. Torrey letters, *ASB*, April 17, 1846, August 14, 1846.

CHAPTER 3

1 "Society at Green Plains, Ohio," *GUE*, March 1833. On the founding of the Green Plain group, see "Stores for the Productions of Free Labor," *GUE*, December 1832.

2 Ohio FPA, September 4, 1849.

3 See Norton, *Liberty's Daughters*; Kerber, *Women of the Republic*; Barbara Clark Smith, "Food Rioters."

4 Drake, *Quakers and Slavery*, 115–16.

5 Nuermberger, *Free Produce Movement*, 6.

6 Heyrick, *Immediate Not Gradual Emancipation*; Heyrick, *Appeal*; Heyrick, *Apology*. See also Fladeland, *Men and Brothers*, 178–83; Holcomb, "'Cement of the Whole Antislavery Building'"; Midgley, *Women against Slavery*, 75–76.

7 The Female Association for Promoting the Manufacture and Use of Free Cotton is also referred to as the Ladies Free Cotton Society. See "Ladies Free Produce Society," *GUE*, November 27, 1829; "Report of the Ladies' 'Free Cotton' Society," *GUE*, April 1830; "Free Labor Cotton Manufactures," *GUE*, June 1830; "Colored Females' Free Produce Society," *GUE*, May 1831; "Coloured Female Free Produce Society," *GUE*, August 1831. See also Nuermberger, *Free Produce Movement*, 16–17, 19.

8 For more on the Green Plain group, see "To the Editor," *GUE*, January 1834. For more on Chandler, see Davidson, "Profile of Hicksite Quakerism"; Dillon, "Elizabeth Chandler"; Lundy, *Poetical Works*; Chandler, *Remember the Distance*.

9 Lundy, *Poetical Works*, 108.

10 Ruth Evans to Jane Howell, October 22, 1832, Elizabeth Margaret Chandler Papers, Bentley Historical Library, University of Michigan, Ann Arbor. See also Chandler, *Remember the Distance*, xxxiii, 394–95 n. 49.

11 Ruth Evans to Jane Howell, October 22, 1832, Chandler Papers.

12 Chandler's fame resulted in part from *Poetical Works*, Lundy's 1836 memoir of her, which included many of her poems and letters. Free produce groups across the North cited Chandler and republished her writings. The Ohio Free Produce Association published several of Chandler's articles. See Ohio FPA, November 14, 1854, February 9, 1856. Chandler also had a transnational influence. The Birmingham, England, Female Anti-Slavery Society lamented Chandler's death in "Our Female Friends in England," *GUE*, December 1836.

13 "On the Use of Free Produce," *GUE*, January 1832.

14 *Liberator*, May 28, 1831, January 21, 1832, January 28, 1832, February 4, 1832, February 11, 1832, February 18, 1832.

15 *Proceedings of the Anti-Slavery Convention, 1837*, 13. For a discussion of the role of free produce at the three antislavery conventions of American women, see Margaret Hope Bacon, "By Moral Force Alone," 279–81; Ira Brown, "'Am I Not a Woman and a Sister?'" 12–15.

16 *Proceedings of the Anti-Slavery Convention, 1838*, 7.

17 As Jeffrey (*Great Silent Army*, 20) and Faulkner ("Root of the Evil") have argued, popular ideas about women's natural ability to make moral sacrifices melded nicely with free produce. Women's increasingly important role in purchasing and consuming goods also made them appropriate leaders of free produce movement. As managers of the household economy, women would employ their superior virtue to fill their homes with products untainted by the blood of slaves. See also Nuermberger, *Free Produce Movement*, 21.

18 Nuermberger, *Free Produce Movement*, 102–3; Kraditor, *Means and Ends*, 217–20. See also Faulkner, "Root of the Evil"; Glickman, "'Buy for the Sake of the Slave,'" 893–94; Wilkinson, "'Touch Not.'" Garrisonian lecturers began objecting to free produce resolutions at antislavery meetings as early as 1845.

19 "The Products of Slave Labor," *Liberator*, March 5, 1847. See also "Abstinence from Slave Produce," *Liberator*, February 19, 1847; "The Slave Produce Question," *Liberator*, April 9, 1847; "Ransom of Douglass—Free Produce," *Liberator*, June 18, 1847.

20 They similarly objected to providing Bibles to slaves or helping slaves escape (Kraditor, *Means and Ends*, 219–20). See SSF's opposition to free produce at the Indiana State Anti-Slavery meeting in 1845: "Anniversary of the Indiana State Anti-Slavery Society," *FLAASC*, November 21, 1845.

21 Wilkinson, "'Touch Not,'" 5–8.

22 Blackett, *Building an Antislavery Wall*, 119–23; Faulkner, "Root of the Evil."

23 Midgley, *Women against Slavery*, 138. See also Billington and Billington, "'Burning Zeal,'" 87–88.

24 Sterling, *We Are Your Sisters*, 160. On Harper's poetry, see Harper, *Brighter Day Coming*, 81.

25 "Duty of Avoiding Slave Produce," *NS*, September 5, 1850.

26 See "Free Produce Convention," *NS*, January 23, 1851.

27 Nuermberger, *Free Produce Movement*, 33–34. See also Edgerton, *History*; Hamm, *Antislavery Movement*, 10–13; Ketring, "Charles Osborn." The *FLAASC* was published in New Garden, Indiana, between 1841 and 1848. Arnold Buffum edited the paper during its first year before being replaced by Benjamin Stanton.

28 Nuermberger, *Free Produce*, 34.

29 "Foster . . . contended that it was right for *himself* to use the products of slave labor—but for such as do not do nor think and act as he and those with him do, it is theft and robbery to do so" (*Aurora*, June 27, 1846). See also *Aurora*, November 8, 1845; "Theory vs. Practice," *Aurora*, November 22, 1845.

30 Wickersham was one of the most important leaders in Indiana antislavery. She

held executive positions with several antislavery groups (both female and mixed-sex) in the state until her death in 1845 (Hamm, *Antislavery Movement*, 61–66).

31 Henry FASS, April 3, 1841.

32 Ibid.

33 Ibid., September 20, 1841.

34 Ohio FPA, September 9, 1851.

35 Ibid., April 3, 1841.

36 Ibid., September 20, 1841.

37 "Report," *FLAASC*, February 16, 1842.

38 The Wayne County Female Anti-Slavery Society instructed ministers to practice free produce in a public address in January 1842; the Newport Female Anti-Slavery Society passed a free produce resolution at its November 1841 meeting; and the Union County Female Anti-Slavery Society passed a free produce resolution in October 1842. See *FLAASC*, January 8, 1842, November 9, 1841, October 15, 1842.

39 The following mixed-sex groups supported free produce: Marion County (Ohio) Free Produce Association (*FLAASC*, November 5, 1842); Hamilton County (Indiana) Anti-Slavery Society (*FLAASC*, December 10, 1842); Grant County (Indiana) Free Labor Association (*FLAASC*, April 29, 1843); Young's Prairie (Michigan) Free Labor Association (*FLAASC*, March 9, 1844); and Ohio Free Produce Association (Ohio FPA).

40 Ohio FPA.

41 See, for example, "Constitution and Proceedings," *WC*, April 6, 1843.

42 Dixon argues that the free produce movement challenged gender roles by bringing abolitionist women into "the outside world of business and politics" (*Perfecting the Family*, 97).

43 Henry FASS, "Address," June 6, 1841.

44 Henry FASS, July 23, 1843. For more on the abolitionist image of female slaves, see Yellin, *Women and Sisters*.

45 Henry FASS, July 23, 1843.

46 "Annual Report," *Non-Slaveholder*, November 1853.

47 "Free Labor Convention," *FLAASC*, November 7, 1846.

48 Henry FASS, "To the Women of Kentucky," June 30, 1849.

49 Ohio FPA, September 8, 1852.

50 Glickman discusses the use of metonymy to link slave products with the suffering of slaves ("'Buy for the Sake of the Slave,'" 899).

51 "The Union Co.," *FLAASC*, October 15, 1846.

52 "Products of Slave Labor," *ASB*, March 22, 1851. This letter is signed "HEH, Edinburgh." Because the writer notes, "It is out of my province to write for publication," the author was likely a woman. She could be Hannah Hiatt, Hannah Hinshaw, or Harriet Hoyt, all of whom were Indiana abolitionists.

53 Lundy, *Poetical Works*, 53–57.

54 *FLAASC*, November 9, 1841.

55 "Encouraging," *FLAASC*, August 18, 1843. There is one other reference to an abolitionist woman in Indiana requesting a burial in free produce clothes. Rachel Williams made this appeal before she died in 1849 (Miller, "Antislavery Movement," chap. 3).

56 "Annual Report," *Non-Slaveholder*, November 1853. For the membership of the committee that wrote the annual report, see Ohio FPA, June 11, 1853.

57 "The Marion County Free Labor Convention," *FLAASC*, November 5, 1842.

58 "At a Meeting," *FLAASC*, December 10, 1842.

59 "Free Labor Anniversary," *FLAASC*, August 25, 1843.

60 "Western Anti-Slavery Fair," *ASB*, April 9, 1847.

61 "Western Anti-Slavery Fair," *ASB*, May 14, 1847.

62 For a concise summery of the relationship between Quakers and abolitionism, see Jordan, "Quakers, 'Comeouters,' and the Meaning of Abolitionism."

63 Many Quakers, particularly those living in the South, developed a fairly moderate attitude toward slavery. See Weeks, *Southern Quakers and Slavery*.

64 "Friends Convention," *FLAASC*, February 25, 1843. See also Drake, *Quakers and Slavery*, 162–66; Jordan, "Indiana Separation"; Nuermberger, *Free Produce Movement*, 33–34, 48–49.

65 McKivigan, "Antislavery 'Comeouter' Sects."

66 Edgerton, *History*, 48; Coffin, *Reminiscences*, 231.

67 Henry FASS, "Address," August 22, 1842.

68 "Address of the Female Anti-Slavery Society of Wayne County, Indiana; to the Professors of Christianity in the United States," *FLAASC*, January 8, 1842.

69 *FLAASC*, April 15, 1843.

70 "Female Anniversary," *FLAASC*, November 1, 1842.

71 Henry FASS, August 6, 1844.

72 Dixon, *Perfecting the Family*, 84–100. See also Kelly, *In the New England Fashion*.

73 Nuermberger, *Free Produce Movement*, 61.

74 Ibid.

75 Margaret Hope Bacon, "By Moral Force Alone," 279.

76 Billington and Billington, "'Burning Zeal,'" 87–88; Midgley, *Women against Slavery*, 138–39.

77 "Ladies Repository," *GUE*, May 1830.

78 Hamm, *Antislavery Movement*, 6.

79 "Free Labor Association," *FLAASC*, March 9, 1844.

80 "Free Labor Convention," *FLAASC*, November 7, 1846.

81 Ibid.

82 "Proceedings of the Free Labor Convention," *FLAASC*, November 18, 1847.

83 Nuermberger, *Free Produce Movement*, 52–56.

84 Most recently, see Faulkner, "Root of the Evil." Glickman says, "Philadelphia was the capital of free produce agitation, but, over time, more than fifty stores opened

in eight other states, including Ohio, Indiana, and New York, and in England as well" ("'Buy for the Sake of the Slave,'" 890).

85 For an excellent summary of the debate between Garrison and Philadelphia free produce advocates, see Wilkinson, "'Touch Not.'"

86 Ibid.

87 Ohio FPA, September 9, 1851: "The Board of Managers were directed to open a correspondence with other similar Associations and endeavor to secure their cooperation in an effort to secure the resuscitation of the Non Slaveholder."

88 Ohio FPA, September 9, 1851, October 12, 1851, February 7, 1852, March 14, 1852, April 10, 1852, May 8, 1852, September 9, 1852, September 11, 1852, September 13, 1852, October 9, 1852, November 13, 1852, December 11, 1852, January 9, 1853, February 12, 1853, March 12, 1853.

89 Ibid., February 7, 1852, March 14, 1852, April 10, 1852, May 8, 1852, September 8, 1852.

90 Ibid., December 11, 1852.

91 Ibid., December 11, 1852, January 8, 1852.

92 "The Free Produce Association of Friends of Ohio Yearly Meeting," *Non-Slaveholder*, February 1853.

93 Ohio FPA, February 12, 1853.

94 "Annual Report," *Non-Slaveholder*, November 1853.

95 See, for example, Ohio FPA, May 14, 1853, June 11, 1853, October 8, 1853, November 1, 1853, December 10, 1853, March 12, 1854.

96 Ibid., November 1, 1853.

97 Ibid., November 14, 1854.

98 "Ladies Repository," *GUE*, May 1830.

99 "Female Association for the Manufacture and Use of Free Cotton," *GUE*, May 1831.

100 "Report of the Executive Committee of the Female Anti-Slavery Society at Economy," *FLAASC*, February 16, 1842.

101 *Extracts from the Minutes of the Annual Meeting of the Free Produce Association*, 2–3. See also Ohio FPA, September 3, 1850.

102 "Proceedings of the Free Labor Convention," *FLAASC*, November 18, 1847.

103 Billington and Billington, "'Burning Zeal,'" 87–88.

104 Nuermberger, *Free Produce Movement*, 58. See also Halbersleben, *Women's Participation*; Midgley, *Women against Slavery*, 137–38.

105 "Communications: From the Henry County (Indiana) Female Anti-Slavery Society, to the Women of Edinburg, (Scotland)," *FLAASC*, April 8, 1847. See also Henry FASS, March 5, 1847.

106 "Communications: From the Henry County (Indiana) Female Anti-Slavery Society, to the Women of Edinburg, (Scotland)," *FLAASC*, April 8, 1847.

107 Huldah Wickersham to Elizabeth Pease, October 18, 1843, BPL, MS A.1.2, vol. 13, no. 65. However, the British Friends failed to recognize the Indiana Yearly Meeting of Anti-Slavery Friends.

108 "The Marion County Free Labor Convention," *FLAASC*, November 5, 1842.

109 For more on antislavery and labor reform, see Eric Foner, "Abolitionism and the Labor Movement"; Glickstein, "'Poverty Is Not Slavery'"; Roediger, "Ira Steward."

110 "Free Labor Convention," *FLAASC*, November 7, 1846. Although the Western Free Produce Association in 1846 included no women as executive officers, several women served on the Business Committee that proposed the resolution regarding English goods.

111 "Marion County Free Labor Convention," *FLAASC*, November 5, 1842.

112 Henry FASS, December 7, 1847.

113 Ibid., June 6, 1841.

114 Ibid., June 30, 1849.

115 On racism among the Quakers, see Hamm et al., "'Great and Good People.'"

CHAPTER 4

1 Sarah MacMillan to AWW, April 15, 1852, BPL, MS A.9.2, vol. 25, no. 25.

2 Parker Pillsbury described AWW's letter and the Salem response in his letter to AWW, April 20, 1852, BPL, MS A.9.2, vol. 26, no. 26. See also Pillsbury to AWW, November 18, 1851, BPL, MS A.9.2, vol. 25, no. 134.

3 On the relationship between the Boston bazaar and other fairs, see Chambers-Schiller, "'Good Work'"; Alice Taylor, "'It Was a Kind of Ladies Exchange.'" Chamber-Schiller emphasizes the positive bonds between the Boston women and other fairs, while Taylor points out some of the friction and conflict that developed over the issue of what types of goods to sell.

4 Sarah MacMillan to AWW, April 15, 1842, BPL, MS A.9.2, vol. 25, no. 25.

5 The advertisement for the 1845 fair read, "The Twelfth Massachusetts Anti-Slavery Fair" (*Liberator*, September 5, 1845). In 1846, the ad read "The Twelfth National Anti-Slavery Bazaar" (*Liberator*, January 23, 1846).

6 Cheek and Cheek, *John Mercer Langston*, 48–83; Ford, "Black Churches"; Glazer, *Cincinnati in 1840*, 7–36; James Oliver Horton and Flaherty, "Black Leadership"; McClellan, "Cincinnati's Response."

7 James Oliver Horton and Flaherty, "Black Leadership"; Cheek and Cheek, "John Mercer Langston"; Nikki M. Taylor, *Frontiers of Freedom*.

8 "Cincinnati," *NS*, June 9, 1848.

9 James Oliver Horton and Flaherty, "Black Leadership." On public education for blacks in Cincinnati, see Calkins, "Black Education."

10 "Cincinnati," *NS*, June 9, 1848.

11 Ibid.; "Communication," *NS*, August 25, 1848.

12 Nikki M. Taylor, *Frontiers of Freedom*, 2; Cheek and Cheek, "John Mercer Langston," 32; Middleton, "Cincinnati."

13 *Daily Cincinnati Republican and Commercial Register*, January 18, 1835, quoted in Aaron, *Cincinnati*, 298.

14 "List of Abolitionists of Cincinnati," *Cincinnati Post and Anti-Abolitionist*, March 26, 1842.

15 See, for example, the following articles in the *CG*: "Debate on Slavery," September 10, 1845; "Sinfulness of Slavery," October 7, 1845, October 8, 1845, October 10, 1845, November 1, 1845; "The Parkersburg Case," October 22, 1845; "Negroes—The Herald," January 1 and 6, 1846; "The Black Laws," February 8, 1847; "The Black Laws and Law Making," February 17, 1847; "Colored Persons," February 27, 1852; "Again in Slavery," July 8, 1853; "A Fugitive Slave Case in Cincinnati," August 17, 1853; "The Cuban Slave Trade," August 30, 1853; "The Indiana Slave Case," August 31, 1853; "The Fugitive Slave Case," February 13, 1854.

16 Gamble, "Moral Suasion," 1.

17 Calkins, "Black Education."

18 Fladeland, *James Gillespie Birney*, 129.

19 See Gamble, "Moral Suasion"; Aaron, *Cincinnati*, 298–314; Harrold, "Forging an Antislavery Instrument"; Middleton, "Cincinnati."

20 Nikki M. Taylor, *Frontiers of Freedom*, 143–45.

21 Middleton, "Cincinnati."

22 Aaron, *Cincinnati*, 298–314. See also Middleton, "Cincinnati"; Cheek and Cheek, "John Mercer Langston."

23 "Highhanded Outrage—Judge Flinn Assaulting Mr. Joliffe in Market—Arrest of Flinn," *CG*, September 3, 1853; "Trial of Judge Jacob Flinn," *CG*, September 6, 1853; "Where Are We? What Are We Coming To?," *CG*, September 7, 1853.

24 "Cincinnati," *NS*, May 7, 1848.

25 For an excellent discussion of the development of moderate antislavery in Cincinnati, see Harrold, "Perspective."

26 James Oliver Horton and Flaherty, "Black Leadership," 73.

27 Fladeland, "James G. Birney's Anti-Slavery Activities"; *Philanthropist*, February 13, 1846; Gamble, "Moral Suasion," 93.

28 Gamble, "Moral Suasion," 143.

29 SOE to AWW, July 28, 1850, BPL, MS A.9.2, vol. 25, no. 16.

30 Mary Donaldson to AK, February 19, 1846, Foster Papers.

31 The 1850 U.S. Census lists A. H. Ernst's personal wealth at $200,000. In 1860, after his death, the Census valued Sarah's real estate at $25,000 and her personal assets at $1,000. His obituary blames the loss of income on irresponsible family members. In the 1870 U.S. Census, however, Sarah's personal estate totals $170,000. See "Death of A. H. Ernst," *Cincinnati Daily Gazette*, February 14, 1860; Sarah and Andrew's wills at the Cincinnati Courthouse; "Died," *Cincinnati Daily Times*, February 14, 1860; *Cincinnati Commercial*, February 18, 1860; Eliot, *Biographical History*; Otis, *Genealogical and Historical Memoir*; "Married," *Cincinnati Daily Gazette*, September 25, 1841. The biographical entry on SOE at *Dictionary of Unitarian and Universalist Biography* Web site is excellent: <http://www25.uua.org/uuhs/duub/articles/sarahotisernst.html> (July 10, 2009). I thank Kathy

Ernst for sharing her extensive files on the Ernsts with me. Andrew Ernst was often mentioned in the *Cincinnati Gazette* in relation to the Horticultural Society. See, for example, "Horticultural Society," April 30, 1847; "Horticultural Society," May 14, 1847; "The Horticultural Show," June 3, 1847; "The Cincinnati Horticultural Society," April 5, 1852; "The Cincinnati Horticultural Society," April 13, 1852; "The Cincinnati Horticultural Society," April 26, 1852; "Spring Exhibition of the Cincinnati Horticultural Society," May 13, 1852. Ernst's gardens were so well known that they were used as a reference point. See, for example, an article about a new Catholic institution: "The Seminary is located, we believe, in Storrs township, nor far from the gardens of A. H. Ernst" ("City News and Notices," *CG*, February 3, 1852). The Ernsts were also very prominent in Cincinnati as a wealthy, generous couple: "On Monday afternoon the members of the Baptist Convention, that has just closed its session here, to the number of about one hundred, took a ride out to the Spring Garden Nursery, on invitation of the Proprieter, Mr. A. H. Ernst. After a stroll through his beautiful grounds, Mr. E. accompanied them in carriages to the Cemetery at Spring Grove; the whole party returned thence to Spring Garden, and took supper at the hospitable table of Mrs. Ernst. The evening passed off in the most agreeable manner, and the Delegates, many of them from New England, (and not less than eleven of them Missionaries on a visit from India,) expressed great satisfaction at the beautiful appearance of the city and its environs, and the profuse hospitality that had been pressed on them by the liberal minded of all denominations" ("Spring Garden," *CG*, May 27, 1847).

32 "Education Society," *Philanthropist*, August 2, 1843.

33 SOE to AWW, July 28, 1850, BPL, MS A.9.2, vol. 25, no. 16.

34 See the *Philanthropist* editorial on the visit of AK and SSF in November 1845: "The Last Week in Cincinnati," *Philanthropist*, November 26, 1845. See also Harrold, *Gamaliel Bailey*, 72–73.

35 Gordon, *Bazaars and Fair Ladies*.

36 "Ladies A-S Fair," *NS*, August 11, 1848.

37 On antislavery fairs, see Chambers-Schiller, "'Good Work'"; Gordon, "Playing at Being Powerless"; Debra Gold Hansen, *Strained Sisterhood*; Hewitt, "Social Origins"; Jeffrey, "'Stranger, Buy'"; Lawes, *Women and Reform*; Soderlund, "Priorities and Power"; Alice Taylor, "Selling Abolitionism"; Van Broekhoven, "'Better Than a Clay Club.'"

38 "Ladies A-S Fair," *NS*, August 11, 1848; "Pittsburgh," *NS*, November 5, 1848.

39 Debra Gold Hansen, *Strained Sisterhood*, 138.

40 Soderlund, "Priorities and Power," 82–83.

41 The Concord, New Hampshire, fair, for example, gave most of its money to the locally based *Herald of Freedom*. See Salerno, *Sister Societies*, 133.

42 Soderlund, "Priorities and Power," 83.

43 Ibid., 84–85.

44 Harrold, "Perspective." An 1840 editorial by Bailey in the *Philanthropist* asserted that aside from the Ladies Education Society and Jonathan Blanchard's abolitionist church, antislavery in Cincinnati was moribund. The members of the female society "are ardent and judicious, and their efforts put to shame those of the men's society of this place. Indeed, we should not know whether this society were dead or alive, if we had nothing to judge by but the action of its executive committee" ("Ladies' Cincinnati Anti-Slavery Society," *Philanthropist*, January 21, 1840). During the late 1840s and 1850s, the reform-minded *CG* rarely mentioned antislavery activities in the city aside from those initiated by Ernst.

45 SOE to AWW, November 14, 1852, BPL, MS A.9.2, vol. 26, no. 70.

46 Chambers-Schiller, "'Good Work.'"

47 SOE to AWW, July 28, 1850, BPL, MS A.9.2, vol. 25, no. 16.

48 Clarissa Olds to AWW, November 29, 1852, BPL, MS A.9.2, vol. 26, no. 73.

49 See Alice Taylor, "It Was a Kind of Ladies Exchange"; Van Broekhoven, "'Better Than a Clay Club.'"

50 McDaniel, "Fourth and the First."

51 SOE to AWW, July 28, 1850, BPL, MS A.9.2, vol. 25, no. 16.

52 *CG*, October 21, 1853; "City Notices and News," *CG*, October 21, 1852.

53 SOE to AWW, July 28, 1850, BPL, MS A.9.2, vol. 25, no. 16.

54 See "Mass Convention of Ladies at Carthage—Formation of a Hamilton County Temperance Association," *CG*, September 2, 1853; "Home for the Friendless," *CG*, May 9, 1854.

55 SOE to AWW, July 28, 1850, BPL, MS A.9.2, vol. 25, no. 16.

56 Ibid.

57 Ibid.

58 Salerno, *Sister Societies*, 135. See also Debra Gold Hansen, *Strained Sisterhood*, 127–28.

59 Salerno, *Sister Societies*, 135.

60 "The Third Anti-Slavery Bazaar," *FDP*, November 5, 1852; "Cincinnati A.S. Bazaar," *Liberator*, November 18, 1853.

61 SOE to AWW, July 28, 1850, BPL, MS A.9.2, vol. 25, no. 16.

62 On gambling in the nineteenth century, see Fabian, *Card Sharps*. See also Masur's review of *Card Sharps*, "Bettor Nation." Masur highlights the lack of gender analysis in *Card Sharps*.

63 "Ladies Anti-Slavery Sewing Circle," *Genius of Liberty*, January 15, 1853.

64 "Cincinnati Anti-Slavery Bazaar," *ASB*, November 6, 1853.

65 On tensions between morality and consumption at antislavery fairs, see Jeffrey, "'Stranger, Buy.'" On the critique of women for entering the commercial arena through their fair activism, see Gordon, *Bazaars and Fair Ladies*, 1.

66 "Cincinnatti [sic] Anti-Slavery Bazaar," *ASB*, November 29, 1851; "Ladies Anti-Slavery Sewing Circle," *Genius of Liberty*, January 15, 1853; "Anti-Slavery Bazaar,"

ASB, November 12, 1853; "Cincinnati Anti-Slavery Bazar [*sic*]," *ASB*, December 2, 1854; "Anti-Slavery Bazaar," *ASB*, November 10, 1855.

67 The Philadelphia fair donated 85 percent of its profits to the state society. See Soderlund, "Priorities and Power," 83.

68 "Cincinnati Anti-Slavery Convention," *ASB*, March 8, 1851.

69 "Anti-Slavery Convention in Cincinnati, O," *ASB*, January 21, 1852.

70 "Cincinnati Convention," *ASB*, February 12, 1853.

71 "Cincinnati Anti-Slavery Convention," *Free West*, May 11, 1854.

72 "Anti-Slavery Convention," *CG*, April 28, 29, 30, 1852, April 20, 21, 22, 23, 1853; "Ohio Anti-Slavery Convention; Frederick Douglas [*sic*], Miss Lucy Stone, and Other Noted Speakers Present," *CG*, April 12, 1854; "Ohio Anti-Slavery Convention/Frederick Douglas [*sic*], Miss Lucy Stone, and Other Noted Speakers Present," *CG*, April 13, 15, 1854.

73 Joseph Treat, "The Cincinnati Convention," *ASB*, May 3, 1851.

74 Ibid.

75 For the official report of the gathering, see "Anti-Slavery Convention at Cincinnati," *ASB*, May 10, 1851.

76 Joseph Treat, "The Cincinnati Convention," *ASB*, May 3, 1851.

77 Joseph Treat, "The Cincinnati Convention," *ASB*, May 8, 1852.

78 Ibid.

79 "Anti-Slavery Convention," *CG*, April 29, 1852.

80 "Cincinnati Convention," *ASB*, April 30, 1853.

81 "Anti-Slavery Convention," *CG*, April 23, 1853.

82 "The Cincinnati Anti-Slavery Convention," *FDP*, April 7, 1854.

83 "The Cincinnati Convention," *FDP*, April 28, 1854.

84 Ibid. For a full account of this meeting, see "Ohio Anti-Slavery Convention; Frederick Douglas [*sic*], Miss Lucy Stone, and Other Noted Speakers Present," *CG*, April 12, 1854; "Ohio Anti-Slavery Convention/Frederick Douglas [*sic*], Miss Lucy Stone, and Other Noted Speakers Present," *CG*, April 13, 15, 1854.

85 "Anti-Slavery Convention," *FDP*, June 3, 1853.

86 "Cincinnati Anti-Slavery Convention," *ASB*, March 8, 1851.

87 "Anti-Slavery Convention in Cincinnati, O," *ASB*, January 21, 1852; "Great Mass Anti-Slavery Convention, in Cincinnati, Ohio," *FDP*, April 15, 1852.

88 "Annual Anti-Slavery Convention in Cincinnati, Ohio," *ASB*, March 17, 1855.

89 J. G. Griffing, "Indiana Correspondence," *ASB*, May 26, 1855.

90 Joseph Treat, "The Cincinnati Convention," *ASB*, May 3, 1851.

91 Ibid.

92 "Anti-Slavery Convention," *CG*, April 29, 1852.

93 "Anti-Slavery Convention," *CG*, April 28, 1852.

94 "Anti-Slavery Convention," *CG*, April 30, 1852.

95 "Cincinnati Annual Anti-Slavery Convention," *ASB*, April 22, 1854.

96 "The Cincinnati Convention," *FDP*, April 28, 1854.

97 "Cincinnati Bazaar," *ASB*, September 8, 1855.

98 The best study of Garrisonianism in the West is Gamble, "Moral Suasion."

99 See Cincinnatti [*sic*] Anti-Slavery Bazaar," *ASB*, November 29, 1852; SOE to AWW, November 14, 1851, BPL, MS A.9.2, vol. 26, no. 70; "Cincinnati Bazaar," *ASB*, November 12, 1853; "Cincinnati Anti-Slavery Bazar [*sic*]," *ASB*, December 2, 1854; "Cincinnati Bazaar," *ASB*, November 3, 1855; "Treasurer's Report," *ASB*, March 28, 1857.

100 "Cincinnati Bazaar," *ASB*, September 8, 1855.

101 SOE to AWW, November 14, 1852, BPL, MS A.9.2, vol. 26, no. 70.

102 SOE to AWW, February 1, 1852, BPL, MS A.9.2, vol. 26, no. 8.

103 Ibid.; SOE to AWW, November 14, 1852, BPL, MS A.9.2, vol. 26, no. 70.

104 SOE to AWW, November 14, 1852, BPL, MS A.9.2, vol. 26, no. 70; McFeely, *Frederick Douglass*, 146–47, 168–69. The Cincinnati Anti-Slavery Sewing Circle gave one hundred dollars to Douglass's *North Star* in 1850, when he was still a Garrisonian ("Receipts," *NS*, October 31, 1850).

105 "Anti-Slavery Bazaar," *ASB*, November 12, 1853.

106 "The Cincinnati Convention," *FDP*, March 24, 1854. See also "The Fifth Cincinnati Anti-Slavery Bazaar," *FDP*, September 22, 1854; "Anti-Slavery Convention," *FDP*, March 3, 1854.

107 SOE to AWW, November 14, 1852, BPL, MS A.9.2, vol. 26, no. 70; SOE to WLG, January 8, 1853, BPL, MS A.1.2, vol. 22, no. 6; "Anti-Slavery Bazaar," *ASB*, November 12, 1853.

108 SOE to WLG, January 8, 1853, BPL, MS A.1.2, vol. 22, no. 6.

109 SOE to AWW, July 28, 1850, BPL, MS A.9.2, vol. 25, no. 16.

110 Ibid.

111 In 1854, the Michigan Anti-Slavery Society, reacting to a missive from the *Bugle*'s parent organization, the Western Anti-Slavery Society, resolved that if the *Bugle* was to change location, it should come north to Cleveland rather than south to Cincinnati (Constitution and Bylaws of the Michigan Anti-Slavery Society, Constitution Preamble, January 27, 1854, Harriet deGarmo Fuller Papers, William L. Clements Library, University of Michigan, Ann Arbor). A year later, abolitionist Jane Nicholson informed her Garrisonian friend, Abram Brooke, that she had received a letter from Ernst "upon the subject of the move of the Bugle to Cincinnati, which she has deeply at heart but is disappointed in the prospect for at present." Nicholson reminded Brooke that Ernst was a "very sincere and thorough A[nti] S[lavery] worker" and requested him to "sustain" her effort and asked, "Would not Lizzie [Jones] feel like making an effort in that direction?" (Jane Nicholson to Abram Brooke, June 22, 1855, Valentine Nicholson Collection, Indiana Historical Library, Indianapolis).

112 SOE to AWW, July 28, 1850, BPL, MS A.9.2, vol. 25, no. 16.

113 SOE to AWW, November 14, 1852, BPL, MS A.9.2, vol. 26, no. 70.

114 Andrew H. Ernst to WLG, January 24, 1853, BPL, MS A.1.2, vol. 22, no. 12.

115 *Liberator*, May 6, 1853.

116 "Cincinnati Anti-Slavery Bazar [*sic*]," *ASB*, December 2, 1854.

117 Holley, *Life for Liberty*.

118 Mary De Graw to WLG, December 17, 1854, BPL, MS A.1.2, vol. 24, no. 173.

119 "William Wells Brown," *ASB*, March 17, 1855.

120 "Ohio Anti-Slavery Convention," *CG*, April 13, 1854.

121 Only Blackwell's letters in relation to this incident are available: Henry Blackwell to WLG, August 1, 1854, BPL, MS A.1.2, vol. 24, no. 109; October 10, 1854, MS A.1.2, vol. 24, no. 152; October 16, 1854, MS A.1.2, vol. 24, no. 154.

122 SOE to AWW, February 1, 1852, BPL, MS A.9.2, vol. 26, no. 8.

123 Sarah MacMillan to AWW, April 15, 1842, BPL, MS A.9.2, vol. 25, no. 25.

124 "The Ninth Annual Report of the Cincinnati Anti-Slavery Sewing Circle," *ASB*, March 13, 1852.

125 "The Cincinnati Convention," *ASB*, May 3, 1851.

126 "Cincinnati," *NS*, May 7, 1848. Delany refers to Boynton as "Boyington."

127 "The Christian Anti-Slavery Convention at Cincinnati," *Oberlin Evangelist*, May 8, 1850; "Cincinnati Correspondence," *ASB*, May 31, 1851; *Oberlin Evangelist*, July 16, 1851.

128 "From Our Iowa Correspondent," *Independent*, January 6, 1853; *National Era*, January 20, 1853.

129 "Anti-Slavery Men in Pro-Slavery Organizations," *Liberator*, August 13, 1852. Douglass reprinted the editorial (*FDP*, October 19, 1852).

130 "Matters in and about the City," *CG*, December 5, 1853. Mary Blanchard, wife of former Cincinnati minister Jonathan Blanchard, received a letter from a Cincinnati friend who explained, "A gentleman in the city said to me last week that Dr. Rices' church and Mr. Boynton's were the most popular churches in [Cincinnati]" (Elizabeth Corwin to Mary Blanchard, November 16–17, 1847, Blanchard Papers).

131 Boynton envisioned women as "help-meets" to men in reform movements ("The Christian Idea of the Nature and Position of Woman," *CG*, June 7, 1852).

132 SOE to AWW, February 1, 1852, BPL, Ms A.9.2, vol. 26, no. 8.

133 "The Ninth Annual Report of the Cincinnati Anti-Slavery Sewing Circle," *ASB*, March 13, 1852.

134 "The Cincinnati Convention," *ASB*, May 8, 1852.

135 SOE to AWW, November 14, 1852, BPL, MS A.9.2, vol. 26, no. 70.

136 *ASB*, November 20, 1852.

137 SOE to AWW, November 14, 1852, BPL, MS A.9.2, vol. 26, no. 70.

138 Garrison reprinted Boynton's editorial: "Anti-Slavery Bazaar," *Liberator*, December 24, 1852.

139 SOE to WLG, January 8, 1853, BPL, MS A.1.2, vol. 22, no. 6.

140 The editor of the *Genius of Liberty*, Elizabeth Aldrich, noted that she copied "Rights and Wrongs of Women" from the *Christian Press* (*Genius of Liberty*,

March 15, 1853). See also the notice of the convention, *Christian Press*, April 1, 1853. Ernst's lecture stemmed from a meeting of "a small circle of philanthropists at Cincinnati" in which Cassius M. Clay gave a talk referring to woman's rights. The attendees desired to hear more on the topic and invited Ernst, who was present, to address the association's next monthly meeting. Her speech became "Rights and Wrongs of Women" (*FDP*, February 25, 1853).

141 See the accounts of the convention in the *CG*, April 20–23, 1853.

142 "Rev. Mr. Boynton and the Cin. Convention," *ASB*, May 21, 1853.

143 Ibid.

144 "From the Ohio Anti-Slavery Bugle: Denying Christ," *Liberator*, July 29, 1853.

145 "From the Anti-Slavery Standard: Sectarian Mendacity," *Liberator*, October 7, 1853.

146 "The Cincinnati Convention," *ASB*, April 22, 1854. See also the coverage of the convention in the *CG*, April 12–15, 1854.

147 "Ohio Anti-Slavery Convention," *CG*, April 15, 1854.

148 "Twelfth Annual Report of the Cincinnati A.S. Sewing Circle," *ASB*, January 27, 1855.

149 "Address to the Cincinnati Anti Slavery Sewing Circle at the Annual Meeting, January 17th, 1855," *ASB*, January 27, 1855.

150 Ibid.; "Cincinnati A.S. Sewing Circle—Mrs. Ernst's Address," *ASB*, January 27, 1855.

151 "Cincinnati Anti-Slavery Bazaar," *ASB*, September 8, 1855.

152 "Cincinnati Bazaar," *ASB*, November 3, 1855.

153 SOE to AWW, January 13, 1856, BPL, MS A.9.2, vol. 28, no. 69.

154 Ibid.

155 Ibid.

156 "Annual Report of the Cincinnati A.S. Bazaar Committee," *ASB*, April 6, 1856.

157 "Rochester Ladies Anti-Slavery Sewing Society," *FDP*, October 16, 1851.

158 Gamble, "Moral Suasion," 18.

159 Middleton, *Black Laws: Race and the Legal Process*, 90.

160 "First of August," *ASB*, August 15, 1845. On the political significance of mottos on goods at fairs, see Van Broekhoven, "Needles, Pens, and Petitions," 138.

161 *ASB*, October 2, 1846.

162 BMC to Henry Cowles, February 14, 1846, Fletcher Papers, Box 3, Folder 18; Timothy Hudson to BMC, March 5, 1846, Fletcher Papers, Box 5, Folder 9; AK to BMC, June 29, 1846, Fletcher Papers, Box 5, Folder 9.

163 *ASB*, September 4, 1846.

164 Ibid., October 2, 1846.

165 Ibid.

166 AK to BMC, November 8, 1846, Fletcher Papers, Box 5, Folder 9.

167 "Western Anti-Slavery Fair," *ASB*, April 9, 1847.

168 "Anti-Slavery Fair," *ASB*, April 9, 1847.

169 Alice Taylor, "It Was a Kind of a Ladies Exchange"; Van Broekhoven, "'Better Than a Clay Club,'" 37.

170 Van Broekhoven, "Needles, Pens, and Petitions"; Lawes, *Women and Reform*, 45.

171 Van Broekhoven, "'Better Than a Clay Club,'" 32.

172 "Sewing Circles," *ASB*, January 22, 1847.

173 "Encouragement," *ASB*, December 3, 1847.

174 Ibid.

175 "Fair at Ravenna," *ASB*, August 27, 1847.

176 Ibid.

177 "Western Anti-Slavery Fair," *ASB*, April 21, 1848.

178 Ibid.

179 "The Fair," *ASB*, August 25, 1848.

180 "Encouraging," *ASB*, February 9, 1849.

181 Ibid.

182 "The Fair," *ASB*, August 4, 1849.

183 "Western Anti-Slavery Fair," *ASB*, May 11, 1850.

184 "The Fair," *ASB*, January 7, 1854.

185 "Thoughts for the Bugle," *ASB*, January 25, 1851.

186 Ibid.

187 Gordon, *Bazaars and Fair Ladies*, 48.

188 "Anti-Slavery Fairs," *Philanthropist*, December 7, 1842.

189 "Address of the Cadiz Anti-Slavery Committee," *ASB*, December 28, 1842.

190 Hise Diaries, July 11, 1851.

191 "The Fair," *ASB*, August 30, 1851; Hise Diaries, October 23, 1851, December 4, 1851, December 18, 1851, November 10, 1852, December 22, 1852.

192 Hise Diaries, December 18, 1851.

193 Ibid., December 4, 1851.

194 Ibid., December 23, 1851.

195 Ibid., January 1, 1852, December 31, 1852.

196 "Western Anti-Slavery Fair," *ASB*, January 10, 1852.

197 See, for example, the following in the *ASB*: "Report of the Managers of the Western Anti-Slavery Fair," January 19, 1856; "The Fair," December 20, 1856; "The Fairs," January 15, 1857; "Report of the Managers of the Western Anti-Slavery Fair," January 9, 1858; "Report of the Committee of the Western Anti-Slavery Fair," January 15, 1859; "Fair Report," December 31, 1859.

198 "Notes from the Lecturing Field," *ASB*, August 9, 1851.

199 "Notes from the Lecturing Field," *ASB*, February 14, 1852.

200 "Letter from Henry C. Wright," *ASB*, July 10, 1852.

201 Gamble, "Moral Suasion," 406.

202 Gordon, *Bazaars and Fair Ladies*, 17.

203 "Official Report of the Western A.S. Fair," *ASB*, January 18, 1851.

204 "Western Anti-Slavery Fair," *ASB*, August 16, 1851.

205 "Western Anti-Slavery Fair," *ASB*, January 10, 1852.

206 On the connection between fairs and social events, see Gordon, *Bazaars and Fair Ladies*, 19.

207 Hise Diaries, December 26, 1852.

208 "Western Anti-Slavery Fair," *ASB*, January 10, 1852.

209 "Fourth Annual Western Anti-Slavery Bazaar," *ASB*, August 20, 1852.

210 "The Western Anti-Slavery Fair," *ASB*, December 14, 1850.

211 "Western Anti-Slavery Fair," *ASB*, April 9, 1847.

212 "Anti-Slavery Fairs," *Philanthropist*, December 7, 1842.

213 Alice Taylor, "'It Was a Kind of Ladies Exchange,'" 33.

214 "Western Anti-Slavery Fair," *ASB*, November 12, 1853.

215 "The Fair," *ASB*, November 29, 1851.

216 "Western Anti-Slavery Fair," *ASB*, January 10, 1852.

217 "Anti-Slavery Fairs," *Philanthropist*, December 7, 1842.

218 "Anti-Slavery Fair," *ASB*, April 9, 1847.

219 "Western Anti-Slavery Fair," *ASB*, July 30, 1847.

CHAPTER 5

1 "Orthodox Yearly Meeting," *ASB*, September 13, 1845.

2 "The Quaker Drag-Out at Mt. Pleasant," *ASB*, October 10, 1845.

3 "First of August—A Repentant Slave-Holder," *ASB*, August 27, 1853.

4 In fact, other women had spoken at the meeting prior to Kelley. See "Orthodox Yearly Meeting," *ASB*, September 13, 1845.

5 For a good introduction to the critique of separate spheres, see Boydston, *Home and Work*; Kerber, "Separate Spheres"; Ryan, "Gender and Public Access"; Stanley, "Home Life."

6 Sterling, *We Are Your Sisters*, 153–59.

7 Sterling offers an excellent description of the Grimkés' first "promiscuous" lecture in Lynn, Massachusetts (*Ahead of Her Time*, 51–55). See also Browne, *Angelina Grimké*; Lerner, *Grimké Sisters*; Lumpkin, *Emancipation*.

8 Sterling, *Ahead of Her Time*, 64.

9 Ibid., 230–31. Women abolitionists often embraced the term with pride. See Jane D. McNeely to AK, April 8, 1846, Foster Papers; BMC letter, *ASB*, September 4, 1846.

10 "Woman's Rights and Duties," *Oberlin Quarterly Review*, July 1849.

11 Gamble, "Moral Suasion," 191–218.

12 M. H. Grisell letter, *Liberator*, June 19, 1840.

13 Gamble, "Moral Suasion," 208.

14 Ibid., 247.

15 Hannah Brooke, Ruth Galbreath, and Elizabeth Wileman were among the first women "to serve on the executive committee of any state or national abolition

society" (ibid., 253). On the history of Quaker women's roles in abolition, see Margaret Hope Bacon, *Mothers of Feminism*; Hewitt, "Social Origins"; Wellman, "Women and Radical Reform."

16 "Anniversary of the Ohio American Antislavery Society," *NLA*, June 19, 1844.

17 The Ohio American Anti-Slavery Society invited AK and JEH to attend the group's anniversary in 1845 and to lecture in the state. The society assured the women of a "cordial reception and a welcome home" (Jesse Holmes to AK and JEH, March 7, 1845, Foster Papers).

18 "Anniversary," *NLA*, May 7, 1845.

19 "Annual Meeting of the Ohio American Anti-Slavery Society," *ASB*, June 20, 1845. This was the first issue of the *Anti-Slavery Bugle*. It was published in New Lisbon until September 5, 1845, when it moved to Salem, Ohio.

20 "Meeting of the Ohio American Anti Slavery Society," *NLA*, June 11, 1845.

21 "Our Cause in Ohio," *Liberator*, July 25, 1845; AK to SSF, June 9, 1845, Abby Kelley Foster Papers, American Antiquarian Society, Worcester, Massachusetts (from the Worcester Historical Society).

22 "Annual Meeting of the Ohio American Anti-Slavery Society," *NLA*, June 18, 1845.

23 "Annual Meeting of the Ohio American Anti-Slavery Society," *ASB*, June 20, 1845. This report of the meeting notes that the resignation was accepted but that "on motion of Jesse Holmes, Cyrus McNeely was re-elected President of the Society for the ensuing year."

24 Within a short period of time, Cyrus McNeely would embrace disunionism and no-voting. See Jane McNeely to AKF and SSF, February 25, [1846], Foster Papers.

25 *NLA*, August 1, 1846.

26 Gamble, "Moral Suasion," 305.

27 "Liberty Party Slang from the *Ohio America*," *ASB*, July 25, 1845.

28 Ibid.

29 "The Liberty Party in Northern Ohio," *Philanthropist*, July 17, 1845.

30 Ibid.

31 Even some eastern Garrisonians concurred with Bailey about the distinctive hospitality of the West. After lecturing for a few weeks in Ohio, Giles Stebbins described the region's Liberty supporters as "warm-hearted, sincere friends of the oppressed" and concluded that they "manifested a fairness and candor that would put to shame their brethren in the East." Stebbins also extolled Ohio Whig Joshua Giddings, who hosted the radical during his stay in Ashtabula, for "bold and fearless advocacy of human rights in Congress." See "Our Cause in Ohio," *Liberator*, July 25, 1845.

32 "The Last Week in Cincinnati," *Philanthropist*, November 26, 1845. Toward the end of 1845, Bailey invited Kelley and Foster to his home, where they insulted Bailey and his wife, Margaret (Harrold, *Gamaliel Bailey*, 72–73).

33 "The Anniversary," *ASB*, November 21, 1845.

34 "The Liberty Party," *NLA*, August 15, 1846.

35 The issue of the *Bugle*'s editorship proved very complex. In a June 1845 letter to SSF, AK incorrectly announced that Milo Townsend had agreed to serve as editor, although she hoped that Parker Pillsbury would become the permanent editor (AK to SSF, June 9, 1845, Abby Kelley Foster Papers). See also AK to MWC, July 17, 1845, BPL, MS A.9.2, vol. 21, no. 25; MWC to AK, September 14, 1845, Foster Papers. The August 15, 1845, issue of the *Anti-Slavery Bugle* announced, "Benj. S. Jones and J. Elizabeth Hitchcock will have charge of the Editorial department of the Bugle for the present." AK regretted that she was forced to pull BJ and JEH out of the lecturing field to edit (AK to Sister, November 8, 1845, Abby Kelley Foster Papers).

36 JEH may have had some editorial experience. Kelley wrote to Foster in 1844 that JEH's brother did not want her to lecture because he needed her editorial skills for his commune's newspaper (AK to SSF, February 16, 1844, Foster Papers).

37 BJ and JEH to AK, July 14, 1845, Foster Papers.

38 Sterling, *Ahead of Her Time*, 215.

39 See, for example, AK to MWC, November 2, 1853, BPL, MS A.1.2, vol. 23, no. 91.

40 For the *ASB*'s subscription lists, see James Barnaby Papers, MSS 1007, Western Reserve Historical Society, Cleveland, Ohio.

41 AK to SSF, March 22, 1845, Foster Papers.

42 AK to MWC, July 17, 1845, BPL, MS A.9.2, vol. 21, no. 25; AK to Sister, November 8, 1845, Abby Kelley Foster Papers.

43 AK to MWC, January 14, 1846, BPL, MS A.9.2, vol. 22, no. 5.

44 AK to MWC, September 21, 1846, BPL, MS A.9.2, vol. 22, no. 89.

45 AK to MWC, January 14, 1846, BPL, MS A.9.2, vol. 22, no. 5.

46 AK to MWC, July 17, 1845, BPL, MS A.9.2, vol. 21, no. 25; AK to MWC, January 14, 1846, BPL, MS A.9.2, vol. 22, no. 5. AK also highlighted BMC's contributions to radical antislavery in the West (AK to MWC, February 18, 1846, BPL, MS A.9.2, vol. 22, no. 21).

47 MWC to AK, [February 8,] 1846, Foster Papers.

48 Gamble, "Moral Suasion," 321.

49 Harriet N. Torrey letter, *ASB*, August 15, 1845.

50 Mary Donaldson to AK, February 19, 1846, Foster Papers.

51 "Editors of the Anti-Slavery Bugle," *ASB*, December 5, 1845.

52 AK to BMC, August 1, 1846, BMC Papers, Box 1, Folder 14.

53 Barnaby Papers.

54 "Comeouterism," *ASB*, February 6, 1846; U.S. Census, 1850.

55 H. E. Smith letter, *ASB*, January 9, 1846.

56 Ibid.

57 Hise Diaries, April 21, 1850.

58 AK to BMC, January 28, 1846, Fletcher Papers, Box 5, Folder 9.

59 BMC to Cornelia Cowles, February 3, 1846, BMC Papers, Box 1, Folder 14.

60 See Fletcher, *History*; Ginzberg, "Women in an Evangelical Community."

61 BMC to Henry Cowles, February 14, 1846, Fletcher Papers, Box 3, Folder 18.

62 Alice Welch Cowles to Henry Cowles, July 19, 1840, Fletcher Papers, Box 3, Folder 19.

63 "Mr. and Mrs. Foster in Oberlin," and "Mrs. Foster versus the Federal Constitution," *Oberlin Evangelist*, March 4, 1846.

64 Helen Cowles to A. Y. Hawkins, March 3, 1846, Fletcher Papers, Box 5, Folder 3.

65 "Woman's Rights and Duties," *Oberlin Quarterly Review*, July 1849. AKF supporter Charles Foote responded with a defense of his friend: "Woman's Rights and Duties," *Oberlin Quarterly Review*, October 1849.

66 Betsy Hudson to BMC, February 27, 1846, Fletcher Papers, Box 5, Folder 9.

67 Kelley was often accused of violating "true womanhood," as were other female abolitionist speakers. See, for example, William Corwin's description of some friends' reaction to his support for Kelley: "They said they were much surprised that a man of my age and experience should follow that worthless girl who was traveling about the country, with young men, sometimes with one and then with another, in a disgraceful manner" ("'No Union with Slave Holders,'" *ASB*, October 31, 1845).

68 Timothy Hudson to BMC, March 5, 1846, Fletcher Papers, Box 5, Folder 9.

69 See Boydston, *Home and Work*; Kerber, "Separate Spheres"; Ryan, "Gender and Public Access."

70 AK to BMC, March 15, 1846, BMC Papers, Box 1, Folder 14.

71 Because of the revival, the Fosters asked to return to Oberlin again at a more propitious time. The Oberlin community spent the summer of 1846 debating whether to invite the Fosters back. According to an Oberlin historian, "A group of students and Negroes was anxious to have them come; [Oberlin president Charles Grandison] Finney and most of the faculty opposed it." The Fosters were allowed to speak in September 1846 but did not seem to make inroads (Fletcher, *History*, 267–69).

72 Stone emphasized the long-term impact of the Fosters' visit: "You set a ball in motion, that is still rolling, and it will roll, for there are a few, who are pushing it, and who will *continue* to do so" (Lucy Stone to AK and SSF, March 25, 1846, Foster Papers).

73 AK to BMC, March 15, 1846, BMC Papers, Box 1, Folder 14.

74 Kelley also invited Cowles to attend the East Coast antislavery annual meetings and chaperoned her when she agreed. Kelley ensured that Cowles was elected to the important business committees at both the American and New England Anti-Slavery Society conventions (*Liberator*, May 22, 1846, June 5, 1846).

75 Immediately after meeting Cowles, Kelley wrote to MWC that Cowles "speaks to excellent effect in public meetings. . . . We hope she will leave the Institute and

devote herself to lecturing" (AK to MWC, February 18, 1846, BPL, MS A.9.2, vol. 22, no. 21). This is likely the type of comment to which Hudson referred.

76 AK to BMC, February 9, 1847, BMC Papers, Box 1, Folder 14. On Kelley's pregnancy, see Sterling, *Ahead of Her Time*, 234–42.

77 Ibid.

78 AK to BMC, November 8, 1846, Fletcher Papers, Box 5, Folder 9.

79 Sarah Hallowell to BMC, January 17, 1847, BMC Papers, Box 1, Folder 15.

80 AK to BMC, November 8, 1846, Fletcher Papers, Box 5, Folder 9.

81 BMC to Martha Cowles, September 28, 1842, BMC Papers, Box 1, Folder 10; BMC letter, *ASB*, September 4, 1846.

82 "Anti-Slavery Fair," *ASB*, April 9, 1847.

83 "Outrage upon Human Rights," *ASB*, February 2, 1849. This was an unusual practice for Garrisonian newspapers. The Ohio legislature partially repealed some Black Laws in 1849.

84 See Pillsbury's letter to the *Liberator*: "Annual Meeting of the Lake and Ashtabula Counties Ladies' Anti-Slavery Society," *ASB*, August 14, 1846. See also excerpts from the *Plea for the Oppressed*, *ASB*, March 5, 1846.

85 JEH to BMC, January 4, 1847, BMC Papers, Box 1, Folder 14.

86 For Kelley's comment on sewing societies, see AK to BMC, August 1, 1846, Box 1, Folder 14, BMC Papers. For her request to see the Cowleses' "Anti-Black-Law Sheet," see AK to BMC, November 8, 1846, Fletcher Papers, Box 5, Folder 9.

87 Sterling, *Ahead of Her Time*, 189, 193, 197–201.

88 AK to SSF, February 16, 1844, Foster Papers. While JEH reported that concerns about her health motivated her family's resistance, Kelley surmised that JEH's brother opposed the idea because he needed his sister's editorial talents for his new commune's paper. See also AK to SSF, April 2, 1845, Foster Papers.

89 AK to SSF, November 14, 1844, Foster Papers. "J. E. Hitchcock is doing grandly," AK wrote (AK to Friend, November 30, 1844, Foster Papers). A few months later, AK had even more praise for JEH: "Elizabeth is improving fast. I consider her one of our most efficient speakers. Indeed she is truly eloquent at times. She has learned to extemporize with great power" (AK to SSF, February 5, 1845, Foster Papers). Parker Pillsbury agreed, stating that JEH captured a New Hampshire audience with "her sweetness of manner and acuteness of reasoning" ("Anti-Slavery Convention at Milford, N.H.," *Liberator*, November 15, 1844).

90 Susan Fulton to AK, May 4, 1845, Foster Papers.

91 AK and JEH to SSF, January 21, 1845, Foster Papers; JEH to MWC, December 15, 1844, BPL, MS A.9.2, vol. 20, no. 123.

92 AK to SSF, November 14, 1844, Foster Papers.

93 The women were traveling with other speakers by March 1845. See AK to SSF, March 25, 1845, Foster Papers. For an example of their romance, see BJ and JEH to AK, July 14, 1845, Foster Papers.

94 "On behalf all our anti-slavery friends I earnestly and would with all emphasis, insist on your presence," implored Jesse Holmes (Jesse Holmes to AK and JEH, March 7, 1845, Foster Papers).

95 Sterling, *Ahead of Her Time*, 210–12.

96 BJ and JEH to AK, July 14, 1845, Foster Papers.

97 Ibid.

98 AK to MWC, July 17, 1845, BPL, MS A.9.2, vol. 21, no. 25. For Kelley's illness, see also BJ and JEH to AK, July 14, 1845, Foster Papers.

99 *Liberator*, June 27, 1845.

100 *ASB*, September 4, 1846.

101 JEH to MWC, October 16, 1845, BPL, MS A.9.2, vol. 21, no. 72.

102 AK to MWC, January 14, 1846, BPL, MS A.9.2, vol. 22, no. 5. On JEH's background, see Moser, "J. Elizabeth Jones."

103 See AK to MWC, January 14, 1846, BPL, MS A.9.2, vol. 22, no. 5. Their marriage was also mentioned in the *ASB*, January 16, 1846. Jane McNeely offered her congratulations in February 1846 (Jane McNeely to AKF and SSF, February 25, [1846], Foster Papers).

104 JEH to SSF and AK, January 23, 1848, Foster Papers; JEH to AK, April 28, 1848, Foster Papers.

105 By January 1847, JEH described her Salem home to BMC as "the most delightful spot on earth. . . . Were I to spend the remainder of my days in a palace, I should ever recur with fond pleasure to this our first home" (JEH to BMC, January 4, 1847, BMC Papers, Box 1, Folder 14). The radicals proved particularly sensitive to the need to support one another. Mary Donaldson, for example, responded to a criticism of the *Bugle* written by MWC by defending the paper and its editors: "I feel a strong sympathy for our friends, particularly Elizabeth. She has sacrificed so much from a sense of duty to the cause, and still bears her privations & performs all her arduous duties with so much cheerfulness & fidelity, that I cannot bear to think hardly of her" (Mary Donaldson to MWC, September 2, 1846, BPL, MS A.9.2, vol. 22, no. 87).

106 Margaret [Burleigh] and Mary [Grew] to WLG and Helen E. Garrison, August 5, 1853, BPL, MS A.1.2, vol. 25, no. 81. For a sense of Salem in the 1850s, see Hise Diaries.

107 See, for example, Hise Diaries, September 5, 1856.

108 Ibid., December 26, 1852. For more on Hise, see Atherton, "Daniel Howell Hise."

109 JEH to AK, November 4, 1856, Foster Papers.

110 See, for example, BJ to BMC, February 7, 1847, November 15, 1847, Samuel Hendry Collection, MSS 3399, Miscellaneous Correspondence, Container 2, Folder 2, Western Reserve Historical Society, Cleveland, Ohio.

111 WLG to Helen E. Garrison, September 5, 1847, in Garrison, *Letters*, 3:524; WLG to Helen E. Garrison, October 14, 1858, BPL, MS A.1.1, vol. 5, no. 75a.

112 WLG to Helen E. Garrison, October 20, 1858, BPL, MS A.1.1, vol. 5, no. 79.

113 Margaret Burleigh and Mary Grew to WLG and Helen E. Garrison, August 5, 1853, BPL, MS A.1.2, vol. 25, no. 81.

114 See, for example, JEH to AK, November 4, 1856, Foster Papers.

115 "Our Cause in Ohio," *Liberator*, July 3, 1846.

116 JEH warned AK in April 1848 that "the Bugle cannot live six months unless we have help pecuniarily, or have [agents] in the field to get subscribers" (JEH to AK and SSF, April 18, 1848, Foster Papers).

117 BJ and JEH to AK, July 14, 1845, Foster Papers; AK to MWC, July 17, 1845, BPL, MS A.9.2, vol. 21, no. 25; MWC to AK, September 14, 1845, Foster Papers; MWC to AK, February 8, 1846, Foster Papers; Mary Donaldson to MWC, September 2, 1846, BPL, MS A.9.2, vol. 22, no. 87; AK to MWC, October 5, 1847, BPL, MS A.9.2, vol. 23, no. 49; BJ and JEH to BMC, October 6, 1847, BMC Papers, Box 1, Folder 14; JEH to AK and SSF, January 23, 1848, Foster Papers; JEH to AK and SSF, April 18, 1848, Foster Papers; JEH to AWW, March 21, 1849, BPL, MS A.9.2, vol. 24, no. 68.

118 Parker Pillsbury to SSF, October 27, 1847, Foster Papers.

119 JEH to SSF and AK, January 23, 1848, Foster Papers.

120 Ibid.

121 JEH wrote, "You know Benj. has a good trade, & we think if his brother would come out & open a shop here with him, they would do very well. We should get a good living" (JEH to SSF and AK, 23 January 1848, Foster Papers). A later letter suggests that this trade may have been bookbinding (AK to SSF, August 11, 1850, Foster Papers). The 1850 Census lists him as a cabinetmaker (U.S. Census, Columbiana County, Ohio, 1850).

122 JEH to AK, January 23, 1848, April 18, 1848, Foster Papers.

123 Ibid.

124 JEH to AK, January 23, 1848, Foster Papers.

125 JEH to AK, April 18, 1848, Foster Papers.

126 Maria Giddings to SSF, September 19, 1848, Foster Papers.

127 On her fair activities, see JEH to AWW, March 21, 1849, BPL, MS A.9.2, vol. 24, no. 68.

128 "Our Cause in Ohio," *Liberator*, July 3, 1846.

129 JEH to BMC, January 4, 1847, BMC Papers, Box 1, Folder 14.

130 "Sewing Circles," *ASB*, January 22, 1847.

131 BJ and JEH wanted to leave the *Bugle* earlier and tried to induce Douglass to edit the paper in 1847 (BJ and JEH to BMC, October 6, 1847, BMC Papers, Box 1, Folder 14). For an early reference to JEH's lecturing, see BMC to Louisa Cowles, August 6, 1850, BMC Papers, Box 1, Folder 16.

132 On JEH's health lectures, see Hise Diaries, November 24, 1851, January 21, 1852, April 29, 1852, November 24, 1852, January 2, 1853, August 18, 1853, September 1, 1853, October 1, 1853, October 4, 1853, March 17, 1854, March 22, 1854, July 1, 1854.

See also BMC to Louisa, August 6, 1850, BMC Papers, Box 1, Folder 16. See also JEH to Roccena B. Vaill Norris, February 14, 1851, February 21, 1851, March 1, 1851, March 24, 1851, August 5, 1851, September 7, 1851, Norris Papers.

133 AK to SSF, August 6, 1850, Foster Papers.

134 JEH to Roccena B. Vaill Norris, February 21, 1851, Norris Papers.

135 Hise Diaries, March 22, 1854.

136 JEH to Roccena B. Vaill Norris, March 24, 1851, Norris Papers.

137 On woman's rights, see "To the Women of Ohio," *ASB*, April 6, 1850; "Woman's Rights in Akron," *ASB*, May 11, 1850; "Trip to Akron," *ASB*, June 1, 1850. For evidence of her continuing support for abolition, see "Tenth Annual Report of the Western Anti-Slavery Society," *ASB*, August 28, 1852; "Mrs. Jones," *ASB*, January 12, 1856; *ASB*, October 7, 1857.

138 BJ and JEH to AK, January 23, 1857, Foster Papers. BJ copied a letter that JEH had written to a Salem friend into this letter.

139 According to Hise, the Joneses moved to Kennett Square, Pennsylvania, in 1861. BJ died in 1862. See Hise Diaries, October 11, 1862.

140 Sterling, *Ahead of Her Time*, 261. Oliver Johnson wrote to Kelley in February 1851 that Griffing's "domestic arrangements have kept her at home" but that he expected she would be in the field by early spring (Oliver Johnson to AK, February 6, 1851, Foster Papers).

141 "The ravages of Fire, Insanity in its most hopeless form, long and dreary sickness, terminating in two instances, in the death of those most near and dear, all these bitter elements have been mingled in their cup of suffering, within the last three years" ("Letter from Parker Pillsbury," *ASB*, November 6, 1852). The Griffings lost their eldest daughter in 1852 (*ASB*, September 25, 1852). At this time they had two other children, Emma, age thirteen, and Helen, five. They would have one more child in 1856 (U.S. Census, 1850, 1860; "Funeral Discourse by Henry C. Wright," *Liberator*, October 15, 1852).

142 "Letter from Parker Pillsbury," *ASB*, November 6, 1852.

143 "Letter from C. S. S. Griffing," *ASB*, January 1, 1853.

144 "Letter from Mrs. Griffing," *ASB*, August 12, 1854.

145 Hoffert, *When Hens Crow*, 100.

146 A. Mantor letter, *ASB*, April 9, 1853.

147 "Letter from C. S. S. Griffing," *ASB*, November 13, 1852.

148 "First of August—A Repentant Slave-Holder," *ASB*, August 27, 1853.

149 "Anti-Slavery Convention," *ASB*, November 25, 1854.

150 See "Correspondence from the Lecturing Field," *ASB*, October 4, 1854; "Correspondence," *ASB*, October 11, 1854. For more on Foote and the politics of antislavery in Canada, see chap. 6.

151 See Emily Rakestraw Robinson to AWW, July 22, 1855, BPL, MS A.9.2, vol. 28, no. 55. The 1860 Census confirms that Griffing had a four-year-old daughter, Cora.

152 "Mrs. Griffing's Meeting," *ASB*, June 9, 1860.

153 "Letter from Mrs. J. S. Griffing," *Liberator*, August 31, 1860.

154 See, for example, the following articles in the *Liberator*: "Letter from Mrs. J. S. Griffing," August 31, 1860; "In the West," November 30, 1860; "Convention at Livonia," February 15, 1861; "Letter from Mrs. J. S. Griffing," February 15, 1861; "Shameful Persecution," June 28, 1861.

155 C. S. S. Griffing to Samuel May Jr., March 1, 1863, BPL, MS B.1.6, vol. 9, no. 87. See also Griffing's other letters to May: February 10, 1863, BPL, MS B.1.6, vol. 9, no. 83; April 27, 1863, BPL, MS B.1.6, vol. 9, no. 92; May 25, 1863, BPL, MS B.1.6, vol. 9, no. 94.

156 "Things at the West," *Liberator*, February 4, 1853.

157 "Letter from Harriet N. Torrey," *ASB*, August 15, 1845.

158 Harriet N. Torrey letter, *ASB*, April 17, 1846.

159 On the Liberty Party, see "Confessing and Forsaking," *ASB*, August 14, 1846.

160 "Mob at Troy," *ASB*, January 15, 1847.

161 Ibid.

162 "Geauga Female A.S. Society," *ASB*, June 25, 1847.

163 On third-party politics, see, for example, Torrey's letters in *ASB*, May 29, 1848, July 14, 1848, October 27, 1848. On the Western Anti-Slavery Society, see "Anniversary Meeting," *ASB*, August 27, 1847. On the Salem Woman's Rights Convention, see Gamble, "Moral Suasion," 368.

164 Hannah T. Thomas letter, *ASB*, May 15, 1847.

165 Hannah T. Thomas letter, *ASB*, April 21, 1848.

166 Ibid.

167 Ibid.

168 Harriet deGarmo Fuller Papers, William L. Clements Library, University of Michigan, Ann Arbor. On Michigan antislavery, see Quist, "'Great Majority.'"

169 "The Campaign in Michigan," *ASB*, December 29, 1855.

170 "From Mrs. Philleo," *ASB*, February 23, 1856.

171 Frances D. Gage to Ruth and Joseph Dugdale, April 23, [1855], Joseph Dugdale Papers, Friends Historical Library, Swarthmore College, Swarthmore, Pennsylvania.

172 Colby Diary, October 17, 1857. See also Brakebill, *"Circumstances Are Destiny."*

173 "Lecture of Mrs. Severance," *ASB*, March 19, 1853.

174 "Letter from Mr. Philleo," *ASB*, February 23, 1856.

175 Harper, *Brighter Day Coming*.

176 "Border Ruffianism in Fairfield Township," *ASB*, November 27, 1858. See also "Letter from Frances E. Watkins," *ASB*, November 13, 1858.

177 Hise Diaries, October 17, 1858.

178 "Proslavery in Indiana," *Liberator*, October 15, 1858. For a thoughtful discussion of this incident, see Painter, *Sojourner Truth*, 138–42.

179 For more on Truth's lecturing experiences, see Ortiz, *Sojourner Truth*, 68–73. See also three recent biographies of Truth: Mabee and Newhouse, *Sojourner Truth*;

Painter, *Sojourner Truth*; Washington, *Sojourner Truth's America*. For references to Truth's early lectures in the Old Northwest, see *NLA*, August 27, 1851, March 3, 1852.

180 "Treason in Disguise," *Liberator*, June 21, 1861.

181 "Shameful Persecution," *Liberator*, June 28, 1861.

182 Ibid. For more on this and other violent incidents, see Washington, *Sojourner Truth's America*, 292–97.

183 Cott, "Passionlessness."

CHAPTER 6

1 By the 1850s, definitions of the "West" had expanded to include Iowa, Minnesota, Kansas, and Nebraska. Save for the controversy over the Kansas-Nebraska Act, I do not include these states in this study.

2 "Proceedings of the Twelfth Anniversary of the Western Anti-Slavery Society," *ASB*, September 2, 1854. See also "An Application of Principles—A Case of Emancipation," *ASB*, September 2, 1854.

3 According to Daniel Hise, the members of the committee included Benjamin Bown, Abram Brooke, Nathan Thomas, and Henry Blackwell (Hise Diaries, August 28, 1854).

4 "An Application of Principles—A Case of Emancipation," *ASB*, September 2, 1854; Hise Diaries, August 28, 1854; "Salem Emancipationists—The Facts," *FDP*, September 22, 1854 (reprinted from the *Cleveland Leader*); "The Salem Rescue," *Cleveland Morning Leader*, August 31, 1854; "The Salem Rescue," *Cleveland Morning Leader*, September 1, 1854; "The Salem Rescue," *Cleveland Morning Leader*, September 14, 1854; "Anti-Slavery Doings in Salem—Release of a Slave—Exciting Scene," *Ashtabula Sentinel*, September 7, 1854.

5 "An Application of Principles—A Case of Emancipation," *ASB*, September 2, 1854. I thank Patricia Cline Cohen for her expertise in tracking down J. J. Robinson in the 1860 Census.

6 "An Application of Principles—A Case of Emancipation," *ASB*, September 2, 1854.

7 The *ASB* announced, "The rescue of a little colored girl, last week, from the hands of the slave claimant, has excited much attention and remark from the press" ("The Salem Rescue," September 9, 1854). For the southern perspective, see "The Salem Robbery," *Memphis Daily Appeal*, October 18, 1854; "The Cincinnati Merchants in a Quandary," *Louisville Daily Journal*, October 5, 1854.

8 "A Specimen," *ASB*, September 9, 1854 (reprinted from the *Cleveland Herald*).

9 According to a Memphis newspaper, "A big buck negro, called John Gibson, conveyed [the slave child] away" ("Southern People Wake Up," *Memphis Daily Appeal*, September 10, 1854). The man was probably John Gibbons, a forty-two-year-old African American whose occupation in the 1850 U.S. Census was listed

as "restaurant." The *ASB* mentions John I. Gaines as the only African American participating in the annual meeting, but I was unable to find any such person in the U.S. Census for 1850 or 1860 ("Proceedings" and "The Anniversary," *ASB*, September 2, 1854).

10 Alice Stone Blackwell, *Lucy Stone*, 148.

11 See excerpts of Blackwell's letter in ibid., 148–53.

12 "The Vermin of an Eagle's Nest," *Memphis Daily Appeal*, September 12, 1854; "Meeting of the Citizens," *Memphis Daily Appeal*, September 17, 1854.

13 "The Cincinnati Merchants in a Quandary," *Louisville Daily Journal*, October 5, 1854.

14 "Correspondence with Blackwell, the Abolitionist & Negro Stealer," *Memphis Daily Appeal*, October 26, 1854.

15 "From the Ohio Anti-Slavery Bugle: Don't Give It Up," *Liberator*, November 10, 1854; "Fayette County Indignation Meeting," *Memphis Daily Appeal*, October 1, 1854.

16 "The Salem Rescue and Cincinnati," *ASB*, September 16, 1854.

17 For more on the interracial character of the Underground Railroad in the Ohio River Valley, see Griffler, *Front Line*.

18 "The discussions were mainly on the distinctive principles of our principles of our friends—the Constitution, non-voting and disunion. Mr. Henry Blackwell, of Cincinnati, was the prominent opponent of these measures, and very earnest advocate of voting against slavery. Mr. Blackwell is an anti-slavery man, thoroughly in earnest, a fluent, agreeable and energetic speaker—who can give and take card raps with good temper" ("The Anniversary," *ASB*, September 2, 1854).

19 "The Salem Rescue," *ASB*, September 9, 1854.

20 See, for example, Harrold, *Subversives*.

21 Kerr, *Lucy Stone*, 80.

22 Abby Kelley Salem initially stayed with Josephine and Charles Griffing but then moved in with Joel and Sarah McMillan, local Quaker abolitionists. There is no record of her in the 1860 or 1870 Census. See "An Application of Principles—A Case of Emancipation," *ASB*, September 2, 1854; "The Drouth—A General Gloom—The Salem Rescue—The Pittsburgh Rescue—The Fusionists—Romanism—Know-Nothingism," *Liberator*, September 15, 1854 (letter from Henry C. Wright); "Salem Emancipationists—The Facts," *FDP*, September 22, 1854; Galbreath, "Anti-Slavery Movement," 381–87. Hise does not mention Abby Kelley Salem again in his diary.

23 Siebert claims that thousands of slaves escaped to the northern United States and Canada (*Underground Railroad*; *Mysteries*). Gara, *Liberty Line*, and others have since suggested that no more than one thousand slaves escaped each year during the antebellum period. Crew argues that Ohio, in particular, was a "hotbed" for the Underground Railroad (foreword, ix).

24 Many historians of the Underground Railroad have emphasized the central role that slaves played in escaping. See, for example, most of the essays in Blight, *Passages to Freedom*; Griffler, *Front Line*.

25 Harriet Beecher Stowe's *Uncle Tom's Cabin* is based on her knowledge of fugitive escapes through Cincinnati and the work of Rankin, Parker, and the Coffins. For more on Stowe, see Hedrick, *Harriet Beecher Stowe*; Coffin, *Reminiscences*; Parker, *His Promised Land*. For more on the myths of the Underground Railroad, see Gara, *Liberty Line*; Blight, "Introduction."

26 The 1859 Oberlin-Wellington Rescue grabbed the most headlines among rescues in the West. See Shipherd, *History*; Cochran, *Western Reserve*, 118–57.

27 For a characteristic example of free blacks' participation in a Cincinnati fugitive slave capture, see "A Fugitive Slave Case in Cincinnati," *CG*, August 17, 1853.

28 See, for example, "Slave Case in Ohio," *FDP*, July 28, 1854.

29 "Cor. of the NY Tribune; A Slave Rescued in Ohio," *FDP*, September 8, 1854.

30 Charles Torrey, for example, disapproved of women's public role in antislavery meetings but nonetheless worked respectfully with white and black women in aiding fugitives. See Harrold, "On the Borders."

31 As cited in Gara, *Liberty Line*, 75.

32 SOE to AWW, July 28, 1850, BPL, MS A.9.2, vol. 25, no. 16.

33 "Sewing Societies," *ASB*, January 22, 1847.

34 Michigan Anti-Slavery Society Executive Committee Minutes, October 1, 1854, Harriet deGarmo Fuller Papers, William L. Clements Library, University of Michigan, Ann Arbor.

35 Ibid.

36 The Griffings would return from Canada to attend the annual meeting of the Michigan Anti-Slavery Society ("Proceedings of the First Annual Meeting of the Michigan Anti-Slavery Society," *ASB*, October 28, 1854).

37 The Female Anti-Slavery Society of Jerseyville, Illinois, the Western Free Produce Association, and the Illinois Female Anti-Slavery Society provided clothes and other forms of aid to fugitives in Canada ("Southern Convention," *WC*, November 2, 1847; "To the Managers of the Ill. Female A.S. Society," *WC*, September 19, 1844; "Free Labor Convention," *FLAASC*, November 7, 1846).

38 See "A Letter from Mrs. Griffing," *ASB*, October 28, 1854; "Correspondence from the Lecturing Field," *ASB*, November 4, 1854; "Correspondence," *ASB*, November 11, 1854. The Griffings do not mention the conflict between Henry and Mary Bibb, associated with the Refugee Home Society, and Mary Ann Shadd (Cary). Shadd disapproved of the Bibb's "begging" for funds for fugitives (Hine, Brown, and Terborg-Penn, *Black Women in America*, 224–25; Murray, "*Provincial Freeman*"). Charles C. Foote was a New York Liberty Party activist who became a minister to the White Lake, Michigan, Presbyterian congregation in the mid-1840s. He served as an agent for the Refugee Home Society in the 1850s, raising

funds to purchase land for fugitives in Canada (Ripley, *Black Abolitionist Papers*, 2:245–52). Foote was a strong supporter of women's equality. See his essay, "Woman's Rights and Duties," *Oberlin Quarterly Review*, October 1849, 400.

39 On Mahan, see Hagedorn, *Beyond the River*. "Anti-Slavery Meeting," *ASB*, March 20, 1846.

40 See Collison, *Shadrach Minkins*; Harrold, "On the Borders"; Griffler, *Front Line*.

41 On the importance of black women's work on the Underground Railroad, see Jeffrey, *Great Silent Army*, 181–83. See also Yee's discussion of how black women's work on the Underground Railroad pointed to the larger differences between white and black abolitionism (*Black Women Abolitionists*, 98–100).

42 Coffin, *Reminiscences*; Gara, *Liberty Line*; Jeffrey, *Great Silent Army*, 88; Middleton, "Fugitive Slave Crisis"; Quarles, *Black Abolitionists*, 153; Parker, *His Promised Land*; Vlach, "Above Ground."

43 On the Blackburn Rescue, see Frost, *I've Got a Home*; Kooker, "Antislavery Movement," 63–77. See also Lumpkin, "'General Plan.'"

44 See Formisano, "Edge of Caste," 21; Frost, *I've Got a Home*, 182; "Riot and Outrage," *Liberator*, June 29, 1833.

45 Frost, *I've Got a Home*, 189.

46 Ibid., 267–69.

47 Ibid., 178, 184. Only blacks were convicted in this case.

48 For a description of the biracial network developed by Charles Torrey, Thomas and Elizabeth Smallwood, and many others, see Harrold, "On the Borders."

49 Glesner, "Laura Haviland." See also Haviland, *Woman's Life-Work*.

50 Haviland, *Woman's Life-Work*.

51 Gara, *Liberty Line*, 120. See, for example, Bibb's speech as described in "Anti-Slavery Convention," *CG*, April 29, 1852.

52 "The Central Committee at Detroit to the Ladies of the State of Michigan," *Signal of Liberty*, April 27, 1846.

53 Ripley, *Black Abolitionist Papers*, 2:109–10.

54 The *Signal of Liberty* kept track of the development of the women's groups. See June 13, 1846, June 20, 1846, July 11, 1846, July 25, 1846, August 10, 1846, September 5, 1846, November 1, 1846, November 7, 1846. See also Ardath Hagaman, "Women of the Old Northwest in the Antislavery Movement," 37–43, May 1941, Box 1, History 431, 432, Student Papers, Department of History, University of Michigan, Bentley Historical Library, Ann Arbor.

55 "Ella Thomas's History of the Underground Railroad," December 1892, Nathan Thomas Papers, Bentley Historical Library, University of Michigan, Ann Arbor. According to a 1904 reminiscence of the Underground Railroad, Pamela Thomas was "one of the first teachers in the school established for colored people by the gift of Benjamin Thomas" (Huff, "Unnamed Anti-Slavery Heroes," 141).

56 Lovina Bissell to BMC, n.d., BMC Papers, Box 2, Folder 9. Bissell served as president of the Ashtabula County Female Anti-Slavery Society in 1835 and 1836

(Ashtabula County Female Anti-Slavery Society Records, Western Reserve Historical Society, Cleveland, Ohio).

57 BMC to Cornelia Cowles, February 3, 1843, BMC Papers, Box 1, Folder 14. BMC's biographer, Geary, notes that the Cowles home in Austinburg probably housed fugitive slaves, although no evidence of such activity appears in the antebellum family correspondence (*Balanced in the Wind*, 104 n. 84).

58 "Female Anti-Slavery State Society," *WC*, June 20, 1844. See also Garman, "'Altered Tone of Expression,'" 128.

59 See the following examples in the *WC*: "Tales of the Star-Gazers, No. 1: Jesse and Dysa," April 6, 1843; "Tales of the Star-Gazers, No. 4: Not the Star-Led, but the Stream-Led," April 6, 1843; "Tales of the Star-Gazers, No. 5: The Oppressed Widow," June 29, 1843; "The Captive of the Bake-House," June 29, 1843; "Tales of the Fugitives, No. III," January 4, 1844; "Kidnapping in Winchester," February 8, 1844; "Adventures of a Fugitive," February 6, 1845.

60 "Adventures of a Fugitive," *WC*, February 6, 1845.

61 Anne Thomas to Nathan Thomas, April 2, 1839, Thomas Papers.

62 See Haviland, *Woman's Life-Work*.

63 See Galbreath, "Anti-Slavery Movement," 381–87.

64 Jeffrey discusses women's arduous domestic work for fugitives in *Great Silent Army*, 184–85.

65 "Ella Thomas' History of the Underground Railroad," December 1892, Thomas Papers.

66 Coffin, *Reminiscences*, 112.

67 "Ella Thomas' History of the Underground Railroad," December 1892, Thomas Papers.

68 Thomas was probably referring to the Crosswhite case, in which a large interracial group rescued a family of fugitives in Marshall, Michigan. Several of the men involved with the rescue were prosecuted. See Fields, "Free Negroes"; Patterson, "Marshall Men"; Ndukwu, "Antislavery in Michigan."

69 "Ella Thomas' History of the Underground Railroad," December 1892, Thomas Papers.

70 Lovina Bissell to BMC, n.d., BMC Papers, Box 2, Folder 9.

71 Haviland, *Woman's Life-Work*.

72 "Correspondence," *ASB*, November 11, 1854.

73 Salerno argues that women turned to aiding fugitives only in the 1850s, with the passage of the Fugitive Slave Act in 1850 and the 1854 Kansas-Nebraska conflict (*Sister Societies*, 149).

74 Yellin and Van Horne, *Abolitionist Sisterhood*, contains only three brief references to the Underground Railroad (28, 94, 164) and no references to vigilance committees. Debra Gold Hansen has few references to the Underground Railroad in her monograph on the Boston Female Anti-Slavery Society, *Strained Sisterhood*. The one exception is the role of the Boston Female Anti-Slavery

Society in the rescue of and legal defense of a fugitive slave in the Med case in Boston in 1837. Salerno, *Sister Societies*, has one reference to the Underground Railroad (149). She also briefly discusses the efforts of female antislavery societies in Salem, Boston, and Philadelphia to aid fugitives, particularly in the 1840s (138–43). Van Broekhoven, *Devotion of These Women*, has no references to the Underground Railroad. Petrulionis argues that individual women associated with Massachusetts's Concord Female Anti-Slavery Society may have housed fugitives, but she does not refer to any formal position on the Underground Railroad adopted by the group ("'Swelling That Great Tide'"). Mary Grew of the Philadelphia Female Anti-Slavery Society occasionally supported fugitives (Ira Brown, *Mary Grew*).

75 In one of the first histories of the antislavery movement, one historian claimed that western women often took on the roles of men in their Underground Railroad work. See Macy, *Anti-Slavery Crusade*, 47.

76 The resolutions passed by many northern communities after the passage of the Fugitive Slave Law reflected the earlier resolutions of the female antislavery societies in the West. See Land, "John Brown's Ohio Environment."

77 *FLAASC*, October 15, 1842.

78 Ibid., November 1, 1843.

79 See Hamm, *Antislavery Movement*.

80 Henry FASS, April 3, 1841.

81 Ibid., March 18, 1843.

82 Ibid., December 2, 1832.

83 "Address to the Men of Indiana, from the Henry County Female Anti-Slavery Society," *FLAASC*, December 22, 1843.

84 See Pierson, *Free Hearts*, 57–64.

85 "Females 2nd Annual Report," *FLAASC*, July 11, 1843.

86 "Constitution and Proceedings," *WC*, April 6, 1843.

87 "Putnam Co. Female Anti-Slavery Society," *WC*, September 7, 1843.

88 "Putnam County," *WC*, February 22, 1844.

89 Turner, *Underground Railroad*, 62–63.

90 "Putnam Co.," *WC*, October 3, 1844.

91 Henry FASS, June 29, 1844.

92 "Union Co. A.S. Society," *FLAASC*, December 31, 1842.

93 See Lois E. Horton, "Kidnapping and Resistance," 157–58.

94 "Constitution of the Female A.S. Society, of Princeton, Bureau Co., Ill.," *WC*, November 9, 1843.

95 Blue, *No Taint of Compromise*, 95–96.

96 "To the Managers of the Ill. Female A.S. Society," *WC*, August 15, 1844.

97 Waldrip, "Station," 70.

98 Henry FASS, April 3, 1847, [summer] 1847.

99 Ibid., December 7, 1847.

100 "Quarterly Report of the Ladies of the Orwell Female Anti-Slavery Society," August 4, 1846, BMC Papers, Box 1, Folder 14.

101 "Southern Convention," *WC*, November 2, 1847.

102 Irene Ball Allan letter, *WC*, May 16, 1844.

103 "From the Newport (Ky) News: Free Soil Ladies," *ASB*, May 2, 1857.

104 SOE to AWW, July 28, 1850, BPL, MS A.9.2, vol. 25, no. 16.

105 A columnist for the *Philanthropist* wrote that "from ten to twelve or fifteen" women met with the sewing circle every week in Cincinnati ("To the Female Abolitionists of Cincinnati," *Philanthropist*, February 7, 1844). See also Coffin, *Reminiscences*, 301.

106 SOE to AWW, November 14, 1852, BPL, MS A.9.2, vol. 26, no. 70.

107 Coffin, *Reminiscences*, 301.

108 "To the Female Abolitionists of Cincinnati," *Philanthropist*, February 7, 1844.

109 "The Ninth Annual Report of the Cincinnati Anti-Slavery Sewing Circle," *ASB*, March 13, 1852.

110 Ibid.

111 "Anti Slavery Meeting," *FLAASC*, December 22, 1843.

112 Henry FASS, January 25, 1845.

113 Ibid., May 31, 1845.

114 "Constitution and Proceedings," *WC*, April 6, 1843.

115 This "higher law" doctrine was familiar to Garrisonians and was used by abolitionists protesting the Fugitive Slave Law in 1850 (Land, "John Brown's Ohio Environment," 36).

116 "Address to the Females," *FLAASC*, July 11, 1843.

117 Henry FASS, January 25, 1845.

118 Levy, "'Abolition Riot.'"

119 Ibid., 90.

120 Pease and Pease, "Confrontation and Abolition." Pease and Pease primarily discuss men's actions.

121 Siebert, "Quaker Section," 498.

122 Prince, "Rescue Case of 1857," 295. See also Watts, "History."

123 On the kidnapping of free African Americans, see Griffler, *Front Line*, 18–20.

124 Formisano, "Edge of Caste," 33.

125 Middleton, "Fugitive Slave Crisis," 20–32.

126 Ibid., 24.

127 Crenshaw, *"Bury Me in a Free Land,"* 32–33.

128 Cashin, "Black Families," 472.

129 Haviland, *Woman's Life-Work*, 76; for a detailed description of this episode, see 53–90. For a historian's interpretation of this event, see Glesner, "Laura Haviland," 83–99.

CHAPTER 7

1 "From Indiana," *ASB*, March 22, 1856.

2 See Hersh, *Slavery of Sex*; DuBois, *Feminism and Suffrage*, 21–52; DuBois, "Women's Rights and Abolition."

3 Keyssar, *Right to Vote*, 51–60.

4 Ginzberg, *Untidy Origins*. Twelve years prior to the New York petition, a group of Harrisburg, Ohio, women petitioned Congress for emancipation in the District of Columbia and included a request for universal suffrage (Zaeske, *Signatures of Citizenship*, 68–69).

5 Basch, *In the Eyes of the Law*.

6 "To the Women of Ohio," *ASB*, April 6, 1850.

7 Audretsch, *Salem, Ohio 1850 Women's Rights Convention Proceedings Women's*, 66. Audretsch notes that several newspapers reported an audience of between four hundred and five hundred, but the meetinghouse where most of the gathering took place could not have accommodated such a large crowd.

8 "The Women's Convention," *ASB*, April 6, 1850.

9 Ibid.

10 Ibid.

11 "The Women's Convention," *ASB*, June 8, 1850.

12 "Letter from Parker Pillsbury," *ASB*, November 16, 1850.

13 "Ohio Women's Convention," *ASB*, April 27, 1850.

14 "The Rights of Women," *Saturday Evening Post*, July 6, 1850. On Swisshelm's woman's rights position, see Hoffert, *Jane Grey Swisshelm*, 141–43.

15 "The Ladies Astir," *Home Journal*, May 11, 1850.

16 Conventions occurred across the North, mostly at the state level. See Hoffert, *When Hens Crow*; Isenberg, *Sex and Citizenship*; Stanton, Anthony, and Gage, *History of Woman Suffrage*, vol. 1.

17 "Woman's Rights Convention: Sojourner Truth," *ASB*, June 21, 1851. On Frances Dana Gage's reconstruction of Truth's speech in 1862 and the historical inaccuracies that followed, see Painter, *Sojourner Truth*, 164–78. On Coe, see Stanton and Anthony, *Selected Papers*, 234 n. 5.

18 "Women's Rights Convention," *ASB*, April 17, 1852; "Annual Meeting of the Ohio Woman's Rights Association," *ASB*, April 1, 1853; "Proceedings of the First Annual Meeting of the Ohio Woman's Rights Association," *ASB*, June 4, 1853.

19 "National Woman's Rights Convention," *ASB*, October 15, 1853; "Woman's Rights Convention," *ASB*, August 25, 1855.

20 "Woman's Rights Convention," *ASB*, October 4, 1851; "Woman's Rights Convention in Indiana," *ASB*, October 30, 1852; "Letter from Josephine Griffing," *ASB*, October 29, 1853; "The Indiana Woman's Rights Association," *ASB*, September 30, 1854; "Indiana Woman's Rights Convention," *ASB*, November 11, 1854; "Woman's Rights Convention—A Call!!," *ASB*, April 24, 1857. Woman's rights conventions

were often linked to state constitutional conventions (Isenberg, *Sex and Citizenship*, 213).

21 Eastern woman's rights conventions also included many abolitionists. According to Wellman, Seneca Falls participants included Quakers, Free-Soilers, and legal reformers ("Seneca Falls").

22 JEH was asked to give the keynote only days before the meeting. "It was a question to wh[ich] I had devoted no thought, I had not a single fact or argument in my mind in relation to it," she explained to a friend. "But they insisted, & I sat down & wrote an address, wh[ich] I read at the Convention, & I supposed that would be the last of it, but the entire address was published, in one of our papers, & then copied by a Boston print, & commended in extravagant terms, & a flattering review of its went into [Horace] Greel[e]y's paper [the *New York Tribune*], who has a circulation of some 40,000, so all at once I found myself before the world as an advocate of Woman's Rights" (JEH to Roccena B. Vaill Norris, February 21, 1851, Norris Papers). For JEH's address, see Stanton, Anthony, and Gage, *History of Woman Suffrage*, 1:106–10.

23 Stanton and Anthony, *Selected Papers*, 1:349.

24 "Eastern Correspondence," *Free West*, October 16, 1854; "Correspondence," *Free West*, November 16, 1854; "Personal and Local," *Free West*, November 23, 1854.

25 "People's Portrait Gallery," *Free West*, December 7, 1854.

26 See, for example, Hersh, *Slavery of Sex*; DuBois, *Feminism and Suffrage*.

27 "Indiana Woman's Rights Convention," *ASB*, September 27, 1851.

28 "Letter from Indiana," *ASB*, November 8, 1851.

29 "Editorials by the Wayside," *ASB*, October 22, 1853.

30 "Woman, Her Position and Duties," *ASB*, May 17, 1851.

31 "Letter from Joseph Treat," *ASB*, January 21, 1852.

32 "Women Lecturers," *Philanthropist*, June 12, 1838.

33 MBD, *Oquakwa Spectator*, October 26, 1853. Other female reformers and journalists, among them Clarina Howard Nichols and Jane Swisshelm, agreed with MBD that men and women had different natures but nevertheless embraced woman's suffrage. See Marilyn Schultz Blackwell, "Meddling in Politics"; Pierson, *Free Hearts*, 71–96; Hoffert, *Jane Grey Swisshelm*.

34 MBD, *Oquakwa Spectator*, February 22, 1854.

35 Kelley, *Learning to Stand and Speak*, 68.

36 "Ohio Woman's Convention," *Liberator*, May 17, 1850.

37 "Letter from Josephine Griffing," *ASB*, October 29, 1853.

38 See "Woman's Rights Convention," *ASB*, October 18, 1851; "Letter form Mary F. Thomas," *ASB*, November 29, 1851; "Woman's Rights Convention," *ASB*, April 17, 1852.

39 "Proceedings of the Women's Rights Convention," *ASB*, June 7, 1851; "Speech of Mrs. H. M. Tracy," *ASB*, June 14, 1851.

40 "Woman's Sphere," *ASB*, June 29, 1850.

41 "Proceedings of the Women's Rights Convention," *ASB*, June 7, 1851. Swisshelm accepted Barker's compromise, which involved the removal of the words "criminal" and "gross" from the resolution.

42 "To the Women of Ohio," *ASB*, April 6, 1850.

43 "'Go and Do Likewise,'" *ASB*, May 21, 1847; "Tenth Annual Report of the Western Anti-Slavery Society," *ASB*, August 28, 1852; "Proceedings of the Eighteenth Anniversary of the Western Anti-Slavery Society," *ASB*, September 29, 1860; "Western Anti-Slavery Fair," *ASB*, April 9, 1847.

44 Garrison, *Letters*, 3:517.

45 "Woman's Rights in Akron," *ASB*, May 11, 1850.

46 "Rights of Woman," *ASB*, April 13, 1850.

47 "Address to the Men of Indiana, from the Henry County Female Anti Slavery Society," *FLAASC*, December 22, 1843.

48 "Editorials by the Wayside," *ASB*, October 22, 1853.

49 "Boots for Girls," *Ohio Cultivator*, [February 1857], Celestia Rice Colby Papers, Box 14, Scrapbooks ca. 1854–1861, Illinois State University, Special Collections, Bloomington.

50 "Letter from Indiana," *ASB*, November 8, 1851.

51 On the Bloomer costume, see Fischer, *Pantaloons and Power*; Leach, *True Love*, 243–60.

52 "For the Spectator and Observer," *Oquakwa Spectator*, July 16, 1851.

53 Hise Diaries, July 6, 1851.

54 "Bloomerism in the Church," *ASB*, November 29, 1851.

55 On free love, see Passet, *Sex Radicals*; Leach, *True Love*; Sears, *Sex Radicals*.

56 "Notes from the Lecturing Field," *ASB*, March 6, 1852.

57 "Mrs. Bloomer's Lecture," *Western Citizen and Chicago Weekly*, October 18, 1853.

58 JEH to Roccena B. Vaill Norris, February 21, 1851, Norris Papers.

59 Berbrugge, *Able-Bodied Womanhood*, 8.

60 Ibid.

61 JEH to Roccena B. Vaill Norris, February 21, 1851, Norris Papers.

62 Ibid., March 24, 1851.

63 Ibid., August 5, 1851.

64 Kansas became such an important part of the new understanding of the West in the 1850s that I include it here. My focus remains on the Old Northwest, but because many western abolitionists moved to Kansas, I have incorporated their experiences. For more on Kansas, see Oertel, *Bleeding Borders*.

65 Tegtmeier, "Ladies of Lawrence Are Arming!"

66 "Kansas," *ASB*, July 7, 1855.

67 "The Ladies of Lawrence," *ASB*, January 12, 1856.

68 Ibid.

69 "Women in Kansas," *ASB*, August 27, 1857.

70 Sarah Grimké to Sarah G. Wattles, February 13, 1856, Weld-Grimké Papers, William L. Clements Library, University of Michigan, Ann Arbor.

71 There is conflicting evidence about when the Wattleses moved to Kansas. The *Anti-Slavery Bugle* reported that the family arrived there in the spring of 1855 ("Kansas," *ASB*, July 7, 1855), but a June 1854 letter from Sarah Grimké indicates that the Wattleses were already in Kansas (Sarah Grimké to Augustus and Sarah G. Wattles, June 10, 1854, Weld-Grimké Papers).

72 Sarah Grimké to Augustus and Sarah G. Wattles, June 10, 1854, Weld-Grimké Papers.

73 Ibid., March 23, 1856, January 27, 1859.

AFTERWORD

1 Emily Rakestraw Robinson to My Dear Friend, n.d., MRR Papers; "Our Old Anti-Slavery Tent," MRR Papers.

2 Haviland, *Woman's Life-Work*. See Haviland's letters to various members of the American Missionary Society, Laura Haviland Collection, Bentley Historical Library, University of Michigan, Ann Arbor.

3 DeBlasio, "Her Own Society," 209–10.

4 Faulkner, *Women's Radical Reconstruction*.

5 Ibid.

6 Ibid.; Venet, *Neither Ballots nor Bullets*, 118, 135, 139.

Bibliography

PRIMARY SOURCES

Manuscripts

American Antiquarian Society, Worcester, Massachusetts
    Abby Kelley Foster Papers (from the Worcester Historical Society)
    Abby Kelley Foster–Stephen S. Foster Papers
Bentley Historical Library, University of Michigan, Ann Arbor
    Robert D. Aldrich Collection
    Martha A. Brown Letter
    Elizabeth Margaret Chandler Papers
    George W. Clark Papers
    Deland Family Papers
    Laura Haviland Collection
    Lucian H. Jones Papers
    Arthur Raymond Kooker Papers
    Berenice Bryant Lowe Papers
    Michigan Anti-Slavery Society Papers
    Norris Family Papers
    Presbyterian Church, Marshall, Papers
    Student Papers, Department of History, University of Michigan
    Swift Family Papers
    Taylor Family Papers

Nathan Thomas Papers

Seymour Treadwell Papers

Boston Public Library, Department of Rare Books and Manuscripts, Boston,
    Massachusetts

Antislavery Collection

Chicago Historical Society, Chicago, Illinois

Zebina Eastman Papers

Cincinnati Historical Society Library, Cincinnati, Ohio

Ohio Anti-Slavery Society

Friends Historical Library, Swarthmore College, Swarthmore, Pennsylvania

Joseph Dugdale Papers

Historical Society of Pennsylvania, Philadelphia

Philadelphia Female Anti-Slavery Society Papers

Illinois State Historical Library, Springfield

Ichabod Codding Papers

Illinois State University, Special Collections, Bloomington

Celestia Rice Colby Papers

Indiana Historical Library, Indianapolis

Valentine Nicholson Collection

Martha White Talbert Diaries

Indiana State Library, Indiana Division, Manuscripts Collection, Indianapolis

Henry Charles Collection, S251

Records of the Henry County Female Anti-Slavery Society, S1672

Neel's Creek Anti-Slavery Society Collection

Charles H. Test Letters, 1840–43, S1296

Kent State University Libraries, Special Collections and Archives, Kent, Ohio

Betsey Mix Cowles Papers

Knox College Library, Galesburg, Illinois

William Hayes Family Papers

Massachusetts Historical Society, Boston

Boston Female Anti-Slavery Society Letterbook

Oberlin College Library, Oberlin, Ohio

Ball-Curtis Genealogy

Betsey Mix Cowles Papers

Robert S. Fletcher Papers

Ladies' Literary Society Records

Elizabeth Lord Papers

Emilie Palmer Diary

Mary Sheldon Papers

Ohio Historical Society, Columbus

Daniel Howell Hise Diaries

Edward Chestor Lampson Papers

Alice McMillan Papers

Ripley Anti-Slavery Society Papers

Western Reserve Historical Society, Cleveland, Ohio

Mrs. S. G. Andrews Letter, MSS v.f. A

Ashtabula County Female Anti-Slavery Society Records, MSS 387

James Barnaby Papers, MSS 1007

Brocton Ladies Aid Society Records, MSS 443

Canton Ladies Anti-Slavery Society Records, MSS 26

Cleveland Anti-Slavery Society Records, MSS v.f. C

Mary Lukens Gilbert Papers, MSS 3101

George E. Jenkins Papers, Ohio Free Produce Association Papers, MSS 100

New Lyme Anti-Slavery Circle Papers, MSS v.f. N

Portage County Ladies Anti-Slavery Society Papers, MSS v.f. L

Marius R. Robinson Papers, MSS 1660

Wheaton College, Wheaton, Illinois

Jonathan Blanchard Papers, RG 2.1

William L. Clements Library, University of Michigan, Ann Arbor

African-American Collection

James G. Birney Papers

Lydia Maria Child Papers

Elizabeth Comstock Papers

Harriet deGarmo Fuller Papers

Weld-Grimké Papers

Newspapers

Anti-Slavery Bugle (Salem, Ohio)

Anti-Slavery Record (New York and Boston)

Ashtabula (Ohio) Sentinel

Aurora (New Lisbon, Ohio)

Chicago Daily Tribune

Cincinnati Daily Commercial

Cincinnati Daily Gazette

Cincinnati Daily Times

Cincinnati Post and Anti-Abolitionist

Cincinnati Weekly Herald and Philanthropist

Cleveland Morning Leader

Cleveland Plain Dealer

Daily Cincinnati Republican and Commercial Register

Daily Commercial Register (Sandusky, Ohio)

Daily Free Democrat (Milwaukee)

Emancipator (New York)

Frederick Douglass' Paper (Rochester, New York)

Free Labor Advocate and Anti-Slavery Chronicle (New Garden, Indiana)

Free West (Chicago)

Genius of Liberty (Cincinnati)

Genius of Universal Emancipation

Independent

Liberator (Boston)

Lily (Mt. Vernon, Ohio)

National Anti-Slavery Standard (New York)

National Era (Washington, D.C.)

New Lisbon (Ohio) Aurora

Non-Slaveholder (Philadelphia)

North Star (Rochester, New York)

Oberlin (Ohio) Evangelist

Oberlin Quarterly Review

Ohio American (Cleveland)

Oquakwa (Illinois) Spectator

Painesville (Ohio) Telegraph

Peoria (Illinois) Register and North-Western Gazetteer

Philanthropist (Cincinnati)

Signal of Liberty (Ann Arbor, Michigan)

Western Citizen (Chicago)

Western Citizen and Chicago Weekly

Books and Articles

1850 Census Columbiana Co. Ohio. Mansfield: Ohio Genealogical Society, 1973.

Audretsch, Robert W., ed. *The Salem, Ohio 1850 Women's Rights Convention Proceedings*. Salem, Ohio: Salem Area Bicentennial Committee and Salem Public Library, 1976.

Beecher, Catharine E. *An Essay on Slavery and Abolitionism, with Reference to the Duty of American Females*. Philadelphia: Perkins, 1837.

Beecher, Edwin. *Narrative of the Riots at Alton in Connection with the Death of Rev. Elijah P. Lovejoy*. Alton, Ill.: Halton, 1837.

Birney, James Gillespie. *Letters of James Gillespie Birney, 1831–1857*. Edited by Dwight L. Dumond. 2 vols. New York: Appleton-Century, 1938.

Bradford, Arthur B. *Address Delivered at the Re-Union Convention of the Old Abolitionists of Eastern Ohio and Western Pennsylvania: October 1st, 1879, at Alliance, Ohio*. Alliance, Ohio: Garrison's, 1879.

Chandler, Elizabeth Margaret. *Remember the Distance That Divides Us: The Family Letters of Philadelphia Quaker Abolitionist and Michigan Pioneer Elizabeth Margaret Chandler, 1830–1842*. Edited by Marcia J. Heringa Mason. East Lansing: Michigan State University Press, 2004.

Cockrum, William Monroe. *History of the Underground Railroad as It Was conducted by the Anti-Slavery League; Including Many Thrilling Encounters between Those Aiding the Slaves to Escape and Those Trying to Recapture Them*. New York: Negro Universities Press, 1969.

Coffin, Levi. *Reminiscences of Levi Coffin*. New York: Arno, 1968.

Colman, Lucy N. *Reminiscences*. Buffalo, N.Y.: Green, 1891.

Comstock, Elizabeth L. *Life and Letters of Elizabeth L. Comstock*. Compiled by C. Hare. London: Headley, 1895.

Dugdale, Joseph A. *Extemporaneous Discourses*. Poughkeepsie, N.Y.: Plat and Schram, 1850.

Eastman, Zebina. "History of the Anti-Slavery Agitation and the Growth of the Liberty and Republican Parties in Illinois." In *Discoveries and Conquests of the Northwest with the History of Chicago*, edited by Rufus Blanchard. Chicago: Blanchard, 1900.

Edgerton, Walter. *A History of the Separation in Indiana Yearly Meeting of Friends,*

Which Took Place in the Winter of 1842 and 1843, on the Anti-Slavery Question.
Cincinnati: Pugh, 1856.

Gibbons, Abby Hopper. *Life of Abby Hopper Gibbons, Told Chiefly through Her Correspondence.* Edited by Sarah Hopper Emerson. 2 vols. New York: Putnam's, 1897.

Extracts from the Minutes of the Annual Meeting of the Free Produce Association of Ohio Yearly Meeting (1850). Mount Pleasant, Ohio: Harris, 1851.

First Annual Report of the Ladies' New-York City Anti-Slavery Society. New York: Dorr, 1836.

Foner, Philip A., and George E. Walker, eds. *Proceedings of the Black State Conventions, 1840–1865.* Vol. 1, *New York, Pennsylvania, Indiana, Michigan, Ohio.* Philadelphia: Temple University Press, 1979.

Garrison, William Lloyd. *The Letters of William Lloyd Garrison.* Edited by Walter M. Merrill. 6 vols. Cambridge: Belknap Press of Harvard University Press, 1973.

Hallowell, Anna Davis, ed. *James and Lucretia Mott: Life and Letters.* Boston: Houghton Mifflin, 1884.

Harper, Frances Ellen Watkins. *A Brighter Day Coming: A Frances Ellen Watkins Harper Reader.* Edited by Frances Smith Foster. New York: Feminist, 1990.

Haviland, Laura S. *A Woman's Life-Work: Including Thirty Years' Service on the Underground Railroad and in the War.* Grand Rapids, Mich.: Shaw, 1881.

Heyrick, Elizabeth. *Apology for Ladies' Anti-Slavery Associations.* London: Hatchard, 1828.

———. *Appeal to the Hearts and Consciences of British Women.* Leicester: Cockshaw, 1828.

———. *Immediate Not Gradual Emancipation; or, An Inquiry into the Shortest, Safest, and Most Effectual Means of Getting Rid of West Indian Slavery.* London: Hatchard, 1824.

Holley, Sallie. *A Life for Liberty: Anti-Slavery and Other Writings of Sallie Holley.* Edited by John White Chadwick. 1899; New York: Negro Universities Press, 1969.

Jacobs, Harriet. *Incidents in the Life of a Slave Girl: Written by Herself.* Edited by Jean Fagan Yellin. Cambridge: Harvard University Press, 2000.

Jones, J. Elizabeth. *The Young Abolitionists; or, Conversations on Slavery.* 1848; Freeport, N.Y.: Books for Libraries, 1971.

Lovejoy, Owen. *His Brother's Blood: Speeches and Writings, 1838–64.* Edited by William F. Moore and Jane Ann Moore. Urbana: University of Illinois Press, 2004.

Lundy, Benjamin. *Poetical Works of Elizabeth Margaret Chandler with a Memoir of Her Life and Character.* Philadelphia: Howell, 1836.

Minutes of the Christian Anti-Slavery Convention Held July 3d, 4th, and 5th, 1851, at Chicago, Ill. Chicago: Western Citizen, 1851.

Old Anti-Slavery Days: Proceedings of the Commemorative Meeting, Held by the Danvers Historical Society at the Town Hall, Danvers, April 26, 1893. Danvers, Mass.: Danvers Mirror, 1893.

Parker, John P. *His Promised Land: The Autobiography of John P. Parker, Former Slave and Conductor on the Underground Railroad*. Edited by Stuart Seely Sprague. New York: Norton, 1996.

Porter, Mary H. *Eliza Chappell Porter: A Memoir*. Chicago: Revell, 1892.

Proceedings of the Anti-Slavery Convention of American Women, Held in the City of New-York, May 9th, 10th, 11th, and 12th 1837. New York: Dorr, 1837.

Proceedings of the Anti-Slavery Convention of American Women, Held in Philadelphia, May 15th, 16th, 17th, and 18th, 1838. Philadelphia: Merrihew and Gunn, 1838.

Proceedings of the Black State Conventions, 1840–1865. Philadelphia: Temple University Press, 1979.

Proceedings of the First Annual Meeting of the Ohio State Anti-Slavery Society: Held in Xenia, Ohio, January 3rd, 4th, and 5th, 1860. N.p., n.d.

Proceedings of the Ohio Women's Convention held at Salem, April 19th and 20th, 1850; with an Address by J. Elizabeth Jones. Cleveland: Smead and Cowles, 1850.

Proceedings of the Woman's Rights Convention Held in Akron, Ohio, 28 and 29 May 1851. New York: Lenox Hill, 1973.

Report of the Second Anniversary of the Ohio Anti-Slavery Society, Held in Mount Pleasant, Jefferson County, Ohio, on the Twenty-seventh of April 1837. Cincinnati: Ohio Anti-Slavery Society, 1837.

Report of the Third Anniversary of the Ohio Anti-Slavery Society, Held in Granville, Licking County, Ohio, on the 30th of May, 1838. Cincinnati: Ohio Anti-Slavery Society, 1838.

Report of the Fourth Anniversary of the Ohio Anti-Slavery Society, Held in Putnam, Muskingum County, Ohio, on the 29th of May, 1839. Cincinnati: Ohio Anti-Slavery Society, 1839.

Report of the Proceedings of the Anti-Slavery State Convention, Held at Ann Arbor, Michigan, the Tenth and Eleventh of November, 1836. Detroit: Snow and Fisk, 1836.

Ripley, C. Peter, ed. *The Black Abolitionist Papers*. 5 vols. Chapel Hill: University of North Carolina Press, 1985–92.

Sanborn, F. B., ed. *The Life and Letters of John Brown, Liberator of Kansas, and Martyr of Virginia*. 1885; New York: Negro Universities Press, 1969.

Shipherd, Jacob R., comp. *History of the Oberlin-Wellington Rescue*. 1859; New York: Negro Universities Press, 1969.

Southwick, Sarah H. *Reminiscences of Early Anti-Slavery Days*. Cambridge, Mass.: Riverside, 1893.

Stanton, Elizabeth Cady, and Susan B. Anthony. *The Selected Papers of Elizabeth Cady Stanton and Susan B. Anthony*. Edited by Ann D. Gordon. Vol. 1, *In the School of Anti-Slavery, 1840 to 1866*. New Brunswick: Rutgers University Press, 1997.

Stanton, Elizabeth Cady, Susan B. Anthony, and Matilda Joslyn Gage, eds. *History of Woman Suffrage*. 6 vols. New York: Fowler and Wells, 1881–1922.

Stebbins, Giles. *Upward Steps of Seventy Years*. New York: U.S. Books, 1890.

Still, William. *The Underground Railroad*. Chicago: Johnson, 1970.

Stone, Lucy, and Antoinette Brown. *Soul Mates: The Oberlin Correspondence of Lucy Stone and Antoinette Brown, 1846–1850*. Edited by Carol Lasser and Marlene Merrill. Oberlin, Ohio: Oberlin College, 1983.

Stowe, Harriet Beecher. *The Oxford Harriet Beecher Stowe Reader*. Edited by Joan D. Hedrick. New York: Oxford University Press, 1999.

Swisshelm, Jane G. *Half a Century*. Chicago: Swisshelm, 1880.

Thome, James A. *Address to the Females of Ohio Delivered at the State Anti-Slavery Anniversary, April 1836*. Cincinnati: Ohio Anti-Slavery Society, 1836.

Weld, Theodore Dwight, Angelina Grimké Weld, and Sarah Grimké. *The Letters of Theodore Dwight Weld, Angelina Grimké Weld, and Sarah Grimké*. Edited by Gilbert H. Barnes and Dwight L. Dumond. 2 vols. Gloucester, Mass.: Smith, 1965.

SECONDARY SOURCES

Aaron, Daniel. *Cincinnati, Queen City of the West: 1819–1838*. Columbus: Ohio State University Press, 1992.

Abzug, Robert H. "The Influence of Garrisonian Abolitionists' Fears of Slave Violence on the Antislavery Argument, 1829–40." *Journal of Negro History* 55 (January 1970): 15–28.

———. *Passionate Liberator: Theodore Dwight Weld and the Dilemma of Reform*. New York: Oxford University Press, 1980.

Aptheker, Bettina. *Woman's Legacy: Essays on Race, Sex, and Class in American History*. Amherst: University of Massachusetts Press, 1982.

Ashley, Martin L. "Frances Titus: Sojourner's 'Trusted Scribe.'" *Heritage Battle Creek* 8 (Fall 1997). <<www.sojournertruth.org/Library/Archive/Titus-TrustedScribe .htm>> (February 28, 2010).

Atherton, Lewis E. "Daniel Howell Hise, Abolitionist and Reformer." *Mississippi Valley Historical Review* 26 (December 1939): 343–58.

Atkin, Andrea. "'When Pincushions Are Periodicals': Women's Work, Race, and Material Objects in Female Abolitionism." *ATQ* 11 (June 1997): 93–113.

Bacon, Jacqueline. *Freedom's Journal: The First African-American Newspaper*. Lanham, Md.: Lexington, 2007.

Bacon, Margaret Hope. "By Moral Force Alone: The Antislavery Women and Nonresistance." In *The Abolitionist Sisterhood: Women's Political Culture in Antebellum America*, edited by Jean Fagan Yellin and John C. Van Horne, 275–97. Ithaca: Cornell University Press, 1994.

———. *I Speak for My Slave Sister: The Life of Abby Kelley Foster*. New York: Crowell, 1974.

———. *Mothers of Feminism: The Story of Quaker Women in America*. New York: Harper and Row, 1986.

———. "'One Great Bundle of Humanity': Frances Ellen Watkins Harper." *Pennsylvania Magazine of History and Biography* 113 (January 1989): 21–43.

Baker, H. Robert. *The Rescue of Joshua Glover: A Fugitive Slave, the Constitution, and the Coming of the Civil War.* Athens: Ohio University Press, 2006.

Baker, Paula. "The Domestication of Politics: Women and American Political Society, 1780–1920." *American Historical Review* 89 (June 1984): 620–47.

Barbour, Hugh, ed. *Quaker Crosscurrents: Three Hundred Years of Friends in the New York Yearly Meetings.* Syracuse, N.Y.: Syracuse University Press, 1995.

Barnes, Charles E. "Battle Creek as a Station on the Underground Railroad." *Historical Collections* (Michigan Pioneer and Historical Society) 38 (1912): 279–85.

Basch, Norma. *In the Eyes of the Law: Women, Marriage, and Property in Nineteenth-Century New York.* Ithaca: Cornell University Press, 1982.

———. "Marriage, Morals, and Politics in the Election of 1828." *Journal of American History* 80 (December 1993): 890–918.

Bass, Dorothy. "The Best Hopes of the Sexes: The Woman Question in Garrisonian Abolitionism." Ph.D. diss., Brown University, 1980.

Baum, Dale. "Woman Suffrage and the 'Chinese Question': The Limits of Radical Republicanism in Massachusetts, 1865–1876." *New England Quarterly* 56 (March 1983): 60–77.

Bederman, Gail. "The Women Have Had Charge of the Church Work Long Enough." *American Quarterly* 41 (September 1989): 435–40.

Beeton, Beverly. *Women Vote in the West: The Woman Suffrage Movement, 1869–1896.* New York: Garland, 1986.

Berbrugge, Martha H. *Able-Bodied Womanhood: Personal Health and Social Change in Nineteenth-Century Boston.* New York: Oxford University Press, 1988.

Berlin, Ira. *Slaves without Masters: The Free Negro in the Antebellum South.* New York: New Press, 1974.

Berwanger, Eugene Harley. "Evidences of Anti-Slavery Sentiment in Sangamon County, 1848–1860." Master's thesis, Illinois State University, 1952.

———. *The Frontier against Slavery: Western Anti-Negro Prejudice and the Slavery Extension Controversy.* Urbana: University of Illinois Press, 1967.

Bethel, Elizabeth Rauh. *The Roots of African-American Identity: Memory and History in Free Antebellum Communities.* New York: St. Martin's, 1997.

Billington, Louis, and Rosamund Billington. "'A Burning Zeal for Righteousness': Women in the British Anti-Slavery Movement, 1820–1860." In *Equal or Different: Women's Politics, 1800–1914,* edited by Jane Rendall, 82–111. Oxford: Oxford University Press, 1987.

Blackett, R. J. M. *Building an Antislavery Wall: Black Americans in the Atlantic Abolitionist Movement, 1830–1860.* Ithaca: Cornell University Press, 1989.

Blackwell, Alice Stone. *Lucy Stone.* Boston: Little, Brown, 1930.

Blackwell, Marilyn Schultz. "Meddling in Politics: Clarina Howard Nichols and Antebellum Political Culture." *Journal of the Early Republic* 24 (Spring 2004): 27–63.

Blanchard, Rufus. *Discovery and Conquests of the Northwest with the History of Chicago.* 2 vols. Chicago: Blanchard, 1898.

Blazer, D. N. *History of the Underground Railroad of McDonough County, Illinois.* Aledo, Ill.: Times Record, 1922.

Blight, David W. "'For Something beyond the Battlefield': Frederick Douglass and the Struggle for the Memory of the Civil War." *Journal of American History* 75 (March 1989): 1156–78.

———. *Frederick Douglass' Civil War: Keeping Faith in Jubilee.* Baton Rouge: Louisiana State University Press, 1989.

———. "Introduction: The Underground Railroad in History and Memory." In *Passages to Freedom: The Underground Railroad in History and Memory*, edited by David W. Blight, 1–12. New York: Smithsonian Books, 2001.

———, ed. *Passages to Freedom: The Underground Railroad in History and Memory.* New York: Smithsonian Books, 2001.

Blockson, Charles L. *The Underground Railroad: Dramatic Firsthand Accounts of Daring Escapes to Freedom.* New York: Berkley, 1989.

Blue, Frederick J. *The Free Soilers: Third Party Politics, 1848–54.* Urbana: University of Illinois Press, 1973.

———. *No Taint of Compromise: Crusaders in Antislavery Politics.* Baton Rouge: Louisiana State University Press, 2005.

Bluestone, Donald M. "'Steamboats, Sewing Machines, and Bibles': The Root of Antislaveryism in Illinois and the Old Northwest, 1818–1860." Ph.D. diss., University of Wisconsin, Madison, 1973.

Bowen, A. L. "Anti-Slavery Convention Held in Alton, Illinois, October 26–28, 1837." *Journal of the Illinois State Historical Society* 20 (October 1927): 329–56.

Boyd, Melba Joyce. *Discarded Legacy: Politics and Poetics in the Life of Frances E. W. Harper, 1825–1911.* Detroit: Wayne State University Press, 1994.

Boydston, Jeanne. *Home and Work: Housework, Wages, and the Ideology of Labor in the Early Republic.* New York: Oxford University Press, 1990.

Boylan, Anne M. "Benevolence and Antislavery Activity among African American Women in New York and Boston, 1820–1840." In *The Abolitionist Sisterhood: Women's Political Culture in Antebellum America*, edited by Jean Fagan Yellin and John C. Van Horne, 119–37. Ithaca: Cornell University Press, 1994.

———. *The Origins of Women's Activism: New York and Boston, 1797–1840.* Chapel Hill: University of North Carolina Press, 2002.

———. "Women and Politics in the Era before Seneca Falls." *Journal of the Early Republic* 10 (Fall 1990): 363–82.

———. "Women in Groups: An Analysis of Women's Benevolent Organizations in New York and Boston, 1797–1840." *Journal of American History* 71 (December 1984): 497–523.

Bradley, A. Day. "Progressive Friends in Michigan and New York." *Quaker History* 52 (Autumn 1963): 95–103.

Brakebill, Tina Stewart. *"Circumstances Are Destiny": An Antebellum Woman's Struggle to Define Sphere.* Kent, Ohio: Kent State University Press, 2006.

Brandt, Nat. *The Town That Started the Civil War*. Syracuse, N.Y.: Syracuse University Press, 1990.

Braude, Anne. *Radical Spirits: Spiritualism and Women's Rights in Nineteenth-Century America*. Boston: Beacon, 1989.

Breen, Patrick H. "The Female Antislavery Petition Campaign of 1831–32." *Virginia Magazine of History and Biography* 110, no. 3 (2002): 377–98.

Brown, Ira. "'Am I Not a Woman and a Sister?': The Anti-Slavery Convention of American Women, 1837–39." *Pennsylvania History* 102 (January 1983): 1–19.

———. "Cradle of Feminism: The Philadelphia Female Antislavery Society, 1833–1840." *Pennsylvania Magazine of History and Biography* 102 (April 1978): 143–66.

———. *Mary Grew: Abolitionist and Feminist*. Selinsgrove, Pa.: Susquehanna University Press, 1991.

Brown, Lois. "Out of the Mouths of Babes: The Abolitionist Campaign of Susan Paul and the Juvenile Choir of Boston." *New England Quarterly* 75 (March 2002): 52–79.

Browne, Stephen Howard. *Angelina Grimké: Rhetoric, Identity, and the Radical Imagination*. East Lansing: Michigan State University Press, 2000.

Buechler, Steven M. *The Transformation of the Woman Suffrage Movement: The Case of Illinois, 1850–1920*. New Brunswick: Rutgers University Press, 1986.

Burroughs, Wilbur Greeley. "Oberlin's Part in the Slavery Conflict." *Ohio State Archaeological and Historical Quarterly* 20 (1911): 269–334.

Caccamo, James F. *Hudson, Ohio and the Underground Railroad*. Hudson, Ohio: Friends of the Hudson Library, 1992.

Calkins, David L. "Black Education and the Nineteenth Century City: An Institutional Analysis of Cincinnati's Colored Schools, 1850–1887." *Cincinnati Historical Society Bulletin* 33 (Fall 1975): 160–73.

Cardinal, Eric J. "Antislavery Sentiment and Political Transformation in the 1850s: Portage County, Ohio." *Old Northwest* 1 (1975): 223–38.

———. "The Development of an Anti-Slavery Political Majority: Portage County, Ohio, 130–1856." Master's thesis, Kent State University, 1973.

Carwardine, Richard J. *Evangelicals and Politics in Antebellum America*. New Haven: Yale University Press, 1993.

Cashin, Joan E. "Black Families in the Old Northwest." *Journal of the Early Republic* 15 (Fall 1995): 449–75.

———. "Introduction: Culture of Resignation." In *Our Common Affairs: Texts from Women in the Old South*, edited by Joan E. Cashin, 1–44. Baltimore: Johns Hopkins University Press, 1996.

Cavanaugh, Helen M. "Antislavery Sentiment and Politics in the Northwest, 1844–1860." Ph.D. diss., University of Chicago, 1938.

Cayton, Andrew R. L. "Introduction: The Significance of Ohio in the Early American Republic." In *The Center of a Great Empire: The Ohio Country in the Early American Republic*, edited by Andrew R. L. Cayton and Stuart D. Hobbs, 1–10. Athens: Ohio University Press, 2005.

Cayton, Andrew R. L., and Stuart D. Hobbs, eds. *The Center of a Great Empire: The Ohio Country in the Early American Republic*. Athens: Ohio University Press, 2005.

Cazden, Elizabeth. *Antoinette Brown Blackwell: A Biography*. Old Westbury, N.Y.: Feminist Press, 1983.

Chambers-Schiller, Lee. "'A Good Work among the People': The Political Culture of the Boston Antislavery Fair." In *The Abolitionist Sisterhood: Women's Political Culture in Antebellum America*, edited by Jean Fagan Yellin and John C. Van Horne, 249–74. Ithaca: Cornell University Press, 1994.

Cheek, William F. "John Mercer Langston: Black Protest Leader and Abolitionist." *Civil War History* 16 (June 1970): 101–20.

Cheek, William F., and Aimee Lee Cheek. "John Mercer Langston and the Cincinnati Riot of 1841." In *Race and the City: Work, Community, and Protest in Cincinnati, 1820–1970*, edited by Henry Louis Taylor Jr., 29–69. Urbana: University of Illinois Press, 1993.

———. *John Mercer Langston and the Fight for Black Freedom, 1829–65*. Urbana: University of Illinois Press, 1989.

Churchman, Keith David. "The Social and Economic Status of the Negro in Ohio in 1860." Master's thesis, Miami University, 1939.

Cincinnati: A Guide to the Queen City and Its Neighbors. Cincinnati: Wiesen-Hart, 1943.

Clifford, Amy. "Feminism in Ohio, 1848–1857." Master's thesis. Kent State University, 1972.

Clinton, Catherine. *Harriet Tubman: The Road to Freedom*. New York: Little, Brown, 2004.

Cochran, William C. *The Western Reserve and the Fugitive Slave Law: A Prelude to Civil War*. 1920; New York: Da Capo, 1972.

Coleman, Willie Mae. "Keeping the Faith and Disturbing the Peace: Black Women from Anti-Slavery to Women's Suffrage." Ph.D. diss., University of California, Irvine, 1982.

Collison, Gary. *Shadrach Minkins: From Fugitive Slave to Citizen*. Cambridge: Harvard University Press, 1997.

Copeland, Robert M. "The Reformed Presbyterian Theological Seminary in Cincinnati, 1845–1849." *Cincinnati Historical Society Bulletin* 31, no. 3 (1973): 151–63.

Cormany, Clayton Douglas. "Ohio's Abolitionist Campaign: A Study in the Rhetoric of Conversion." Ph.D. diss., Ohio State University, 1981.

Cott, Nancy F. "Passionlessness: An Interpretation of Victorian Sexual Ideology, 1790–1880." *Signs* 4 (Winter 1988): 219–36.

Crenshaw, Gwendolyn J. *"Bury Me in a Free Land": The Abolitionist Movement in Indiana, 1816–1865: The Catalog*. Indianapolis: Indiana Historical Bureau, 1986.

Crew, Spencer. Foreword to *Passages to Freedom: The Underground Railroad in History and Memory*, edited by David W. Blight, vii–xi. New York: Smithsonian Books, 2001.

Cunningham, Patricia A. *Reforming Women's Fashion, 1850–1920: Politics, Health, and Art*. Kent, Ohio: Kent State University Press, 2003.

Davidson, Carlisle G. "A Profile of Hicksite Quakerism in Michigan, 1830–1860." *Quaker History* 59 (Autumn 1970): 106–12.

Davis, Hugh. *Leonard Bacon: New England Reformer and Antislavery Moderate*. Baton Rouge: Louisiana State University Press, 1998.

DeBlasio, Donna Marie. "Her Own Society: The Life and Times of Betsy Mix Cowles, 1810–1876." Ph.D. diss., Kent State University, 1980.

DeBoer, Clara Merritt. *Be Jubilant My Feet: African American Abolitionists in the American Missionary Association, 1839–1861*. New York: Garland, 1994.

DeFiore, Jayne Crumpler. "COME, *and Bring the Ladies*: Tennessee Women and the Politics of Opportunity during the Presidential Campaigns of 1840 and 1844." *Tennessee Historical Quarterly* 51, no. 4 (1992): 197–212.

Demos, John. "The Antislavery Movement and the Problem of Violent 'Means.'" *New England Quarterly* 37 (December 1964): 501–26.

Dillon, Merton L. "Abolitionism Comes to Illinois." *Journal of the Illinois State Historical Society* 53 (Winter 1960): 389–403.

———. "The Antislavery Movement in Illinois, 1809–1844." Ph.D. diss., University of Michigan, 1951.

———. "The Antislavery Movement in Illinois: 1824–1835." *Journal of the Illinois State Historical Society* 47 (Summer 1954): 149–66.

———. *Elijah P. Lovejoy, Abolitionist Editor*. Urbana: University of Illinois Press, 1961.

———. "Elizabeth Chandler and the Spread of Antislavery Sentiment to Michigan." *Michigan History* 39 (December 1955): 481–94.

———. "Sources of Early Antislavery Thought in Illinois." *Journal of the Illinois State Historical Society* 50 (Spring 1957): 36–50.

Dixon, Christopher. "'An Equal and Permanent Relationship': Abolitionism, Gender, and Family Reform in the Nineteenth Century United States." Ph.D. diss., University of New South Wales, 1992.

———. *Perfecting the Family: Antislavery Marriages in Nineteenth-Century America*. Amherst: University of Massachusetts Press, 1997.

Donaldson, Charles Robert. "The Antislavery Career of Marius Robinson." Master's thesis, Ohio State University, 1970.

Drake, Thomas E. *Quakers and Slavery in America*. Gloucester, Mass.: Smith, 1965.

DuBois, Ellen Carol. *Feminism and Suffrage: The Emergence of an Independent Women's Movement in America, 1848–1869*. Ithaca: Cornell University Press, 1978.

———. "Women's Rights and Abolition: The Nature of the Connection." In *Antislavery Reconsidered: New Perspectives on the Abolitionists*, edited by Lewis Perry and Michael Fellman, 238–51. Baton Rouge: Louisiana State University Press, 1979.

Earle, Jonathan H. *Jacksonian Antislavery and the Politics of Free Soil, 1824–1854*. Chapel Hill: University of North Carolina Press, 2004.

Edwards, G. Thomas. *Sowing Good Seeds: The Northwest Suffrage Campaigns of Susan B. Anthony*. Portland: Oregon Historical Society Press, 1990.

Edwards, Rebecca. *Angels in the Machinery: Gender in American Party Politics from the Civil War to the Progressive Era*. New York: Oxford University Press, 1997.

Eisan, Frances K. *Saint or Demon?: The Legendary Delia Webster Opposing Slavery*. New York: Pace University Press, 1998.

Eliot, Samuel Atkins, ed. *Biographical History of Massachusetts: Biographies and Autobiographies of the Leading Men in the State*. Vol. 5. Boston: Massachusetts Biographical Society, 1914.

Ellsworth, Clayton Sumner. "Oberlin and the Anti-Slavery Movement Up to the Civil War." Ph.D. diss., Cornell University, 1930.

Etcheson, Nicole, *The Emerging Midwest: Upland Southerners and the Political Culture of the Old Northwest, 1787–1861*. Bloomington: Indiana University Press, 1996.

Evans, Linda Jeanne. "Abolitionism in the Illinois Churches, 1830–1865." Ph.D. diss., Northwestern University, 1981.

Fabian, Ann. *Card Sharps, Dream Books, and Bucket Shops: Gambling in Nineteenth-Century America*. Ithaca: Cornell University Press, 1990.

Fahs, Alice. "The Feminized Civil War: Gender, Northern Popular Literature, and the Memory of the War, 1861–1900." *Journal of American History* 85 (March 1999): 1461–94.

Faulkner, Carol. "The Root of the Evil: Free Produce and Radical Antislavery, 1820–1860." *Journal of the Early Republic* 27 (Fall 2007): 377–405.

———. *Women's Radical Reconstruction: The Freedman's Aid Movement*. Philadelphia: University of Pennsylvania Press, 2004.

Fehr, Nancy Gail. "The Underground Railroad in Western Illinois." Master's thesis, Western Illinois University, 1977.

Field, Phyllis. "Party Politics and Antislavery Idealism: The Republican Approach to Racial Change in New York, 1855–1860." In *Crusaders and Compromisers: Essays on the Relationship of the Antislavery Struggle to the Antebellum Party System*, edited by Alan M. Kraut, 123–39. Westport, Conn.: Greenwood.

Fields, Harrold B. "Free Negroes in Cass County before the Civil War." *Michigan History* 44 (December 1960): 375–83.

Filler, Louis, ed. "John Brown in Ohio: An Interview with Charles S. S. Griffing." *Ohio State Archaeological and Historical Quarterly* 58 (January 1949): 213–18.

Finkelman, Paul. "Evading the Ordinance: The Persistence of Bondage in Indiana and Illinois." *Journal of the Early Republic* 9 (Spring 1989): 21–51.

———, ed. *Slavery and the Law*. Madison, Wisc.: Madison House, 1997.

Fischer, Gayle V. *Pantaloons and Power: Nineteenth-Century Dress Reform in the United States*. Kent, Ohio: Kent State University Press, 2001.

Fladeland, Betty. "James G. Birney's Anti-Slavery Activities in Cincinnati, 1835–1837." *Bulletin of the Historical and Philosophical Society of Ohio* 9 (October 1951): 251–65.

————. *James Gillespie Birney: Slaveholder to Abolitionist.* Ithaca: Cornell University Press, 1955.

————. *Men and Brothers: Anglo-American Antislavery Cooperation.* Urbana: University of Illinois Press, 1972.

Fletcher, Robert Samuel. *A History of Oberlin College from Its Foundation through the Civil War.* 2 vols. Oberlin, Ohio: Oberlin College, 1943.

Foner, Eric. "Abolitionism and the Labor Movement in Antebellum America." In *Antislavery, Religion, and Reform: Essays in Memory of Roger Anstey*, edited by Christine Bolt and Seymour Drescher, 254–71. Hamden, Conn.: Archon, 1980.

Ford, Bridget. "Black Churches and the Making of an Antebellum Borderland, 1840–1860." Paper presented at the annual meeting of the Society for Historians of the Early American Republic, 2008.

Formisano, Ronald P. "The Edge of Caste: Colored Suffrage in Michigan, 1827–1861." *Michigan History* 56 (Spring 1972): 19–41.

Friedman, Lawrence J. *Gregarious Saints: Self and Community in American Abolitionism, 1830–1870.* New York: Cambridge University Press, 1982.

Frost, Karolyn Smardz. *I've Got a Home in Glory Land: A Lost Tale of the Underground Railroad.* New York: Farrar, Straus, and Giroux, 2008.

Fuller, Robert H. *Underground to Freedom: An Account of the Anti-Slavery Activities in Ashtabula County prior to the Civil War.* Jefferson, Ohio: Gazette, 1977.

Galbreath, Charles Burleigh. "Anti-Slavery Movement in Columbiana County." *Ohio Archaeological and Historical Quarterly* 30 (1921): 355–95.

Gamble, Douglas A. "Garrisonian Abolitionists in the West: Some Suggestions for Study." *Civil War History* 23 (March 1977): 52–68.

————. "Joshua Giddings and the Ohio Abolitionists: A Study in Radical Politics." *Ohio History* 88 (Winter 1979): 37–56.

————. "Moral Suasion in the West: Garrisonian Abolitionism, 1831–1861." Ph.D. diss., Ohio State University, 1973.

————. "The Western Anti-Slavery Society: Garrisonian Abolitionism in Ohio." Master's thesis, Ohio State University, 1970.

Gara, Larry. "A Glorious Time: The 1874 Abolitionist Reunion in Chicago." *Journal of Illinois State Historical Society* 65 (Autumn 1972): 280–92.

————. *The Liberty Line: The Legend of the Underground Railroad.* Lexington: University of Kentucky Press, 1967.

Garman, Mary Van Vleck. "'Altered Tone of Expression': The Anti-Slavery Rhetoric of Illinois Women." Ph.D. diss., Northwestern University, 1989.

Geary, Linda L. *Balanced in the Wind: A Biography of Betsey Mix Cowles.* Cranbury, N.J.: Associated University Presses, 1989.

Geers, Bonnie Arlene. "Elizabeth Margaret Chandler: A Third Sphere." Master's thesis, Michigan State University, 1988.

Gerteis, Louis S. "Antislavery Agitation in Wisconsin, 1836–1848." Master's thesis, University of Wisconsin, Madison, 1966.

Getz, Lynne Marie. "Partners in Motion: Gender, Migration, and Reform in Antebellum Ohio and Kansas." *Frontiers* 27, no. 2 (2007): 102–35.

Gienapp, William. *The Origins of the Republican Party, 1852–1856*. New York: Oxford University Press, 1987.

Ginzberg, Lori D. "Moral Suasion Is Moral Balderdash: Women, Politics, and Social Activism in the 1850s." *Journal of American History* 73 (December 1986): 601–22.

———. *Untidy Origins: A Story of Woman's Rights in Antebellum New York*. Chapel Hill: University of North Carolina Press, 2005.

———. *Women and the Work of Benevolence: Morality, Politics, and Class in the Nineteenth Century United States*. New Haven: Yale University Press, 1990.

———. "Women in an Evangelical Community: Oberlin 1835–1850." *Ohio History* 89 (Winter 1980): 78–88.

Glazer, Walter Stix. *Cincinnati in 1840*. Columbus: Ohio State University Press, 1999.

Glesner, Anthony P. "Laura Haviland: Neglected Heroine of the Underground Railroad." *Michigan Historical Review* 21 (Spring 1995): 83–99.

Glickman, Lawrence. "'Buy for the Sake of the Slave': Abolitionism and the Origins of American Consumer Activism." *American Quarterly* 56, no. 4 (2004): 889–912.

Glickstein, Jonathan A. "'Poverty Is Not Slavery': American Abolitionists and the Competitive Labor Market." In *Antislavery Reconsidered: New Perspectives on the Abolitionists*, edited by Lewis Perry and Michael Fellman, 195–218. Baton Rouge: Louisiana State University Press, 1979.

Goitein, Patricia L. "'Her Whole Heart Went Out in Behalf of Freedom, Justice and Education': The Early Anti-Slavery Movement along the Galena Trail." Paper presented at the Illinois History Symposium, 2003.

Goldfarb, Joel. "The Life of Gamaliel Bailey prior to the Founding of the *National Era*: The Orientation of a Practical Abolitionist." Ph.D. diss., University of California, Los Angeles, 1958.

Goodheart, Lawrence B. *Abolitionist, Actuary, Atheist: Elizur Wright and the Reform Impulse*. Kent, Ohio: Kent State University Press, 1990.

Goodman, Paul. "The Manual Labor Movement and the Origins of Abolitionism." *Journal of the Early Republic* 13 (Fall 1993): 355–402.

———. *Of One Blood: Abolitionism and the Origins of Racial Equality*. Berkeley: University of California Press, 1998.

Gordon, Beverly. *Bazaars and Fair Ladies: The History of the American Fundraising Fair*. Knoxville: University of Tennessee Press, 1998.

———. "Playing at Being Powerless: New England Ladies Fairs, 1830–1930." *Massachusetts Review* 26 (September 1986): 144–60.

Gray, Susan E. *The Yankee West: Community Life on the Michigan Frontier*. Chapel Hill: University of North Carolina Press, 1996.

Griffler, Keith P. *Front Line of Freedom: African Americans and the Forging of the Underground Railroad in the Ohio Valley*. Lexington: University Press of Kentucky, 2004.

Grimsted, David. *American Mobbing, 1828–1861: Toward Civil War*. New York: Oxford University Press, 1998.

Gross, Cecilia Rosenblum. "Antislavery in Stark County, Ohio, 1831–1856." Master's thesis, University of Akron, 1962.

Grover, Kathryn. *The Fugitive's Gibraltar: Escaping Slaves and Abolitionism in New Bedford, Massachusetts*. Amherst: University of Massachusetts Press, 2001.

Gunderson, Robert Gray. *The Log-Cabin Campaign*. Lexington: University of Kentucky Press, 1957.

Gustafson, Melanie Susan. *Women and the Republican Party, 1854–1924*. Urbana: University of Illinois Press, 2001.

Hagedorn, Ann. *Beyond the River: The Untold Story of the Heroes of the Underground Railroad*. New York: Simon and Schuster, 2002.

Halbersleben, Karen I. *Women's Participation in the British Antislavery Movement, 1824–1865*. Lewiston, N.Y.: Mellen, 1993.

Hamm, Thomas D. *The Antislavery Movement in Henry County, Indiana*. New Castle: Indiana County Historical Society, 1987.

———. *God's Government Begun: The Society for Universal Inquiry and Reform, 1842–1846*. Bloomington: Indiana University Press, 1995.

———. *The Transformation of American Quakerism: Orthodox Friends, 1800–1907*. Bloomington: Indiana University Press, 1988.

Hamm, Thomas D., April Beckman, Marissa Florio, Kirsti Giles, and Marie Hopper. "'A Great and Good People': Midwestern Quakers and the Struggle against Slavery." *Indiana Magazine of History* 100 (March 2004): 1–34.

Hansen, Debra Gold. "The Boston Female Anti-Slavery Society and the Limits of Gender Politics." In *The Abolitionist Sisterhood: Women's Political Culture in Antebellum America*, edited by Jean Fagan Yellin and John C. Van Horne, 45–65. Ithaca: Cornell University Press, 1994.

———. *Strained Sisterhood: Gender and Class in the Boston Anti-Slavery Society*. Amherst: University of Massachusetts Press, 1993.

Hansen, Karen. *A Very Social Time: Crafting Community in Antebellum New England*. Berkeley: University of California Press, 1994.

Harris, N. Dwight. *The History of Negro Servitude in Illinois and the Slavery Agitation in that State, 1719–1864*. Chicago: McClurg, 1904.

Harrold, Stanley. *The Abolitionists and the South, 1831–1861*. Lexington: University of Kentucky Press, 1995.

——— "Forging an Antislavery Instrument: Gamaliel Bailey and the Foundation of the Ohio Liberty Party." *Old Northwest* 2 (1976): 371–87.

——— *Gamaliel Bailey and Antislavery Union*. Kent, Ohio: Kent State University Press, 1986.

——— "On the Borders of Slavery and Race: Charles T. Torrey and the Underground Railroad." *Journal of the Early Republic* 20 (Summer 2000): 273–92.

———— "The Perspective of a Cincinnati Abolitionist: Gamaliel Bailey on Social Reform in America." *Cincinnati Historical Society Bulletin* 35 (Fall 1977): 173–90.

————. *Subversives: Antislavery Community in Washington, D.C., 1828–1865*. Baton Rouge: Louisiana State University Press, 2003.

Haynes, April. "The Trials of Frederick Hollick: Obscenity, Sex Education, and Medical Democracy in the Antebellum United States." *Journal of the History of Sexuality* 12 (October 2003): 543–74.

Hedrick, Joan D. *Harriet Beecher Stowe: A Life*. New York: Oxford University Press, 1994.

Herbig, Katherine. "Friends for Freedom: The Lives and Careers of Sallie Holley and Caroline Putnam." Ph.D. diss., Claremont Graduate School, 1977.

Hersh, Blanche G. *The Slavery of Sex: Feminist-Abolitionists in America*. Urbana: University of Illinois Press, 1978.

Hewitt, Nancy A. "Feminist Friends: Agrarian Quakers and the Emergence of Woman's Rights in America." *Feminist Studies* 12 (Spring 1986): 27–49.

————. "The Fragmentation of Friends: The Consequences for Quaker Women in Antebellum America." In *Witnesses for Change: Quaker Women over Three Centuries*, edited by Elisabeth Potts Brown and Susan Mosher Stuard, 93–119. New Brunswick: Rutgers University Press, 1989.

————. "On Their Own Terms: A Historiographical Essay." In *The Abolitionist Sisterhood: Women's Political Culture in Antebellum America*, edited by Jean Fagan Yellin and John C. Van Horne, 23–30. Ithaca: Cornell University Press, 1994.

————. "The Social Origins of Women Antislavery Politics in Western New York." In *Crusaders and Compromisers: Essays on the Relationship of the Antislavery Struggle to the Antebellum Party System*, edited by Alan M. Kraut, 205–33. Westport, Conn.: Greenwood, 1983.

————. *Women's Activism and Social Change: Rochester, New York, 1822–1872*. Ithaca: Cornell University Press, 1984.

Hine, Darlene Clark, Elsa Barkley Brown, and Rosalyn Terborg-Penn, eds. *Black Women in America: An Historical Encyclopedia*. Bloomington: Indiana University Press, 1993.

Hinerman, Mary Jo. "The Antislavery Movement in Columbiana County, Ohio." Master's thesis, University of Mississippi, 1977.

Hobart, William W. "The Crosswhite Case." *Historical Collections* (Michigan Pioneer and Historical Society) 38 (1912): 257–79.

Hoffert, Sylvia D. *Jane Grey Swisshelm: An Unconventional Life, 1815–1884*. Chapel Hill: University of North Carolina Press, 2004.

————. *When Hens Crow: The Woman's Rights Movement in Antebellum America*. Bloomington: Indiana University Press, 1995.

Holcomb, Julie. "'Cement of the Whole Antislavery Building': Women, Consumption, and Abolitionism in the Transatlantic World." Paper presented at the annual meeting of the Western Conference on British Studies, 2006.

Horowitz, Helen Lefkowitz. *Rereading Sex: Battles over Sexual Knowledge and Suppression in Nineteenth-Century America*. New York: Knopf, 2002.

Horton, James Oliver. *Free People of Color: Inside the African American Community*. Washington, D.C.: Smithsonian Institution Press, 1993.

Horton, James Oliver, and Stacy Flaherty. "Black Leadership in Antebellum Cincinnati." In *Race and the City: Work, Community, and Protest in Cincinnati, 1820–1970*, edited by Henry Louis Taylor Jr., 70–95. Urbana: University of Illinois Press, 1993.

Horton, James Oliver, and Lois E. Horton. *In Hope of Liberty: Culture, Community, and Protest among Northern Free Blacks, 1700–1860*. New York: Oxford University Press, 1997.

Horton, Lois E. "Kidnapping and Resistance: Antislavery Direct Action in the 1850s." In *Passages to Freedom: The Underground Railroad in History and Memory*, edited by David W. Blight, 149–73. New York: Smithsonian Books, 2004.

Howard, Victor B. "The 1856 Election in Ohio: Moral Issues in Politics." *Ohio History* 80 (Winter 1971): 24–44.

Howe, Henry. "Granville Riot." In *Historical Collections of Ohio*, 2:80–81. Norwalk, Ohio: Lansing, 1896.

Huff, O. N. "Unnamed Anti-Slavery Heroes of Old Newport." *Indiana Magazine of History* 3 (September 1907): 133–43.

Isenberg, Nancy. *Sex and Citizenship in Antebellum America*. Chapel Hill: University of North Carolina Press, 1998.

Jeffrey, Julie Roy. *The Great Silent Army of Abolitionism: Ordinary Women in the Antislavery Movement*. Chapel Hill: University of North Carolina Press, 1999.

———. "'Stranger, Buy ... Lest Our Mission Fail': The Complex Culture of Women's Abolitionist Fairs." *American Nineteenth Century History* 4, no. 1 (2003): 1–24.

Jennings, Judith. "A Trio of Talented Women: Abolition, Gender, and Political Participation, 1780–91." *Slavery and Abolition* 26 (April 2005): 55–70.

Johnson, Reinhard O. *The Liberty Party, 1840–1848: Antislavery Third-Party Politics in the United States*. Baton Rouge: Louisiana State University Press, 2009.

———. "The Liberty Party in Massachusetts, 1840–1848: Antislavery Third Party Politics in the Bay State." *Civil War History* 28 (Fall 1982): 241–43.

Jones, Martha S. *All Bound Up Together: The Woman Question in African American Public Culture, 1830–1900*. Chapel Hill: University of North Carolina Press, 2007.

Jordan, Ryan. "The Indiana Separation of 1842 and the Limits of Quaker Anti-Slavery." *Quaker History* 89 (Spring 2000): 1–27.

———. "Quakers, 'Comeouters,' and the Meaning of Abolitionism in the Antebellum Free States." *Journal of the Early Republic* 24 (Winter 2005): 55–70.

Karcher, Carolyn L. *The First Woman in the Republic: A Cultural Biography of Lydia Maria Child*. Durham: Duke University Press, 1998.

Kellow, Margaret M. R. "'For the Sake of Suffering Kansas': Lydia Maria Child, Gender, and the Politics of the 1850s." *Journal of Women's History* 5 (Fall 1993): 32–49.

Kelley, Mary. *Learning to Stand and Speak: Women, Education, and Public Life in America's Republic*. Chapel Hill: University of North Carolina Press, 2006.

Kelly, Catherine E. *In the New England Fashion: Reshaping Women's Lives in the Nineteenth Century*. Ithaca: Cornell University Press, 1999.

Kennon, Donald. "'An Apple of Discord': The Women's Question at the World's Antislavery Convention of 1840." *Slavery and Abolition* 5 (December 1984): 244–66.

Kephart, John E. "A Pioneer Michigan Abolitionist." *Michigan History* 45 (March 1961): 34–42.

———. "A Voice for Freedom: *The Signal of Liberty*, 1841–1844." Ph.D. diss., University of Michigan, 1960.

Kerber, Linda K. "The Paradox of Women's Citizenship in the Early Republic." *American Historical Review* 97 (April 1992): 349–78.

———. "Separate Spheres, Female Worlds, Woman's Place: The Rhetoric of Women's History." *Journal of American History* 75 (June 1988): 9–39.

———. *Women of the Republic: Intellect and Ideology in Revolutionary America*. Chapel Hill: University of North Carolina Press, 1980.

Kerr, Andrea Moore. *Lucy Stone: Speaking Out for Equality*. New Brunswick: Rutgers University Press, 1992.

Ketring, Ruth Anna. *Charles Osborn in the Anti-Slavery Movement*. Columbus: Ohio State Archaeological and History Society, 1937.

Keyssar, Alexander. *The Right to Vote: The Contested History of Democracy in the United States*. New York: Basic Books, 2000.

Kooker, Arthur Raymond. "The Antislavery Movement in Michigan, 1796–1840." Ph.D. diss., University of Michigan, 1941.

Kraditor, Aileen S. *Means and Ends in American Abolitionism: Garrison and His Critics on Strategy and Tactics, 1834–1850*. New York: Pantheon, 1967.

Kraut, Alan M. "Partisanship and Principles: The Liberty Party in Antebellum Political Culture." In *Crusaders and Compromisers: Essays on the Relationship of the Antislavery Struggle to the Antebellum Party System*, edited by Alan M. Kraut, 71–100. Westport, Conn.: Greenwood, 1983.

Land, Mary. "John Brown's Ohio Environment." *Ohio State Archaeological and Historical Quarterly* 57 (January 1948): 24–47.

Lapsanky, Emma Jones. "Feminism, Freedom, and Community: Charlotte Forten and Women Activists in Nineteenth-Century Philadelphia." *Pennsylvania Magazine of History* 63 (January 1989): 3–19.

———. "The World the Agitators Made: The Counterculture of Agitation in Urban Philadelphia." In *The Abolitionist Sisterhood: Women's Political Culture in Antebellum America*, edited by Jean Fagan Yellin and John C. Van Horne, 91–99. Ithaca: Cornell University Press, 1994.

Lapsansky, Phillip. "Graphic Discord: Abolitionist and Antiabolitionist Images." In *The Abolitionist Sisterhood: Women's Political Culture in Antebellum America*, ed. Jean Fagan Yellin and John C. Van Horne, 201–30. Ithaca: Cornell University Press, 1994.

Large, Moina W. *History of Ashtabula County Ohio*. 2 vols. Topeka and Indianapolis: Historical Publishing, 1924.

Lasser, Carol. "Abolitionist Appeals to Women: Gender and Rhetoric in the Early Writings of James Thome and Angelina Grimké." Paper presented at the annual meeting of the Society for Historians of the Early American Republic, 1998.

———. "A Tale of Two Josephines: Class, Gender and Self-Sovereignty in Gilded Age Cleveland." *Gender and History* 13 (April 2001): 65–96.

Laughlin, Bonnie E. "'Endangering the Peace of Society': Abolitionist Agitation and Mob Reaction in St. Louis and Alton, 1836–1838." *Missouri Historical Review* 95 (October 2000): 1–22.

Laurie, Bruce. *Beyond Garrison: Antislavery and Social Reform*. Cambridge: Cambridge University Press, 2005.

Lawes, Carolyn J. *Women and Reform in a New England Community, 1815–1860*. Lexington: University Press of Kentucky, 2000.

Leach, William. *True Love and Perfect Union: The Feminist Reform of Sex and Society*. New York: Basic Books, 1980.

Lerner, Gerda. *The Grimké Sisters from South Carolina: Pioneers for Woman's Rights and Abolition*. New York: Schocken, 1967.

———. "The Political Activities of Antislavery Women." In *The Majority Finds Its Past: Placing Women in History*, 112–28. New York: Oxford University Press, 1979.

———. "Women and Slavery." *Slavery and Abolition* 4 (December 1983): 173–98.

Lesick, Lawrence Thomas. *The Lane Rebels: Evangelicalism and Antislavery in Antebellum America*. London: Scarecrow, 1980.

Levy, Leonard. "The 'Abolition Riot': Boston's First Slave Rescue." *New England Quarterly* 25 (March 1952): 85–92.

Litwack, Leon F. *North of Slavery: The Negro in the Free States, 1790–1860*. Chicago: University of Chicago Press, 1961.

Lockard, Joe. "'A Light Broke Out over My Mind': Mattie Griffith, *Madge Vertner*, and Kentucky Abolitionism." *Filson History Quarterly* 57 (March 2005): 129–51.

Logan, Shirley Wilson. "Frances Ellen Watkins Harper." In *With Pen and Voice: A Critical Anthology of Nineteenth-Century African-American Women*, 30–46. Carbondale: Southern Illinois University Press, 1995.

———, ed. *With Pen and Voice: A Critical Anthology of Nineteenth-Century African-American Women*. Carbondale: Southern Illinois University Press, 1995.

Loomis, Willard D. "The Antislavery Movement in Ashtabula County, Ohio, 1834–1854." Master's thesis, Western Reserve University, 1934.

Lumpkin, Katharine DuPre. *The Emancipation of Angelina Grimké*. Chapel Hill: University of North Carolina Press, 1974.

———. "'The General Plan Was Freedom': A Negro Secret Order on the Underground Railroad." *Phylon* 28 (Spring 1967): 63–77.

Lupold, Harry Forrest. "Anti-Slavery Activities in a Western Reserve County: 1820–1860." *Negro History Bulletin* 38 (1975): 468–69.

Lutz, Alma. *Crusade for Freedom: Women of the Antislavery Movement.* Boston: Beacon, 1968.

Mabee, Carleton. *Black Freedom: The Nonviolent Abolitionists from 1830 through the Civil War.* New York: Macmillan, 1970.

Mabee, Carleton, and Susan Mabee Newhouse. *Sojourner Truth: Slave, Prophet, Legend.* New York: New York University Press, 1993.

Macy, Jesse. *The Anti-Slavery Crusade: A Chronicle of the Gathering Storm.* New Haven: Yale University Press, 1919.

Magdol, Edward. "A Window on the Abolitionist Constituency: Antislavery Petitions, 1836–1839." In *Crusaders and Compromisers: Essays on the Relationship of the Antislavery Struggle to the Antebellum Party System,* edited by Alan M. Kraut, 45–70. Westport, Conn.: Greenwood, 1983.

Maher, William J. "The Antislavery Movement in Milwaukee and Vicinity, 1842–1860." Master's thesis, Marquette University, 1954.

Maizlish, Stephen E. *The Triumph of Sectionalism: The Transformation of Ohio Politics, 1844–1856.* Kent, Ohio: Kent State University Press, 1983.

Marsh, Owen Robert. "Anti-Slavery Sentiment in Eight Counties of Central Illinois, 1850–1860." Master's thesis, Illinois State University, 1958.

Masur, Louis R. "A Bettor Nation." *Reviews in American History* 19 (December 1991): 505–10.

Matijasic, Thomas D. "Abolition vs. Colonization: The Battle for Ohio." *Queen City Heritage* 45 (Spring 1987): 27–40.

————. "Conservative Reform in the West: The African Colonization Movement in Ohio, 1826–1839." Ph.D. diss., Miami University, 1982.

Mayer, Henry. *All on Fire: William Lloyd Garrison and the Abolition of Slavery.* New York: St. Martin's, 1998.

McBride, Genevieve G. *On Wisconsin Women: Working for Their Rights from Settlement to Suffrage.* Madison: University of Wisconsin Press, 1993.

McCarthy, Timothy Patrick, and John Stauffer, eds. *Prophets of Protest: Reconsidering the History of American Abolitionism.* Cambridge: Harvard University Press, 2006.

McClellan, Bernard E. "Cincinnati's Response to Abolitionism, 1835–1845." Master's thesis, University of Cincinnati, 1963.

McClure, Stanley W. "The Underground Railroad in South Central Ohio." Master's thesis, Ohio State University, 1932.

McClymer, John F., ed. *This High and Holy Moment: The First National Woman's Rights Convention, Worcester, 1850.* San Diego: Harcourt Brace College, 1999.

McDaniel, W. Caleb. "The Fourth and the First: Abolitionist Holidays, Respectability, and Radical Interracial Reform." *American Quarterly* 57 (March 2005): 129–51.

McFeely, William S. *Frederick Douglass.* New York: Simon and Schuster, 1991.

McGerr, Michael. "Political Style and Women's Power, 1830–1930." *Journal of American History* 77 (December 1990): 864–85.

McGlone, Robert E. "Deciphering Memory: John Adams and the Authorship of the

Declaration of Independence." *Journal of American History* 85 (September 1998): 411–38.

———. "Rescripting a Troubled Past: John Brown's Family and the Harpers Ferry Conspiracy." *Journal of American History* 75 (March 1989): 1179–1200.

McGuire, Joseph F. "Owen Lovejoy, Congressman from the Prairie." Master's thesis, Illinois State Normal University, 1951.

McKivigan, John R. "Antislavery 'Comeouter' Sects: A Neglected Dimension of the Abolitionist Movement." *Civil War History* 26 (June 1980): 142–60.

———. "Vote as You Pray and Pray as You Vote: Church-Oriented Abolitionism and Antislavery Politics." In *Crusaders and Compromisers: Essays on the Relationship of the Antislavery Struggle to the Antebellum Party System*, edited by Alan M. Kraut, 179–204. Westport, Conn.: Greenwood, 1983.

———. *The War against Proslavery Religion: Abolitionism and the Northern Churches, 1830–1865.* Ithaca: Cornell University Press, 1984.

McKivigan, John R., and Mitchell Snay, eds. *Religion and the Antebellum Debate over Slavery.* Athens: University of Georgia Press, 1998.

McManus, Michael J. *Political Abolitionism in Wisconsin, 1840–1861.* Kent, Ohio: Kent State University Press, 1998.

———. "'A Redeeming Spirit Is Busily Engaged': Political Abolitionism and Wisconsin Politics, 1840–1861." Ph.D. diss., University of Wisconsin, Madison, 1991.

McMillen, Sally G. *Seneca Falls and the Origins of the Women's Rights Movement.* Oxford: Oxford University Press, 2008.

McMurry, Sally Ann. *Transforming Rural Life: Dairying Families and Agricultural Change, 1820–1885.* Baltimore: Johns Hopkins University Press, 1995.

McMurry, Stephanie. "The Two Faces of Republicanism: Gender and Proslavery Politics in Antebellum South Carolina." *Journal of American History* 78 (March 1992): 1245–64.

McTighe, Michael J. *A Measure of Success: Protestants and Public Culture in Antebellum Cleveland.* Albany: State University of New York Press, 1995.

Melder, Keith. "Abby Kelley and the Process of Liberation." In *The Abolitionist Sisterhood: Women's Political Culture in Antebellum America*, edited by Jean Fagan Yellin and John C. Van Horne, 231–48. Ithaca: Cornell University Press, 1994.

———. *Beginnings of Sisterhood: The American Woman's Rights Movement, 1800–1850.* New York: Schocken, 1977.

Melish, Joanne Pope. *Disowning Slavery: Gradual Emancipation and "Race" in New England, 1780–1860.* Ithaca: Cornell University Press, 1998.

Meltzer, Milton. *Tongue of Flame: The Life of Lydia Maria Child.* New York: Crowell, 1965.

Merrill, Walter M. *Against Wind and Tide: A Biography of William Lloyd Garrison.* Cambridge: Harvard University Press, 1963.

Middleton, Stephen. *The Black Laws: Race and the Legal Process in Early Ohio.* Athens: Ohio University Press, 2005.

———. *The Black Laws in the Old Northwest: A Documentary History.* Westport, Conn.: Greenwood, 1993.

———. "Cincinnati and the Fight for the Law of Freedom in Ohio, 1830–1856." *Locus* 4 (Fall 1991): 59–73.

———. "The Fugitive Slave Crisis in Cincinnati, 1850–1860: Resistance, Enforcement, and Black Refugees." *Journal of Negro History* 72 (Winter–Spring 1987): 20–32.

———. *Ohio and the Antislavery Activities of Attorney Salmon Portland Chase, 1830–1849.* New York: Garland, 1990.

Midgley, Clare. *Women against Slavery: The British Campaigns, 1780–1870.* London: Routledge, 1992.

Miller, Marion C. "The Antislavery Movement in Indiana." Ph.D. diss., University of Michigan, 1938.

Moger, Elizabeth H. "Quakers as Abolitionists: The Robinsons of Rokeby and Charles Marriott." *Quaker History* 92 (Fall 2003): 52–59.

Moore, Charles Edwin. "Anti-Slavery Movements in Ohio." Master's thesis, Miami University, 1933.

Morrison, Michael A. *Slavery and the American West: The Eclipse of Manifest Destiny and the Coming of the Civil War.* Chapel Hill: University of North Carolina Press, 1997.

Moser, I. Kathleen. "J. Elizabeth Jones: The Forgotten Activist." Honors paper, Kent State University, 1996.

Moses Pettengill. Chicago: Thompson, n.d.

Muelder, Hermann R. *Fighters for Freedom: The History of Anti-Slavery Activities of Men and Women Associated with Knox College.* New York: Columbia University Press, 1959.

———. "Galesburg: Hot-Bed of Abolitionism." *Journal of the Illinois State Historical Society* 35 (September 1942): 216–35.

Murray, Alexander L. "The *Provincial Freeman*: A New Source for the History of the Negro in Canada and the United States." *Journal of Negro History* 44 (April 1959): 123–35.

Myers, John L. "Antislavery Activities of Five Lane Seminary Boys in 1835–36." *Bulletin of the Historical and Philosophical Society of Ohio* 21 (April 1963): 95–111.

Ndukwu, Maurice Dickson. "Antislavery in Michigan: A Study of Its Origin, Development, and Expression from Territorial Period to 1860." Ph.D. diss., Michigan State University, 1979.

Neely, Ruth. *Women of Ohio.* 3 vols. Cincinnati: Clarke, 1937.

Newman, Richard S. *The Transformation of American Abolitionism: Fighting Slavery in the Early Republic.* Chapel Hill: University of North Carolina Press, 2002.

Newman, Simon Peter. *Parades and the Politics of the Street: Festive Culture in the Early American Republic.* Philadelphia: University of Pennsylvania Press, 1997.

Norton, Mary Beth. *Liberty's Daughters: The Revolutionary Experience of American Women, 1750–1800.* Boston: Little, Brown, 1980.

Nuermberger, Ruth. *The Free Produce Movement: A Quaker Protest against Slavery*. Durham: Duke University Press, 1942.

Nye, Russel B. "Marius Robinson: A Forgotten Abolitionist Leader." *Ohio State Archaeological and Historical Quarterly* 55 (April–June 1946): 138–54.

———. *William Lloyd Garrison and the Humanitarian Reformers*. Boston: Little, Brown, 1955.

Oates, Stephen B. *To Purge This Land with Blood: A Biography of John Brown*. New York: Harper and Row, 1970.

Oertel, Kristen Tegtmeier. *Bleeding Borders: Race, Gender, and Violence in Pre–Civil War Kansas*. Baton Rouge: Louisiana State University Press, 2009.

Ortiz, Victoria. *Sojourner Truth: A Self-Made Woman*. Philadelphia: Lippincott, 1974.

Otis, William A. *A Genealogical and Historical Memoir of the Otis Family in America*. Chicago: Schulkins, 1924.

Padgett, Chris. "Abolitionists of All Classes: Political Culture and Antislavery Community in Ashtabula County, Ohio, 1800–1850." Ph.D. diss., University of California, Davis, 1993.

———. "Comeouterism and Antislavery Violence in Ohio's Western Reserve." In *Antislavery Violence: Sectional, Racial, and Cultural Conflict in Antebellum America*, edited by John R. McKivigan and Stanley Harrold, 193–214. Knoxville: University of Tennessee Press, 1999.

Painter, Nell Irvin. "Difference, Slavery, and Memory: Sojourner Truth in Feminist Abolitionism." In *The Abolitionist Sisterhood: Women's Political Culture in Antebellum America*, edited by Jean Fagan Yellin and John C. Van Horne, 139–58. Ithaca: Cornell University Press, 1994.

———. *Sojourner Truth: A Life, a Symbol*. New York: Norton, 1996.

Palmer, Beverly Wilson. "Towards a National Antislavery Party: The Giddings-Sumner Alliance." *Ohio History* 99 (Winter–Spring 1990): 51–71.

Pasley, Jeffrey L. "The Cheese and the Words: Popular Political Culture and Participatory Democracy in the Early American Republic." In *Beyond the Founders: New Approaches to the Political History of the Early American Republic*, edited by Jeffrey L. Pasley, Andrew Robertson, and David Waldstreicher, 31–56. Chapel Hill: University of North Carolina Press, 2003.

Passet, Joanne E. *Sex Radicals and the Quest for Women's Equality*. Urbana: University of Illinois Press, 2003.

Patterson, John C. "Marshall Men and Marshall Measures in State and National History." *Historical Collections* (Michigan Pioneer and Historical Society) 38 (1912): 220–78.

Pease, Jane H. "The Freshness of Fanaticism: Abby Kelley Foster: An Essay in Reform." Ph.D. diss., University of Rochester, 1969.

Pease, Jane H., and William H. Pease. "Confrontation and Abolition in the 1850s." *Journal of American History* 58 (March 1972): 923–37.

———. *They Who Would Be Free: Blacks' Search for Freedom, 1830–1861*. New York: Atheneum, 1974.

Penney, Sherry H., and James D. Livingston. *A Very Dangerous Woman: Martha Wright and Women's Rights*. Amherst: University of Massachusetts Press, 2004.

Perry, Lewis. "Black Abolitionists and the Origins of Civil Disobedience." In *Moral Problems in American Life: New Perspectives on Cultural History*, edited by Karen Halttunen and Lewis Perry, 103–21. Ithaca: Cornell University Press, 1998.

Petrulionis, Sandra Harbert. "'Swelling That Great Tide of Humanity': The Concord, Massachusetts, Female Anti-Slavery Society." *New England Quarterly* 74 (September 2001): 385–418.

———. *To Set This World Right: The Antislavery Movement in Thoreau's Concord*. Ithaca: Cornell University Press, 2006.

Pierson, Michael D. "'All Southern Society Is Assailed by the Foulest Charges': Charles Sumner's 'The Crime against Kansas' and the Escalation of Republican Anti-Slavery Rhetoric." *New England Quarterly* 68 (December 1995): 831–57.

———. "Antislavery Politics in Harriet Beecher Stowe's *The Minister's Wooing* and *The Pearl of Orr's Island*." *American Nineteenth Century History* 3 (Summer 2002): 1–24.

———. "Between Antislavery and Abolition: The Politics and Rhetoric of Jane Grey Swisshelm." *Pennsylvania History* 60 (July 1993): 305–21.

———. *Free Hearts and Free Homes: Gender and American Antislavery Politics*. Chapel Hill: University of North Carolina Press, 2003.

———. "'Free Hearts and Free Homes': Representations of Family in the American Antislavery Movement." Ph.D. diss., State University of New York at Binghamton, 1993.

———. "'Prairies on Fire': The Organization of the 1856 Mass Republican Rally in Beloit, Wisconsin." *Civil War History* 48 (June 2002): 101–22.

Pih, Richard W. "Negro Self-Improvement Efforts in Ante-Bellum Cincinnati, 1836–1850." *Ohio History* 78 (1969): 179–87.

Porter, Dorothy B. "The Organized Educational Activities of Negro Literary Societies, 1828–1846." *Journal of Negro Education* 5 (October 1936): 555–76.

Praus, Alexis A., ed. "The Underground Railroad at Schoolcraft." *Michigan History* 37 (June 1953): 177–82.

Price, Robert. "Further Notes on Granville's Anti-Abolition Disturbances of 1836." *Ohio Archaeological and Historical Quarterly* 45 (October 1936): 365–68.

———. "The Ohio Anti-Slavery Convention of 1836." *Ohio State Archaeological and Historical Quarterly* 45 (April 1936): 173–88.

Prince, Benjamin F. "The Rescue Case of 1857." *Ohio Archaeological and Historical Quarterly* 16 (July 1907): 292–309.

Quarles, Benjamin. *Allies for Freedom: Blacks and John Brown*. New York: Oxford University Press, 1974.

———. *Black Abolitionists*. London: Oxford University Press, 1969.

———. "Sources of Abolitionist Income." *Mississippi Valley Historical Review* 32 (June 1945): 63–76.

Quist, John W. "'The Great Majority of Our Subscribers Are Farmers': The Michigan Abolitionist Constituency of the 1840s." *Journal of the Early Republic* 14 (Fall 1994): 325–58.

———. *Restless Visionaries: The Social Roots of Antebellum Reform in Alabama and Michigan.* Baton Rouge: Louisiana State University Press, 1998.

———. "Social and Moral Reform in the Old North and the Old South: Washtenaw County, Michigan, and Tuscaloosa County, Alabama, 1820–1860." Ph.D. diss., University of Michigan, 1992.

Rakow, Lana F., and Cheris Kramarae, eds. *The Revolution in Words: Righting Women, 1868–1871.* New York: Routledge, 1990.

Rayback, Joseph G. "The Liberty Party Leaders of Ohio: Exponents of Antislavery Coalition." *Ohio Archaeological and Historical Quarterly* 57 (1948): 165–78.

Reilly, Edward C. "The Early Slavery Controversy in the Western Reserve." Ph.D. diss., Western Reserve University, 1940.

Rendall, Jane, ed. *Equal or Different: Women's Politics, 1800–1914.* Oxford: Oxford University Press, 1987.

Rhodes, Jane. *Mary Ann Shadd Cary: The Black Press and Protest in the Nineteenth Century.* Bloomington: Indiana University Press, 1998.

Richards, Leonard L. *"Gentlemen of Property and Standing": Anti-Abolition Mobs in Jacksonian America.* Oxford: Oxford University Press, 1970.

Richardson, Marilyn. "'What If I Am a Woman?': Maria Stewart's Defense of Black Women's Political Activism." In *Courage and Conscience: Black and White Abolitionists in Boston,* edited by Donald M. Jacobs, 191–206. Bloomington: Indiana University Press for Boston Athenaeum, 1993.

Ripley, C. Peter, ed. *Witness for Freedom: African American Voices on Race, Slavery, and Emancipation.* Chapel Hill: University of North Carolina Press, 1993.

Roediger, David. "Ira Steward and the Anti-Slavery Origins of American Eight-Hour Theory." *Labor History* 27 (Summer 1986): 410–26.

Rozinek, Erika. "Trembling for the Nation: Illinois Women and the Election of 1860." *Journal of Illinois History* 5 (Winter 2002): 309–24.

Runyon, Randolph Paul. *Delia Webster and the Underground Railroad.* Lexington: University Press of Kentucky, 1996.

Russo, Ann, and Cheris Kramarae, eds. *The Radical Women's Press of the 1850s.* New York: Routledge, 1991.

Ryan, Mary P. "Gender and Public Access: Women's Politics in Nineteenth-Century America." In *Habermas and the Public Sphere,* edited by Craig Calhoun, 259–88. Boston: MIT Press, 1992.

———. *Women in Public: Between Banners and Ballots, 1825–1880.* Baltimore: Johns Hopkins University Press, 1990.

Salerno, Beth A. *Sister Societies: Women's Antislavery Organizations in Antebellum America*. De Kalb: Northern Illinois University Press, 2005.

Salitan, Lucille, and Eve Lewis Perera, eds. *Virtuous Lives: Four Quaker Sisters Remember Family Life, Abolitionism, and Women's Suffrage*. New York: Continuum, 1994.

Saunders, Delores T. *Illinois Liberty Lines: The History of the Underground Railroad*. Farmington, Ill.: Farmington Shopper, 1982.

Scholten, Pat Creech. "A Public 'Jollification': The 1859 Women's Rights Petition before the Indiana Legislature." *Indiana Magazine of History* 72 (December 1976): 347–59.

Schwalm, Leslie Ann. "The Antislavery and Reform Activities of Women in Wisconsin." Master's thesis, University of Wisconsin, Madison, 1984.

Sears, Hal D. *The Sex Radicals: Free Love in High Victorian America*. Lawrence: Regents Press of Kansas, 1977.

Seibert, Wilbur. "A Quaker Section of the Underground Railroad in Northern Ohio." *Ohio Archaeological and Historical Quarterly* 39 (July 1930): 479–502.

Seigel, Peggy. "The Fort Wayne *Standard*: A Reform Newspaper in the 1850s Storm." *Indiana Magazine of History* 97 (September 2001): 168–89.

———. "Moral Champions and Public Pathfinders: Antebellum Quaker Women in Eastcentral Indiana." *Quaker History* 81 (Fall 1992): 87–106.

SenGupta, Gunja. "Bleeding Kansas." *Kansas History* 24 (Winter 2001–2): 318–41.

———. "'A Model New England State': Northeastern Antislavery in Territorial Kansas, 1854–1860." *Civil War History* 34 (March 1993): 31–46.

Sewell, Richard H. *Ballots for Freedom: Antislavery Politics in the United States, 1837–1860*. New York: Oxford University Press, 1976.

———. "Slavery, Race, and the Free Soil Party, 1848–1854." In *Crusaders and Compromisers: Essays on the Relationship of the Antislavery Struggle to the Antebellum Party System*, edited by Alan M. Kraut, 101–24. Westport, Conn.: Greenwood, 1983.

Shapiro, Samuel. "The Rendition of Anthony Burns." *Journal of Negro History* 44 (June 1959): 34–51.

Siebert, Wilbur Henry. *Mysteries of Ohio's Underground Railroads*. Columbus, Ohio: Long's College Book, 1951.

———. "A Quaker Section of the Underground Railroad in Northern Ohio." *Ohio Archaeological and Historical Quarterly* 39 (July 1930): 479–502.

———. *The Underground Railroad from Slavery to Freedom*. New York: Macmillan, 1899.

Silbey, Joel H. "'There Are Other Questions beside That of Slavery Merely': The Democratic Party and Antislavery Politics." In *Crusaders and Compromisers: Essays on the Relationship of the Antislavery Struggle to the Antebellum Party System*, edited by Alan M. Kraut, 143–78. Westport, Conn.: Greenwood, 1983.

Simeone, James. "Making the People's Republic: Culture and Politics in Early Illinois." Ph.D. diss., University of Chicago, 1992.

Sklar, Kathryn Kish. *Catharine Beecher: A Study in American Domesticity.* New York: Norton, 1976.

———. "'Women Who Speak for an Entire Nation': American and British Women at the World Anti-Slavery Convention, London, 1840." In *The Abolitionist Sisterhood: Women's Political Culture in Antebellum America,* edited by Jean Fagan Yellin and John C. Van Horne, 301–33. Ithaca: Cornell University Press, 1994.

Sklar, Kathryn Kish, and James Brewer Stewart, eds. *Women's Rights and Transatlantic Antislavery in the Era of Emancipation.* New Haven: Yale University Press, 2007.

Smith, Barbara Clark. "Food Rioters and the American Revolution." *William and Mary Quarterly* 51 (January 1994): 3–38.

Smith, Theodore Clarke. *The Liberty and Free Soil Parties in the Northwest.* New York: Longmans, Green, 1897.

Soderlund, Jean R. "Priorities and Power: The Philadelphia Female Anti-Slavery Society." In *The Abolitionist Sisterhood: Women's Political Culture in Antebellum America,* edited by Jean Fagan Yellin and John C. Van Horne, 67–88. Ithaca: Cornell University Press, 1994.

Speicher, Anna M. *The Religious World of Antislavery Women: Spirituality in the Lives of Five Abolitionist Lecturers.* Syracuse, N.Y.: Syracuse University Press, 2000.

Sponagle, Carol. "Reform and Resistance: Abolitionism of the East in Illinois, 1830–1840." Master's thesis, University of Illinois, Springfield, 1998.

Stanley, Amy Dru. "Home Life and the Morality of the Market." In *The Market Revolution in America: Social, Political and Religious Expressions, 1800–1880,* edited by Melvyn Stokes and Stephen Conway, 74–96. Charlottesville: University Press of Virginia, 1996.

Stauffer, John. *The Black Hearts of Men: Radical Abolitionists and the Transformation of Race.* Cambridge: Harvard University Press, 2002.

Steinhagen, Carol. "The Two Lives of Frances Dana Gage." *Ohio History* 107 (Winter 1998): 22–38.

Sterling, Dorothy. *Ahead of Her Time: Abby Kelley and the Politics of Antislavery.* New York: Norton, 1991.

———. "The Antislavery Ladies." In *We Are Your Sisters: Black Women in the Nineteenth Century,* edited by Dorothy Sterling, 119–50. New York: Norton, 1984.

———, ed. *We Are Your Sisters: Black Women in the Nineteenth Century.* New York: Norton, 1984.

Stewart, James Brewer. "Abolitionists, Insurgents, and Third Parties: Sectionalism and Partisan Politics in Northern Whiggery, 1836–1844." In *Crusaders and Compromisers: Essays on the Relationship of the Antislavery Struggle to the Antebellum Party System,* edited by Alan M. Kraut, 25–44. Westport, Conn.: Greenwood, 1983.

———. *Holy Warriors: The Abolitionists and American Slavery.* New York: Hill and Wang, 1997.

———. *Joshua R. Giddings and the Tactics of Radical Politics*. Cleveland: Press of Case Western University, 1970.

———. "Peaceful Hopes and Violent Experiences: The Evolution of Reforming and Radical Abolitionism, 1831–1837." *Civil War History* 17 (December 1971): 293–309.

Strane, Susan. *A Whole-Souled Woman: Prudence Crandall and the Education of Black Women*. New York: Norton, 1990.

Stricker, Leslie A. "Stealing Themselves: Fugitive Slaves, the Underground Railroad, and the Quest for Freedom: The Ohio Experience." Master's thesis, Wright State University, 1993.

Strong, Douglas M. *Perfectionist Politics: Abolitionism and the Religious Tensions of American Democracy*. Syracuse, N.Y.: Syracuse University Press, 1999.

Sumler-Lewis, Janice. "The Forten-Purvis Women of Philadelphia and the American Antislavery Crusade." *Journal of Negro History* 66 (Winter 1981–82): 281–88.

Sussman, Charlotte. *Consuming Anxieties: Consumer Protest, Gender, and British Slavery, 1713–1833*. Palo Alto, Calif.: Stanford University Press, 2000.

Swerdlow, Amy. "Abolition's Conservative Sisters: The Ladies' New York City Anti-Slavery Societies, 1834–1840." In *The Abolitionist Sisterhood: Women's Political Culture in Antebellum America*, edited by Jean Fagan Yellin and John C. Van Horne, 31–44. Ithaca: Cornell University Press, 1994.

Taylor, Alice. "From Petitions to Partyism: Antislavery and the Domestication of Maine Politics in the 1840s and 1850s." *New England Quarterly* 77 (March 2004): 70–88.

———. "'It Was a Kind of Ladies Exchange': The Transatlantic Female Economy of the Boston Female Anti-Slavery Fair." Paper presented at the Great Lakes History Conference, 2007.

———. "Selling Abolitionism: The Commercial, Material, and Social World of the Boston Antislavery Fair, 1834–58." Ph.D. diss., Western Ontario University, 2007.

Taylor, Clare. *Women of the Anti-Slavery Movement: The Weston Sisters*. New York: St. Martin's, 1995.

Taylor, Henry L. "Spatial Organization and the Residential Experience: Black Cincinnati in 1850." *Social Science History* 10 (Spring 1986): 45–69.

Taylor, Nikki M. *Frontiers of Freedom: Cincinnati's Black Community, 1802–1868*. Athens: Ohio University Press, 2005.

Tegtmeier, Kristen A. "The Ladies of Lawrence Are Arming!: The Gendered Nature of Sectional Violence in Early Kansas." In *Antislavery Violence: Sectional, Racial, and Cultural Conflict in Antebellum America*, edited by John R. McKivigan and Stanley Harrold, 215–35. Knoxville: University of Tennessee Press, 1999.

Thelen, David. "Memory and American History." *Journal of American History* 75 (March 1989): 1117–29.

Thomas, John L. *The Liberator, William Lloyd Garrison: A Biography*. Boston: Little, Brown, 1963.

Thompson, Carol L. "Women and the Antislavery Movement." *Current History* 70 (May 1976): 198–201.

Thorne, Irene. "The Anti-Slavery Movement in Ohio as Illustrated by the Abolition Movement and the Underground Railroad." Master's thesis, Kent State University, 1942.

Travers, Len. *Celebrating the Fourth: Independence Day and the Rites of Nationalism in the Early Republic.* Amherst: University of Massachusetts Press, 1997.

Turner, Glennette Tilley. *The Underground Railroad in DuPage County, Illinois.* Wheaton, Ill.: Newman Educational, 1986.

Van Broekhoven, Deborah Bingham. "'Better Than a Clay Club': The Organization of Anti-Slavery Fairs, 1835–60." *Slavery and Abolition* 19 (April 1998): 24–45.

———. "'A Determination to Labor': Female Antislavery Activity in Rhode Island." *Rhode Island History* 44 (May 1985): 35–45.

———. *The Devotion of These Women: Rhode Island in the Antislavery Network.* Amherst: University of Massachusetts Press, 2002.

———. "'Let Your Names Be Enrolled': Method and Ideology in Women's Antislavery Petitioning." In *The Abolitionist Sisterhood: Women's Political Culture in Antebellum America*, edited by Jean Fagan Yellin and John C. Van Horne, 179–99. Ithaca: Cornell University Press, 1994.

———. "Needles, Pens, and Petitions: Reading Women into Antislavery History." In *The Meaning of Slavery in the North*, edited by David Roediger and Martin H. Blatt, 125–55. New York: Garland, 1998.

Varon, Elizabeth R. "Tippecanoe and the Ladies, Too: White Women and Party Politics in Antebellum Virginia." *Journal of American History* 82 (September 1995): 494–521.

———. *We Mean to Be Counted: White Women and Politics in Antebellum Virginia.* Chapel Hill: University of North Carolina Press, 1998.

Venet, Wendy Hamand. *Neither Ballots nor Bullets: Women Abolitionists and the Civil War.* Charlottesville: University Press of Virginia, 1991.

Vlach, John Michael. "Above Ground on the Underground Railroad: Places of Flight and Refuge." In *Passages to Freedom: The Underground Railroad in History and Memory*, edited by David W. Blight, 95–116. New York: Smithsonian Books, 2004.

Volpe, Vernon L. *Forlorn Hope of Freedom: The Liberty Party in the Old Northwest, 1838–1848.* Kent, Ohio: Kent State University Press, 1990.

———. "The Ohio Election of 1838: A Study in the Historical Method?" *Ohio History* 95 (Summer–Autumn 1986): 85–100.

———. "Theodore Dwight Weld's Antislavery Mission in Ohio." *Ohio History* 100 (Winter–Spring 1991): 5–18.

Waldrip, W. D. "A Station of the Underground Railroad." *Indiana Magazine of History* 7 (June 1911): 64–76.

Washington, Margaret. *Sojourner Truth's America.* Urbana: University of Illinois Press, 2009.

Watts, Ralph M. "History of the Underground Railroad in Mechanicsburg." *Ohio Archaeological and Historical Quarterly* 43 (July 1934): 209–54.

———. *History of the Underground Railroad in Mechanicsburg*. Columbus, Ohio: Herr, 1934.

Weeks, Stephen. *Southern Quakers and Slavery: A Study in Institutional History*. New York: Bergman, 1968.

Weiner, Dana E. "Anti-Abolition Violence and Freedom of Speech in Peoria, Illinois." *Journal of Illinois History* 11 (Autumn 2008): 179–204.

Weisenburger, Steven C. *Modern Medea: A Story of Slavery and Child-Murder from the Old South*. New York: Hill and Wang/Farrar, Straus, and Giroux, 1998.

Wellman, Judith. *The Road to Seneca Falls: Elizabeth Cady Stanton and the First Woman's Rights Convention*. Urbana: University of Illinois Press, 2004.

———. "The Seneca Falls Women's Rights Convention: A Study of Social Networks." *Journal of Women's History* 3 (Spring 1991): 9–35.

———. "Women and Radical Reform in Antebellum Upstate New York: A Profile of Grassroots Female Abolitionists." In *Clio Was a Woman: Studies in the History of American Women*, edited by Mabel Deutrich and Virginia Purdy, 113–27. Washington, D.C.: Howard University Press, 1980.

Wheeler, Adade Mitchell, and Marlene Stein Wortman. *The Roads They Made: Women in Illinois History*. Chicago: Kerr, 1977.

Wheeler, Leslie. "Lucy Stone: Wife of Henry Blackwell." *American History Illustrated* 16 (December 1981): 38–45.

White, Marie S. "The Methodist Antislavery Struggle in the Land of Lincoln." *Methodist History* 10 (July 1972): 33–52.

Whitlock, Martha, ed. *Women in Ohio History*. Columbus: Ohio Historical Society, 1976.

Wilkinson, E. C. "'Touch Not, Taste Not, Handle Not': The Abolitionist Debate over the Free Produce Movement." *Columbia Historical Review* 2 (Winter 2002): 2–14.

Williams, Carolyn. "The Female Antislavery Movement: Fighting against Racial Prejudice and Promoting Women's Rights in Antebellum America." In *The Abolitionist Sisterhood: Women's Political Culture in Antebellum America*, edited by Jean Fagan Yellin and John C. Van Horne, 159–77. Ithaca: Cornell University Press, 1994.

———. "Feminist Abolitionists in Boston and Philadelphia: Liberal Religion and the Reform Impulse in Antebellum America." In *The Meaning of Slavery in the North*, edited by David Roediger and Martin H. Blatt, 94–123. New York: Garland, 1998.

———. "Religion, Race, and Gender in Antebellum American Radicalism: The Philadelphia Female Anti-Slavery Society, 1833–70." Ph.D. diss., University of California, Los Angeles, 1991.

Wimberly, Ware William, II. "Missionary Reforms in Indiana, 1826–1860: Education, Temperance, Antislavery." Ph.D. diss., Indiana University, 1977.

Winch, Julie. *A Gentleman of Color: The Life of James Forten*. Oxford: Oxford University Press, 2002.

——— "'You Have Talents—Only Cultivate Them': Philadelphia's Black Female Literary Societies and the Abolitionist Crusade." In *The Abolitionist Sisterhood:*

Women's Political Culture in Antebellum America, edited by Jean Fagan Yellin and John C. Van Horne, 101–18. Ithaca: Cornell University Press, 1994.

Wyatt-Brown, Bertram. "Abolition and Antislavery in Hudson and Cleveland: Contrasts in Reform Styles." In *Cleveland: A Tradition of Reform*, edited by David D. Van Tassel and John J. Grabowski, 91–112. Kent, Ohio: Kent State University Press, 1986.

Wyman, Lillie B. Chace. "Sojourner Truth." *New England Magazine*, March 1901, 59–66.

Yannessa, Mary Ann. *Levi Coffin, Quaker: Breaking the Bonds of Slavery in Ohio and Indiana*. Richmond, Ind.: Friends United Press, 2001.

Yee, Shirley J. *Black Women Abolitionists: A Study in Activism, 1828–1860*. Knoxville: University of Tennessee Press, 1992.

Yellin, Jean Fagan. *Women and Sisters: The Antislavery Feminists in American Culture*. New Haven: Yale University Press, 1989.

Yellin, Jean Fagan, and John C. Van Horne, eds. *The Abolitionist Sisterhood: Women's Political Culture in Antebellum America*. Ithaca: Cornell University Press, 1994.

Zaeske, Susan. *Signatures of Citizenship: Petitioning, Antislavery, and Women's Political Identity*. Chapel Hill: University of North Carolina Press, 2003.

Zagarri, Rosemarie. "Gender and the First Party System." In *Federalists Reconsidered*, edited by Doron Ben-Atar and Barbara B. Oberg, 118–34. Charlottesville: University Press of Virginia, 1998.

———. *Revolutionary Backlash: Women and Politics in the Early American Republic*. Philadelphia: University of Pennsylvania Press, 2007.

Zboray, Ronald J., and Mary Saracino Zboray. "Gender Slurs in Boston's Partisan Press during the 1840s." *Journal of American Studies* 34 (December 2000): 413–46.

———. "Whig Women, Politics, and Culture in the Campaign of 1840: Three Perspectives from Massachusetts." *Journal of the Early Republic* 17 (Summer 1997): 277–315.

Zorn, Roman. "Garrisonian Abolitionism, 1828–1839." Ph.D. diss., University of Wisconsin, Madison, 1953.

Index

Bailey, Gamaliel, 4; and Abby Kelley, 134, 243 (n. 32); editor of *Philanthropist*, 94; and Liberty Party, 130, 217 (n. 7); and moderate antislavery, 95; and western antislavery, 4, 95; on women's equality, 53–54, 189

Bailey, Margaret, 32, 96, 217 (n. 19)

Ballou, Adin, 96

Banners. *See* Politics: banners and

Barber, Amzi D., 30

Barker, Joseph, 191

Beardsley, Leonard E., 21

Beckley, Guy, 52, 56

Beecher, Catharine, 55, 129, 190

Beecher, Lyman, 209–10 (n. 16)

Beeson, Rebecca, 78, 90

Bibb, Henry, 27, 45, 105, 106, 167, 180, 253–54 (n. 38)

Bierce, Lucius V., 192

Birmingham Female Anti-Slavery Society, 87

Birney, James, 4, 13, 18, 19, 38, 94, 95, 201, 209 (n. 14)

Bishop, Emeline, 15, 18

Bissell, Lovina, 169, 171–72

Black abolitionists: and antislavery fairs, 97–98; in Cincinnati, 93–95, 97–98; early leadership of, 2; and education, 28–29; and free produce, 70, 72–73, 89–90; issues of concern, 7; lecturers, 157–59; and Salem Rescue, 162; and Underground Railroad, 163, 164, 166–69, 179–81; and Union Anti-Slavery Conventions, 105–6; in West, 7; and white abolitionists, 7, 166–70. *See also* Bibb, Henry; Blackburn, Ruthy and Thornton; Black Laws; Black women; Brown, William Wells; Colored conventions; Delany, Martin; Douglass, Frederick; Stewart, Maria; Truth, Sojourner; Watkins, Frances Ellen

Blackburn, Ruthy and Thornton, 166

Black Laws, 9, 28, 37, 94, 160, 175, 183–84; background of, 7, 183–84, 191; Betsey Mix Cowles's campaign against, 60, 143–44; and education, 93, 191; Garrisonians on, 60, 143–44; and Liberty Party, 59–65; Sojourner Truth and, 159; and Underground Railroad, 172–73, 180; and woman's rights, 188–89, 191

Blackwell, Henry, 109, 162–63

Black women: and colored conventions, 40, 47–48; and education, 28–29; and fairs, 97–98; and free produce, 70; lecturers, 157–59;

and Liberty Party, 40; and Ohio female antislavery societies, 209 (n. 8); and postwar work, 203; and stereotypes, 61; and Underground Railroad, 254 (n. 41); and white abolitionists, 169. *See also* Black abolitionists; Blackburn, Ruthy and Thornton; Black Laws; Colored conventions; Stewart, Maria; Truth, Sojourner; Watkins, Frances Ellen

Blanchard, Jonathan, 96

Blanchard, Mary, 32, 96, 239 (n. 130)

Bloomer, Amelia, 195

Bloomers, 195–97. *See also* Woman's rights

Bonsall, Daniel, 122

Booth, Sherman, 54

Bosfield, Titus, 22

Boston Female Anti-Slavery Society, 1, 5, 12, 35, 91–92, 96, 98, 110

Bown, Benjamin, 121

Bown, Sarah, 121

Boylan, Anne, 55

Boynton, Charles, 111–13, 126

Brisbane, William H., 104

Brooke, Abram, 130, 239 (n. 111), 251 (n. 3)

Brooke, James, 130

Brown, John, 153

Brown, William Wells, 108–9

Burleigh, Charles, 104–5, 108, 113, 130

Burleigh, Margaret, 147

Burritt, Elihu, 86

Cadiz (Ohio) Female Anti-Slavery Society, 22, 28, 121, 212 (n. 84)

Canada: fugitives in, 143, 152–53, 164, 165, 166, 171, 176, 180, 181; Garrisonians and, 165; missions in, 149, 153; Refugee Home Society and, 153, 165, 253–54 (n. 38); refugee schools in, 172; western female antislavery societies and, 175–76

Candler, John, 87

Canton (Ohio) Female Anti-Slavery Society, 18

Carpenter, Sarah, 17, 18

Chandler, Elizabeth Margaret: and British abolitionism, 87; and free produce, 67, 70, 71 (ill.), 72, 73, 76, 78, 84, 228 (n. 12); and Laura Smith Haviland, 167

Chapman, Maria Weston, 116–17, 136, 146, 165, 182

Chase, Salmon P., 94

Cheese, 1–2, 79, 80, 123, 124, 207 (n. 5)

163, 164–66; and interracial networks, 166–70; and rescues, 179–81; Salem Rescue, 162–64. *See also* Underground Railroad

Gage, Frances Dana, 42, 156, 258 (n. 17)
Garner, Margaret, 115
Garnet, Henry Highland, 72
Garretson, Mrs., 24–25
Garrison, William Lloyd, 1, 2, 13, 49, 96, 126, 131, 147, 153; in Cincinnati, 108, 109, 112–13, 126; and Cincinnati Union Anti-Slavery Convention, 103; and free produce, 72–73, 85; and Liberty Party, 38; and western abolitionism, 5; and woman's rights, 55
Garrisonianism, 4, 202; in *Anti-Slavery Bugle*, 106, 135; and anti-slavery fairs, 79–80, 91–92, 116–17; and Black Laws, 60, 143–44; Canadian fugitives and, 152–53; in Cincinnati, 9, 95–96, 97, 99–100, 106–15; and education for blacks, 32, 60; and 1840 divide, 3, 95; and free produce, 73, 77, 79–80; and Liberty Party, 45, 130–36, 154, 243 (n. 31); and Underground Railroad, 143, 152–53, 161, 163–66, 172, 177; in West, 6, 9, 45, 90, 92, 98, 130–60 passim; and woman's rights, 75, 103
Geauga Female Anti-Slavery Society, 155
Genius of Universal Emancipation, 43, 67–69, 70, 84
Giddings, Joshua, 1, 4, 116, 153, 192
Giddings, Maria, 1, 192
Glasgow Female Anti-Slavery Society, 165
Gordon, Lavenia, 18
Gordon, Susannah, 178
Gove, Sallie, 122
Gray, Isaac, 61
Green, Beriah, 209 (n. 10)
Green Plain (Ohio) Free Produce Society, 67–69, 70, 125
Grew, Mary, 147, 207 (n. 16)
Griffing, Charles, 128, 151–53, 249 (n. 141)
Griffing, Josephine, 105, 108, 156, 160; and Abby Kelley, 128, 151; and antislavery lecturing, 128–29, 151–54; background of, 151, 249 (n. 141); and Canadian fugitives, 152–53, 165; divorce of, 153, 159; pregnancy of, 153; on Sojourner Truth, 157–59; and Underground Railroad, 152–53, 161, 164, 165; and Western Anti-Slavery Society, 151, 161; on woman's rights, 186, 190

Grimké, Angelina, 11, 26, 129, 184
Grimké, Sarah, 11, 40, 129, 184, 199
Griswold, Eleanor, 18

Hallowell, Sarah, 143
Hamilton, Elsie and Willis, 181
Harpers Ferry, 153
Harrison, William Henry, 47
Harwood, Edward, 104
Haviland, Laura Smith, 9, 164; and House of Refuge, 202–3; post–Civil War work, 202–3; and Underground Railroad, 167, 168 (ill.), 170, 172, 181–82
Heaton, Jacob, 191
Henry County (Indiana) Female Anti-Slavery Society, 45, 50, 56, 57; addresses of, 27; and Black Laws, 62, 64; and free produce, 73–77, 82, 83, 88; lack of black members in, 88–89; and Liberty Party, 50, 56, 57, 58; and transatlantic abolitionism, 88; and Underground Railroad, 172–73, 175, 176, 178; and vigilance committee, 88; and woman's rights, 193
Hewitt, Nancy, 40
Heyrick, Elizabeth, 70, 87–88
Hicks, Elias, 69–70
"Higher law," 174
Hinshaw, Seth, 84
Hise, Daniel, 121, 122–23, 124, 150, 157
Hise, Margaret, 124, 195
Hitchcock, Jane Elizabeth "Lizzie," 1, 2, 125, 156, 200; and Abby Kelley, 136, 144–46, 149; on antislavery fairs, 117, 118–19, 192; and antislavery lecturing, 128–29, 131, 145–47, 149, 150, 153–54, 160, 246 (n. 89); background of, 145–47; and dancing, 122–23; editor of *Anti-Slavery Bugle*, 106, 135, 143, 145–49; and family life, 146–47; home of, 146–47, 247 (n. 105); and hygiene lecturing, 149–51, 196–97; and Salem Woman's Rights Convention, 259 (n. 22); and Underground Railroad, 161, 164, 165; on woman's rights, 184, 186, 188, 189; and *The Young Abolitionists; or, Conversations on Slavery*, 148;
Hoffert, Sylvia, 151–52
Holley, Myron, 38, 108
Holley, Sallie, 108–9, 156, 203
Home Journal, 187–88
Hudson, Betsy, 139–40
Hudson, Timothy, 140–42

Porter, Jeremiah, 42
Putnam (Illinois) Female Anti-Slavery
Society, 27, 45, 56, 58; and Black Laws,
64–65; and Liberty Party, 222 (n. 87); and
Underground Railroad, 174–75, 178

Quakers: attack on Abby Kelley, 127–28; and
come-outerism, 137; and free produce,
4, 8–9, 69–70, 72, 73, 76, 77, 78, 80, 82, 84;
Hicksite, 131; and internal conflict, 80–83;
and Liberty Party, 38, 81

Raffles. *See* Fairs, antislavery
Raisin Institute, 167
Rakestraw, Emily. *See* Robinson, Emily
(Rakestraw)
Rankin, John, 105, 164
Rayner, Kenneth, 75
Refugee Home Society, 152–53, 165, 253–54
(n. 38)
Republican Party, 38–39, 40, 153
Robinson, Emily (Rakestraw), 15, 22–24, 28,
191, 201–2
Robinson, J. J., 162
Robinson, Marius, 14, 15, 22–25, 156–57; on
Salem Rescue, 162–63; on woman's rights,
188–89, 191, 193, 195
Rochester Ladies Anti-Slavery Sewing
Society, 115
Rulin, Ephraim, 122

Salem, Abby Kelley, 162, 252 (n. 22)
Salem, Ohio, 2, 9, 115–25. *See also* Woman's rights
Salem Rescue, 161–64, 170
Salerno, Beth A., 5, 100
School Fund Institute (Ohio), 28
Seneca Falls Woman's Rights Convention,
184, 185, 186
Sewing societies, antislavery, 7, 27, 90, 95, 97,
99, 101, 102, 106, 108–9, 110, 113, 114, 115, 116,
117–18, 121–22, 125, 137, 149, 175–77. *See also*
names of individual groups
Sexuality. *See* Woman's rights
Sheldon, Mary, 56–57
Shugart, Zachariah, 170, 171
Signal of Liberty, 56, 167
Smith, Harriet, 137–38
Stanton, Benjamin, 134

Stanton, Elizabeth Cady, 186
Stebbins, Giles, 132, 243 (n. 31)
Stereotypes: gender, 80, 148, 159; racial, 27, 61,
63, 163, 170
Stewart, Alvan, 38
Stewart, Maria, 28, 129
Stone, Lucy, 108, 109, 114, 141, 162, 163
Storr, Charles, 209 (n. 10)
Stowe, Harriet Beecher, 174, 209–10 (n. 16)
Sturges, Maria, 21, 26, 32, 33–36, 209 (n. 14), 214
(n. 120), 215 (n. 136)
Sumner, Charles, 96
Swift, Adeline, 192
Swisshelm, Jane, 187–88, 191, 216 (n. 4)

Third parties. *See* Politics: third parties
Thomas, Anne, 170
Thomas, Hannah, 155–56
Thomas, Nathan, 170
Thomas, Pamela, 167, 169, 171
Thome, James, 17–19, 26, 209 (n. 14)
Tilden, Daniel, 192
Tilden, Martha, 192
Torrey, Harriet N., 60, 136, 154–55, 189, 192
Tracy, Hannah M., 191
Treat, Joseph, 102–3, 105, 120, 121, 189
Truth, Sojourner, 47, 157–59, 188, 191, 202

Uncle Tom's Cabin, 174
Underground Railroad, 9, 89, 149, 152, 160;
Black Laws and, 172–73; black women and,
254 (n. 41); Canada and, 175; Cincinnati and,
95, 104, 115; clothing production and, 175–77;
cooperation across abolitionist party lines
and, 160, 163, 164–66; female antislavery societies and, 172–78, 255–56 (n. 74); Garrisonians and, 143, 149, 152–53; household labor
and, 170–72; housing fugitives and, 167, 168,
170–72; racism and, 173; religion and, 177–78;
rescues and, 179–81; West and, 161–82
Union County (Indiana) Female Anti-Slavery
Society, 77, 82, 173, 175
Updegraff, Rebecca, 217 (n. 19)

Van Broekhoven, Deborah Bingham, 5, 118
Vigilance committees: Cleveland, 48; Henry
County, 89; New York, 165
Voice of the Fugitive, 27, 106–7